Dietrich Bonhoeffer's Ecumenical Quest

Also by Keith Clements

Faith (1981)

Baptists in the Twentieth Century (1983)

A Patriotism for Today: Love of Country in Dialogue with the Witness of Dietrich Bonhoeffer (edited, 1984).

The Theology of Ronald Gregor Smith (1986)

Friedrich Schleiermache: Pioneer of Modern Theology (1987)

Lovers of Discord: Twentieth Century Theological Controversies in England (1988)

What Freedom? The Persistent Challenge of Dietrich Bonhoeffer (1990)

Learning to Speak: The Church's Voice in Public Affairs (1995)

Faith on the Frontier: A Life of J.H. Oldham (1999)

The Churches in Europe as Witnesses to Healing (2003)

Bonhoeffer and Britain (2006)

Dietrich Bonhoeffer Works, Volume 13, London 1933-1935 (edited, 2007)

The SPCK Introduction to Bonhoeffer (2010)

The Moot Papers. Faith, Freedom and Society 1938-1944 (edited, 2010)

Ecumenical Dynamic: Living in More than One Place at Once (2013)

Dietrich Bonhoeffer's Ecumenical Quest

KEITH CLEMENTS

World Council of Churches Publications

WCC Publications is the book publishing programme of the World Council of Churches. Founded in 1948, the WCC promotes Christian unity in faith, witness and service for a just and peaceful world. A global fellowship, the WCC brings together 345 Protestant, Orthodox, Anglican and other churches representing more than 550 million Christians in 110 countries and works cooperatively with the Roman Catholic Church.

Opinions expressed in WCC Publications are those of the authors.

Scripture quotations are from the New Revised Standard Version Bible, © copyright 1989 by the Division of Christian Education of the National Council of the Churches of Christ in the USA. Used by permission.

Cover and book design: Michelle Cook / 4 Seasons Book Design
Cover image and photo gallery courtesy of Bonhoeffer Bildarchive and Gütersloher Verlagshaus

ISBN: 978-2-8254-1656-3

World Council of Churches
150 route de Ferney, P.O. Box 2100
1211 Geneva 2, Switzerland
http://publications.oikoumene.org

Contents

Preface / ix
Abbreviations / xi
Citations and Translations / xiii

Introduction: "With Him, I Believe": The Ecumenical Witness / 1
An Ecumenist—Really? / 3
An Inspiration Still to Be Claimed / 8

1. Young Bonhoeffer: A Case Study in Ecumenical Formation / 17
Upbringing / 19
Rome 1924 / 22
Berlin and *Sanctorum Communio* / 26
The Spanish Experience: Barcelona 1928–1929 / 35
Berlin Again—and America / 38

2. Enter a New Recruit—On His Own Terms / 45
Enter Bonhoeffer / 49
Why So Many Churches? A New Catechism / 54
The Cambridge Conference and After / 55
Cooperation: Absolutely Necessary but Impossible? / 58

3. Ecumenism and Peace: Theological Foundations / 65
The Ecumenical Youth Secretary at Work / 67
Peace: Theological Critique / 74
The Ecumenical Movement: A Theological Basis? / 78
Ecumenical Bodies: Functional Organizations or Forms of Church? / 84

4. Crisis 1933: Church, Nation, and *Oikoumene* / 89
The Church Struggle to September 1933: An Ecumenical Issue / 91
Theology of Church and Ecumenism / 97
September 1933: Battle Joined / 100
Ecumenical Responsibility: A New Stage / 104

5. Ecumenical Friendship: 1933–1935 / 109
London: October 1933–Summer 1934 / 111
Friendship with George Bell / 117

6. "The Hour Is Late": Fanø 1934 in Context / 127
The Context: Rising Peril and the Need for Self-Examination / 128
The Fanø Conference: Its Nature and Purpose / 132
Fanø: 22–30 August 1934 / 136
Recollections and Perspectives on Fanø / 144

**7. "The Question Has Been Posed": Is the Ecumenical
   Movement Church? / 157**
Political and Ecumenical Developments to May 1938 / 160
The Seminary: An Intense Life, but Still Ecumenical / 162
Confessing Church and Ecumenical Movement:
    The Mutual Challenge / 165
Maintaining the Links / 174
Bonhoeffer at Oxford? / 178

**8. Christian, Ecumenical, German: Shifting Priorities,
   1938–1939 / 183**
The Slide to War / 184
The Ecumenical Scene / 185
Bonhoeffer's Path to War / 190
Transatlantic Ecumenism: The American Episode / 199
In a Germany at War: Entry into the Resistance / 208

9. In Ecumenical Conspiracy: 1939–1943 / 211
Bonhoeffer and the Changing Ecumenical Scene / 212
The Nature of the German Resistance / 213
The Three Swiss Visits / 222
The Norwegian Visit / 229
The Meeting with George Bell: Sigtuna, May 1942 / 230
The Italian Visit / 234
A New Catholic Encounter / 235
The Wider Ecumenical Dialogue: Preparing for Peace / 241
Conspiratorial Ecumenist / 246

10. Ecumenism from Prison / 249
Continuing Contacts / 251
A Continuing Ecumenical Formation / 253
Ecumenism in the World Come of Age / 260
Contradiction or Fulfillment of Earlier Thinking
    on Church and Ecumenism? / 265

11. Still Ahead of Us? The Continuing Quest / 271
The Making of an Ecumenical Saint / 271
The Ecumenical Movement: Tracking Bonhoeffer's Influence / 274
1. The Ecumenical Role Model / 282
2. Is the Ecumenical Movement Church? / 285
3. Belonging "Wholly to the World" / 293
". . . And That Our Victory Is Certain" / 330

Notes / 301
Index / 325

PREFACE

This book aims to show how and why for Dietrich Bonhoeffer, from the conclusion of his student years in Berlin to his death on the Nazi gallows at Flossenbürg, the ecumenical movement was central to his concerns. Of course, during these years he fulfilled several distinct roles: academic theologian and teacher, leading protagonist for the Confessing Church, pastor, seminary director and—most dramatically and controversially—willing participant in the German resistance and the conspiracy to overthrow Hitler. But it is his commitment to and active involvement in the ecumenical movement that form the most continuous thread of his life and activity, and links all his various engagements. Equally, the challenge that he laid down to that movement in his time remains a legacy which has still to be fully claimed by the ecumenical world today. This book therefore has two potential readerships particularly in view: enthusiastic admirers of Bonhoeffer who need convincing of the significance of ecumenism for him; and ecumenists who, content to leave Bonhoeffer in effigy safely in the martyr's niche, have yet to consider what so invigoratingly he has to say—or, rather, what he has to question—about their contemporary concerns.

In writing this book, my own assumptions have been challenged or corrected at a number of points. As one who had been studying Bonhoeffer closely for more than forty years, and for much of that time also involved in full-time ecumenical work, I had had a sense of journeying with Bonhoeffer. But any notion that I had absorbed all there was to know about his role in the ecumenical movement of his time, and what his significance may be for the cause in ours, was soon dispelled. I hope that readers may be as creatively surprised as I have been.

Thanks and acknowledgments are due to a number of friends and colleagues. First of all, I must thank Michael West, publisher at the World Council of Churches (WCC), who first suggested that I write on this topic, especially in view of the 70th anniversary of Bonhoeffer's death being observed in 2015, and whose advice, help, and encouragement have been vital from start to finish. Also in Geneva, Hans von Rütte, WCC archivist, was most helpful in locating materials in the ecumenical collections and so enabling me to draw on documentation that sheds new light on the context in which Bonhoeffer was operating during the German Church Struggle, thus setting him in greater relief. Victoria Barnett, general editor of the *Dietrich Bonhoeffer Works* English edition and scholar of the churches and the Holocaust, not only answered queries on historical detail but pointed me to further important sources and documentation, in particular relating to the American ecumenist Henry Smith Leiper; moreover, she went the third mile by reading the book in draft and making a number of factual corrections and very helpful suggestions. Others to whom I am grateful for advice or information on either the Bonhoeffer story or the wider ecumenical history, or both, are Stephen Brown, David Carter, Andrew Chandler, Alan Falconer, Wesley Granberg-Michaelson, Clifford Green, Ulrich Möller, Larry Rasmussen, Mary Tanner, David Thompson, and Mark Woodruff. I must also thank my wife, Margaret, for additional help in surveying the almost-final manuscript with an eagle eye for lapses in English usage. The final result, remaining faults and all, is of course my own.

Portishead, England

ABBREVIATIONS

BBC	British Broadcasting Corporation
CIMADE	*Comité Inter-Mouvement auprès des Évacués*
CCBI	Council of Churches for Britain and Ireland
CTBI	Churches Together in Britain and Ireland
DBW	*Dietrich Bonhoeffer Werke*, German edition
DBWE	*Dietrich Bonhoeffer Works*, English edition
IMC	International Missionary Council
JPIC	Justice, Peace and the Integrity of Creation
MSC	Missionary Structure of the Congregation
NSDAP	*Nationalsozialistische Deutsche Arbeiterpartei* ["Nazi" Party]
PCR	Programme to Combat Racism
SA	*Sturmabteilung*
SCM	Student Christian Movement
SPCK	Society for the Promotion of Christian Knowledge
SS	*Schutzstaffel*
WCC	World Council of Churches
WSCF	World Student Christian Federation
YWCA	Young Women's Christian Association
YWCA	Young Men's Christian Association

CITATIONS AND TRANSLATIONS

All citations of Bonhoeffer are from the Dietrich Bonhoeffer Works English Series (DBWE), published by Fortress Press, Minneapolis, and used with permission of Fortress Press.

Vol. 1, *Sanctorum Communio: A Theological Study of the Sociology of the Church.* Ed. Clifford J. Green. Trans. Reinhard Krauss and Nancy Lukens. 1998.

Vol. 2, *Act and Being: Transcendental Philosophy and Ontology in Systematic Theology.* Ed. Wayne Whitson Floyd and Hans-Richard Reuter. Trans. Martin Rumscheidt. 1996.

Vol. 3, *Creation and Fall: A Theological Exposition of Genesis 1-3.* Ed. John W. de Gruchy. Trans. Douglas S. Bax. 1997.

Vol. 4, *Discipleship.* Ed. Geffrey B. Kelly and John D. Godsey. Transl. Barbara Green and Reinhard Krauss. 2000.

Vol. 5, *Life Together* and *Prayerbook of the Bible: An Introduction to the Psalms.* Ed. Geffrey B. Kelly. Trans. Daniel W. Bloesch and James H. Burtness. 1996.

Vol. 6, *Ethics.* Ed. Clifford J. Green. Trans. Reinhard Krauss, Charles West, and Douglas W. Stott. 2005.

Vol. 7, *Fiction from Tegel Prison.* Ed. Clifford J. Green. Trans. Nancy Lukens. 2000.

Vol. 8, *Letters and Papers from Prison*. Ed. John W. de Gruchy. Trans. Isabel Best, Lisa E. Dahill, Reinhard Krauss, and Nancy Lukens. 2009.

Vol. 9, *The Young Bonhoeffer: 1918–1927*. Ed. Paul D. Matheney, Clifford J. Green, and Marshall D. Johnson. Trans. Mary Nebelsick and Douglas W. Stott. 2003.

Vol. 10, *Barcelona, Berlin, New York: 1928–1931*. Ed. Clifford J. Green. Trans. Douglas W. Stott. 2008.

Vol. 11, *Ecumenical, Academic, and Pastoral Work: 1931–1932*. Ed. Victoria J. Barnett, Mark Brocker, and Michael B. Lukens. Trans. Isabel Best, Nicholas S. Humphreys, Marion Pauck, Anne Schmidt-Lange, and Douglas W. Stott. 2012.

Vol. 12, *Berlin: 1932–1933*. Ed. Larry L. Rasmussen. Trans. Douglas W. Stott, Isabel Best and David Higgins. 2009.

Vol. 13, *London: 1933–1935*. Ed. Keith Clements. Trans. Isabel Best. 2007.

Vol. 14, *Theological Education at Finkenwalde: 1935–1937*. Ed. H. Gaylon Barker and Mark S. Brocker. Trans. Douglas W. Stott. 2013.

Vol. 15, *Theological Education Underground: 1937–1940*. Ed. Victoria J. Barnett. Trans. Claudia D. Bergmann, Scott A. Moore, and Peter Frick. 2011.

Vol. 16, *Conspiracy and Imprisonment: 1940–1945*. Ed. Mark Brocker. Trans. Lisa E. Dahill and Douglas W. Scott. 2006.

Further Note on Translation and English Usage

Where Bonhoeffer wrote originally in English, as for example to English-speaking correspondents, DBWE preserves his exact wording, even if this is not standard or absolutely correct English usage (for example "ecumenic" for "ecumenical"). In addition, both Bonhoeffer and many English-speaking writers of the time referred to *die Bekennende Kirche* as the "Confessional Church." Today it is generally recognized that "Confessing Church" is the more accurate rendering and is so used in this book, but "Confessional" is retained when found in original English citations by Bonhoeffer or his contemporaries.

"With Him, I Believe": The Ecumenical Witness

"Tell him . . . With him I believe in the principle of our universal Christian brotherhood which rises above all national interests, and that our victory is certain."

These are the last recorded words of Dietrich Bonhoeffer, a message to George Bell, bishop of Chichester. It was a bright spring morning on 8 April 1945, the first Sunday after Easter, and the war in Europe had barely four weeks to run. In the village of Schönberg, in southern Germany, a school had been turned into a makeshift jail to house a group of special prisoners being transported south from Buchenwald concentration camp. The prisoners were mostly Germans who for one reason or another had fallen foul of the Nazi regime, and were in some cases accompanied by their families. But they also included two British and a Russian. Lutheran pastor Dietrich Bonhoeffer was the only clergyman in the group, and both in Buchenwald and on the unpleasant week-long journey south he had endeared himself to the other prisoners by his calmness, kindness, courage, and cheerfulness. So on this Sunday morning, when hopes were rising that release or even escape might soon be in sight, several of the prisoners asked if he would conduct a prayer service for them in the upstairs room where they were being kept. Bonhoeffer was at first diffident: most of the company were Roman Catholics and he did not wish to impose a Protestant style on a (literally) captive audience. Not only so but the Russian, Vasily Kokorin, nephew of the Soviet foreign minister Vyacheslav Molotov, was an atheist (though no doubt of Orthodox descent). Yet even Kokorin—with whom Bonhoeffer had spent time explaining Christianity in exchange for being taught some Russian—was in favour! The British prisoners, Captain Payne Best and Squadron Leader Hugh Falconer, have left us vivid and poignant recollections of what followed. In a way which met the conflicting hopes and anxieties of all his hearers, Bonhoeffer read and explained the biblical texts for the day, "With his wounds we are healed" (Isa. 53:5) and "Blessed be the God and Father of our Lord Jesus Christ! By his great mercy we have been born anew into a living hope through the resurrection of Jesus Christ from the dead" (1 Pet. 1:3), and prayed on their behalf. Then, good Catholics included, all sang Luther's great hymn *Ein' feste Burg ist unser Gott* ("A Mighty Fortress Is Our God"). Hearing the sound, the families downstairs hoped they might smuggle Bonhoeffer in to minister to them, too. But it was too late. A car had arrived. Two Gestapo in civilian clothes came in and demanded that prisoner Bonhoeffer come with them. All knew what that meant.[1]

Bonhoeffer, hastily packing his bag, was able to whisper to Payne Best, "This is the end—for me the beginning of life," and asked him, if ever he had the opportunity, to convey to his closest English friend and ecumenical collaborator, George Bell, the message placed at the start of this chapter: "With him I believe . . ." Together with another prisoner, General Friedrich von Rabenau, he was taken back north to Flossenbürg execution camp. The next morning, with six others convicted for high treason on account of their involvement in the conspiracy to overthrow Hitler, he was hanged—almost certainly with prolonged barbarity.

A Lutheran pastor conducting a service for a group of fellow prisoners of various Christian traditions or none, and of diverse nationalities and languages: this was a very ecumenical occasion! If this was so by accident rather than design, Bonhoeffer's message to George Bell (which, on his eventual return to England, Best was indeed able to give to the bishop) was a very different matter. This was a decidedly emphatic credo of ecumenical vision and commitment, all the more striking for where and when it was uttered. All around, Germany was falling into chaos amid the military collapse. No longer heard were the cries of *Heil!* ("Victory!"), which had accompanied the twelve-year Nazi Reich, and much of the rest of Europe lay in ruins. But Bonhoeffer, his own death imminent, dared to speak of victory, "our" victory, a victory of no one nationality or grouping—not even of the conquering Allies closing in on Berlin—but of the new community of Jesus Christ arising in the world, among all nations and as such the sign of a new world. Bonhoeffer was staking his soul on the certainty of that victory no less than on the triumph of the resurrection of Jesus Christ and that living hope on which he had just preached and to which he now dared to look forward via the gallows at Flossenbürg.

We may thus describe this scene at Schönberg as a parable of ecumenical commitment. But it is more than that. It is the summation of a whole career of ecumenical engagement, that is, of commitment to the unity of the church of Christ in and for the *oikoumene*, the "whole inhabited earth." Bonhoeffer was an ecumenist, and this book seeks to explore what the ecumenical movement meant for Bonhoeffer, and what Bonhoeffer meant and can still mean for the ecumenical movement today.

An Ecumenist—Really?

To describe Bonhoeffer as an ecumenist will no doubt surprise some. The foremost popular image of him is of "the pastor who opposed Hitler"; who was a stalwart figure in the Confessing Church, that section of German Protestantism which resisted the nazification of the Evangelical Church's life and theology; who led an underground seminary of pastors, teaching and writing powerfully about "costly grace and discipleship"; who joined the political resistance and became part of the plot actually to overthrow Hitler; who endured two years of imprisonment during which, in secret letters smuggled out to a friend, he set out astonishingly original ideas about a new form of Christianity—a "religionless Christianity"—for "a world come of age"; who died a martyr's death, yet whose ideas about God, Christ, the church, and faith still have living force today, as radical and revolutionary as they did when first publicized over 60 years ago. But an ecumenist? Certainly, the skeptics may acknowledge, Bonhoeffer attended a number of ecumenical meetings and conferences, speaking powerfully at them, but were these any more than stage settings for his prophetic activity and utterances? Was he really occupied with what is often thought of as ecumenical activity, that is, promoting the unity or at least the closer collaboration of the churches nationally and internationally? Is not all this interchurch doctrinal dialogue and ecclesiastical engineering a manifestation of the self-concern of the churches and therefore just the opposite of what Bonhoeffer stood for? Bonhoeffer was surely above all set on making Christ real in the secular world, in politics and social life, in the struggle for peace, justice, and human rights. Indeed, at the end was he really concerned about churchly matters at all?

It is certainly the case that one can be among the most enthusiastic admirers of Bonhoeffer without manifesting equal interest in or regard for the ecumenical movement, whether of Bonhoeffer's time or ours. All this serves to highlight a major factor in the reluctance to deal adequately with Bonhoeffer's ecumenism, namely, the generally low esteem in which ecumenical life is now held relative to former times, together with the crisis in which even many of its most committed supporters now perceive it to be. Ecumenism, for many people today, even if they are not opposed to it, is simply not interesting as compared with the epic of a heroic pastor, radical theologian, and martyr for truth and justice. Even an informed and scholarly interest in Bonhoeffer can be accompanied by a dismissal of the ecumenical movement, at least as it has developed.[2] The same is even truer of writings at a more popular level.[3] A negative attitude toward the present ecumenical movement, while in some respects understandable, increases the potential to excise a fair slice from the core Bonhoeffer story. There is in fact a major problem here for any biographer of Bonhoeffer, for the ecumenical story of the 1930s *is* in many respects complex and daunting in its close-up detail, and the sensible biographer will wish to give a map sufficient to navigate the wood without getting lost in the trees. But to know fully the Bonhoeffer story does involve appreciating the specific detail of the work and why he was so passionate about it. Among the biographies, the most adequate treatment of Bonhoeffer's ecumenical role is still that provided by Eberhard Bethge.[4] But even there the reader of today is liable to feel that the ecumenical scene amid which Bonhoeffer walked is a foreign country, whose customs and history require more explanation than time allows.

On the other hand, if interest in Bonhoeffer does not automatically mean an interest in his ecumenical involvement, does an ecumenical engagement today naturally breed an interest in Bonhoeffer? The answer has to be "Often yes, but . . ." The "Often yes" is due to two main factors. First, few Christian figures and theologians of the 20th century have had such an *ecumenically wide* reception and impact. Bonhoeffer's posthumous appeal and influence, whether as a courageous resister to tyranny or as a daringly innovative theologian, have been felt far beyond his native German Lutheran home, in every branch of Protestantism (including Pentecostal churches) in every part of the world, in the Anglican Communion, and among Roman Catholics and Orthodox, too. Not surprisingly, in view of his response to Nazism and the Holocaust, he is also a significant figure for many Jews and for Jewish–Christian dialogue (although for reasons which can be somewhat discomforting for Christians, Jewish responses to Bonhoeffer are rarely as straightforward as might be expected). As a figure now posthumously inhabiting the *oikoumene*, therefore, Bonhoeffer serves as a common reference point for people of all Christian traditions, and often well beyond Christianity, too. He belongs naturally to the ecumenical scene.

The second factor prompting the "Often yes" answer is that many people who are engaged ecumenically, whether at local, national, or international levels, if they have more than a smattering of knowledge of the ecumenical story of the 20th century, will know at least something of Bonhoeffer's own involvement in that story: his active association with such pioneering and influential ecumenical figures as J. H. Oldham, W. A. Visser't Hooft, Reinhold Niebuhr, Pierre Maury, C. F. Andrews, and Karl Barth, and above all his close friendship with Bishop George Bell. They will know of his participation in organizations like the World Alliance for Promoting International Friendship through the Churches and the Universal Christian Council for Life and Work. They will know that he provided a vital link between the Confessing Church in Germany and the ecumenical community abroad, and so forth. It was, moreover, largely through the ecumenical network that Bonhoeffer—who was almost unknown even in Germany at the time of his death—and his life and work came to be publicized in the years immediately following the Second World War. There is a sense, then, still today in ecumenical circles that Bonhoeffer belongs to the ecumenical scene: he is, one could say, one of us. Indeed, historian and Holocaust scholar Victoria Barnett can describe Bonhoeffer as an "ecumenical saint."[5]

This, however, brings us to the "but . . ." part of the answer. It is one thing to claim an illustrious figure as belonging to one's church, party, cause, or movement, but quite another to take that person seriously for what they have actually said and done and for what they really represent. There is always the danger of using the hero—especially the martyr—as a kind of mascot or figurehead to promote the cause at the expense of asking whether the person in question would really have approved of the cause itself—or, at any rate, as it has developed. The saint can be adopted as patron in order to bestow reflected glory rather than to promote serious self-examination: an idealized projection of ourselves rather than a standard against which we are to be measured. This is not to say that the ecumenical movement as a whole or any organization within it has actually done this with Bonhoeffer, although one writer on student ecumenism went so far as to describe Bonhoeffer as "a martyr of the WSCF [World Student Christian Federation]."[6] It is, rather, a matter of presuming that Bonhoeffer sits easily within the ecumenical story past and present, a presumption born out of the assumption that because he was involved in the ecumenical life of his time he was giving it his unqualified approval, and that by the same token we have his ecumenical imprimatur for it today. It is an assumption fed in turn by lack of serious study of how Bonhoeffer actually acted in the ecumenical scene of the day and, above all, how his own theology of ecumenism developed. If many Bonhoeffer enthusiasts tend to ignore his ecumenism, ecumenical enthusiasts are apt to fight shy of looking in any depth at the nature of his ecumenical commitment, especially its theological dimension, and, above all, the *challenge* which he brought and still brings to ecumenism. For, as this study will show, Bonhoeffer did not sit comfortably with any of the ecumenical agencies of his own time. "The history of Bonhoeffer's connection with the ecumenical movement is fascinating because it is full of tensions,"[7] states Eberhard Bethge, who lived with him through many of those tensions day to day. We should not assume he would be any less of a discomfitting presence in our own context and activities, either. He was a disturber of the ecumenical peace, not because he was opposed to the movement but precisely because he believed in the ecumenical cause with a passion equal to none, and wanted it to take itself more seriously than it typically did.

"There is still no theology of the ecumenical movement." So declared Dietrich Bonhoeffer at the start of his address to a meeting in Czechoslovakia in 1932.[8] Feathers might well have been ruffled by the directness, or arrogance, of such a claim being made by a relative newcomer to ecumenical life, a mere 26-year-old (and therefore in the "youth" category according to the protocols that still operate today for most ecumenical gatherings). After all, the modern movement had been running for at least a quarter of the century, and much had been written about it by theologians. The Edinburgh World Missionary Conference of 1910 had inaugurated a new era of worldwide cooperation in evangelism and service. The World Alliance, which Bonhoeffer was now addressing, and the Life and Work movement were grappling with issues of peace and disarmament, and with social and economic problems, as ethical imperatives for the churches. Moreover, the Faith and Order movement was promoting theological dialogue between the major Christian traditions. No theology in all this? Of course there was, but Bonhoeffer was perceiving that while there was indeed much theological talk about the tasks of the churches and the needs of the world in all the areas covered by these organizations, there was a notable blind spot: how the ecumenical movement evaluated *itself*, theologically. Or was it all just a pragmatic affair? When Christians from different traditions and from various nations met together, what was actually happening? Was it just a gathering of like-minded religious people sharing some common concerns on behalf of the churches? Or was it in some way not just a meeting *about* the churches and their work in the world, but a meeting *of* the one church of Jesus Christ witnessing to the world? Bonhoeffer repeatedly pressed this question, sometimes to the embarrassment of his colleagues, because, in his view, unless it was settled the ecumenical movement had no firm basis on which to stand, no rock that could outface the competing tidal surges of nationalism, racism, war, and confessional chauvinism, no sense of mandate to speak God's word to the world. It had to dare to believe in itself as the church of the *oikoumene*, and venture to *act* accordingly. This was provocative at the time, and is no less so today.

An Inspiration Still to Be Claimed

"There is still no theology of the ecumenical movement." Placed alongside Bonhoeffer's 1932 statement, a comment made 64 years later by Konrad Raiser, the then general secretary of the World Council of Churches (WCC), sounds with a telling resonance: "The organized ecumenical movement still has to claim Dietrich Bonhoeffer as one of its great sources of continuing inspiration."[9] Raiser's comment comes in the opening paragraph of a paper which still stands as one of the most important overall surveys of both Bonhoeffer's ecumenical activity and the significance of his legacy for the ecumenical movement. As far as the historical record of Bonhoeffer's ecumenical activity is concerned, there has been no shortage of material on the subject. The pioneering documentation by the Danish scholar Jørgen Glenthøj in the 1950s, together with the historical treatment of the German Church Struggle and its ecumenical dimensions by Armin Boyens in the 1960s and 1970s, not to mention the monumental and definitive biography by Bonhoeffer's closest friend Eberhard Bethge, have laid essential and sure foundations.[10] Moreover, all the relevant historical sources are now readily available in the new German and English editions of the entire Dietrich Bonhoeffer Works.[11] Nor are we entirely lacking in discussion and analysis of the continuing significance of Bonhoeffer for ecumenism. In addition to Raiser's presentation, there are substantial published papers by such experts as W. A. Visser't Hooft,[12] Ulrich Duchrow,[13] Victoria Barnett,[14] and John Moses.[15] Yet it remains the case that, as Raiser states: "In the mainline discussion about the significance of Dietrich Bonhoeffer, his involvement in the ecumenical movement has received relatively little attention."[16] We can demonstrate this relative paucity with some precision. Since the 1940s, the recorded books and published articles on Bonhoeffer number almost 4,000.[17] To date, those whose titles indicate a dealing in any way, even the most tangential, with his ecumenical activity and theology, or their continuing significance for the *oikoumene*, number 66—well under 2 percent of the total. Such themes as God, "death of God theology," world, religion, religionless Christianity, resistance, secularization, and (especially) ethics score far more heavily.[18]

Some disparity in treatment is of course to be expected. It was, after all, his exceptional status as "the pastor who resisted Hitler" to the point of martyrdom, together with the radical content of his prison letters, which so immediately brought Bonhoeffer to centre stage in international attention in the first place. That initial impact was so great as virtually to ensure a continuing momentum of interest in those directions. By contrast with this nearly universal interest in political ethics and the nature of faith in face of modernity and secularization, active ecumenical engagement is evidently a more specialized concern; one, moreover, in which, as has been noted for various reasons, interest has progressively diminished in recent decades. Nevertheless, quite apart from the contemporary slackening in enthusiasm for the quest for unity, it is worth probing a little more deeply to identify other issues which can inhibit a serious study of Bonhoeffer's ecumenism or divert attention away from it. A study such as this will need to address these factors, which, moreover, readers may need to recognize and even admit to owning themselves, if what follows in these pages is to be fruitful. I suggest three in particular.

The first is that in treating Bonhoeffer's ecumenical engagement we are dealing to a significant extent with *history*, and a truly historical interest and awareness—as distinct from a vague sense of the past—cannot be taken for granted today, at least in Western society and its churches. I have written elsewhere[19] of a virtual amnesia even among church leaders about the story of their respective communities and therewith the ecumenical story, too. Of course, too great a preoccupation with the past is unhealthy, but so, too, is a loss of memory and therewith is a loss of direction and sense of identity, from which follow an inability and lack of courage to live and write the next chapter in the story. This is a feature of a society where, under globalizing pressures and instantaneous communication, everything is fixated on the present, where not only do pressing contemporary problems vociferously call for immediate answers and solutions, but where wants and desires—created and manipulated by powerful economic interests—demand instant gratification. It is a situation that Bonhoeffer himself perceived, writing in his *Ethics* during the Second World War:

> There is no future and no past. There remains only the present moment rescued from nothingness and the desire to grasp the next moment. Already yesterday's concerns are consigned to forgetfulness, and tomorrow's are too far away to obligate us today. The burden of yesterday is shaken off by glorifying shadowy times of old; the task of tomorrow is avoided by talking about the coming millennium. Nothing is fixed, and nothing holds us. The film, vanishing from memory as soon as it ends, symbolizes the profound amnesia of our time.[20]

In our own time, Rowan Williams has similarly written about how, in the contemporary West, it has been forgotten that as persons we are produced, formed in our biology and psychology "by the passage of time," and instead have adopted a worldview "of timeless consuming egos, adopting and discarding styles of self-presentation and self-assertion."[21] In such a situation where the past becomes seemingly irrelevant and the future unimaginable, it is not easy to persuade ourselves to take any history seriously. In our particular case, we have to beware of simply conjuring up a Bonhoeffer figure as an example to supply a ready dose of inspiration in our present difficulties. To look at him and listen to him in his actual context is an exercise of a different order.

Second, if we are dealing with history, then we have to combat the tendency in all of us simply to make that history tell the story we wish to hear in order to suit and bolster our present commitments or prejudices. We have grown used to recognizing that the writing and teaching of history easily falls prey to contemporary ideological interests: hence, for example, the way that history is taught in schools is a matter for perennial debate in many countries because it brings political interests to the surface. What was the really great period in your country's history? Before the revolution? After independence? Or when? Or, our view of history can be coloured by a pervasive assumption about the way the world is or how we would like it to be. The English historian Herbert Butterfield (1900–1979), who was a devout Christian, coined the term "the Whig interpretation of history"[22] to denote the assumption that history is a story of continual progress toward ever greater human enlightenment and betterment, particularly in political conditions. Awkward facts, like new despotisms or global economic disasters or environmental catastrophes, which do not fit into such a scheme tend to be discounted or explained away. No less, Christian and church history, including ecumenical history, has to beware lest it construct a history largely determined by theological interests, and nowhere is this more so than with a figure like Bonhoeffer.

Andrew Chandler, a British historian with a special interest in the German Church Struggle, the resistance, and the roles of such as Bonhoeffer and Bishop George Bell, has spoken of historians' irritation at theologians whose high regard for Bonhoeffer tempts them to a cavalier treatment of the actual history of which he was a part.[23] Theological lauding of Bonhoeffer's significance can easily lead to exaggerated or otherwise distorted claims for what he actually did, which in turn lead to an obscuring of his truer and actually more important significance. For example, to say that Bonhoeffer was a courageous and outspoken opponent of Hitler (and therefore according his theology a special moral validity) can prompt a picture of him as leading from the front, and on all fronts, in the resistance and conspiracy. In terms of effective engagement, Bonhoeffer came into the active political resistance quite late in the day (in the second year of the war) and in a relatively minor role. Granted, that was a fateful step to take, since after the failure of the assassination attempt of 20 July 1944 any known involvement in the conspiracy was to lead to almost certain death. But the point that Chandler makes is that theological statements about Bonhoeffer need to be checked out against the actual history, not in order to diminish his significance, but to identify more precisely what that significance is, what form his courage actually took, and the specific point to which he applied it. Only so can proper connections be made between him and our own context. The same must hold for assessing his ecumenical significance. Ecumenical history can itself be prone to a "Whig interpretation," a march of continual progress,[24] and Bonhoeffer can be conveniently slotted into it as a martyr figure to add lustre to it. In contrast, there has to be a discipline of checking whether the weight of the theology we ascribe to Bonhoeffer can be borne by the actual story in which it is set, and whether we might be missing some vital clues. The contribution he makes to our ecumenical enterprise may then prove to be not quite what we imagined, yet indeed more pertinent.

Third, following from the above, there is the innate tendency to become so focused on the renowned subject as an individual that we lose a full sense of the matrix of *relationships* which constitute such a large a part of anyone's life. This is always a special temptation with Bonhoeffer, who, because in many ways he was indeed an exceptional person in his context, becomes extracted from those with whose lives he was bound up at so many levels. He is turned into a lone knight-errant riding out against the dragons and demons, rather than a member of a larger company. This becomes particularly evident in the various attempts that have been made to dramatize Bonhoeffer's story on stage or screen. Neither the play nor the film are forms that really allow the multilayered world of relationships to be dealt with adequately. They are reduced to leaving Bonhoeffer an excessively lone and romanticized, heroic figure.[25] The novel offers better possibilities for keeping the dimension of relationships in view.[26] With Bonhoeffer,

moreover, abstraction from his relationships constitutes a gross viola-
tion of who he was. His relationships with family, close friends, colleagues near and far, with fellow prisoners (and even his guards in
some cases), were not an extra to his life, or merely its setting, but its
very substance. Even in his prison writings he was not communing just
with himself, but with others and, above all, with Eberhard Bethge. It
is very doubtful whether without Bethge, that "daring, trusting spirit"
as a friend to hand, he would have written as he did.[27]

Further, not only in his being but in his thought, *sociality*, human
life as relational, was central. This has an obvious bearing on what to
expect when we explore Bonhoeffer's vision and commitment to the
ecumenical movement, for if nothing else the ecumenical movement
is about the *community* of Christ becoming more visibly one for the
sake of the whole inhabited earth, the *oikoumene*. We should expect
ecumenism, as the fullest manifestation of true community in Christ,
to be of prime importance to someone for whom human beings are
created in and for mutual relationships as the true form of freedom[28]
and for whom the church itself is "Christ existing as community." But
such an expectation will have to compete with the innate individualistic impulses of the reader, an impulse which these days is liable to be
fed by a quest for a rather restricted and precious kind of spirituality.
A selective reading of Bonhoeffer on discipleship, in particular, can
too readily feed an individual's ego with aspirations after becoming an
exceptional person oneself. True, Bonhoeffer's stunning book *Discipleship* stresses the personal call of Jesus to follow him, and has a whole
chapter on "Discipleship and the Individual": "Jesus' call to discipleship makes the disciple into a single individual. Whether disciples
want to or not, they have to make a decision; each has to decide alone.
It is not their own choice to desire to be single individuals. Instead,
Christ makes everyone he calls into an individual. Each is called alone.
Each must follow alone."[29] In the context in which it was written, this
was clearly a riposte to the appeal of Nazism as a movement in which
all sense of individuality was submerged in the mass appeal of the
party and *Volk*, and all personal responsibility surrendered to the will
of the *Führer*. But note that the individual who remains subject to the
call of Jesus is not left to him- or herself in isolation. Nearly half of

Discipleship is devoted to the *community* of the disciples led by Jesus, and to the church as the body of Christ, and it concludes with an emphatic depiction of Christ as the one who unites us in his solidarity with all who suffer, and by whom we are thereby "delivered from the isolation caused by sin, and at the same time restored to the whole of humanity."[30]

What is more, it is striking how often Bonhoeffer throughout his career writes in the first-person plural "we," not the singular "I." He communicates both to and on behalf of a community, as one of its members. Whenever he preaches, he stands in and with his congregation invoking God's judgment and grace upon "us." He is a member of the resistance but is not himself the resistance in its entirety, nor one of its leaders. He is a minor player, but he articulates a theology and ethics for the resistance as a whole. "Are *we* still of any use?" he asks in his short wartime essay "After Ten Years," a Christmas gift for his family members and close friends in the resistance.[31] His moving poem *Who Am I?*, written in Tegel Prison, is all the more striking because in his "lonely" enforced isolation and predicament Bonhoeffer is nevertheless "helplessly fearing for friends so far away."[32] Notice, too, how in his final message to George Bell it is "*with* him"—not "as" or "like"—he believes in the reality of the ecumenical fellowship. To become attuned to Bonhoeffer we must repeatedly adapt to his communal tone.

In this study, therefore, we shall move through Bonhoeffer's career and the ecumenical movement of his time, seeking to do justice to both, and tracing the interconnections and interactions at a number of levels. We shall in chapter 1 observe Bonhoeffer's personal ecumenical formation through his upbringing and his student years, including his remarkable fundamental theology of the church which he set out in his youthful doctoral thesis, and see how both this and his widening experiences of the world outside Germany were woven seamlessly into his first ecumenical engagement and responsibility. We shall then (ch. 2) map out as clearly as possible the main features, organizations, and leaders of the ecumenical scene which Bonhoeffer entered in the early 1930s, and describe how Bonhoeffer began to make an impact on them. In chapters 3 through 7, we shall focus on Bonhoeffer's ecumenical witness for peace and role in the German Church Struggle, with his efforts to represent the Confessing Church and the ecumenical fellowship to each other. In chapter 8, we move with Bonhoeffer toward the Second World War and the shifting priorities of ecumenism and political opposition, leading in chapter 9 into the wartime resistance and thence in chapter 10 to his imprisonment and death. His new theological explorations into a "religionless Christianity," it will be argued, did not mean a departure from his ecumenical engagement but a continuation of it in a new key. Finally (ch. 11) we shall survey Bonhoeffer's ecumenical impact since his death and conclude with a discussion of his relevance for the ecumenical movement of today and tomorrow. In the end, it is to be hoped, at least some readers will be encouraged to say with renewed confidence: "With *him*—Bonhoeffer—we too believe in . . ."

CHAPTER 1

Young Bonhoeffer: A Case Study in Ecumenical Formation

In November 1930, while an exchange student in the USA, Dietrich Bonhoeffer received a letter from his cousin Hans Christoph von Hase, who was also a theologian, hoping to find out "the extent to which you still belong to domestic theology or have already become an ecumenist."[1] How one *becomes* an ecumenist takes us to the heart both of Bonhoeffer's life and thought, and the story of the modern ecumenical movement. For over 50 years, few topics have exercised the World Council of Churches (WCC) and kindred bodies more than "ecumenical formation" or "ecumenical learning."[2] The very fact that at least two terms are used, often interchangeably but sometimes with arguments as to whether they mean quite the same thing[3] (and for good measure joined by "ecumenical education"), is significant. It shows that a range of elements may be in view when considering how people are brought into a committed, knowledgeable, and active engagement in the ecumenical movement, at any level from the local to the international. In 1983, the WCC sixth assembly at Vancouver listed six features of ecumenical learning as "a constitutive dimension for the church as church": (1) it transcends barriers of birth and context because it responds to the word of God and the horizons of God's promise; (2) it is action oriented, not seeking information only; (3) it is done in community, in which relationships are established with others both near and far; (4) it means learning together, "detecting the global in the local, the unfamiliar in the context of one's own environment"; (5) it is intercultural; and (6) it is a total process, in which social and religious learning are unified.[4] My own preference is to speak of "formation," provided it is not taken to imply that it is ever complete or final (there are no finishing schools in Christianity).[5] More than "learning" or "education," it does justice to the multiplicity of factors in what is an inclusive, open-ended process of growth embracing personal experience, encounters with others, widening knowledge of other traditions and environments in the *oikoumene*, intellectual discovery, deepening spirituality, and committed action, as well as prescribed courses of learning.

This preference grows even stronger in considering the case of Dietrich Bonhoeffer. Here is a prime example of someone who did not suddenly emerge as a ready-made ecumenist but surprisingly *became* one, having started from what at first sight was an unlikely background. He did so, moreover, at a time long before ecumenical formation was conceived of in any formal educational or programmatic sense.[6] We might say that with Bonhoeffer it simply happened, or, rather, that he was formed ecumenically without having consciously sought to be an ecumenist or being subjected to any educational programme designed to move him in that direction. Through a variety of factors, including family and upbringing, foreign travel and experiences abroad, and the forging of friendships and relationships with people from contexts very different from his own, Dietrich Bonhoeffer's early life brilliantly illustrates all six features listed by the Vancouver Assembly and to that extent powerfully endorses the received wisdom on ecumenical formation.

At the same time, however, he was driven by a peculiarly powerful impulse, one which was unique to his youthful formation: his discovery of a particular theology of the church which proved to be intrinsically ecumenical. More than he himself probably realized at the time, this was to have enormous significance for his struggles in the political and religious upheavals that lay ahead. Further, the story of his ecumenical formation includes a result not specified in the Vancouver assembly list and which indeed does not sit readily into any type of programme. It was, however, crucial: the emergence of a new kind of *self-consciousness and sense of identity.*

Hans Christoph von Hase, at least, suspected that his cousin's life was on a certain trajectory. In this chapter we shall examine this trajectory of Dietrich Bonhoeffer's ecumenical formation from childhood to his return from studies in the USA, aged 25, in June 1931.

Upbringing

The births of Dietrich and his twin sister Sabine in Breslau on 4 February 1906 were additions to an already sizeable and still growing family: three older brothers and two sisters, with another sister to arrive three years later.[7] The father, Karl Bonhoeffer, was a leading psychiatrist and neurologist, and the family moved to Berlin in 1912 on his appointment as professor and director of the University Psychiatric Clinic. The Bonhoeffer household was privileged in every way typical of an upper-class family of the time: servants, private tutors for the children, the enjoyments of high culture, and, for good measure, a country house for the summer holidays. Birth into this home, however, was introduction not just into the immediate family and its comforts but into a longstanding family tradition. The mother, Paula (née von Hase), came from an aristocratic Prussian line that had produced distinguished artists, musicians, and scholars (including theologians). The paternal ancestry lay in Schwäbisch Hall, Württemberg, where successive generations of Bonhoeffers had served as pastors, doctors, city councillors, and mayors, and (in the case of Karl Bonhoeffer's father) a high judiciary official for the state of Württemberg. Eberhard Bethge sums up the effect of this: "The rich world of his ancestors set the standards for Dietrich Bonhoeffer's own life. It gave him a certainty of judgment and manner that cannot be acquired in a single generation. He grew up in a family that believed that the essence of learning lay not in a formal education but in the deeply rooted obligation to be guardians of a great historical heritage and intellectual tradition."[8] To be guardian, however, did not imply slavish adherence. It meant assessing contemporary issues and challenges in the light of the tradition, and in turn reflecting on how that tradition of responsibility might need to take new forms in face of those challenges. It meant the capacity to think independently and critically, not just repetitively. Here Karl Bonhoeffer, retiring by nature and a man of few but well-chosen words, had a profound influence on all his children. As a psychiatrist, he was cautious in his judgments, averse to the Freudian theories then coming into vogue, preferring to study the empirical data of disorders rather than speculate on what might lie beneath them. Dietrich's sister Sabine writes: "Above all, he hoped that we would truly learn to distinguish the essential from the inessential, and would come to recognize our own limitations. His great tolerance left no room for narrow-mindedness, and broadened the horizons of our home."[9] Anyone wishing to know where ecumenical education begins might usefully ponder this parental example.

Part of the family tradition was, of course, German Lutheranism. There had been pastors on both sides of the family, most notably and recently the maternal. Paula Bonhoeffer's father, Karl Alfred von Hase (1842–1914), had been professor of practical theology at Jena, and performed the baptisms of the Bonhoeffer children. But the Bonhoeffers were not a church-going family. Karl Bonhoeffer was an agnostic: not antireligious but quietly skeptical while respectful of others' beliefs. As with many middle-class German Protestants of the time, for the Bonhoeffers religion was a matter of the rites of passage and, if desired, domestic piety. The latter was certainly practiced in the Bonhoeffer household since Paula Bonhoeffer, as well as providing the basic education of her children in their earliest years, also saw to their religious instruction through Bible stories, hymns, and prayers. She had in her youth spent some time with the Moravian community at Herrnhut and imbibed its spirit of warm, Bible-based personal devotion to Christ. The Herrnhuter piety may have had to be restrained to suit the sophisticated regime of the Bonhoeffer home, but it also came to be reaffirmed with the arrival in 1908 of a governess, Maria Horn, a member of the Herrnhut community who taught the children for the next 15 years and was dearly loved by all the family. Much later in life, Dietrich would adopt the Moravians' biblical *Losungen* (the "Watchwords") for his daily meditations.

It was, then, a family which accepted as a matter of course that it belonged to the Lutheran church but sat loose to its institutional life. Church was there, but nothing to get too excited about. If there was to be religion, then personal devotion mattered more than public practice and liturgical observance. Certainly there was no anti-Catholic chauvinism or obsession with the Lutheran confessional formulae. It came therefore as a surprise to his parents and siblings when, still a boy, Dietrich announced his wish to become a theologian, in contrast to the older offspring who were on their way to becoming (or marrying) scientists or lawyers. For a time it had seemed that Dietrich's future lay in music (he was proving a brilliant pianist), but even his agnostic father did not stand in his way. His brothers taunted him with the idea that the church was dead. "Then I'll change it," retorted Dietrich. Perhaps, as youngest son, he was wishing to assert his independence. But a deeper motivation may well have been at work. The 1914–18 war did not spare the Bonhoeffers their share of tragedy. All three older sons, Karl-Friedrich, Walter, and Klaus, were called up. Walter, aged barely 18, died of wounds in 1918. The stability and happiness of this family, close-knit in unswerving mutual loyalty, was for a time shattered and never wholly recovered. Dietrich never forgot his mother's grief, which traumatized her for long months. The fact and significance of Walter's death certainly left an indelible mark on his youngest brother, stained with the real horror of war. It may well also have turned him toward the question he was to raise again and again until his last year: "Who is God?"

Meanwhile, Dietrich continued his studies at the local *Gymnasium* (high school). In the summer of 1920 while on a walking tour in the Harz Mountains he wrote to his parents an account of a visit to Nordhausen and its Romanesque cathedral:

We were in it. It is obviously still used as a Catholic church. It truly was the first time that I had been in a Catholic church, and I was completely surprised by the splendor. The entire altar was covered with gold, and there were paintings of the saints and the Virgin Mary everywhere. They had probably been painted a long time ago. Having seen this, one can understand how something like it can attract simple people.[10]

If this shows the naïve first impressions of a 14-year-old, with a slightly condescending tone in the last sentence, it also reveals a straightforward curiosity about what is there, a willingness to be surprised and to reconsider presuppositions. His home nurturing of respectfulness was manifesting itself.

In April 1923 Dietrich, aged 17, began a year of theological studies at Tübingen University. He immersed himself in a wide range of student activities (even including a spell of military training) but evidently had no time for or interest in the lively branch of the Student Christian Movement there. Indeed, his most memorable religious encounter was once again provided by Roman Catholicism, a Corpus Christi procession in Rottenburg "which made a great impression on me. . . . It really makes a very distinct impression when you hear the approaching people in the procession praying from a long way off. . . . Everyone seems to be earnestly participating."[11] When he left Tübingen in the spring of 1924 he remained as committed as ever to theology, but the readiness for new encounters and widening experiences was about to be rewarded in ways he could not have imagined.

Rome 1924

In April 1924 Dietrich, accompanied by his brother Klaus, embarked on a two-and-a-half-month visit to Italy, most of the time to be spent in Rome ostensibly for study (either in the German college or the Gregorian University—the details are unclear). For a cultivated young German, Italy promised an exciting pilgrimage to the classical roots of his culture. His travel diary records: "It feels strange when one first crosses the Italian border. Fantasy begins to transform itself into reality. Will it really be nice to have all one's wishes fulfilled? Or might I return home completely disillusioned after all? But reality is, quite certainly, more beautiful than fantasy."[12] As expected, he revelled in the Roman sites and artifacts of antiquity, but what he was not prepared for was the impact of Roman Catholicism on full display on its home ground. Already on the journey south he was in continual lively discussion and argument with a Catholic seminarian. Then came a succession of stunning encounters with St. Peter's and the other great churches of Rome, and above all during the services of Holy Week and Easter. It was not just the glorious music that impressed him (though it did, rapturously). In St Peter's on Palm Sunday the gospel passion narrative was read, with many priests, seminarians, and monks of different nationalities standing with the cardinal at the altar: "The universality of the church was illustrated in a marvellously effective manner. White, black, yellow members of religious orders—everyone was in clerical robes united under the church. It truly seems ideal."[13] Nor could this be described only as outward observance. That evening in Trinità dei Mondi he was moved by the singing of the novice nuns—"unbelievable simplicity, grace and great seriousness." "The ritual was truly no longer merely ritual. Instead, it was worship in the true sense. The whole thing gave one an unparalleled impression of profound, guileless piety."[14] The sincerity of devotion was no less evident to him next day, an important day of confession, in Santa Maria Maggiore:

All the confessionals are occupied and densely surrounded by people praying. It is gratifying to see so many serious faces; nothing that you can say against Catholicism applies to them. The children also confess with true fervor. It is very touching to see that for many of these people confession has not become an obligation, but a necessity. . . . For those people who are religiously astute, it is the concretization of the idea of the church that is fulfilled in confession and absolution.[15]

So to the climax of Holy Week, "unbelievably impressive,"[16] hour after hour in St Peter's from Maundy Thursday to Easter Day, with an

Italian priest alongside him to explain everything, and more discussions about Protestant–Catholic differences.

The eighteen-year-old German Lutheran was being given profound cause for reflection by these experiences. He wrote to his parents: "The unification of Catholicism and Protestantism is probably impossible, although it would do both parties much good. Catholicism will be able to exist for a long time without Protestantism. The people are still very devoted [to it]. The Protestant church often seems like a small sect when compared to the enormous range of the local festivals."[17] Clearly he was asking if, compared with Catholicism, his easy-going, bourgeois, individualistic, non-church-attending Protestantism, took *church* seriously. Four years later, in Barcelona, he would begin a sermon on "the body of Christ" (1 Cor. 12:26f.) by contrasting how the feelings of awe and bliss, a sense of a beloved "home," which the word "church" evokes for Catholics, compares with the indifference and banality typical of Protestants when they hear the same word.[18] It is clear that in Rome Bonhoeffer was allowing his curiosity and interest to take him beyond any ignorance and prejudice, to see and see into what was there in this other tradition; to try to understand it on its own terms and to empathize with what it meant for its participants; and not only so, but then to reflect further on what this encounter revealed about himself and his native background, upbringing, and faith tradition. He was learning about himself through encountering and learning about the other, and so forming a wider conception of the world of which both were part. This was at the heart of his ecumenical formation. Clearly, he was not being swept off into a mindless romanticization of this exotically new world (an audience with the pope made an "indifferent" impression on him[19]), though he always did regard Rome as his favourite spot on earth and once confessed that at times he was tempted to become a Catholic.[20] But he was learning to see things more objectively as they were, and by the same token to view his own tradition in a new way.

It was not, however, only Catholicism that was prompting such reflection. At home in Germany Bonhoeffer would probably have had very little if any acquaintance with the small free churches such as the Baptists, Methodists, and the *freie evangelische Gemeinde*, apt to be

regarded by the historic Protestant churches, the *Volkskirche*, as "sects."
But then as today, the Protestant minority communities were also to
be found in Rome,[21] and on Ascension Day, 29 May, while visiting the
Trastevere district, Bonhoeffer's diary records: "*Baptism* in a small sect
with good choral music."[22] It is now known that this was the Baptist
Church of Roma Trastevere, located at Via della Lungaretta 124, and
that on this day two adult believers were baptized.[23] Bonhoeffer muses:
"Maybe Protestantism should not have tried to become an established
church; perhaps it should have remained a large sect, which always
have an easier time, and so might have avoided the present calamity."[24]
By "calamity" he means the effective end of the territorial church's
claim on the masses, its ability "to give everyone something." The end
of the tie between church and state confronts Protestantism with the
truth that it has now nothing distinctive to offer to the people. "If
Protestantism had never become an established church, the situation
would be completely different. It would still have a not inconsequential
number of enthusiastic adherents. In view of its size, it would hardly
be designated as a sect but would represent an unusual phenomenon
of religious life and serious thoughtful piety. It would therefore be the
ideal form of religion, which is sought after in so many ways today."
This no less than the fundamental Catholic emphasis on *church* was,
at least in the form of a question if not an idea, to be an important
souvenir to take home to Germany, a creative irritant in the working
out of his first major theological enterprise in *Sanctorum Communio*.
We should note how Bonhoeffer uses the word *ideal* to describe both
the universality of the multinational Catholicism that he glimpsed in
St Peter's on Palm Sunday, and the possibility of Protestantism as a
"large sect," drawing its strength from the enthusiasm of its members
and not dependent on the state.

The Bonhoeffer brothers did not confine themselves to Rome.
They travelled south to Naples and Sicily, from where they even ventured across to Tripoli in Libya. This brief venture into the fascinating
Arab world of North Africa pushed the horizons of experience still
further: "In general, it seems to me that there is immense similarity
between Islam and the lifestyle and piety recorded in the Old Testament," he wrote to his parents, for "In Islam, everyday life and religion

are not separated at all";[25] and "It would really be interesting to study Islam on its own soil . . . ," he comments wistfully afterwards. But for reasons which are not clear, the Libyan experience had to be curtailed hurriedly and Dietrich, at least, was evidently glad to be back in Europe again: there was simply so much that was new to absorb in Africa, with too little time to reflect upon it. At any rate, on his return to home in Berlin in June 1924 he had proved to himself the value of seeing and learning from other worlds and other traditions.

Berlin and *Sanctorum Communio*

In the summer of 1924 Dietrich Bonhoeffer resumed his studies not in Tübingen but at his home university of Berlin, and plunged into intensive courses in biblical studies, systematic theology, philosophy, and church history. The Berlin theology faculty, from the time of its founding genius F. D. E. Schleiermacher (1768–1834), had been renowned for its leading role in liberal Protestant thought. In the light of modern scientific and critical thought, liberal theologians sought to present Christian belief on the basis not of the dogmatic foundations of the past, but based instead on the nature of actual religious experience and on what could be reliably reconstructed, by modern historical research, of the teaching and history of Jesus embedded in the gospel records and the New Testament as a whole. Reigning over Berlin theology from the turn of the century was Adolf von Harnack (1851–1930), renowned internationally for his erudition in New Testament and church history. His acclaimed lectures in 1899–1900 on the essence of Christianity[26] succinctly summarized the liberal credo: the teaching of Jesus comprised the fatherhood of God, the human soul so ennobled as to unite with him, and the moral influence of faith in spreading the brotherhood of humankind over the earth. Scarcely less erudite was Ernst Troeltsch (1865–1923) who, notwithstanding his death the year before Bonhoeffer began his Berlin studies, was to remain a powerful force in the philosophy of history and, especially, the study of the various social forms in which Christianity manifested itself.[27]

The liberal ethos of Berlin meant that theology was essentially the study of human religious experience, thought, and history. From the end of the First World War, however, a different theological wind had started to blow across continental Europe. The Swiss theologian Karl Barth (1886–1968) had sounded the alarm call for a decisive about-turn in theology, from talk about the religious aspirations of humanity to the holiness, judgment, and grace of the "wholly other" God who is known only in his self-revelation in Jesus Christ. His famous commentary on Romans[28] turned Paul's attack on "the law" as the way to salvation into a full-scale onslaught on contemporary theology's focus on "religion." Naturally, this sounded dangerously irrational and retrograde to many liberal theologians and a war of words ensued between Harnack and Barth, who from 1921 was teaching in Germany.

It is known that Bonhoeffer was reading Barth's *The Word of God and the Word of Man* by the summer of 1925. He would have read, for example:

> It is not the right human thoughts about God which form the content of the Bible, but the right divine thoughts about men. The Bible tells us not how we should talk with God but what he says to us; not how we find the way to him, but how he has sought and found the way to us; not the right relation in which we must place ourselves to him, but the covenant which he has made with all who are Abraham's spiritual children and which he has sealed once and for all in Jesus Christ. It is this which is within the Bible. The word of God is within the Bible.[29]

Bonhoeffer was captured. He had found the one who would be his chief theological mentor to the end of his days. Henceforth, he could justly be labelled a Barthian, which made him a somewhat unusual figure in liberal Berlin. He was not, however, an uncritical disciple, as will be seen. Moreover, and very unusually for a young and enthusiastic convert, becoming pro-Barth did not for him mean *ipso facto* becoming anti-Harnack in every respect. Indeed, Bonhoeffer retained a deep personal appreciation and respect for the aged scholar. He even considered majoring in church history under him, and on

Harnack's retirement delivered the congratulatory address on behalf of his students. There was a generous spirit at work here, certainly committed to a particular line but free from any strident, arrogant partisanship. As Eberhard Bethge says of Bonhoeffer at this stage: "His own upbringing and his father's example gave Bonhoeffer a broader perspective, enabling him to respect and learn from those who taught something different from what he believed."[30] For while Bonhoeffer was completely at one with Barth in affirming that it is only through his word in Jesus Christ that the hidden God makes himself known, he was also wanting to know just where and how this revelatory word is made real and accessible in the life that humans experience. Here is where he believed that philosophy, history, and—not least—sociology offered important resources for theology, even the astringent dialectical theology of the Barthians. A sound theology should be secure enough to know when it can make room for others.

So Bonhoeffer maintained a devoted yet critical engagement with his Berlin teachers, and not just Harnack. Prominent among them was the exponent of Martin Luther, Karl Holl (1866–1926). Bonhoeffer drew deeply from Holl's research into the original sources of the German reformer's teaching, which were just then creating a renewal of interest in Luther as distinct from what later Lutheranism had made of him. Bonhoeffer thus became thoroughly immersed in the wellspring of his own Protestant tradition—so much so that he took issue with Holl on an important aspect of the latter's interpretation of Luther. Holl argued that Luther's distinctive discovery was the inwardness of faith and the role of conscience in the believer's relation to God. To Bonhoeffer, this did not touch the radicality of Luther's view: faith looks away from itself and all its own feelings—even including that of conscience—to the God whose grace is *extra nos*, other than us, coming to us from outside ourselves and all our feelings, however pious. Also important to him was Reinhold Seeberg (1859–1935), professor of systematic theology, who laid great stress on the sociality of human existence, and it was under Seeberg that in 1925 Bonhoeffer decided he would write his doctoral thesis.

This brings us to the intellectual heart of Bonhoeffer's ecumenical formation. In choosing *Sanctorum Communio*—"The Communion of

Saints"—as the title of his doctoral thesis, he was taking up the theme which had begun to excite him in Rome: the church. But he was to approach it in a quite novel way, combining a theology of revelation through the word of God with the sociological tools he was learning about in his Berlin studies—one might almost say it was an attempt to yoke together, of all people, Karl Barth and Ernst Troeltsch. That he completed the dissertation in just two years and at the age of 21 is some cause for wonder. Nearly 30 years later, Barth was to praise the book highly and even hailed it as a "theological miracle."[31] Unsurprisingly for such a youthful enterprise, it manifests both high sophistication and some rough-hewn or incomplete arguments, but it is now widely recognized as foundational for an understanding of much of his later thought. A full exposition of the book will not be attempted here, simply enough to demonstrate that in working out his understanding of the church Bonhoeffer was, perhaps barely consciously at the time, arguing the ecumenical case.

"In this study," Bonhoeffer begins, "social philosophy and sociology are employed in the service of theology."[32] It is not therefore an attempt to derive a theology from social science; rather, it seeks to describe the social form of the church which is in keeping with its theological self-understanding as the body of Christ, bearing in mind that "*the concepts of person, community, and God* are inseparably and essentially interrelated."[33] First of all drawing upon much of the personalist social philosophy of the time,[34] Bonhoeffer lays out a decidedly relational view of human existence. Self-consciousness only arises in community: "By recognizing a You, a being of alien consciousness, I recognize myself as an 'I,' and so my self-consciousness awakens."[35] One can be oneself only through being in the other. The theological question is how community and relationality are realized in the church. To describe the church as the body of Christ is of course a theological commonplace on any reading of the Pauline letters. But Bonhoeffer makes a quite daring leap beyond the usual view of the church as the community which believes in God's self-revelation in Christ. The church is itself that revelation *having taken concrete, earthly, human social form.* Hence his most famous sentence in the thesis: *Die Kirche ist Christus als Gemeinde existierend*: "The church is Christ existing as

Gemeinde.[36] *Gemeinde* is generally understood as German for "community," that is, as a grouping formed by interpersonal bonds and a conscious sense of shared belonging, as distinct from the more impersonal "society" or "association," and it can also denote "parish" or "congregation." In *Sanctorum Communio*, Bonhoeffer uses it in relation to "church" with a range of such allusions and references although never as "community" in a completely undefined sense. Hence the preferred rendering of *Gemeinde* in the now-standard English translation of *Sanctorum Communio* as "church-community."[37] Bonhoeffer is not saying that wherever some form of human community is found (however "genuine"!), there is Christ. Neither is he saying that any institution bearing the name "church" can be assumed to be where Christ is present as community. The church is the community that lives under the word of God in Christ and is defined by that word; the word is not defined by the church but the church by the word. But the word desires to take social form and that is the theological foundation of the church.

What makes the church distinctive among other forms of human community is therefore a matter of how its members are related to one another in a common life, as Christ-existing-as-community. The nature of these relationships is defined and enabled solely by Christ, which leads us to another of Bonhoeffer's key terms, one which recurs repeatedly throughout his theological writings: *Stellvertretung.* A conventional English translation of this would be "action as representative or deputy." Bonhoeffer, however, invests it with deeper meaning by using it to describe the saving work of Christ, Christ who vicariously bears the sins of others. If somewhat clumsy, the rendering in the most recent translations of Bonhoeffer does it more justice: "vicarious representative action."[38] This both describes the work of Christ and indicates the relationships between members of his body, relationships which are of love, not just in a conventional form of nice goodwill, but of bearing one another's burdens and sufferings and, most specifically, in forgiving one another's sins and in intercessory prayer. Here, in fact, Bonhoeffer is following most closely Martin Luther:

Bear one another's burdens (Gal. 6:2). The possibility of this 'being with one another' does not rest on human will. It exists only in the community of saints, and goes beyond the ordinary sense of 'being-with-one-another'. It belongs to the sociological structure of the church-community. In the *Tesseradecas* Luther expounds his thoughts on this point with incomparable beauty. My burden is borne by the others, their strength is my strength, in my fear and trembling the faith of the church comes to my aid. And even when I come to die, I should be confident that not I, or at least not I alone, am dying, but that Christ and the community of saints are suffering and dying with me. We walk the path of suffering and death accompanied by the whole church.[39]

The church is therefore identified by the Christ-formed, vicarious relationality of its members to one another—which at its most specific yet most profound level is expressed in the forgiveness of sins. Church is therefore a relational community of persons, "being-with-each-other" and "being-for-each-other."[40] It is not a "religious community" or association. It is *Christus praesens*, the present Christ in his word and sacrament and in the relationships of vicarious representative action that he establishes by his own such action in the forgiveness of sins. It is therefore not a manifestation of "religion," for it is nothing less than *the new humanity*, in contrast to the old humanity in Adam.

Although completed six years before the advent of Hitler and the onset of the Church Struggle, *Sanctorum Communio* lays out several key weapons for Bonhoeffer to wield in the coming conflict. That the church is *Christ*—not the national spirit or the Aryan race—existing as community is an obvious example. That Christ exists as *community* formed the basis for the underground seminary life he established at Finkenwalde and its exposition in *Life Together*. But equally, *Sanctorum Communio* sets the compass for his ecumenical venturing. His identification of the church as the relational community under the word, Christ existing as church-community, gives him the freedom to range widely over the scenery of Christian traditions with a combination of generous appreciation and respectful criticism. The essential church can be looked for wherever the word of God is preached and where

Christ takes shape in its community. All else is relative. He writes as a Lutheran—the church is under the word—but not as an advocate of Lutheranism over against all other traditions. In *Sanctorum Communio*, he rejects on both theological and sociological grounds the significance of the famous distinction made by Ernst Troeltsch between "church" and "sect" types of Christianity:[41] so long as it has the word, the sect no less than the church is the "community of Christ."[42] His critique of Roman Catholicism is firm but measured, as when, following an exposition of how each member of the church-community is called to be "a Christ to the other," he asks:

> But do we not come alarmingly close here to the Roman Catholic teaching of the treasury of merits that stands at the center of all more recent Roman Catholic views on the *sanctorum communio*? We are indeed, and do so quote consciously. With Luther we want to be sure that the sound core . . . is preserved in Protestant theology. The decisive difference lies in the fact that we do not acknowledge any person as having overflowing merits that could be used on behalf of another. The 'treasury of merits' is God's love that in Christ created the church-community; it is nothing else.[43]

Roman Catholic teaching and practice are a rationalization of "the irrational fact that human beings can never do more than they ought" and that within the church-community, as Luther says, God lets each person "enjoy" the other. The Catholic teaching is thus to be regarded as distortion of a basal truth—which by implication Protestantism itself is in danger of forgetting. Bonhoeffer recognizes the clear distinction between the Roman Catholic and Protestant concepts of the church—the former linking the Spirit and ecclesiastical office, the latter assuming the connection between Spirit and church-community as a whole.[44] But this is not the final conclusion, for

> It is the miracle of the divine promise that wherever the word of God is proclaimed, it will create a church-community through its own power. Within the Roman Catholic church, as a place where God's word is proclaimed, we therefore must assume the existence

of such a church-community that belongs together with the Protestant and sectarian church-communities.[45]

Where the Catholic church may be judged to have failed is not on the question of its having the word, but on the purity of its doctrine and the consequent compulsory nature of its sociological structure. But even here matters are relative: "That there is a quest for pure doctrine is just as self-evident as the fact that no church can claim to possess it fully." At this point Bonhoeffer even dares to criticize, of all things, that touchstone of Lutheran orthodoxy, the Augsburg Confession!

> We must consider the Augsburg Confession to be in error when, in Article 7, it links *recte docetur* [being rightly taught] to the *congregatio sanctorum* [congregation of saints]. . . . The community of saints will no doubt always strive for pure doctrine; but through historical circumstances this effort can remain ineffective. We are therefore bound to believe and acknowledge that in principle the *sanctorum communio* is present both in the Roman Catholic church and in the sect.[46]

Memories of St Peter's and of the Baptist church in Trastevere were evidently operative here. Likewise, while defending the value of the *Volkskirche* or "church of the people," he also acknowledges the need in principle for the voluntary church, which is indeed the essential nature of the church,[47] and which circumstances (as was to happen in 1933) may at any time drive to the forefront. *Sanctorum Communio* thus manifests a readiness to search for and find the essential church, Christ as existing as church-community, within a diversity of ecclesiastical forms and in a variety of historical contexts. It is written in a spirit transcending the boundaries of the existing traditions.

There is only one point in *Sanctorum Communio* where Bonhoeffer explicitly mentions the matter of unifying the churches. He notes:

It is particularly important not to forget that unification from below is not identical with unity given from above; further, we must also remember that the will to unify should be practiced, first of all, in the smaller and even the smallest congregation. The way toward unification, however, is fraught with the fiercest resistance; for the stronger the will, the more partisan individuals behave. However, there will presumably be a basic goal that can be built upon and that provides a relative unity. And this common goal may be assumed in the church even where it cannot yet be formulated, but a conceptual expression is still being sought. In spite of recognizing that we can never achieve the absolute unanimity that would correspond to the unity of Spirit, the will seeking the greatest possible realization of unanimity will be alive in the church, and will take comfort from the prayer of Jesus, "that they may all be one, just as you Father are in me and I am in you" (John 17:21). And it will be to the honor of the church-community to praise through its unity the glory of Jesus before the world (v. 23).[48]

Bonhoeffer's chief concern here, as elsewhere in *Sanctorum Communio*, is to safeguard the proper place and freedom of the individual person in his or her relation with others in face of an abstract notion of "community" which effectively suppresses individuality and diversity. Likewise, faith in the church is very different from "romantic feelings of solidarity between kindred spirits."[49] Faith experiences the church "where there is no other link between the individuals than that of the community that exists within the church; where Jew and Greek, pietists and liberal, come into conflict, and nevertheless in unity confess their faith, come together to the Lord's Table, and intercede for one another in prayer."[50] By contrast, says Bonhoeffer harshly, the "communal impulses of the Youth Movement," such a feature of Germany at the time, have been great but have not added to the experience of the church.

We shall have cause to refer again to *Sanctorum Communio* at several later points along Bonhoeffer's ecumenical journey. For the present, it has been shown that with its emphasis on the relationality of human life and on the essential nature of the church as

Christ-existing-as-community, the logic of an ecumenical commitment was being laid out. Here is an ecclesiology which is intrinsically ecumenical, in contrast to those understandings of the church to which "ecumenical considerations" come as extras, or as preliminary thoughts which are then forgotten in the desire to secure a confessional identity. Put more dynamically, here was a vision about human life and the church in particular which was to drive its author into the ecumenical movement, and not only into it but through it to the point where he was to call for the church to discover a wholly new relation to the *oikoumene*.

The Spanish Experience: Barcelona 1928–1929

Bonhoeffer successfully defended his doctoral thesis *Sanctorum Communio* in December 1927. A brilliant academic career was now in prospect. But it was also to the pastorate that he felt called, and while working on his dissertation he had also been preparing for the theologian examinations for ordination in the Church of Berlin-Brandenburg. This included practical work such as teaching in Sunday school. His experience of the wider world, however, was about to be widened again thanks to Max Diestel, superintendent of Bonhoeffer's church district in Berlin and a committed ecumenist. Diestel recommended Bonhoeffer for the post of assistant pastor in the German congregation at Barcelona, and he willingly accepted, spending 12 months there from February 1928. While once again in a Mediterranean Catholic environment, this proved in many ways a contrasting experience to Rome three years earlier, as well as to his native Berlin. After he had been settled in Barcelona for some time, Diestel wrote to him:

> The problem is often, especially among us theologians, that we grow up much too academically and much too unworldly, and then our view of the real world, a world oriented quite differently, ends up being shortsighted. For this reason I also think it quite good that you are dealing with a completely different kind of congregation in Spain than we have here. . . . I can imagine . . . that it would also

be interesting for you if, once you have learned to speak Spanish fluently, you might have some contract with authentic Spanish life itself.[51]

Bonhoeffer needed little encouragement. He had plenty of opportunity to enjoy the country and pursue his intellectual interests, although his energies were of necessity largely focussed on the parochial—in every sense—life of the German congregation and to some extent the wider expatriate German community. For the sophisticated and cultured Berliner, this self-enclosed world of small businessmen and their families with their often petty and gossipy concerns was a strange and constricting environment. But it was one to which he gave himself unreservedly, not only in pastoral visiting and preaching but in developing new youth work and presenting a series of lectures on Christianity and vital contemporary issues. Relating to such a community provided a test of Bonhoeffer's capacity to empathize with a hitherto unknown context as it actually was and what it felt it needed, and in this he was patently successful. If the horizons of his flock were restricted he sought to widen, not mock, them. He was greatly liked by the congregation, its young people especially, and they wished him to stay longer—even if the pastor Friedrich Olbricht showed some signs of insecurity at his younger colleague's popularity.

Olbricht gave him little encouragement to relate to Spanish Catholicism, which in any case proved something of a disappointment. In contrast to the Italian expression it was, Bonhoeffer judged, the most gloomy form of the faith. Small wonder, he felt, that the bullfight with its passion and drama was so popular (Bonhoeffer's own enjoyment of the brutal spectacle disconcerted his family). More impressive was the scene he had witnessed when, en route to Barcelona, during a stopover in Paris he attended high mass in Sacré Coeur and noted the Montmartre prostitutes and their men at worship, "and once again one could see quite clearly how close, precisely through their fate and guilt, these most heavily burdened people are to the heart of the gospel."[52] Nevertheless, in Barcelona Bonhoeffer was struck by the social egalitarianism of the street cafés and the Spanish dislike of all pretentiousness. He spent some hours each week working in the office of the German welfare society, meeting all kinds of cases of need, homelessness, penury, fecklessness, or delinquency. As in Rome, he was joined by his brother Klaus for a time and they journeyed to admire the ancient grandeurs of the south of the country, and also briefly crossed to Morocco.

If Spain was a scene with which, unlike Italy, a German of his background felt little affinity, it was still one that interested him enormously and which he felt had to be appreciated from within. Embedded as it was in its own particular historical experience and culture, Bonhoeffer allowed Spain to challenge his own presuppositions. Not long after arriving in Barcelona, he confessed to his brother-in-law Walter Dress that in Spain, "a country that has known neither war nor revolution, neither a youth movement nor Spengler," he felt that "one really finds oneself forced to reassess one's theology from the ground up."[53] Two months later he again writes to Dress, reflecting on all his new experiences: "You can see that I am glad to be here; and while it is certainly interesting to enter different circles than those to which one is accustomed, one must also add the joy of being in a foreign country and the adjustment to what seems to be an extremely alien culture for us, yet one that is certainly stimulating and serious."[54] Some of that stimulus became evident in his sermons and lectures to the German congregation. His own mind, pulled out of his home environment, was clearly expanding. This is perhaps not surprising, since, as commonly happens, in an expatriate circle "home" is invested with even more nationalist sentiment than at home itself. Some of his speech showed signs of a lingering, traditional German nationalism. In a lecture on Christian ethics, he expounds the very traditional Lutheran justification of war for the sake of the nation, and even: "Strength also comes from God, and power, and victory, for God creates youth in the individual as well as in nations, and God loves youth, for God himself is eternally young and strong and victorious. And fear and weakness will be conquered by courage and strength."[55] Yet not only were such ideas not to be heard from him ever again, but even at that very time they were being implicitly challenged by other notes being sounded, as in a sermon on 1 Corinthians 12:27 ("Now you are the body of Christ . . ."). The church is a people whose members love one another because God loves them: "Not Germany and not France and not America, but a people extending over the entire world, whose members can be found here and there and everywhere—indeed it has and is yet seeking members among us! This is the people of God; this is the church of Christ."[56]

In Spain, therefore, he was discovering more about the *oikoumene*, what it meant to live in strange parts of it, and was reflecting on what it meant to be the *sanctorum communio* of the whole inhabited earth. It was during this time that he started to dream of going far beyond Europe altogether and visiting India. Returning to Berlin via Geneva in February 1929 he visited the League of Nations to get information on the churches and the League and "the question of protection of children, minorities, and calendar reform."[57]

Berlin Again—and America

While in Spain Bonhoeffer had already begun work on his postdoctoral thesis, which would qualify him to teach in university. Back home in Berlin this was his chief preoccupation until he submitted it in March 1930, under the title *Act and Being*. In effect, it was a follow-up to *Sanctorum Communio* but focussing on the question of how in Christ God's freedom is not so much a negative freedom *from*, but a gracious freedom *for*, the world. Relationality remained to the fore in his thinking. Meanwhile, in the faculty he was employed as assistant in systematic theology, and following the satisfactory report on *Act and Being* gave his trial and inaugural lectures. Through all this he was also following the prescribed programme in practical theology leading toward ordination. His career seemed set on course, but as repeatedly happened in his life, a major diversion presented itself: this time, the possibility of a year in the USA as an exchange student at Union Theological Seminary, New York. Once again it was Max Diestel who was instrumental here, in securing the invitation through the German Academic Exchange Service and encouraging Bonhoeffer's acceptance.[58] Bonhoeffer sailed for New York in September 1930, returning at the end of June 1931.

Once again Bonhoeffer found himself in an environment quite unlike anything he had experienced before; or rather, one should say, in several very diverse environments in the land of the free. First there was Union Seminary itself, founded to serve the mainstream Protestant denominations, decidedly progressive and liberal in ethos and having on its faculty some of the most eminent contemporary names in American theology and church life, including Henry Sloane Coffin, Reinhold Niebuhr, William Adams Brown, Harry Emerson Fosdick, and the Scotsmen James Moffat and John Baillie. The intense yet informal conviviality typical of American college life was at first disconcerting to him. Still more so was the approach to theology with its largely humanistic, pragmatic assumptions: doctrine seemed to have been swallowed up in social ethics and behavioural science, the Bible largely lost sight of, Luther laughed at in class, and Barth hardly heard of. Such, at least, was the initial reaction of this sophisticated and perhaps prejudiced German. "There is no theology here," he wrote to Diestel after three months at Union.[59] He himself presented a seminar paper on Barth, prefaced with the warning that in order to understand Barth the listeners would have to give up all their preconceptions as to what theology was about. But even at his most negative Bonhoeffer was prepared to find seams of value in this unpromising mine. Niebuhr's classes on ethics, social analysis, and contemporary literature he found enlivening (and both Niebuhr and Baillie were to be important to him personally in the coming years). If at first he did not like what he met in American thought, he at least decided to study it in depth to understand more, and so he took private tutorials with Eugene Lyman, professor of philosophy of religion. Moreover, he valued greatly the courses on "The Church and Community" taught by C. C. Webber, which involved visits to social and political organizations in the city.

Second, there was the world of the Protestant Sunday and the illustrious pulpits of New York. Here again, he was not overly impressed. Popular preaching aimed to make the hearers feel optimistic about themselves, the world, and God rather than bring them in worship through fear and trembling to holy joy. The churches appeared to have succumbed to the mores of the business world. In a (Methodist) Sunday school, he noted with scorn, "a little girl recently received—right in front of me—a makeup box as a reward for good attendance. And we're supposed to believe we're sitting in a Christian church."[60] He preached in Methodist and Baptist churches, spoke to student conferences, and visited the conference of the Federal Council of Churches in Washington, D.C. If he was not impressed by easy-going theological liberalism, neither was he taken with the opposing fundamentalism which, while it might preserve some elements of Reformation views, also distorted them "by the crassest orthodoxy, especially in the Southern Baptist Church."[61] Fortunately, Bonhoeffer was not left just to the mercy of his European perspectives and instant reactions. At Union he began a close friendship with a doctoral student, Paul Lehmann, and his wife, Marion. In Lehmann, Bonhoeffer found a sympathetic understanding of his European thought-world, and in return Lehmann helpfully interpreted the American scene to him.

Indeed, Bonhoeffer made several important friendships at Union, and it was through one of them that he was able to make the most pivotal social discovery of his time in America. Frank Fisher was one of the few black students in the seminary, and he introduced Bonhoeffer to the huge Abyssinian Baptist Church in Harlem. Bonhoeffer was instantly impressed by the powerful preaching of the church's charismatic pastor Adam Clayton Powell Jr., the fervent worship of the congregation, and the church's prophetic social ministry in the ghetto. Here he found his spiritual home while in New York, and regularly taught a Sunday school class and led a women's Bible study group. "I heard the gospel preached in the Negro churches," he later reported with gratification to Max Diestel.[62] Nor was this simply an enjoyment of the exotic for its own sake. "During my overall stay in America I spent a great deal of time getting to know the Negro problem from every angle *and also observing white America from this rather hidden perspective*."[63] He studied social-survey reports, visited leaders of the young black movement at Howard College in Washington, read novels by contemporary black writers, ostentatiously walked out of restaurants in protest when his friend Fisher was refused service, and on his return to Germany took home a collection of records of spirituals. At home the "Jewish question" was beginning to stir as antisemitism became politically voluble and at times violent. New York was putting him through an important process of conscientization on race, vital not only in understanding the American context but also in alerting him to the sinister trends on his home scene.

Friendships with two fellow Europeans at Union also became significant. Erwin Sutz, a Swiss, had studied under Barth and so readily made common theological cause with Bonhoeffer (and later helped to introduce him personally to Barth). Jean Lasserre of the French Reformed Church on two counts presented a more challenging possibility for a relationship, which in the end proved transformative. First, never until now had Bonhoeffer come into close relationship with a representative of the former enemy nation. Twelve years after the war, the emotional scars were still real on both sides, and above all for Germans who were still smarting under the humiliation of the Versailles Treaty with its imputation to Germany of sole guilt for the war. Bonhoeffer and his family shared that sense of injustice.[64] Second, Lasserre was a convinced pacifist, the first such that Bonhoeffer had really met and engaged with. Bonhoeffer found that his traditional Lutheran view of military action as justified by national need, still so evident in his Barcelona lectures, and the conventional interpretation of the Sermon on the Mount ("turn the other cheek") as words to be taken symbolically and not literally, were now challenged. He started to think seriously about the command of Christ as one to be obeyed concretely, and to face the pacifist option. He was in any case seeing himself as a kind of German peace envoy in America. Several times he addressed youth and student gatherings about the longing of German young people for peace, speaking frankly and with great passion of German feelings during and after the war, of the death of his brother Walter, and the bitter privations caused by the blockade that followed the armistice. Here was no anodyne, forgive-and-forget attitude but, rather, a belief that reconciliation requires the exposure of suffering and grief on all sides. But he also looks to the future:

> Returning to the Christian point of view, it seems to me one of the greatest tasks for our church, to strengthen the work of peace in every country and in the whole world. It must never more happen, that a Christian people fights against a Christian people, brother

against brother, since both have one Father. Our churches have already begun this international work. But more important than that is . . . that every Christian man and woman takes seriously the great idea of the unity of Christianity, above all personal and national desires, of the one Christian people in the whole world, of the brotherhood of mankind, of the charity, about which Paul says . . .[65]

Bonhoeffer's American experience, it should be said, went well beyond New York, and even the USA. It took in Washington, D.C., Philadelphia (where he had relatives), Chicago, the deep South, and over to Cuba where he and Erwin Sutz spent Christmas 1930 with the sister of Käthe Horn, the Bonhoeffer children's governess; and just before his return to Europe he and Jean Lasserre, accompanied part of the way by Paul Lehmann and Erwin Sutz, made it by car to Mexico.

Bonhoeffer concluded his long and detailed American report to Max Diestel with surprising diffidence as to what he had learned there "for our situation," and warned against looking for any "direct application." Rather, he said, "It is simply no more and no less than that one has begun to become acquainted with a different part of the world."[66] Perhaps this diffidence was because Bonhoeffer knew that something very significant but of a rather different kind than could be set down on paper was happening to him while in America. It was not just a further accumulation of experiences, of interesting encounters, nor even of new understandings about societies and churches, though all these played a role. It was a change in his self-consciousness, of who he understood himself to be in the world as he was now perceiving it. German, Protestant, and theologian he still certainly was. But something else had been added, a new way of identifying himself, which marked a qualitative change from how he had been still thinking of himself when in Barcelona. Being translated more radically than ever before out of his home, church, and European contexts into liberal "Anglo-Saxon" America, and still further into black America and its churches, had precipitated a quite new awareness of what it meant to be a Christian human person. It may be seen in the small but give-away phrase "our church" in the words quoted above from his peace lecture, with its recognition of a common task for peace to be taken up by all Christians in every part of the world.[67] In Barcelona, he could certainly talk about the worldwide church, the people of God. Now, he spoke as one who was consciously part of it—"our church"—and personally committed to its reconciling mission. The centre of gravity of his conscious identity had shifted decisively from the national and confessional to the worldwide Christian. "Christ existing as church-community" was now to be understood on a level not perceived before, and not only understood but lived as well.

Eleven years later, in 1942, Bonhoeffer wrote Max Diestel a congratulatory letter on his 70th birthday, full of gratitude for what he owed to him ever since the 1927 telephone call suggesting the Barcelona curacy "set my thinking on a track from which it has not yet deviated,"[68] that is, to ecumenical Christianity, followed by the year at Union Seminary "that has been of the greatest significance for me up to the present day." No less revealing is the remark in his letter to Eberhard Bethge written from Tegel prison in April 1944: "I don't think I've ever changed very much, except perhaps at the time of my first impressions abroad, and under the first conscious influence of Papa's personality. It was then that a turning from the phraseological to the real ensued."[69] The experience of home, and the experiences of being not-at-home, were indeed both vital in his nurturing. Bound up with this was what, as he later confided to a friend, was an inner change around the time in America, from being simply a theologian to becoming a praying Christian, one who read his Bible not just as an intellectual exercise but in order to hear God's word to him.[70] We do not know how, or if, Dietrich Bonhoeffer answered Hans Christoph von Hase's question on whether he had become an ecumenist, but certainly he had undergone an ecumenical formation by the time he sailed back to Germany from New York in June 1931. Awaiting him at home, moreover, was a summons not just to ecumenical interest, but to ecumenical responsibility as well. Diestel had yet further plans for him.

CHAPTER 2

Enter a New Recruit— On His Own Terms

To speak of the ecumenical movement in the singular is, except in the broadest sense, misleading. The movement has always comprised several streams and organizations in varying degrees of harmony, often sharing an overall vision but also with differing and sometimes competing agendas. This was certainly the case when Dietrich Bonhoeffer returned to Berlin from the USA in July 1931 to embark on his career as academic theologian and church pastor. There was as yet not even any single umbrella organization: a constitution for a World Council of Churches (WCC) would not be agreed upon until 1938 and, due to the Second World War, its actual inauguration had to wait ten further years. What did exist in 1931 at the international level was a broad and advancing front led by bodies each with a distinct identity and ethos, some of them newcomers to the field, others with histories reaching back nearly 100 years. The longest-standing players were the Christian youth movements: the Young Men's Christian Association (YMCA), the Young Women's Christian

Association (YWCA), and the World Student Christian Federation (WSCF). The YMCA and YWCA had originated in Britain in the mid-19th century and spread remarkably quickly throughout the British Empire, North America, and beyond. Their strength and vitality lay in their local groups devoted to prayer, Bible study, social service, and evangelism. Although at first largely Protestant, they were irrevocably committed to drawing younger Christians together regardless of denominational allegiance, and equally cultivated an international outlook with meetings and programmes on a world scale. The basis of the YMCA, adopted at its world conference in Paris in 1855, was the uniting in discipleship and service for the reign of God those young men who regarded "Jesus Christ as their God and Saviour according to the Holy Scriptures"[1]—wording which was to echo down the ecumenical movement right into the eventual basis of the WCC. The WSCF, closely related to these youth bodies, coordinated the Student Christian Movement (SCM) groups and Christian Unions in the universities of Europe, North America, and—increasingly—Asia. It had been formed in 1895 under the headstrong command of the American Methodist layman and YMCA leader John R. Mott. The result was an extraordinary burst of international youth and student activity committed to world evangelism and social witness. This was important for its immediate missionary impact and in providing the seedbed from which came many of the next generation of ecumenical leaders. By the early 1930s, the "Ys" and the WSCF were still highly important ecumenical actors in their own right, with fulltime headquarters staff in Geneva.

The International Missionary Council (IMC) was the most visible fruit of that turn-of-the-century missionary impulse which had flowered into the pivotal 1910 Edinburgh World Missionary Conference. But the IMC had not been formed until 1921, the First World War having intervened to prevent any further development beyond the continuation committee of the Edinburgh conference. The IMC secretariat was in London, under the skillful direction of the Scottish layman, theologian, and social thinker J. H. Oldham. Its constituency mainly comprised the boards of (largely Western-based) missions. In terms of official church representation and breadth of membership, the most significant ecumenical body was the Universal Christian Council for Life and Work,[2] child of the 1925 Stockholm Conference on "Life and Work," inspired, planned, and led by Nathan Söderblom, archbishop of Sweden. In the wake of the tragedy of 1914–18, Söderblom's vision was for an ecumenical council of the churches which would seek to bring Christian principles to bear on international relations and on social, industrial, and economic problems—and in so doing enable the churches themselves to grow more visibly united. Life and Work, like the youth organizations, had its secretariat in Geneva which facilitated close contact with international bodies like the League of Nations and the International Labour Organization. Its secretary was a Swiss Reformed theologian, Henry Louis Henriod, sometime secretary of the WSCF. In 1931, also in Geneva, it set up a research office. The latest arrival on the ecumenical scene in terms of organization was the Faith and Order movement, although interest in interchurch dialogue on doctrinal matters had been evident since the turn of the century, and it was during the 1910 Edinburgh conference that the American missionary bishop of the Episcopal Church, Charles Brent, felt led to pursue still more actively what had been on his heart and mind for so long. The movement really got under way with the 1927 Faith and Order Conference at Lausanne and was guided by that conference's continuation committee, which promoted further comparative study of central doctrinal matters such as the nature of the church, the doctrine of grace, Christ, and the sacraments. In 1930 it, too, opened an office in Geneva.

There was, however, another ecumenical body, closely related to Life and Work, with much less official status than either that body or Faith and Order, or even the IMC, in that its membership and governance lay much less with official church representatives and much more with enthusiastic individuals and national groupings— yet it predated all those bodies. The World Alliance for International Friendship through the Churches[3] had been formed on the very eve of war in 1914, having grown out of earlier exchange visits by the British and German churches, and joined by other European and— especially—American church figures. Surviving the bitter estrangements of the war, in the 1920s it promoted renewed encounter and reconciliation between people and churches from former belligerent and neutral countries alike, with increasing participation from the Far East as well as Europe and the Americas. It was more lay oriented, less overtly theological, more pragmatic in its approach to contemporary problems than were the IMC, Faith and Order, and Life and Work. But its kinship to Life and Work was obvious—indeed, Nathan Söderblom was given impetus toward setting up the Stockholm conference by his involvement in the World Alliance's first main postwar conference in Holland in 1919. The relation between the World Alliance and Life and Work was sealed in 1931 with the formation of a joint youth commission of both bodies, and a joint secretariat in Geneva, H. L. Henriod serving as secretary to both bodies.

Such in outline was the international ecumenical scene in 1931. The ecumenical bodies had established themselves, though not entirely securely. They were all caught up in change and uncertainty. Partly it was due to the passage of time and the passing of some founding apostles: Charles Brent died in 1929, Nathan Söderblom in July 1931 (the very month of Bonhoeffer's return from the USA). There had been internal tensions within some of the organizations. Conservative evangelicals were disaffiliating from the Student Christian Movement groups in a number of countries, and the WSCF was embarking on an international study on the essentials of the Christian message, which was to prove both long and contentious. Within the IMC there was some controversy over the emphasis made at the 1928 Jerusalem World Missionary Conference that the real enemy of the gospel was secularism rather than other world religions, while J. H. Oldham at the helm of the IMC was chafing at the restricted view of many of the mission boards in the face of the new challenges in society. Faith and Order was beset by severe financial difficulties in the wake of the world economic crisis and closed its Geneva office in 1932.

On the broader front, Life and Work and Faith and Order, in the view of some, represented contrasting approaches to ecumenicity: "Doctrine divides, service unites" was the glib slogan heard from some socially activist quarters. Within Life and Work itself there were tensions between continental Protestants—especially Germans— and their British and American counterparts, with the continentals declaring that the reign of God could only come in by divine eschatological intervention, and the "Anglo-Saxons" seeking to build that kingdom by human effort in social progress. In some circles, it was the World Alliance that was regarded as a hindrance to greater ecumenical integration. With Life and Work manifesting a concern for unity between the churches as well as their social action, a rapprochement with Faith and Order was not inconceivable[4]—except that in some eyes the closeness of Life and Work with the World Alliance made it guilty by association, given the latter body's liberalism and openness (especially in the USA) to other religions.[5] The World Alliance, in any case, was finding itself in a newly daunting world. If up until 1914 the churches' peace movement had been an expression of pious sentiment and goodwill, following the calamity of 1914–18 it had been appealing to human rationality: surely no one could want a repeat of that catastrophic bloodletting. War no longer made sense; hence the churches' efforts should be put toward bolstering the only sensible ways of running the world, through the League of Nations, arbitration, and disarmament. By 1931, however, it was becoming evident that fewer people and governments were inclined to think or behave rationally. More primeval impulses of nationalism and militarism were stirring again. To what good instincts could Christians now appeal? Perhaps Karl Barth's message of the wholly other God who meets the world in decisive judgment and the unexpected miracle of grace was indeed the word for the hour. Into this scene stepped the 25-year-old Dietrich Bonhoeffer.

Enter Bonhoeffer

When Dietrich Bonhoeffer arrived home in Berlin from the USA at the end of June 1931, he was not immediately recognizable as an ecumenist. He had had no relationship or personal acquaintance with any of the organizations or movements mentioned above, or any of their expressions within Germany. There is no evidence, for example, that while studying in Tübingen and then Berlin he had taken any interest in the activities of the lively SCM branches in those universities.

While in the USA his regard for the Federal Council of Churches had been, at best, mild. Ecumenical commitment certainly marked several of his teachers in the Berlin faculty, notably Adolf Deissmann (1866–1937), professor of New Testament, who was a founder member of the World Alliance and chair of its German section, and a member of the council of Life and Work. Little if any of this interest, however, seems to have been imparted to Bonhoeffer directly from Deissmann, whose only known personal communication with Bonhoeffer on ecumenical matters was a response to his report on his USA visit and his impressions of the American churches: "I have a more positive opinion about the current condition of the Episcopal Church and the predominant Lutheran churches. Perhaps you had less contact with these churches."[6] No less remarkable was Bonhoeffer's lack of contact, as yet, with Friedrich Siegmund-Schultze (1885–1969), pioneer ecumenist from the time of the Anglo-German churches' peace exchanges of 1908–09, a co-founder of the World Alliance, social theologian and researcher, honorary professor in the Berlin faculty—and, moreover, a collaborator with Bonhoeffer's father in his neurological clinic.[7]

As for certain of Bonhoeffer's peers among students and younger pastors, an ecumenical enthusiasm was hardly evident. During his doctoral studies in 1926 he had received a letter from Richard Widmann, a pastor in Württemberg, highly critical of the Stockholm Life and Work conference which he had attended the previous year: "The more one occupies oneself with the subject, the more doubtful it becomes. (The subject would be less doubtful if it didn't strive to be more than an international alliance to promote ethical culture. It does, however, strive to be more! One truly wants to build the kingdom of God!)."[8] While at Union Seminary in New York a long, studious letter came from his erstwhile friend Helmut Rössler, now pastor in Beveringen, Ost-Prignitz, including the comment that he was very moved by Bonhoeffer's description of "the theologically grotesque nature of the American church," which would lead him to see "what a frightful illusion 'world Protestantism' can be as an 'ecumenical idea.'"[9] Still more serious, as will be described in more detail later, was the rising opposition to international ecumenism as being inimical to German interests, which was being manifest in the bourgeoning nationalist movement and was being voiced also by some of the most esteemed academic theologians.

It was precisely at the time when ecumenism was becoming increasingly questionable in Germany that Bonhoeffer made his commitment to it. In doing so, he was neither disadvantaged by having had no previous relations with the ecumenical bodies, nor dissuaded by the coolness of some of his friends, nor intimidated by the rising nationalist hostility. He entered the field impelled by his own vision, gained through his international experiences and encounters, of the church as a worldwide community, and by his innate theological conviction of church, at every level, being *Christ existing as community*. That made ecumenism an imperative for him. He found his own way into it, and he was to plot his own route through it.

The figure in Berlin who, above all others, was responsible for Bonhoeffer's induction into ecumenical activity was Max Diestel (1872–1949), superintendent of the Berlin-Lichterfelde church district, which included the Grunewald parish where Bonhoeffer's home was. A committed ecumenist himself, and from 1927 assigned the task of building an ecumenical youth programme for the Berlin church, Diestel had clearly set his eyes on Bonhoeffer as a potentially important recruit to the cause. As seen in the previous chapter, he had encouraged Bonhoeffer to take up the Barcelona appointment and facilitated his scholarship at Union Seminary. Moreover, he had kept in touch by letter with his protégé in both Barcelona and New York, with advice on how to benefit most fully from his foreign experiences. It was in this self-same year 1931 that Diestel also became secretary of the German section of the World Alliance, which in September that year was to hold its eighth international conference in Cambridge, England. In May, while Bonhoeffer was still in New York, Diestel wrote saying that he was already enrolling him as a youth delegate to Cambridge along with such as Hans Lilje, general secretary of the German Student Christian Federation and a vice president of the WSCF,[10] and scarcely had Bonhoeffer set foot back in Berlin than Diestel was following this up with a phone call. Years later, in 1942, in very different circumstances for them both (Bonhoeffer was by then working in the resistance; Diestel, a Confessing Church pastor, had himself been

interrogated by the Gestapo), Bonhoeffer wrote to Diestel congratu-
lating him on his 70th birthday. Bonhoeffer was full of gratitude for
all the ways in which the older man had opened up opportunities for
him to experience the wider world and church; and the Cambridge
invitation, said Bonhoeffer, was "perhaps the most decisive of all."[11]
In 1931, Bonhoeffer could not have foreseen just what a momentous
step this would prove. For the moment, it was just another step of
exploration into a sphere which was increasingly drawing his interest
and curiosity. An immediate result was that at last he was brought into
direct acquaintance with more of the senior Berlin ecumenists, notably Friedrich Siegmund-Schultze.

It was a step, however, which was already liable to make him a
marked man. A month before his return home there had taken place in
Hamburg a preparatory meeting of the German section of the World
Alliance in order to formulate a position on the three main issues to
be dealt with at Cambridge: national and international obligations,
disarmament, and minority questions. But the meeting from the start
was beset by public controversy. A Hamburg newspaper carried an
article virulently hostile to all such conferences as deadly to German
interests, stating that there could be no understanding between "us
Germans and the victorious nations in the world war," and that " a
Christian and church rapprochement among the peoples is impossible as long as the others are waging a murderous policy against our
people. Whoever believes that understanding can be better served
otherwise disowns the German destiny and confuses consciences at
home and does not honor the truth."[12] These rampantly nationalist
sentiments—given rousing amplification as other right-wing papers
published them in turn—were penned by none other than two of the
country's most eminent Protestant theologians, Paul Althaus of Erlangen and Emanuel Hirsch of Göttingen. Amid the ensuing storm, lasting several months, "internationalism" became a term of abuse, and
the World Alliance and any Germans associated with it were prime
targets of the political right. For Bonhoeffer, the stance of Althaus in
particular must have come as a shock, for hitherto they had seemed to
be on a similar theological wavelength. Althaus, like Bonhoeffer, had
recently written on the church as community.

Already, not just differences but fault lines were appearing on the German Protestant scene. Ecumenism was coming to signify not merely a viewpoint but a commitment facing serious opposition and potentially carrying a price. Perhaps it was this very fact that encouraged Bonhoeffer to go to Cambridge. In New York, for all the questions he had about liberal Anglo-Saxon Protestantism, he had also seen black Christianity taking up the cross, had listened to Jean Lasserre expounding the Sermon on the Mount as meaning actual discipleship—*following*—of the nonviolent Jesus, and had met at least some American theologians who were asking searching questions about society, international order, the war-guilt question, and the legacy of 1914–18. The World Alliance could be the place where this pathway to a more challenging Christianity might, however uncertainly, be pursued. Eberhard Bethge summarizes the situation: "It was both characteristic and incongruous that [Bonhoeffer] entered the ecumenical movement through the World Alliance. . . , the ecumenical organization most dominated by the spirit of liberal and humanist Anglo-Saxon theology. It was also the freest organization, and not nearly as strongly ecclesiastical as the others. With its emphasis on peace work, it was also the group most committed to something."[13] At a further preparatory meeting for Cambridge convened in Berlin by Siegmund-Schultze, Bonhoeffer became fully apprised of the sensitivities to be encountered at the conference—above all, the question of disarmament, about which hardly any German could be expected to say anything in public because of how it would be (mis)represented at home—not to mention the anxieties persisting between German and French participants even at such a meeting.

In the two months between his homecoming and the World Alliance conference, another factor entered into Bonhoeffer's new commitment: he had his first personal encounter with Karl Barth, his main theological inspiration since 1924. He spent three weeks of July in Bonn where Barth was now professor, heard him lecture, attended his seminar, was received in his home, and lunched with him. Previously impressed with his writings and fired by them into becoming a Barthian, he was now even more captivated by the man himself, his extraordinary combination of concentrated intellectual energy and free, open-hearted interest in other people (laced with delicious wit) and, for the sake of the truth, a willingness to hear critical questions. To Erwin Sutz, who had facilitated the introduction, Bonhoeffer wrote excitedly: "He is really fully present. I have never seen anything like it nor thought it possible."[14] Barth and the young German became collegial friends for life. The bearing of Barth on Bonhoeffer's nascent ecumenism may not be readily apparent—after all, Barth at this stage was not himself in the ecumenical vanguard. But his emphasis on the transcendent majesty of God and the utter supremacy of God's word, as well as placing all human projects (including church structures) under judgment, also meant that no human enterprise, however unprepossessing (such as the World Alliance might appear to be!), was necessarily without purpose under the free, elective grace of God. Bonhoeffer, however, was a restless as well as devoted disciple of Barth, and brought to the professor some critical questions. One of them he had already voiced in his postdoctoral thesis *Act and Being*,[15] namely: Does not Barth so stress God's transcendence as to make the divine freedom a freedom *from* the world whereas in Jesus Christ the divine freedom is the freedom of grace, freedom *for* the world? Bonhoeffer was now following this up with a related question: How can faith in the God who is "wholly other" lead to concrete ethical directions for life in this world? He was troubled by Barth's seeming unclarity or even evasiveness here—over lunch Barth talked about "relative ethical criteria," but not in a way that satisfied Bonhoeffer.[16] This passion to find a way in which the church could say, "This you must do," as assuredly as it pronounced, "Your sins are forgiven," was to make Bonhoeffer as impatiently expectant of the ecumenical movement as he was of Barth.

Why So Many Churches? A New Catechism

One particular sign must be noted of how importantly Bonhoeffer regarded the ecumenical cause during this summer of 1931, even prior to the Cambridge Conference, as he was starting to prepare for pastoral ministry as well as academic teaching. During August, he and

Franz Hildebrandt, a young pastor who had been assistant to Friedrich Siegmund-Schultze and whom Bonhoeffer had known since 1927,[17] worked together on drafting a new catechism to replace the traditional Lutheran ones which had been used virtually unchanged since the 16th century. It was a quite revolutionary experiment, for as well as trying to put into contemporary and simplified language the central doctrines of the Reformation faith, it ventured into questions of science and belief, war, peace—and the unity of the church:

> Why . . . are there so many churches?
> We really should be *one* church. Due to our inexplicable disunion, we insist on a new community [*Gemeinschaft*] of all Christians. To have such a new community is never possible for us as human beings other than in expectation and in a faith that is faithful to God's church.
> Where is the true church?
> The true church is where preaching stands and falls with the pure gospel of a gracious God over against all human self-righteousness. It is where the sacraments depend on the word of Christ without any element of magic. It is where the community of the Spirit exists in service and not in domination.[18]

A "new community of all Christians": this hope has to be kept in mind as we trace Bonhoeffer's ecumenical journey from here on.

The Cambridge Conference and After

In late August 1931 Bonhoeffer travelled to England for the first time. The Cambridge Conference was preceded by two preliminary meetings for youth and students, at St Leonards-on-Sea and Westcliffe-on-Sea, while at Cambridge there was a conference for all the 70 youth delegates prior to the opening of the main World Alliance conference which opened on 1 September. The introduction of such a sizeable youth presence was itself a new step for the Alliance, or, indeed, for any major ecumenical gathering of the time. It was to prove a creative irritant, for at their meeting the youth were in no mood simply to add their fresh energy to what they knew was in store at the main conference: calls to outlaw war without a prior resort to arbitration; to provide civil alternatives to military service; and, above all, to support the World Disarmament Conference scheduled to start in Geneva in 1932. Not that the youth were in disagreement with any of these, but they made clear their deep skepticism about *the church* being in a position to say or do anything meaningful given its own history of involvement in wars, its present divisions, the lack of spiritual ardour on the part of so many of its members, and the prevailing skepticism of those outside organized Christianity about the relevance of the church in promoting peace. Some leaders sought to draw up a benign resolution to present to the main conference on the need for Christian principles to be applied to international life, and for a total reconstruction of church, social, and political life. This was voted down. Something other than bland statements of ideals was demanded.

From what transpired during the following days in Cambridge it is very evident that Bonhoeffer was foremost among the skeptics, arguing that it was not for the church to lecture the world without questioning its own assumptions about what it meant *to be church*. He found a sympathetic ally in a young French pastor, Pierre Toureille. Together they were scornful of the poster that welcomed delegates to Cambridge: "World Peace depends on World Disarmament and Disarmament depends on you!"[19] and which seemed to epitomize Anglo-Saxon pragmatism. In fact, meeting his French counterparts was for Bonhoeffer one of the most worthwhile aspects of the Cambridge experience. Much of the conference ran its course as expected, beginning with the sermon at the opening service preached by Miles Krumbine of Cleveland, Ohio, an eloquent statement of the rational, liberal viewpoint Bonhoeffer had come to expect: "The will to war will break down when war no longer serves national interests. That hour has come at last. . . . It is just as logical and timely for the statesman of today to plot peace in the interest of his nation as it seemed necessary to the statesman of the nineteenth century to plot war."[20] Much in the same vein was to be heard during the next five days, on disarmament as a moral issue, as a challenge to the churches, as a factor in national security. On the penultimate day resolutions were passed, the main one, as expected, being on disarmament. After stating, "War considered as an institution for the settlement of international disputes is incompatible with the mind and method of Christ therefore is incompatible with the mind and method of His Church," the declaration welcomed the summoning of the World Disarmament Conference, demanded a reduction in armaments of every form, the fixing of a scale for the armed forces of the nations, and security for all nations against aggression.[21] It was passed unanimously.

There is no doubt that Bonhoeffer supported this resolution, for all his doubts that by itself it represented an adequate statement of Christian witness. His main concern remained: What did it mean *to be church* in a world still wounded by the last war, when nationalism was stirring again and a new arms race was threatening? During the first session of the conference, presided over by Bishop Valdemar Ammundsen of Denmark, four main speakers had addressed the disarmament issue, including the Dane G. Sparring Petersen on "The Responsibility of the Churches"—an impassioned plea against armaments and wars launched with Christian legitimation. Toureille was deputed to respond on behalf of the youth conference and prepared his remarks with the help of Bonhoeffer: "Humanitarian efforts will never make war disappear, the struggle against it must come out of different depths and greater obedience."[22] As Eberhard Bethge remarks, "Here we hear Bonhoeffer's voice in Cambridge."[23] A similar echo from Bonhoeffer is heard in the report by a French delegate, Roger Jézéquel, who shortly afterward spoke of a long, late-night meeting between the French and German youth, and of discovering a striking rapport with a German academic (undoubtedly Bonhoeffer) and their agreement about the ground of rapprochement: "Security? A revision of the treaties? Pacifist propaganda? Perhaps . . . actually, we are being cornered, compelled to make Christianity a reality, to make the church visible . . ."[24] Those rhetorical questions strikingly presage those in Bonhoeffer's famous declaration at the Fanø conference three years later.[25] There was another forecasting of what could be in store for a prophetic witness, in the sermon preached at the closing service of the conference by Edward Arthur Burroughs, Anglican bishop of

Ripon and president of the British section of the World Alliance. The churches' witness for peace, he declared, would open the way for martyrdom: "It will be for every Christian in that way to decide between the two forms of treason, treason to God or treason to the State."[26] Just then, none could have imagined how that was to become poignantly true for the German delegates especially, and for one member of the youth group above all.

For Bonhoeffer, however, the most immediate and crucial significance of the Cambridge Conference lay not in any resolution, declaration, or sermon, or even a new personal encounter, but in an invitation for him to accept a specific position of responsibility in the World Alliance. The youth conference had made a threefold proposal to the main conference: to enlarge the youth committee; to appoint a secretary to work in Geneva and to assist Bishop Burroughs; and to appoint three international youth secretaries who would serve on an honorary basis but with their expenses met by the World Alliance. It was the third of these proposals which now had immediate bearing on Bonhoeffer, for he was invited, and accepted, to be the youth secretary for Germany, central and northern Europe, Hungary, and Austria. Toureille was named for France, Latin America, the Balkans, Poland, and Czechoslovakia; and the Englishman F. W. Tom Craske for the British Empire, the USA, and Far East. These proposals were approved by the management committee and accepted by the World Alliance. Bonhoeffer was thus now linked decisively and, as it proved, irrevocably into the ecumenical movement. He went to Cambridge as an interested participant. He returned to Germany as an actual representative and advocate of the movement as found in the World Alliance.

Cooperation: Absolutely Necessary but Impossible?

Bonhoeffer's state of mind on the World Alliance and the Cambridge Conference in particular is conveyed in the report which he wrote immediately afterward for the journal *Theologische Blätter*.[27] That journal had earlier published the antiecumenical statements of Paul

Althaus and Emanuel Hirsch, and it was clearly with them in mind that Bonhoeffer began: "Those who view the World Alliance with disinterest or resentment should take the opportunity either to confirm their judgment based on the results of the Cambridge meeting or to revise it."[28] For one who had at first in Cambridge resisted strongly the resolution-making attitude, Bonhoeffer is surprisingly positive, indeed fulsome, on the significance (not least for suspicious Germans) of the Cambridge resolution on disarmament and what it demonstrates: "At the very edge of the abyss of yet another complete moral chaos in the lives of the nations, the churches are standing firm and summon all to truthfulness and faithfulness, to respect and honor the foresworn promise."[29] The commitment of the French, Americans, and British delegates to secure peace and mutual confidence among all nations including Germany, he writes, cannot be doubted. Nevertheless, Bonhoeffer seeks to recognize misgivings (no doubt within himself) about some aspects of the procedure under the prevailing "Anglo-Saxon" ethos:

> It will not be possible to avoid the criticism coming from the most diverse sides that too much or too little has been said here, or, one the other hand, that once again something has been merely *said*. . . . The "too much" rests particularly in the theological formulations, which have been determined essentially by Anglo-Saxon theology and grasp the problematic of something like war only in the realization of an already well-established ideal, that is, conceiving the matter as a problem of action rather than as a problem of its essential nature. This is what so often gives the international church resolutions a full-bodied ring and yet to our [German] ear a tone that is devoid of real content.[30]

Rather than continually argue, says Bonhoeffer, about whether the English and Americans "still believe in resolutions more than we do," it is more important that the actual existence and purpose of the World Alliance be highlighted and its resolutions be made known in the respective countries of its members. Conversely, he is concerned to make known to fellow Germans what is being said on peace by

Christians abroad, such as the international YMCA convention in Cleveland, USA, in August 1931, which declared against Germany's sole guilt for the 1914–18 war, and the similar message of the Federal Council of Churches of Christ in the USA in 1930. That latter message, Bonhoeffer points out, was criticized by "serious Americans" as coming ten years too late. He concludes his report: "When will the time come that Christianity speaks the right word at the right time?"[31]

Bonhoeffer was clearly wrestling with the fact that, as far as ecumenical peace work was concerned, it was not just a matter of the churches needing to address the war-torn and war-threatened world. The churches of the European continent and the churches of the English-speaking world were themselves somewhat at odds in their respective approaches to making this address. Put simplistically, the continentals looked to the astringency of divine judgment and grace for insight while the Anglo-Saxons stressed concerted human goodwill and action; and for all the widening of his outlook, Bonhoeffer's basic sympathies at this time remained instinctively within his native tradition, especially encouraged by Barth's rediscovery of the gospel of the wholly other God. Some of his recent experiences of American liberalism no doubt contributed to this sense of where the true gospel was to be found. But, far from prompting a purely negative reaction, these differences made for a truly *ecumenical* issue. Less than two months after Cambridge he was writing to Helmut Rössler: "My stay in America and recently also in England has made one thing clear to me: the absolute necessity of cooperation and at the same time the inexplicable divisions that seem to make such a coming together simply impossible."[32] At times over the next year the sense of "impossibility" was to become uppermost, and Bonhoeffer could write cuttingly of the "Anglo-Saxon" predominance in the World Alliance. To Werner Koch, one of his future seminarians, Bonhoeffer wrote in August 1932, inviting him to the forthcoming World Alliance youth conference at Gland, Switzerland: "Please don't be frightened off by the program. That's just how it has to look to please the Anglo-Saxons. What we do with it is another story."[33] He wrote to Erwin Sutz about the same conference: "At least today I don't feel responsible for running the daily events. The English have already gotten involved much too much in that."[34] His report on Gland would refer again to "the huge gap between Continental and Anglo-Saxon thinking."[35] It was this Anglo-Saxon liberal influence which, he felt, was responsible for current "ecumenical assemblies," unlike the ecumenical councils of the early church, evading the question of *truth* and *heresy*.[36] The time would soon come, early in 1933, when a drastically changed political context would shift preferences and prejudices, and the boundaries between the safety of "home" and the strangeness of "abroad" would become far less clear. With the Nazi revolution and the onset of the Church Struggle, one's foes would be members of one's own church household. Helmut Rössler (to name but one) and Bonhoeffer would part company. It would be from within Germany—indeed, from among some claiming the inheritance of Martin Luther—and not from bland Anglo-Saxon liberalism that the deadliest heresy would raise its head. It would be in London and New York at least as much as in Berlin that friends and comrades would be desperately sought and found. Bonhoeffer would remain critical of aspects of the Anglo-Saxon thought-world but only within an even deeper conviction of the "absolute necessity of cooperation" and, moreover, a growing experience of its actual practice. But even in this initial period (1931–1932) of blustery weather before the real storm broke Bonhoeffer's ecumenical commitment was grounded in a theological conviction deeper than cultural and intellectual inclinations. It was an understanding of community that not only embraced but *required* difference, in encounter with the other, if it was to be genuine. It was in keeping with this that Bonhoeffer shortly after his return from Cambridge sent a copy each of *Sanctorum Communio* and *Act and Being* as a gift to Paul Althaus, along with Emanuel Hirsch the declared opponent of the World Alliance and all its works, "in sincere admiration and gratitude" for the older scholar's help and kindness in encouraging the publication of these works.[37] In *Sanctorum Communio* Bonhoeffer had written of the unity of spirit of the church-community as a fundamental, God-willed, and already established relation:

> Neither unanimity, uniformity, nor congeniality makes it possible, nor is it to be confused with unity of mood. Rather, it is a reality precisely where the seemingly sharpest outward antitheses prevail, where

each person really leads an individual life; and it is perhaps missing just where it seems to prevail most. When one person clashes with another, it might very well lead them to remember the One who is over them both, and in whom both of them are one. Precisely where Greek and Jew clash, out of their completely different psychological dispositions, their intuitive and intellectual perceptions, there unity is established through God's will . . . (Gal. 3:28) . . . —to put it paradoxically—the more powerful the dissimilarity manifests itself in the struggle, the stronger the objective unity. [38]

At the heart of Bonhoeffer's ecumenical theology was the key concept in *Sanctorum Communio*, "Christ existing as church-community," writ large and transposed onto the international level. Later, in the Church Struggle, the emphasis would be placed decisively on *Christ* (as known in his word) existing as church-community. That would mean a sharp separation from such as Althaus. For the present, however, Bonhoeffer had an assured theological compass with which to navigate his way into the complex ecumenical scene and the witness for peace. The significance of the Cambridge Conference for his entry onto that scene cannot be overstated, as was affirmed by Bonhoeffer in his letter to Max Diestel, referred to earlier in this chapter, of 1942. To be a youth secretary of the World Alliance, a body less weighty than the more official ecumenical bodies, might not of itself seem to carry much prestige or influence. But the World Alliance was becoming ever more closely related to the wider ecumenical network described earlier. H. L. Henriod, already secretary of Life and Work in Geneva, was now to combine that role with that of youth secretary of the World Alliance and, moreover, of a joint ecumenical youth commission which was being established for both Life and Work and the World Alliance, and there would be joint meetings of the senior governing bodies of both organizations. In new circumstances, Bonhoeffer himself would be co-opted onto the Council of Life and Work in 1934. Moreover, there were no watertight bulkheads between Life and Work, Faith and Order, the IMC, YMCA, and WSCF as far as their leading personnel were concerned. The same faces were often to be seen at their various meetings. Bonhoeffer was on the way to knowing those leading international ecumenical actors who were to be significant—in some cases, exceedingly so—in his career such as the British figures George Bell, J. H. Oldham, and C. F. Andrews; the Dutchman W.A. Visser't Hooft; the Scandinavian bishops Valdemar Ammundsen and Erling Eidem; and the Americans William Adams Brown and Henry Smith Leiper.

The furthest significance for Bonhoeffer himself of that step taken at Cambridge was hidden at the time. It would lead him even beyond the peace cause to occupy a salient position in the Church Struggle, thence to a specific role in the political resistance and conspiracy and so ultimately to his death. None of this could be foreseen, and in any case he had many other things to occupy him on his return to Berlin: further preparation for pastoral ministry, and his ordination in November 1931; serving as an assistant pastor in north Berlin; conducting a boys' confirmation class in a deprived area of the city; a chaplaincy at the Technical University; and a strenuous programme of lecturing as a *Privatdozent* (freelance lecturer) in the University of Berlin. Moreover, always in the back of his mind, as it had been since his year in America, was the dream of going to India. He took all his Berlin-based activities extremely seriously, but none more so than his work for the World Alliance. We shall turn next to examine that work and the thinking which drove and accompanied it, up to the fateful date of 30 January 1933.

CHAPTER 3

Ecumenism and Peace: Theological Foundations

The period September 1931 to the end of January 1933—that is, the eighteen months from the end of the World Alliance Cambridge Conference to Hitler's accession to power—saw Dietrich Bonhoeffer's first active engagements in ecumenical responsibility. They were undertaken in a context of alarming developments, in Germany and internationally. The financial crash of 1929 was still reverberating across the world, the impact being severe upon Germany and its payment of war reparations, though these were suspended in 1932. International relations overall were taking an ominous turn. The long-awaited Geneva Disarmament Conference opened in May 1932, but from the outset—that is, even before the German place at the table became a Nazi one in 1933—was beset by difficulties. Britain and France, for instance, insisted that any German armaments must be strictly limited by the specifications of the Versailles Treaty, whereas the legitimacy of their own so-called defensive measures was couched only in very general terms. No less discouragingly, the week prior to the opening of the conference saw the outbreak of war between

Japan and China. In Germany, the Weimar Republic was in a state of progressive paralysis in face of economic chaos and social unrest. Unemployment reached an unprecedented high of 6,000,000 in the winter of 1931–32. Successive centrist governments proved unable to accommodate the strident demands of either the extreme left or the extreme right. The complacent belief that the Communists and National Socialists could be left to destroy each other so as to leave the country in the hands of the moderate centre parties proved illusory. The National Socialists proved to be too politically adept with a combination of brutal intimidation, exploitation of middle-class fears of Bolshevism, and a cunning waiting game. The result was that even though Hitler's party never achieved a majority in the Reichstag (and the Nazi vote even declined in late 1932), by early 1933 there seemed no alternative for providing stability of any kind, and on 30 January Hitler was appointed chancellor by President Hindenburg.

The global economic crisis had calamitous consequences for international organizations, including ecumenical bodies. Faith and Order, for example, as mentioned in the previous chapter, was forced to close its Geneva office. Germans were finding it almost impossible to finance their own participation at international events and had to rely on subsidies. Paradoxically, it was the World Alliance—of all ecumenical bodies the least "official" and least beholden to the institutional churches—which had the most financial stability, thanks to major funding from the USA-based Church Peace Union.[1]

Meanwhile, the German churches could not escape the political turmoil in their country and the rise of far-right nationalism, in particular the growing strength of the National Socialist Party (NSDAP or "Nazi" Party) of Adolf Hitler. Many Protestants were proving highly susceptible to the National Socialist brew of racist, Völkisch sentiment and antisemitism, especially when it seemed to promise a spiritual as well as national revival. The antiecumenical outbursts of Paul Althaus and Emanuel Hirsch in the summer of 1931, as described in the previous chapter, were but symptoms of a much wider, and growing, religiously flavoured nationalism. This burst into florid shape in May 1932 with the formation of the "Faith Movement of German Christians," effectively a Protestant ancillary of the Nazi party (complete with its own brown uniform akin to that of the Nazi Storm Troopers) and designed to mobilize Protestant opinion behind the party. The German Christians aspired after "a dynamic national church (*Volkskirche*), which expresses the living faith of our people,"[2] "in the Germanic spirit of Luther and of heroic piety." The movement rallied people to "the decisive battle against Marxism, the enemy of God, and against the unspiritual Centre group." Central to its own credo ("a confession of life") was the tenet: "In race, nation and cultural heritage we see the orders of existence which God has given us in trust; it is the law of God that we should be concerned to preserve them. Therefore racial admixture is to be opposed . . . faith in Christ does not destroy the race, it deepens and sanctifies it."[3] Nor, according to the German Christians, should the church engage in any mission to the Jews in Germany "as long as the Jews have the right to citizenship and there is therefore danger of bastardization and an obscuring of racial differences."[4] Marriage between Germans and Jews must be prohibited. Moreover: "We want a Protestant church rooted in our own culture, and are opposed to the spirit of cosmopolitanism" and all accompanying "degenerate phenomena"—pacifism, international freemasonry, and the like.[5] Clearly, nothing could be more directly opposed to ecumenism, especially as represented by the World Alliance. The German Christians grew into an energetic movement among both clergy and laypeople, publicly committed to capturing the governing bodies of the Protestant churches, in the first instance the large Prussian Church.[6]

The Ecumenical Youth Secretary at Work

As stipulated by the decision of the Cambridge Conference, Dietrich Bonhoeffer's duties as an honorary travelling secretary of the World Alliance were quite specific. As secretary for Germany, central and northern Europe, Hungary, and Austria, he was to promote and encourage the work of the World Alliance among youth in the respective countries, liaising with the national bodies of the Alliance and with the joint youth secretariat of the Alliance and Life and Work in Geneva, now under the charge of H. L. Henriod. He was also to liaise with the other two youth secretaries, Paul Toureille and Tom Craske. The work involved correspondence, organizing meetings and conferences, writing reports, and attending committees of the joint youth commission and the management committee of the Alliance, of which he and the other youth secretaries were now ex officio members. In the course of the 17 months we are reviewing, up to the end of January 1933, the work took him to England, Switzerland, France, and Czechoslovakia.

It also, however, gave him much to do within Germany itself, and in Berlin in particular, which was a main stronghold of the World Alliance thanks to the work of such as Friedrich Siegmund-Schultze, Adolf Deissmann, and Bonhoeffer's chief ecumenical mentor, Max Diestel. The German branch of the World Alliance was in fact a key component of the internal German ecumenical scene which, on paper at least, had a somewhat untidy and cumbersome structure (complaints about the complexity of ecumenical architecture, deserved or not, are nothing new). Key to German ecumenical work were four bodies:

1. *The German Ecumenical Working Committee*,[7] founded and led by August Schreiber, high consistory official in the Church Federation office and director of the German Protestant Mission Society. In this were represented the Protestant Church Federation (the coordinating body for the 28 regional (*Land*) churches), the larger free churches and youth organizations, Faith and Order, Life and Work, and the World Alliance.

2. *The Student Circle for Ecumenical Youth Work*,[8] directed by Herbert Petrick, a Baptist and secretary of the German section of the World Alliance. Faith and Order and the World Alliance were connected to this group.

3. *The Regional Protestant Friends' Circle for Ecumenical Friendship Work*,[9] originally founded by Friedrich Siegmund-Schultze and now led by Herbert Petrick. Participants were from the free churches, independent youth organizations, and the East German Youth League led by Friedrich Peter, a right-wing Protestant, a member of the NSDAP, and a German Christian.

4. *The Provisional Bureau for Ecumenical Youth Work,*[10]
   under the general jurisdiction of August Schreiber, bringing together the Church Federation, the German Section
   of the World Alliance, Faith and Order, the free churches,
   and a range of youth and student organizations (SCM,
   YMCA, YWCA, etc.). Its director was Wilhelm Stählin,
   professor of practical theology at Münster, with Herbert
   Petrick initially as secretary.

Eberhard Bethge states that when Bonhoeffer took up his ecumenical responsibilities in Berlin, the most important of these groups
for him was the Regional Protestant Friends Circle for Ecumenical
Friendship Work.[11] But by virtue of being a youth secretary of the
World Alliance, it was with the Provisional Bureau for Ecumenical
Youth Work that he was to become most directly involved and, after
a short time, he replaced Herbert Petrick as its secretary. The Bureau,
taking on an agenda of theological study of ecumenical problems,
advocacy for the ecumenical idea, and the organizing of conferences
and international exchanges, almost by default extended its clientele
beyond the strict confines of "youth." There were, in addition, a number of study groups in Berlin, mostly relatively informal, such as the
circle of theologically keen pastors who gathered around Hans Jacobi,
pastor of the Kaiser Wilhelm Memorial Church, and which Bonhoeffer joined (it was later to play an important role at the onset of the
Church Struggle).[12] There was also the Working Group of Theologians and Economists[13] that met fortnightly in the Church Federation
Office, but which Bonhoeffer attended only occasionally—whether
because he had reservations about its relatively conservative stance
or because its meetings often clashed with his academic duties is not
clear.[14]

Bonhoeffer, the newcomer to the ecumenical cause, thus found
several ready-made instruments to hand, in particular the Provisional
Bureau, which afforded him a desk in August Schreiber's Church
Federation office. It must have been gratifying to the likes of Diestel and Siegmund-Schultze to have such an energetic and theologically able recruit. But, Bethge comments: "Some groups welcomed

him as a stimulus; others regarded him as an ambitious intruder."[15] Be that as it may, it is clear that in Berlin Bonhoeffer devoted his considerable energies to the day-to-day mechanics of ecumenical work even if he was not a natural bureaucrat and some of the tasks seemed tediously humdrum such as, at Wilhelm Stählin's insistence, compiling a national card-index with details of young people thought suitable to attend international ecumenical events, or seeing into print some minor publications such as the Bureau's newsletter. His overall orientation, however, was provided by the World Alliance office in Geneva. At the end of October 1931 came a circular letter from H. L. Henriod to the World Alliance Youth Secretaries outlining proposals and plans for the next twelve months, including a summer youth conference at Gland, Switzerland, in 1932, and suggestions for regional conferences, Anglo-French, Franco-German, and Balkan. These events alone made for a heavy organizational schedule—with very uncertain finances. Nevertheless, Henriod continued, "This should not delay any action by the Secretaries in establishing contact with their respective areas."[16] Bonhoeffer more than took Henriod at his word here, while making clear that any Germans participating in events aboard would require financial subsidies.

The most significant ecumenical events with which Bonhoeffer was involved during this period, in chronological order, were:

1. *Provisional Bureau for Ecumenical Youth Work, Berlin, 20 October 1931.* This was a regular full meeting of the Provisional Bureau, chaired by Wilhelm Stählin. Reports and exchanges were made on recent events, including the World Alliance Cambridge Conference, and forward planning was discussed, including a proposal to hold a theological conference in the spring of the following year on "The Unity of Christian Churches" and "The Unity of Christian Churches and the Peoples," arrangements being delegated to Stählin and Bonhoeffer.

2. *London and Epsom, April 1932.* The World Alliance International Youth Committee met in London, 4 April 1932, chaired by Arthur Burroughs, bishop of Ripon. This

was followed by the Anglo-French regional conference at Epsom, near London, organized by Bonhoeffer's colleagues Tom Craske and Paul Toureille. Its main theme was the applicability of Christianity to the state and to social and industrial life. In his report for *Die Eiche*,[17] Bonhoeffer's appreciation was outweighed by his criticism of trying to "force results" in such meetings where "discussion of such far-reaching problems lasts only two or three hours"[18] and where much more intensive preparation is required: "This deplorable state of affairs must be confronted most decisively, especially in youth conferences, We must not become so accustomed to the beautiful feeling of international friendship that we lose the time for serious work."[19] Writing to Erwin Sutz, he was downright dismissive of "a very superfluous conference."[20]

3. *Theological Conference of Provisional Bureau for Ecumenical Youth Work, Berlin, April 1932.* This wholly German conference, as proposed in number 1, above, took place in Berlin, 29–30 April 1932. The two main addresses were given by Wilhelm Zoellner, recently retired general superintendent of the Church of Westphalia ("The Church and the Churches"), and Wilhelm Stählin ("The Church and the Peoples"). Bonhoeffer himself responded critically and vigorously to both presentations in the ensuing discussion, as recorded in his own report.[21]

4. *German–French World Alliance Youth Conference, July 1932, Westerburg.* This regional conference, organized by Bonhoeffer, took place in the Westerburg, Rhineland-Palatinate, 12–14 July 1932, on the theme "The Unity of German–French Protestantism between Catholicism and Bolshevism." Bonhoeffer, in contrast to his report on the Epsom meeting, judged it highly successful on account both of its intentionally small size and the quality of its preparatory material, but even more because of the way in which it faced specific issues—including the responsibility of other countries in provoking the rise of German

National Socialism by their policies, in particular the terms of the Versailles Treaty.[22]

5. *International Youth Peace Conference, Ciernohorské-Kúpele, Czechoslovakia, 20–30 July 1932.* This event was sponsored by Czechoslovakian church leaders and World Alliance figures who invited participation by World Alliance officers and members from other countries including Britain and France. The gathering, more in the nature of a retreat than a formal conference, covered a diverse range of topics. Bonhoeffer attended at short notice, deputizing for Max Diestel who was ill, and could only attend part of the time but gave his very substantial paper "On the Theological Foundation of the Work of the World Alliance."[23]

6. *Ecumenical Committees, Geneva, August 1932.* Just prior to the Gland conference (see number 7, below) Bonhoeffer attended the management committee of the International Section of the World Alliance in Geneva, 19–22 August 1932, followed on 23 August by the directing group for the Gland conference. Shortly before these meetings the Council of Life and Work had also met in Geneva and had elected Bishop George Bell as president of the Council. Several of the senior figures in Life and Work remained in Geneva for the World Alliance Committee, including Bishop Ove Ammundsen of Denmark and C. F. Andrews (British Anglican priest, almost naturalized Indian, and close friend of Gandhi). It is not clear whether these days in Geneva also saw Bonhoeffer's first meeting with George Bell, but it was about this time that, at the request of Friedrich Siegmund-Schultze, he obtained a copy of Bell's book *A Brief Sketch of the Church of England* and edited its translation into German.[24]

7. *Youth Conference of World Alliance and Life and Work, Gland, Lake Geneva, 25–31 August 1932.* This conference, organized by the Joint Ecumenical Youth Commission,

was the most substantial event so far for which Bonhoeffer had major responsibility. He had also, as noted in the previous chapter, expressed doubts in advance due to the "Anglo-Saxon" influence in its planning.[25] Some 60 participants came from Europe, America, and the Far East. Presentations were made on the main topics "The Call of Christianity in the Present Crisis," "The Economic Crisis," and "The International Crisis." Bonhoeffer himself felt that the first topic alone should have sufficed. He gave one of the opening speeches of welcome, persistently objected throughout the conference to the British desire for a "declaration," and toward the end gave the summing-up address in place of Bishop Ammundsen who had needed to cancel.

8. *Second Theological Conference of Provisional Bureau for Ecumenical Youth Work, Berlin, 9–10 December 1932.* This was intended as a follow-up to the April conference but was held jointly with the Student Circle for Ecumenical Youth and thus had a wider intake of represented ecumenical bodies. Some tension arose, however, over the invitations, a sign of the growing polarization in the political context: there was a general move to exclude the avowedly right-wing Friedrich Peter. In his place, not without misgivings which were shared by Bonhoeffer, the more moderate Ludwig Weichert of the Berlin Mission, who was nevertheless also a member of the NSDAP and a moderate German Christian, was invited. No report of the meeting was published.[26]

Such a schedule of organizational responsibility and travel, in addition to his heavy academic and pastoral activity in Berlin, could only have been undertaken by someone of extraordinary and passionate commitment to the ecumenical cause. The heart and nerve centre of that commitment, however, are only fully exposed in what he himself was actually saying at these ecumenical gatherings. At this point, for the sake of overall clarity, it is necessary to distinguish his two overriding ecumenical concerns at this time: peace in the world, and the need for a theology of the ecumenical movement itself. These were closely related in his mind, and he often dealt with them on the same occasion or even in the same presentation, but for the moment, in order to do full justice to each, it will be helpful to treat these parallel concerns by turn. With the onset of the Church Struggle in 1933, the twin themes became inextricably fused in the calling to confess Christ above all else in the world. For the present it will be enough to see just how independently and radically Bonhoeffer was viewing the ecumenical movement and its purpose in 1932.

Peace: Theological Critique

Bonhoeffer's first contribution to the ecumenical peace witness was not, as one might expect, simply to denounce (as if it had not been done often enough before) rearmament, militarism, and nationalism, but to attack the *theological* presuppositions that lay behind much of the debate of the time. His most immediate target was the concept, beloved of the nationalist theologians in Germany such as Paul Althaus and Emanuel Hirsch, of "orders of creation." This is the doctrine that certain structures in human life are not merely incidental or historically conditioned phenomena, but are ordained of God as essential and immutable features of divine creation, without which humanity is not humanity as created and intended by God. As such, the concept of orders of creation was not particularly exceptionable. Both Protestant and Catholic thought had traditionally identified features of human existence and social life that are especially significant for the way in which the image of God is reflected in the human creature. Even Karl Barth was not averse in the 1920s to speaking of "the orders" in his teaching on ethics.[27] Since the First World War, however, much effort had been devoted in Germany to finding an explicit metaphysical or theological basis for *nationhood*, and the concept of orders of creation here proved very convenient for nationalist theology: it could be claimed that the supreme order of creation is the people (*das Volk*), race, or nation to which one belongs and thus owes loyalty. Such an understanding could then become the mould for recasting the entire shape of Christian belief. So, for instance, when the creed confesses belief in God as maker of heaven and earth, this becomes the confession that God has specifically created a person with his or her particularly nationality and its unique characteristics. It is in the flowering of a nation's special identity that one sees what creation really is, and God has therefore bound the person to submit oneself to the forces working out the destiny of one's nation and to cooperate with its spirit. Such thinking became the hallmark especially of the German Christian movement and its manifesto, noted above, set out in May 1932.

For Bonhoeffer, by contrast, and in line with Barth's christocentric theology of revelation, all such attempts to talk about creation in a general way were spurious. For him, as he was to make clear in his winter 1932–33 lectures on *Creation and Fall,*[28] it is Jesus Christ through whom both God and the world as God intends it to be are known. God's will and purpose cannot be read off directly from the world as it is, the fallen world of sin and division. Christian faith cannot be redefined in terms of nationhood. Rather, nationhood, like everything else, has to be understood in the light of the word of God, Jesus Christ.

It is remarkable that Bonhoeffer so early in his career was alert to this coming theological clash and engaged himself in it. Well before the actual German Christian manifesto of May 1932, in January of that year he prepared a short presentation on "The Discernible Nature of the Order of Creation" for a meeting in Berlin of the Working Group of Theologians and Economists.[29] It was in April, however, that he launched his attack most publicly at the theological conference of the Provisional Bureau for Ecumenical Youth Work.[30] At the second session of the conference, Wilhelm Stählin gave his presentation on "The Unity of Christian Churches and the Peoples." That Stählin, a moderate theologian who never joined the German Christians, could make such positive use of "orders of creation" as he did in this paper illustrates how well established and widely respected the term was in the Protestant theology of the time. Bonhoeffer, in his response to Stählin, showed no such respect: "It is not possible to lift out certain given elements in the world as orders of creation apart from others and to ground a Christian moral way of acting upon that."[31] Making nationhood an order of creation is a theological presupposition justifying war between the nations. "When the problem of conflict originates in obedience to the specific order of creation of God, why shouldn't a person then understand his fight as a fight for the cause of God?"[32] Bonhoeffer's own report of the meeting continues:

> [The order of creation] is a dangerous and treacherous foundation. Rather, in place of the order of creation, one should introduce the concept of the "order of preservation" of God. The difference would be that, from the perspective of the order of creation, certain orders, that is, given realities that are seen as worthy and original in themselves, will be considered "very good" on the basis of being such orders. Whereas with the concept of the orders of preservation, it would be understood that every given reality is a reality maintained solely from God in grace and wrath, in view of the revelation in Christ. Every order under the preservation of God would then be aligned with Christ and only preserved on his behalf. An order is seen as an order of preservation only as long as it is open to the preservation of the gospel. Wherever an order, even though it appears to be most fundamental, such as marriage, nation, and so on, is fundamentally closed to the proclamation, it must be surrendered. Instead of proceeding from the order of creation, the solution to the overall ethical problem and to the ecumenical problem as well must be sought exclusively from the revelation of God given in Christ.[33]

In the ensuing discussion, Bonhoeffer's radical relativizing of all given realities including nationhood was well received by the ecumenical student leader Hans Lilje and the missiologist Siegfried Knak. The Nazi pastor Friedrich Peter unsurprisingly and stoutly defended "orders of creation." Stählin, for his part, remained nervous about where Bonhoeffer's critique, leading to the possibility of conscientious objection, would leave the statesman charged with the responsibility for defending his country under threat of war. Bonhoeffer replied that such decisions must be risked. Also to be noted is Bonhoeffer's remark that the relativizing of all given realities in the light of Christ was the solution not only to the overall ethical problem but the *ecumenical problem* as well.

Bonhoeffer repeated his attack on orders of creation and his advocacy of orders of preservation three months later in his presentation to the Youth Conference at Ciernohorské Kúpele. This new attack is double-edged, however, for now he turned his sword as sharply against elements in the World Alliance as he did against the nationalist theologians. At Ciernohorské Kúpele, he goes on to criticize (no doubt to the surprise of many of his hearers) the tendency of the World Alliance, allegedly under "Anglo-Saxon" influence, to see "peace" as an *ideal*, a state of affairs regarded as an absolute good in itself. But this, Bonhoeffer holds, is to make as serious an error as the nationalists were making in their exaltation of nationhood as an order of creation. Peace, resting on an external order of freedom, cannot be a good in itself but only for a purpose beyond itself, namely the reception of the gospel of Christ. It is not itself the gospel but the *commandment* of God, and as such not an order not of creation but of preservation. The peace commanded by God has two boundaries: truth and justice: "A community of peace can exist only when it does not rest on *a lie* or on *injustice*. Wherever a community of peace endangers or suffocates truth and justice, the community of peace must be broken and the battle must be declared."[34] It is in "Anglo-Saxon thinking" that truth and justice remain subordinate to the ideal of peace—but such an ideal of peace is illusory. Then, crucially:

> *Struggle* as possible action with respect to Christ becomes understandable if the order of external peace is not timelessly valid but can be disrupted at any moment, precisely because the complete violation of truth and justice would threaten to make hearing about revelation in Christ impossible. Struggle is not an order of creation, but it can be an order of preservation for the future of Christ, toward the new creation. Should the situation arise, the struggle can protect the openness for the revelation in Christ better than external peace, in that it breaks the hardened, self-enclosed order.[35]

By *struggle*, however, Bonhoeffer does not here mean *war*, which in the contemporary world means total annihilation of soul and body[36] and therefore cannot be an order of preservation, "and because war needs to be idealized and idolatrized in order to live, today's war, the next war, must be *condemned* by the church."[37] In criticizing "peace as an ideal," Bonhoeffer was very likely reflecting on his experiences of discussions in World Alliance circles, where Germans had had difficulty in conveying to their foreign counterparts the level of resentment and sense of injustice at the continuing legacy of the Versailles Treaty, and the effect of the rearmament policies of countries like France and Britain on German opinion. Bonhoeffer was thus entering uninhibitedly into the ecumenical peace witness but challenging much of its presuppositions. As well as theologically rebutting the sanctity of nationhood, he was calling for a dethroning of peace as an ideal state where awkward questions of truth and justice were ignored. This, of course, would imperil ecumenism as a painless meeting of minds in easy agreement. It would mean a radical hearing of peace as *God's commandment*, not an ideal state to be endlessly discussed or even advocated, still less justified in merely human terms. Bonhoeffer was set on disturbing the would-be peace of the peacemakers for the sake of a radical obedience to God.

The Ecumenical Movement: A Theological Basis?

"There is still no theology of the ecumenical movement."[38] Nothing could be starker than Bonhoeffer's opening sentence in his address to the Ciernohorské Kúpele youth conference. The paper "On the Theological Foundation of the Work of the World Alliance" was by far the most substantial of his ecumenical writings thus far. As he was attending the conference at short notice in place of Max Diestel, such an intense and coherent piece must either have been written in an astonishing burst of concentrated energy, or else it was a theme that he had been working on seriously for some time independent of any specific occasion in mind; or perhaps it was originally intended for the Gland conference a month later.[39] Quite possibly, the Provisional Bureau conference in April had prompted him to more urgent thinking on the ecumenical movement and the churches. It was there, in discussion of Wilhelm Zoellner's paper on "the Church and the Churches," that Bonhoeffer had warned against evading the question of *truth*, and stated that "the concept of heresy has been lost in the ecumenical movement."[40]

Whatever the genesis of this paper, Bonhoeffer at Ciernohorské Kúpele makes clear that his opening statement is no mere rhetorical flourish. Whenever, he asserts, the church of Christ comes to a new understanding of itself it produces a new theology appropriate to it and "If the ecumenical movement emerges from a new self-understanding of the church, it must and will bring forth a new theology. If it does not succeed in this, it is a sign that the church is nothing but a new church organization in keeping with the times and for a certain purpose."[41] One can imagine at least some of Bonhoeffer's World Alliance hearers wearing puzzled expressions at this point. Was he not denigrating exactly what indeed they thought they were supposed to be: a cooperative organization (an *alliance* after all!) with a practical aim in view? Bonhoeffer anticipates the objection that there is already enough theology being worked on in the ecumenical movement, especially by Faith and Order. The very same critical question, he insists, must be put to Faith and Order: Is it a new ecclesial self-understanding at work there, "or is it ultimately an organization for the purpose of improving mutual understanding among divergent theological languages?"[42] Whatever else, there has grown a fateful dichotomy in ecumenical thinking between "theology" and "practice," with "practitioners" tending to disparage theology. "But it is this very attitude that is destructive and demands our fullest protest, because it has led to the touchy consequence that ecumenical work was at the mercy of fluctuations in the political atmosphere. Because the ecumenical movement has no theology, the ecumenical concept, for example, has currently become powerless and meaningless through the political wave of nationalism among the youth."[43] Bonhoeffer here, of course, is very much speaking from his German context but he was seeking to expose the vulnerability of ecumenism in any situation if it lacks a theological undergirding as distinct from essentially pragmatic aspirations, because pragmatic considerations (however noble) are always liable to be displaced by other pragmatic demands (national honour and security, the need of the hour and so forth, not to mention economic pressures). Moreover, by theology Bonhoeffer does not mean just a theoretical justification (however intellectually accomplished) for the movement. He means a conscious, obedient attachment to the word of Christ no less than should be found in the church itself, and it is here where Bonhoeffer comes to the crux of the matter: the World Alliance considered not just an organization concerned about the churches, *but a form of church itself*.

> The work of our World Alliance . . . is grounded in a very distinct conception of church. The church as the one church-community [*Gemeinde*] of the Lord Jesus Christ, who is the Lord of the world, has the task of speaking his word to the entire world. The range of the one church of Jesus Christ is the entire world. There are local boundaries for the proclamation of each individual church but the *one* church has no boundaries around it.[44] The churches of the World Alliance have joined together in order to express their claim, or rather the claim of our Lord, on the entire world . . . it is not a holy, sacred district of the world that belongs to Christ but rather the entire world.[45]

Bonhoeffer is not only daring to speak prophetically (though he is) as if this was already the self-understanding of the World Alliance. More radically, in this proposed self-understanding he is eliding the assumed distinction between "church" and "ecumenical organization." The Alliance is not just an organization of church representatives: it *is* the church convened together to address the whole world, and demonstrates this by its transnational membership. The Alliance, in speaking to the world, must thereby claim the only authority available to it, the same authority as that under which the church itself stands, the word of Christ. Indeed, "The church is the presence of Christ on earth; the church is *Christus praesens*. This alone gives its word authority."[46] The church in speaking to the world under the authority of the present Christ can speak with authority "only when a word from the deepest knowledge of my humanity hits me in my full reality here and now. The word of the church to the world must therefore touch it out of the deepest knowledge of the world in its complete present if it wishes to be authoritative. The church must here and now be able to speak the word of God, of authority, out of its own knowledge in the most concrete way."[47] But how can a concrete, relevant word to the here and now be spoken authoritatively by a church marked by division and liable to human error? If the validity of its command depends on detailed technical knowledge and analysis of the matter in hand (war and social questions, for example) then it will be trapped in uncertainty, and the church will customarily opt either for evasion or (yet again) generalities. More honestly and authentically, the church should choose either a "qualified silence" *or* take the risk of speaking specifically and decisively to the situation, "out of the clear recognition that it is possible therewith to take the name of God in vain, that the church is in error and is sinful, but it may speak it in faith in the forgiveness of sins that holds true for the church as well."[48]

This is an astonishingly bold (or insightful) assertion by a young newcomer to the ecumenical movement. He was under no illusions about the ecumenical movement as an enterprise. He was not romanticizing it. Far from it, he was repeatedly asking the movement to face the fact of its own weakness and disarray: "the churches that are members of the World Alliance do not have a common recognition of truth but are instead most deeply torn asunder on this very point. When they say Christ or gospel, each of them means something very different. At present, this is our most pressing problem in ecumenical work. We can speak only as the church that proclaims the truth of the gospel. But the truth is torn asunder. And that makes our word powerless, even mendacious."[49] But worst of all, Bonhoeffer says, would be to ignore this or treat it light-heartedly. The hope of the church, and the ecumenical movement, lies in confession of its own "guilt of its ruptured knowledge."[50] He concludes that the church in its crisis must remain humble and must live on the basis of forgiveness alone."[51]

Bonhoeffer was in no less serious mood at the Gland youth conference at the end of August. Indeed, his opening words of welcome as a youth secretary, a sober reflection on 2 Chronicles 20:12 ("We do not know what to do, but our eyes are upon you"),[52] reflect not just his foreboding at the world in general but also his unease at the prevalent confusion on the ecumenical scene itself, its apparent inability to see the crisis as he saw it. He had been only partly successful in his efforts to get the conference agenda more sharply focused on the peace question at the expense of social and economic issues. Bishop Arthur Burroughs, president of the Alliance, regarded Bonhoeffer's reiteration of his Old Testament text as "the expression of a pessimism that verged on passivism"[53] and found more constructive the address of the Russian Nicolas Zernov, with his "picture of an 'organic society' in which the creative principle is love."[54] The address which Bonhoeffer later gave in place of Valdemar Ammundsen repeats much of what he had said at Ciernohorské Kúpele: the church, and therefore the World Alliance, as the community of those who hear the word of Christ in and for the world; the distinction between war and struggle; the requirements of truth and justice not subordinate to peace; Christ as present in his church. The crisis in which the world is caught is, however, stressed and illustrated as never before by reference to hunger, distress, rearmament, and war imminent or actual. Here the challenge for a proper self-understanding of the Alliance is put even more sharply than before, and set in the dramatically eschatological perspective which shapes the whole paper:

> We are not a purely functional organization of church business but rather a distinct form of the church itself. We are the community of those who are startled by the signs of the time, who in the midst of the terrors of the night have heard a penetrating call from whom one they know: it is the Lord, but is he coming to help or to judge? The World Alliance has become the anxious church of Christ, which has become terrified and sensitive, made fearful by the anxiety of the world, and calling upon its Lord.[55]

As the community that waits to hear the word of its Lord, not its own word, the church can afford to recognize that there is truth in the accusation "The church is dead"—an accusation which Bonhoeffer quotes as the opening of his address. "Faith in the living church of Christ only breaks through where one sees most clearly the death of the church in the world."[56] Faith can live with "an ever-new collapse" and the funeral of the church. The believer, says Bonhoeffer, can be neither an optimist nor a pessimist. The church lives in the midst of dying, as it waits for God to create God's world anew. Bonhoeffer expresses his concern that the conference has revealed that "we are no longer obedient to the Bible"[57]—"We read it no longer against ourselves but only for ourselves."[58] But the call of God still comes, as Bonhoeffer notes by concluding with reference to the story in Acts 16:9-10 of Paul hearing the plea of the Macedonian man. "Europe," says Bonhoeffer, "calls a second time: come and help us. Europe, the world wants to be won over a second time by Christ. Are we ready?"[59]

"At a later session the German leader corrected his first pessimistic emphasis by a passionate proclamation of the church," reported Arthur Burroughs and commended Bonhoeffer's final peroration just quoted.[60] Nevertheless, it is not apparent that the actual substance of Bonhoeffer's "passionate proclamation" was fully registered by the president of the World Alliance in his reports for the British church and secular press: "The New City of Friends: Internationalism in the Making" ran the headline over his account of Gland in the *Church of England Newspaper*.[61] Warm tribute was paid to the youth secretaries Toureille, Bonhoeffer, and Craske: "All these are young men, with very obvious gifts for their World Alliance duties, including remarkable talent as musicians and entertainers when an international social evening was decreed." Evidently, Bonhoeffer had displayed his talents at the piano but would surely have preferred that his words had made at least as much impact as his playing. No doubt Bonhoeffer felt that once again, as at the Epsom conference in April, the "beautiful experience of international friendship" was in danger of supplanting serious work. Indeed, "International Friendship—A Hopeful Conference" was the title of Burroughs's report in the *Yorkshire Post*.[62] "On the whole the most characteristic plea was that the Christian individual is everywhere (or should be) himself the germ-cell of 'an organic society based on love'."[63] This was a far cry from Bonhoeffer's eschatological emphasis on judgment and grace, of life through death, and a tremblingly expectant ecumenical community. Zernov's personalism was evidently more congenial to the English bishop and other aspirants after goodwill. Bonhoeffer's Ciernohorské Kúpele and Gland lectures appeared in *Die Eiche*. But the days of that journal, and of the World Alliance itself in Germany, were numbered as the nationalist clamour and pressure rose.

Ecumenical Bodies: Functional Organizations or Forms of Church?

"There is still no theology of the ecumenical movement." How just, in actuality, was Bonhoeffer's contention? All the main ecumenical bodies of the time, and the main instigators of the movement, could well have retorted that their work had a theological motivation, whether this was expressed as the missionary task of bringing the gospel to the whole world, or serving the reign of God in its call for justice and peace, or for making visible the unity of the one body of Christ. There was no shortage of theology in the respective activities of the International Missionary Council, of Life and Work, and of Faith and Order—and, indeed, of the World Alliance. Professional theologians and scholars served on their councils and working groups. Bonhoeffer would not have disputed this, nor that, for example, there was much theological debate in Life and Work circles between liberal Protestants who saw the reign of God as a social order being built by human effort and traditional Lutherans who saw it as a reality to be awaited as an eschatological event; nor that Faith and Order's work consisted almost entirely of the comparative study of central doctrinal and ecclesiological questions. But Bonhoeffer was asking these bodies a rather different question: not about their theological understanding of Christian mission, or of social justice, or the visible unity of the church, *but about their own here-and-now significance as ecumenical bodies and about their relation to the church*. Were they purely functional instruments of the churches, or did they have ecclesial significance as forms of church themselves? What is actually happening when churches or their representatives meet together? Are they discussing how to be more united, or are they even there and then a form of that unity, the one church? A functional self-understanding was perhaps most overtly true of the World Alliance itself, whose constitution stated:

> That in order to enable the different Churches to be brought into touch with one another, steps should be taken to form in every country councils of either a denominational or interdenominational character . . . whose object it will be to enlist the Churches . . . in a joint endeavour to achieve the promotion of international friendship and the avoidance of war, and that for this purpose a central bureau should be established for facilitating correspondence between such councils, collecting and distributing information and generally co-ordinating the work connected with the movement.[64]

The Council of Life and Work was similarly functional in its principal objective "to perpetuate and strengthen the fellowship between the churches in the application of Christian ethics to the social problems of modern life,"[65] although there was always the implied hope that such cooperation might also serve the cause of deeper mutual relations between the churches, especially if there could be closer relations with Faith and Order. But it was at the 1927 Lausanne Faith and Order Conference itself that the greatest hesitations and disagreements were found about what kind of event was taking place and what kind of continuation should result. The conference president Charles Brent had again and again to restate the purpose of the conference as being "an occasion on which 'both agreements and disagreements were to be carefully noted'. 'It is not, he said, "a conference that aims at complete agreement" still less at a united church'."[66] Bonhoeffer was absolutely right in stating that Faith and Order no less than any other ecumenical body was careful to identify itself as no more than an organ of cooperation and coordination. Three years later, his critique of Faith and Order became a sharply polemical attack on what he saw as its evasion of the truth of what was happening in the Church Struggle. The

International Missionary Council, for its part, existed to "stimulate thinking and investigation on missionary questions"; to "help to co-ordinate the activities of the national missionary organizations . . . and to bring about united action where necessary in missionary matters; and help to unite the Christian forces of the world in seeking justice in international and inter-racial relations."[67] In fact, one searches almost in vain through the ecumenical literature and records of the period for any theological reflection within the ecumenical movement on the ecumenical movement itself.[68]

There was, however, one contemporary instance of a theological essay which at certain points does come close to Bonhoeffer's trajectory of thinking. In 1931, there had appeared *Der Weg der dialektischen Theologie durch die kirchliche Welt*,[69] by the celebrated Swiss ecumenist and social activist Adolf Keller (1872–1963). It appeared in English in 1933 as *Karl Barth and Christian Unity*.[70] Keller focusses more on Barthian theology and its relevance for the hour than upon the ecumenical movement as such, but, like Bonhoeffer, he does see the need for the "Stockholm movement" (i.e., Life and Work) to view itself as more than a purely cooperative fellowship which incurs the Barthian critique that it is merely a sum of human ambitions and hopes.[71] The movement must become more than an organization. The fundamental question for both Barthianism and the ecumenical movement is not how they can build a larger and more influential church but, rather, what is the will of God in our day. Further: "The Ecumenical Movement . . . will . . . have to remind all theology, that in all hearing of the Word, in all the seriousness of listening, the chief concern must ever be the *doing* of the divine will, that is *obedience* on our part. What is demanded is a naked, simple, immediate obedience without any reflecting theology, without having an eye on rewards or merits."[72]

This *doing* of the divine will, in face of Lazarus lying before our door and the immensity of the world's needs in the present hour, is what matters above all, insists Keller. "Christian faith is obedience as well as trust. The Ecumenical Movement, as well as Barthianism, is an admonition to the churches, so that in their faith both obedience and trust will not be forgotten."[73] While Keller does not go as far as Bonhoeffer, in that he still distinguishes sharply between the churches and the ecumenical movement, in this wish for concrete obedience there are evident resonances between Keller and Bonhoeffer, and one would have expected that the shared Barthian theology would at least have drawn Keller to Bonhoeffer's attention. But there appears to be no detectable reference to Keller in any of Bonhoeffer's writings from this period, and scarcely in any other period, too, and the virtual absence of Keller from all the received accounts of Bonhoeffer's life is puzzling.[74]

All the organizations stated their aims as being to promote cooperation, fellowship, and dialogue but were studiously avoiding giving themselves any intrinsic theological, let alone ecclesial, status. Bonhoeffer brazenly challenged this as false modesty, a denial of their true calling to be, no less than the churches, under the word of Christ and thus themselves *to be at least a form of the church* witnessing in and to all the world. The ecclesial status of ecumenical bodies remains a contentious issue today, as will be noted in the final chapter. In Bonhoeffer ecclesiology and ecumenism were fused, with radicalizing effects on both, as we shall now see.

CHAPTER 4

Crisis 1933: Church, Nation, and *Oikoumene*

The progress of any organization, cause, or movement is never wholly under the control of its leaders or participants. Other stories intervene, demanding responses, shifting directions, and reordering priorities, often in quite unexpected ways. The ecumenical movement is no exception, as was shown in January 1933. At the end of that month and the beginning of February, the executive bodies of both the World Alliance for International Friendship through the Churches and Life and Work had their routine meetings in Berlin. As well as the formal business meetings, the delegations, which included eminent figures like the bishops Ove Valdemar Ammundsen of Denmark and George Bell of England, together with staff from Geneva, were hosted at receptions provided by Berlin academics and church leaders. Prominent on the German side were the ecumenical theologian Adolf Deissmann and the president of the Evangelical High Church Council in Berlin, Hermann Kapler, who was also one of the four presidents of Life and Work. Dietrich Bonhoeffer as a youth secretary of the Alliance was required to be present at least for the World

Alliance committee. Given his heavy schedule of pastoral and lecturing responsibilities it was highly convenient, for once, not to have to travel outside his own city on ecumenical business. On the Alliance agenda there was much to occupy him, especially the merging of the youth committees of the Alliance and Life and Work, the planning for a small group of French and Germans to meet in Basel, and the preparations for a World Alliance conference planned for September in Sofia, Bulgaria. As well as in formal committee sessions he had preliminary talks with H. L. Henriod on 25 January.

As the ecumenical leaders gathered in Berlin they knew they were entering a tense political scene, but none could have guessed that they were to be immediate eyewitnesses of the most dramatic and fateful event of the decade: on 30 January, Adolf Hitler was sworn in as chancellor of Germany. To huge popular acclaim, the National Socialist revolution was launched with parades, banners, and torch-lit marches across the city. The visitors were by turns stunned and bemused. Their German hosts, for the most part, pointed with some pride to the remarkable "discipline" under which the revolution had occurred. On neither side was it as yet fully appreciated what all this signified, nor was it guessed that these ecumenical meetings would be the last in which Germans and their international partners could meet without any kind of political constraints until October 1945.

Dietrich Bonhoeffer was among the few on the German side who had long seen what was coming and its ominous significance. His critical radio talk on "The Younger Generation's Altered View of the Concept of Leader [*Führer*]" was actually delivered on 1 February, just two days after Hitler's ascension and while the ecumenical meetings were taking place. It had, however, clearly been prepared some time before then.[1] Nevertheless, for him, 30 January 1933 marked a fateful turning point. Eberhard Bethge comments: "It did not require a reorientation of his personal convictions or his theology, but it became increasingly clear that academic discussion must give way to action."[2]

The Church Struggle to September 1933: An Ecumenical Issue

There is no need here to rehearse in detail Bonhoeffer's critical engagements with the mounting German crisis and the onset of the Church Struggle during the months of 1933 up to his emigration to London in October that year. These are narrated fully elsewhere,[3] and it suffices only to note:

- his university lectures on Christology;

- his early alliance with the "Young Reformation" movement in opposition to the German Christians;

- his crucial essay "The Church and the Jewish Question,"[4] published in June;

- his outright opposition, in speaking and writing, to the German Christians and their attempts to gain control of the church and to force the Aryan paragraph on the church and its ministry;

- his work during August on the Bethel Confession, a first major attempt to assert the Reformation understanding of the church over against the German Christians' nationalist and anti-Jewish heresies;

- his revulsion at the election of Ludwig Müller (a former naval chaplain, and a nonentity except for his forthright Nazism) as regional bishop of the Church of the Old Prussian Union and then as "Reich bishop" at the National Synod in September;

- his support for the Pastors' Emergency League, the first major form of church opposition, formed in September under the leadership of Martin Niemöller and others.

It was not just a dramatic time but also an emotionally draining one of propaganda and counterpropaganda, of the forming of alliances and therewith, inevitably, also the breaking of former associations and friendships. But for Bonhoeffer the basic issue was clear: a church which decided to base itself on national or racial criteria, for example by accepting the Nazi Aryan paragraph which would bar those of Jewish descent from office, was ipso facto no longer the church of Jesus Christ as taught by the scriptures and the Reformation. It was indulging in heresy and, moreover, committing idolatry of the state. In Reformation terminology, a *status confessionis* had presented itself.

From the outset, however, an *ecumenical* dimension to the struggle was very apparent to Bonhoeffer. Certain factors made this obvious and unavoidable. For one thing, the very nature of the National Socialist order was inimical to what the ecumenical movement in its internationalism stood for. Whereas ecumenical activists had previously had to bear with strident disapproval from nationalist pressure groups, it was now the state itself—and increasingly a police state at that—with which they were faced. This had immediate practical consequences, as all foreign contacts were now liable to state scrutiny. Phone tapping and censorship of mail had to be reckoned with. Bonhoeffer's friends from New York, Paul and Marion Lehmann, on their visit to Berlin in 1933 noticed how even in their home the Bonhoeffer family members were now wary of open political conversation.[5] This did not deter Dietrich and Klaus Bonhoeffer from discussing with Paul Lehmann ways in which they could send information about what was actually going on in Germany to appropriate contacts in the USA. Technically, this was already treason since among the early Nazi legislation was the "Malicious Practices Act" of 21 March 1933, which forbade the spreading of "an untrue or grossly distorted assertion of a factual nature that is likely to impair the welfare of the Reich . . . or the reputation of the Reich Government" or, indeed, the reputation of a party or association behind the government.[6] Just days after this enactment, several leaders in the German regional and free churches wrote to partners abroad requesting them to oppose any propaganda against the new Germany and assuring them that all was well there. The state itself, however, seemed extraordinarily willing to demonstrate the vanity of such claims: on 21 June Friedrich Siegmund-Schultze, veteran of the World Alliance, became the first ecumenical victim of the regime, dismissed from his chair of social ethics and deported by the Gestapo to Switzerland on account of his aid to Jews. He had, moreover, been planning to include in the July issue of his journal *Die Eiche* "certain information" about the German situation for the benefit of "our foreign friends" as well as German readers.[7]

For its part, the ecumenical leadership outside Germany was increasingly anxious for reliable information. George Bell, an assiduous reader of the almost daily reports from Berlin in the London *Times*, was suspicious of the soothing noises from Hermann Kapler and other German church leaders. In April Bell requested that three key people from the Geneva ecumenical staff—H. L. Henriod (joint secretary of Life and Work and the World Alliance), Hans Schönfeld (head of the research department), and Nils Ehrenström (assistant in the research department)—visit Berlin on his behalf. Right at the start of their visit Bonhoeffer secured a personal meeting with Henriod, whom of course he knew well already, to give his own opinion on the situation and to warn him against the more optimistic tenor of what the delegation was likely to hear from the church leaders: a generalized optimism and gratitude that the revolution, whatever else, had established a safe stronghold against godless Bolshevism.

The atmosphere of extreme sensitivity on the side of the German church leadership and of cautious criticism on the part of the Geneva ecumenicals is well conveyed in the June 1933 issue of the joint bulletin of Life and Work and the World Alliance, *The Churches in Action Newsletter*, in which the American Presbyterian academic and ecumenist William Adams Brown reflected on his recent travels and experiences in Europe. He was not personally on the delegation to Berlin but his report drew upon Henriod's account of that visit:

> During the height of the tension between Germany and other countries, which followed the announcement of the boycott against the Jews and other measures designed to limit freedom in the University and in the Press, the Council received many messages from Christian bodies in different countries calling for some public protest on behalf of the Christian conscience, while from Germany came communications asking for suspension of judgment till the facts were known. As a result of these communications the Secretary of

the Council visited Berlin and had a conference with the leaders of the German Church, as a result of which he gained much valuable information and a deep impression that the leaders of the churches were not unmindful of their responsibility to safeguard the freedom of the Christian conscience, to help the suffering and the oppressed and to maintain the church's independence in every sphere. Further, the importance of creating a real understanding of the widespread changes of this national revolution, which is a revolution in the literal sense of that term, was very apparent. It was particularly valuable to realise the great hope of the church that these vast upheavals would in the end be for the good of the people in every class and that meanwhile great new opportunities would present themselves to the church in its service to the whole nation. All our impressions confirmed the conception clearly expressed by Hitler in his last great speech before the Reichstag[8] that the responsible leaders in Germany desire peace and that the concentrating of all the forces of the nation is designed primarily to mobilize public opinion for the task of internal reconstruction and not for any aggressive design against other countries. On the contrary, Germany is ready to cooperate in a peaceful manner with other countries for the reconstruction of the political and economic conditions of the world.

It was a great joy to feel that the leaders of the church in Germany realized and appreciated the effectiveness of oecumenical co-operation and that they wished to build up still closer oecumenical relations with the churches of other countries. Just at present the energies of these leaders are engrossed in the reorganization of the German Church in such a manner as to pave the way, in close relationship with the great national movement, for the union of the various churches, (*Landeskirchen*) in one German Protestant Church, to strengthen its independence and liberty and to make it thereby of widespread service to the whole nation. This movement of our German fellow-Christians will be followed, I am sure, with the keenest sympathy by all those who are working for a real unity of the church.[9]

This was clearly what the German church leadership was wanting to be aired aboard, betraying little sign of Bonhoeffer's critical
stance and, indeed, manifesting the bland acquiescence that he was
so soon to be targeting mercilessly. But neither did it say quite all that
Henriod himself (as distinct from Brown) knew. In May, the administrative committee of Life and Work had met in London and spent
much time on the German situation.[10] Henriod reported on the correspondence that he and George Bell had had with Kapler and other
German church leaders at the end of March, in which the Germans
had protested against "pronouncements made against Germany as a
result of recent events in that country." Henriod had promised to do
whatever he could to prevent statements based on false information,
"yet at the same time calling attention to the fact that press reports
of utterances by members of the government and other influential
persons in Germany had caused serious and widespread concern, and
that he was in receipt of many protests, and the demand that something be done on behalf of those persons in Germany who found their
existence threatened, or who were condemned to exile."[11] He was convinced that the German churches would face these challenges in a
truly evangelical spirit but at the same time pressed the case for full
and accurate information—hence the visit to Berlin made by Henriod, Schönfeld, and Ehrenström. They had been courteously received
by the church leaders "who had explained to them the difficulties
which the Church was facing, and the steps they were taking to deal
with them, and had requested their fellow Christians to have patience
and not to press them for action which might be premature."[12] The
Life and Work committee endorsed Henriod's actions as secretary,
expressed cordially their support for the German churches and their
confidence that would meet the critical situation "in a truly Christian
spirit" as they had in fact been doing. But the minutes continue: "At
the same time they would not be dealing fairly with their brothers in
the German churches if they did not share with them the concern of
many lovers of Germany in other lands, and not least among their
fellow Christians at reported utterances and actions on the part of
responsible persons in Germany which it is difficult to reconcile with
the Christian spirit." They therefore hoped that very soon "it may be

possible for the leaders of the German church to express in clear terms the spirit in which they are meeting the present crisis—a crisis which affects not Germany alone, but all nations,"[13] while recognizing that no nation is exempt from confession of sin and all are in need of sympathetic understanding.

It was indeed a cloudy, confused, and confusing scene alike for many within and outside Germany and it was precisely the stark clarity of Bonhoeffer's view from within which was soon to make him so important to the ecumenical movement. To note, for example, that at this stage even Martin Niemöller was politically a National Socialist is to underline that the clear battle lines of the Church Struggle had yet to be drawn. Equally pertinent is the case of another Lutheran who was to figure prominently on the international ecumenical scene and with whom Dietrich Bonhoeffer, after a friendly start, was to develop a peculiarly fraught relationship: Theodor Heckel (1894–1967). Brother of the prominent Bonn church lawyer Johannes Heckel, he was a senior consistory officer in the Church Federation Office, industrious and deeply committed to his church. To Henriod, on his April visit to Berlin, Heckel had seemed, like Bonhoeffer, to be highly skeptical of the new situation[14] and, indeed, early in May he was a collaborator with Martin Niemöller and others in founding the oppositional Young Reformation Movement. His official responsibilities in church foreign relations, together with this evidently oppositional stance, meant that Bonhoeffer and he saw each other as potentially important to one another. So it was to prove, but not in the way that either had initially hoped. Heckel saw himself primarily as a church administrator and official representative, and as such desirous of harmonizing the tensions within the German Evangelical Church. His ecumenical duty would be to represent the official church to circles abroad and to request respect for all parties within that church as a whole. This became still more firmly his line once he was appointed director of the new Church Foreign Office in 1934 and was made a bishop. Bonhoeffer, by contrast, saw the crucial issue to be *which was the true church* of the Reformation in Germany, calling for a church based on a confessing of the biblical and Reformation faith and therefore *excluding* groups such as the German Christians which were to be judged

heretical. Therewith he would ask the ecumenical family to acknowledge exclusively the church which truly confessed as the one church
deserving membership in the ecumenical family. Heckel himself never
became a German Christian, but as an officer of the Reich Church led
by the unworthy bishop Müller, a church acquiescing in the German
Christian presence in it, Bonhoeffer deemed him to be the servant of
a church which was tolerating heresy and so was fatally compromised.

Theology of Church and Ecumenism

Eberhard Bethge's comment, that for Bonhoeffer, from 30 January
1933 on, academic discussion had to give way to action, became true
for his ecumenical involvement as much as, and in some ways more
than, any other aspect of his life. To eschew academic discussion did
not, however, mean a departure from serious theology as the basis of
action. As so often with Bonhoeffer, we find a mixture of change and
continuity, a chronological overlapping of major theological concerns
both recollected and anticipated, as he interacted with the immediate
challenges of the hour. Accordingly, in order to understand fully his
decisive ecumenical engagement in the tumultuous year 1933, it is
appropriate at this point to recall a major strand of theological continuity with his earlier academic life.

Bonhoeffer's heavy schedule of university lecturing in Berlin during 1932–33 included courses on twentieth-century systematic theology, creation, and christology—the latter two in particular engaging
critically with the presuppositions of much of the nationalist theology
of the time. But it is highly significant that in the summer of 1932—
just as the nationalist tide was rising in the church no less than society—he had also given a series on "The Nature of the Church."[15] This
demonstrated that his doctoral thesis *Sanctorum Communio*[16] of five
years earlier had not been left behind as a pretentious youthful display
of erudition. These lectures do not simply reproduce *Sanctorum Communio*, but there is much continuity in their emphases upon the church
as Christ existing as church-community (*Gemeinde*); on the church
being constituted by *Christus praesens* and Christ's representative

vicarious action; on the church occurring where the word of God breaks into the world; on the church not as a "religious community" but as the new humanity in Christ. What is also apparent, however, is a much less heavily philosophical and theoretical framework than in *Sanctorum Communio* and an evident, almost nervous, consciousness that decisive challenges and searching questions are building up for the church—his own church—of the day. Moreover, the question of *unity* is seen as crucial—but not in the way that many of his contemporaries assumed. Notes taken by one of the hearers run thus:

> The church as a genuine form is *unity*, basically the unity of God! The form reveals itself under the presupposition of unity. Differentiation: the church over against a religious community (arisen from individual converging wills) [is necessary]. The church is the *primary unity*. Those who do not start with unity confuse the church with a religious community. Unity is not the ideal of a world church; it is not "unity" [*Einigkeit*] of the church" (Roman, ecumenical, Anglicanism). Only faith in [the] unity of God in Christ [is possible]. "Wholeness" is to be understood not as the state of not being broken, but [rather as] the wholeness of the revelation of God.[17]

The true form of the church and its unity, Christ existing as community, is believed but not necessarily visible. The church's oneness consists in the oneness of the God self-revealed in Christ, a oneness that transcends the all-too-human brokenness of the church. Nevertheless, Christ's representative vicarious action being the foundation of the church, there are very concrete ethical requirements to be manifest in its relational structure of its members as "being-with-each-other" and "being-for-each-other." The church-community leads *one* life. Following Luther, "[The] need of the other must be such that I feel it as mine . . . you must allow your heart to feel the infirmity that your brothers experience [as if it were] your own. " Christ and the church-community bear and suffer and die with each member.[18] Such an understanding of mutual responsibility in the body of Christ was, on the international level, to become very apparent in the resolution engineered by Bonhoeffer at the ecumenical meeting in Sofia in September 1933.

In spite of all that he had said about the invisibility of the reality of the church, Bonhoeffer does return to the requirement of the church's proper visibility and unity, though with stringent qualifications:

> *Realization* [Verwicklung] *[occurs] in the world as visible church*! Therefore, [it is the] *una ecclesia*, the believed church. There is a disunity, not only in form but in the truth as well! The church will not want to reach [an] illusory unity. Sincere, bona fida faith [is] not to be confused with the truth of the content of faith (ecumenical danger: [the] question of heresy is no longer noted). Heresy of doctrine is to be combated sharply! [The] church must deny itself the act of [portraying the unity of truth]. Division is to be carried as cross; believing that God [has] called it as *una sancta*.[19]

The visible unity of the church, Bonhoeffer goes on to say, is called for precisely because of its *catholicity* (universality) which has to be expressed in the inescapably worldliness of the church as humanity. Protestantism claims a catholicity of proclaiming the worldwide word of Christ yet remains within given boundaries in the kingdom of the cross (*in regno crucis*) as distinct from the Roman Catholic view of the church (in standard Lutheran polemic) as existing "in the kingdom of glory" in the world.

It is striking how in such passages Bonhoeffer was already arming himself with weapons that were to be crucial in the Church Struggle, both on his German home scene and in the ecumenical world. The question of heresy was to raise its head most directly at home, in the attempt to Nazify the gospel and the church. Likewise, the prospect of an illusory unity was to seduce many into a truly "German church" founded on national and racial lines. But the edge of his critique was to challenge the ecumenical movement, too, on what it believed to be the basis of unity. And no less, his view of the church is that of a true *community* as the form of the present Christ, which is not a "religious community" but the new humanity reconciled in Jesus Christ. This was to nerve his ecumenical venture for peace. He had no "ecumenical theology" other than his theology of the church being Christ existing as community, writ large. The ecumenical movement was to be just that, on the widest level.

September 1933: Battle Joined

It is his tenacious hold on this theology of the church that accounts for Bonhoeffer's sharp reaction to the events of September 1933 and his insistence on a response from the ecumenical movement. Most critical of these events was the notorious "Brown Synod" (so-called because of the majority presence of German Christians in their Nazistyle uniforms) of the Old Prussian Union Church which met 5–6 September in Berlin. Among other measures, it resolved to introduce the state Aryan paragraph into the church, and a number of regional synods soon followed suit. To Bonhoeffer, this was clearly heretical and soon he wrote to Hermann Sasse, professor at Erlangen, and to Karl Barth to seek their views on the implications. Barth had already stated that wherever a church introduces the Aryan paragraph it ceases to be a Christian church, and both he and Sasse in their replies agreed with Bonhoeffer that a *status confessionis* had arisen.[20] Bonhoeffer's most immediate action, however, was ecumenical: on the very day of the Synod, 5 September, he sent a terse telegram to H. L. Henriod in Geneva: "General Assembly finished, all Generalsuperintendents dismissed, only Teutonic Christians admitted to National Synod, Aryan paragraph now in action, please work out memorandum against this and inform press at once, separation at hand, further information at Sofia."[21] "Sofia" referred to the forthcoming meeting of the World Alliance executive in Bulgaria later in the month, which Bonhoeffer was committed to attending; because of the current German events he had cancelled his attendance at the planned ecumenical youth meeting in Switzerland. The Sofia meeting, however, was preceded by the executive committee of Life and Work which met in Novi Sad, Yugoslavia, 9–12 September. Not being (as yet) a member of the executive committee, Bonhoeffer was not present and the small German delegation included Theodor Heckel, who now assumed a dominant role and presented a positive and optimistic picture of the changes taking place in Germany, alike in society, state, and church. This was too much for delegates such as Wilfrid Monod of France, who challenged the Germans' silence on the synodical anti-Jewish measures. A heated debate ensued. George Bell, as chairman, proposed a resolution recording the great anxieties of churches in Europe and North America "in particular with regard to the severe action taken against persons of Jewish origin" and the "serious restrictions placed upon freedom of thought and expression in Germany."[22] This was passed—but with the Germans recording their dissent. A second resolution decided that Bell should convey these concerns to the German government. Divergence was starting to appear between the wider ecumenical community and the official German church leadership. This divergence became still more apparent at the World Alliance executive meeting in Sofia, 15–20 September. Here a major factor was that Heckel was not present and Dietrich Bonhoeffer was. Due to financial difficulties, only 30 delegates managed to attend, and of these only two were from Germany, Bonhoeffer and the veteran missiologist Julius Richter. Several delegates had been at Novi Sad, including Bishop Ove Ammundsen, who was to chair the Sofia meeting, while Henriod had been alerted to how serious a response Bonhoeffer would be expecting following his telegram of 5 September. In any case, the issue of racial minorities was on the Sofia agenda at the request of the French and Dutch.

At Sofia Bonhoeffer employed a tactic that was to become characteristic of him at ecumenical gatherings: to prepare the ground in informal and confidential conversation rather than bringing issues straight to the conference table in plenary. The evening prior to the discussion of the agenda item on racial minorities, at Henriod's request a group met with Bonhoeffer in his hotel room:[23] Ove Ammundsen, William Adams Brown, Henry Atkinson (USA), Pierre Toureille, and Henriod.[24] Some weeks later, in a letter to Friedrich Siegmund-Schultze, Bonhoeffer described what happened: "On this occasion I spoke very frankly about the Jewish question, the Aryan paragraph in the church, and the general synod, and also about the question of the future of the minority, and met with a great deal of understanding . . ." [25] The group also supported Bonhoeffer's suggestion of a delegation to the government of the German church. Henriod's diary account—referring to what the group heard about "the real situation in Germany and the brutal and intransigent attitude of the German Christians"—accords with Bonhoeffer's and concludes: "we closed with prayer together. Bonhoeffer was very moved."[26] The actual resolution that the conference agreed to the next day was a text prepared by Bonhoeffer and amended by Atkinson:

> The members of the Executive Committee of the World Alliance meeting at Sofia . . . taking note of the fact that racial discrimination in any part of the world, whether because of colour or on other grounds, constitutes a great danger to peace and the welfare of humanity, considers necessary an emphatic declaration, in which the super-racial character of the Gospel is avowed.
>
> As members of many churches representing different cultures and coming from many lands, but all united in a common allegiance to our Lord Jesus Christ, we confess with shame our many sins of transgression against our brothers of other races and colour. In a feeling of brotherhood and responsibility with all the Churches of the world, while recognising the right of every country to safeguard the integrity of its own national life, we are nevertheless deeply concerned by the treatment inflicted upon persons of Jewish origin and connection in Germany.
>
> We especially deplore the fact that the State measures against the Jews in Germany have had such an effect on public opinion that in some circles the Jewish race is considered a race of inferior status. We protest against the resolution of the Prussian General Synod and other Synods which apply the Aryan paragraph of the State to the Church, putting serious disabilities upon ministers and church officers who by chance of birth are non-Aryan, which we believe to be a denial of the explicit teaching and spirit of the Gospel of Jesus Christ.[27]

This was a much sharper statement than that made by Life and Work at Novi Sad, and it is certain that Bonhoeffer's direct influence was vital here. Three points, however, need to be noted if its full significance is to be gauged:

First, only later did it emerge that, prior to the meeting, the presidium and secretariat had agreed that the executive, as such, was not empowered to make public statements on behalf of the Alliance. Bonhoeffer's informal meeting, in which the gravity of the German situation had been brought home to the leadership, was evidently crucial in generating the momentum to override that caution. For example, according to Ove Ammundsen it was only during that late-night exchange that William Adams Brown was finally convinced about the menace from the German Christians.[28]

Second, while Bonhoeffer was later to describe the statement as "moderate," with the implication that personally he had wished for a still more critical wording,[29] he nevertheless regarded it as something of a triumph. Ammundsen recalled: "[Bonhoeffer] even said to me that he was very grateful for the resolution; now he would really be able to go back to his friends with a result that was a valuable expression of Christian community and could strengthen their biblical stance."[30]

Third, from the start it was evident to all that the statement, which was directly critical of the general anti-Jewish measures as well as the imposition of the Aryan paragraph on the church, could have serious repercussions back in Germany for the church opposition, the German section of the World Alliance, and, not least, personally for Bonhoeffer and Richter who had actually voted for the resolution. Richter was especially concerned that the statement should not be read as an attack on the state as such, and he and Bonhoeffer visited the German Embassy in Sofia in an attempt to give assurance on this point.[31] Even Friedrich Siegmund-Schultze, now in the safety of Switzerland, feared what damage might ensue to the World Alliance in Germany and his journal *Die Eiche*. A somewhat free translation of the Sofia statement in German did appear in *Die Eiche*, with the (to say the least) misleading comment that "the German representatives who took part in the session [at Sofia] were unable to prevent the passing of a resolution" and, rather disingenuously, that the resolution "contained no criticism of the government of their country."[32] The extent to which Siegmund-Schultze himself really believed this,

or whether he was seeking honourably to protect his colleagues from
an already brutal regime, may be left open. That issue of *Die Eiche* was
the last to appear. Regardless of its reporting of Sofia it surely would
not have survived long anyway.

In short, Sofia saw ecumenical risk taking.

Ecumenical Responsibility: A New Stage

In terms of plotting the course of Bonhoeffer's ecumenical engagement the Sofia statement is of highest significance. Two years earlier in
Cambridge and for a year thereafter he had been strongly against the
passing of resolutions by ecumenical gatherings. Now, in a drastically
changed and critical situation, he had seen the necessity for the ecumenical family to speak out. This change of view was not really contradictory. His earlier opposition had been to declarations of general
principle which remained in the abstract, changed nothing concretely,
and cost nothing. By contrast, Sofia was not only addressing a very
concrete situation in a specific country but was speaking to those actually in that situation, and the church especially, identifying a course of
action ("No!" to the Aryan paragraph) to be taken there—and incur-
ring a potential cost. As such it was *performative* speech, creating a
bond of solidarity between those representing the ecumenical community and those in Germany struggling to resist "a denial of the explicit
teaching and spirit of the Gospel of Jesus Christ." It was putting into
action all that is found in *Sanctorum Communio* and the 1932 Berlin
lectures on the Nature of the Church, on being-for-one-another in
the body of Christ. Also to be noted is the statement's strong emphasis
that it was being spoken out of genuine confession of guilt shared with
all churches and all humanity: it is not the voice of a pretentious self-
righteousness addressing the sins of others, and this recalls Bonhoeffer's recognition, made in his 1932 lecture at Ciernohorské Kúpele,
that when the church does speak it does so confident not in its own
righteousness but in the mercy and forgiveness of God.[33]

Equally the Sofia statement, thanks largely to Bonhoeffer, marked
a new phase in the ecumenical story. Out of the confusing clamour

and smoke of the struggle in Germany and the efforts of those trying to understanding it from outside there was beginning to emerge
an understanding of mutual accountability. Bonhoeffer was thrusting
upon ecumenism the need to identify where the gospel itself was at
stake, and to act accordingly, at the same time calling upon his German church to recognize that its own credibility had to be scrutinized
by the ecumenical community at large. This sense of mutual accountability was a quite new stage of consciousness in the movement as
it had developed from the years immediately before the First World
War. Bonhoeffer's stance at Sofia, provoked by the Brown Synod and
similar assemblies in early September, was also of a piece with the
insistence in his Berlin lectures on the nature of the church, that the
concept of heresy, which the ecumenical movement was apt to evade,
was crucial if the unity of the church was a matter not just of goodwill
but of agreement in the truth. Now, however, it was not the ecumenical movement under the dominant Anglo-Saxon liberal ethos that was
most immediately vulnerable to heresy, but his own German church,
proud heir of the Reformation. Later, when the lines in Germany had
been more clearly drawn, with the Confessing Church established and
making its costly witness, the weight of Bonhoeffer's argument would
lie in presenting the existence and claim of that church to the ecumenical movement rather than vice versa. For the moment he was looking
to the ecumenical community to open the eyes of his compatriots to
the truth of their situation. The Sofia statement, moreover, is strongly
redolent of the whole thrust of *Sanctorum Communio*, the 1932 Berlin
lectures on the Nature of the Church, and his 1932 Ciernohorské
lecture on the church as being Christ existing as church-community,
its members belonging to one another in a supra-racial and supranational community. The Aryan paragraph represented a total reversal
of such an understanding of the church. Bonhoeffer the ecumenist
was bound to reject the German Christian doctrine as heretical for
both the German church and no less for the ecumenical movement
because, to repeat yet again, Bonhoeffer's theology of ecumenism was
but his ecclesiology writ large.

Back in Germany, partly because the German versions of the statement somewhat softened its tone, there was not in the event a huge

outcry over Sofia. The main furor took place within the Foreign Relations Department of the Evangelical Church, where Theodor Heckel had a hard job convincing his superiors that he was equal to the task of keeping the wayward ecumenicals under control. In a circular letter to pastors of German congregations abroad he sought to downplay the significance of Novi Sad and Sofia, dismissing the former's statement as "a comparatively meaningless resolution," and calling for the pastors to counter all negative pictures of what was happening at home. To an extent he even justified the Aryan paragraph (or at any rate opposed public attacks on it) on the grounds that "very strong elements among the National Socialists" would not understand its rejection at just the time when the revolution was opening up new avenues for the church's influence among the people.[34] Through Heckel's bland generalizations ran one clear theme: German church affairs were a matter for Germans alone. Ecumenism as represented by Novi Sad and Sofia constituted unacceptable outside interference. The only appropriate ecumenical activity by Germans would be that which presented a positive picture of what was happening in their homeland and its Protestant church.

This was the fundamental issue between Heckel and Bonhoeffer, and the reason why their relationship was to become so fraught during the next two years. Each had to watch the other carefully. While Heckel rose in seniority within his church—he was appointed head of the new foreign office of the church and was made a bishop in February 1934—Bonhoeffer's stature was increasing within his ecumenical circles. At Sofia, he had shown himself to be more than a scholar committed to the ecumenical movement, and more even than an able youth secretary: he emerged as a genuine strategist and mover within it, seizing the initiative at a crucial moment and reorienting its agenda in reaction to the German situation. This was immediately recognized at Sofia, where plans were made for the major ecumenical conference to take place in 1934,[35] and he was entrusted with a significant piece of the envisaged work, a "catechism of peace." For the moment, however, there were more pressing tasks. Bonhoeffer hurried home in time to observe the much-awaited (or feared) National Synod of the Evangelical Church at Wittenberg where Ludwig Müller was elected Reich bishop. Even more urgently, final preparations had to be made for the next stage of his career, in a move which alarmed some and puzzled many—including himself, to a degree: to leave Germany for a time in order to be a pastor in London, England. If in some ways this was a diversion or interruption in his career, it was not to prove a real disengagement from the struggle in Germany but a continuation of it from another place. Throughout this period it was his ecumenical activity which formed the most consistent thread of continuity in his life.

CHAPTER 5

Ecumenical Friendship: 1933–1935

Dietrich Bonhoeffer's decision to leave Germany in the autumn of 1933 and to spend eighteen months as a parish minister in London was not taken suddenly or rashly but out of a growing inner sense of need. The theological issues of the Church Struggle were to him very clear and he was absolutely certain where he stood. He was, however, increasingly unsure of the strategy and tactics of the campaign. He felt progressively isolated, even from people he highly respected, and was not sure how far his own judgment was to be trusted. In short, somewhat battle fatigued, he wanted some respite so that he could find himself again before returning to the fray. In any case, he had always wanted to be a pastor as well as a teacher, and now an opportunity arose of being minister to two German congregations in London. In July he preached a trial sermon in the church at Sydenham and received a warm invitation to the pastorate. He arrived to settle in London on 17 October 1933, and the Sydenham manse was to be his base until April 1935.

Not everyone approved or understood, even among his closest allies. From Bonn, Karl Barth waxed wrathful, accusing him of deserting his frontline battle post, and demanded that he return to Germany by the next boat or, at any rate, the next but one.[1] Bonhoeffer would no doubt have had qualms of conscience if his interests in coming to London were purely personal but in fact they were not, and one prime concern was the ecumenical dimension. This is clear from exchanges he had with significant figures both in Britain and Germany during the summer as he was making up his mind. In July, Bishop Arthur Burroughs, president of the British section of the World Alliance, responded very positively to an inquiry Bonhoeffer had made to him about the possible move, especially since in coming to England "you might be available as an interpreter of Germany when such interpreters are badly needed."[2] In Germany, the new political climate meant that all appointments to posts abroad, including ecclesiastical ones, came under serious scrutiny from the authorities. Although Bonhoeffer as a junior lecturer did not have tenure in the university, the departure of such an able teacher might arouse suspicion. Wilhelm Lütgert, who now held the chair in systematic theology and to whom Bonhoeffer was assistant, wrote warmly on his behalf to the Ministry of Education and Cultural Affairs, stating quite explicitly: "This position [as pastor in London] also includes a special assignment to ecumenical work."[3] Emil Karov, general superintendent of the church in Berlin, wrote to Bonhoeffer of his sadness that theologians like him felt there was no longer room for them in the German church but added: "However, your decision will have been influenced positively by the foreign connections created by your ecumenical work. So there is in your place at least an apparent connection."[4] There was an evident expectation all around that in London Bonhoeffer would be able to serve the interests of the German church in the ecumenical field to a new degree. But quite what those interests were and, indeed, what ecumenism would now mean soon became a matter of intense debate. Bonhoeffer was by now highly suspect in the church's Foreign-Relations department thanks to his radical oppositional stance taken throughout the summer, his role in the Sofia statement of the World Alliance, and, most particularly, his being a signatory to the protest issued by the Pastors' Emergency League to the National Synod in September, on the Aryan paragraph. Was he a fit person to represent

German Protestantism in the new dispensation? During October, there were heated confrontations between Bonhoeffer and Heckel, with the latter actually stating that permission for him to go to London would be conditional on his agreeing to refrain from ecumenical activity. Bonhoeffer insisted on a meeting with Reich bishop Müller himself. He wished to have official recognition by the church of his appointment to the London parishes but made clear that he could not represent the German Christian cause, and called Heckel's and Müller's bluff by suggesting that if they had doubts about him he should be banned outright from going. The next day he was given authorization to leave. The church evidently wished to avoid a counterproductive public controversy—and also risk losing the attachment of the London congregations that had invited Bonhoeffer. From now on, the London-based pastor and the Berlin church officials would be joined in mutual suspicion and often open hostility.[5]

London: October 1933–Summer 1934

Bonhoeffer's two London congregations,[6] at Sydenham and the St. Paul's Church, Aldgate, were more than enough to occupy him full-time in preaching and pastoral care. He carried out all the normal duties of a pastor assiduously.[7] In addition, he gave himself unstintingly to the support of refugees from Germany, and his Sydenham manse itself became a refuge for friends and former colleagues, such as Franz Hildebrandt, seeking either temporary or permanent escape from the peril. Nor, pace Karl Barth, did leaving Germany mean leaving the Church Struggle. Far from it. In continuous touch with Berlin by telephone and telegram, he remained closely involved in all that was happening, urging Martin Niemöller and other leaders of the opposition to stand firm, and he frequently travelled back to Berlin for vital meetings. Moreover, in a major way he brought the Church Struggle over to Britain by seeking to lead not only his own but all the other German congregations in Britain and their pastors into opposition to the German Christian influence, and eventually into identifying with the Confessing Church. In this he was largely successful, one of the most dramatic points of the campaign being a heated confrontation in February 1934 between the London pastors and Theodor Heckel, who had been sent by the Reich Church government to bring these errant Germans into line. Heckel, empty handed, had to beat a humiliating retreat back to Berlin. Insofar as the German congregations abroad represented part of the *oikoumene*, and keeping them in line with a "positive" view of Germany was such a high priority for the Reich Church, Bonhoeffer's activity on behalf of the oppositional and Confessing movements was itself implicitly ecumenical. But he also engaged in much more explicitly and specifically ecumenical work, and the fact that this was in addition to all his other preoccupations demonstrates such how deep was his commitment. The expectations (or fears) that he had generated were abundantly fulfilled in his time in London. His ecumenical work in London can be broadly categorized as, on the one hand, the formal responsibilities he had been shouldering since becoming a youth secretary of the World Alliance in 1931; and, on the other hand, the relationships that he now developed with leading ecumenists and other significant figures in Britain and elsewhere. This was not just a matter of forming relationships in the abstract, but of making some very specific friendships. These were to prove crucial not only in the functional sense of assisting the bridge building between the Confessing Church and the ecumenical fellowship, but more literally *crucial* in bringing about a shared experience of the cross, the *crux*, on the part of Bonhoeffer and those who were to be closest to him from now on. It was to be an ecumenism under the cross of suffering.

Of course, in coming to London Bonhoeffer relinquished much of his specifically German-related ecumenical work. That which was required of him as a youth secretary of the World Alliance, however, and now also as a member of the joint Youth Commission of the World Alliance and Life and Work, if anything grew more onerous. He attended a meeting of the Youth Commission in Paris in January 1934, and would have travelled to Paris again in April that year for an important study meeting of Life and Work on "Church and State," had not he felt compelled to stay and conduct the funeral of a young German woman. His main preoccupation, however, was as a co-organizer of the conference being planned by the Youth Commission to take place on the Danish island of Fanø in August 1934, coincidentally with the meeting of the Council of Life and Work. As the months went by, this meant an immense amount of correspondence both with the Geneva office and with representatives of the Alliance and senior church figures in different countries, and he called on the assistance of one of his Berlin students, Jürgen Winterhager, who came to live in the Sydenham manse for a time. Questions of the programme, the composition of youth delegations (an especially fraught issue by now in Germany), and, inevitably, of finances in the worsening economic climate all had to be dealt with—as well as his own input into the conference. Bonhoeffer did not shirk the detailed, unglamorous, often tedious, and frustrating kind of work needed to make ecumenical events happen. The same was true for the small conference held at Bruay-en-Artois, France, shortly after Fanø, in September 1934. And as will be seen, if one source of anxiety for Bonhoeffer was the Reich Church office in Berlin, for various reasons neither were his relationships always easy with the offices of the Youth Commission and the Research Department in Geneva.

It was, however, in the making of personal and working relationships with church and public figures in Britain that Bonhoeffer's ecumenical engagement was to prove most vital, for it was through them that he was able to be a mediator and interpreter of the German scene to the *oikoumene*. He arrived in London with warm recommendations from German World Alliance leaders such as Adolf Deissmann[8] and from H. L. Henriod in Geneva.[9] He was, of course, already known to leading British figures in the World Alliance: Lord Willoughby Hugh Dickinson, president of the International Council of the World Alliance; Bishop Arthur Burroughs, sometime president of the British section and chair of the Youth Commission;[10] H. W. Fox, secretary of the British section; and Tom Craske, Bonhoeffer's colleague as a youth secretary of the World Alliance (for the British Empire, USA, and Far East). Bonhoeffer was able to meet them all again soon after his arrival in London, as the executive boards of both the World Alliance and Life and Work met in London 2–4 November. That meeting also triggered a number of further vital contacts.

Important to note is that at this particular time Britain was a crucial nerve centre for the ecumenical movement since leading figures in all three of its organized strands were based here. The Scotsman J. H. Oldham (1874–1969) was secretary of the International Missionary Council (IMC), and since the Edinburgh Missionary Conference of 1910 had been the main organizing genius of the ecumenical movement as a whole, with interests and global influence far beyond the IMC and its specifically missionary agenda. His study *Christianity and the Race Problem* (1924), for example, was a pioneering and prophetic engagement with the issue that was to predominate in so much ecumenical concern for the rest of the 20th century.[11] George Bell, bishop of Chichester (1883–1958), had been president of the Council of Life and Work since 1932, and chairman of its executive committee. Leonard Hodgson (1889–1969), at that time a canon of Winchester Cathedral, was secretary of the Continuation Committee of the Lausanne Conference on Faith and Order. Then, for good measure, there was the towering force known as William Temple (1881–1944), at that time archbishop of York, devoting his considerable powers of leadership, intellect and spiritual charisma to all three main streams of ecumenism.

Moreover, it was in Britain and in this year of 1933 that the first intentional, if informal, discussions took place on the possibility of drawing together the IMC, Life and Work, and Faith and Order, with the main Christian youth organizations into a coordinated whole—a process that was to lead to the formation of the World Council of Churches in embryo in 1938, and fully established in 1948. George Bell in Britain and William Adams Brown of the USA were prime movers in the initial inquiry, monitored closely by J. H. Oldham. The first informal meeting took place at Bishopthorpe Palace, York, in May 1933, hosted by William Temple.[12] Bonhoeffer's arrival in England, enabling his entry into closer dealings with the ecumenical leadership concentrated there, thus coincided with a highly significant phase in the ecumenical movement, a time of heightened urgency and self-awareness. Questions of new organization inevitably raised the primary and underlying questions of purpose. Bonhoeffer himself was not directly concerned in these structural discussions[13] but, as always, he was to put his own challenging questions to the ecumenical movement about its primary nature and purpose, and the questions increasingly stemmed from his involvement in the German Church Struggle. Bonhoeffer saw his primary ecumenical task in Britain as being to inform leading church circles about the German scene, to interpret for them the significance of the Church Struggle, and to engage the support of the British churches and the wider ecumenical fellowship for the church opposition and its consolidation into the Confessing Church in the summer of 1934. To a degree the ground was prepared for him, since there was huge British public interest in the Nazi revolution, alarm at the first anti-Jewish measures, and an instinctive sympathy for those pastors who were taking a stand and paying the price. In the London *Times*, for example, the regular reports from Berlin on the church dramas were highly informative. But not all the issues were clear nor the background understood. What is more, the Nazi religious propaganda machine was at work in Britain. The German Christian movement had its supporters there even in senior church circles, most notably A. C. Headlam, bishop of Gloucester. Headlam, a notable scholar and former occupant of an Oxford chair of divinity, was also a leading figure in the Faith and Order movement and chairman of the Church of England's Foreign Relations Committee. Deeply sympathetic to Hitler's "new Germany," he lent his prestige to a visit to England by the young bishop Joachim Hossenfelder, national leader of the German Christians, in October 1933, just days before Bonhoeffer's arrival in London. The two bishops emerged from their meeting with mutual admiration, but that meeting was the farthest reach of Hossenfelder's attempt to gain publicity in Britain. Most disappointingly for him, the doors of Lambeth Palace, seat of the archbishop of Canterbury, remained firmly closed.[14] By contrast, Bonhoeffer's already existing ecumenical contacts in London gave him notable access. It was H. W. Fox, secretary of the World Alliance in Britain, who secured for him an interview with the archbishop, Cosmo Gordon Lang, who had also been informed about Bonhoeffer by George Bell. Their meeting took place at Lambeth Palace on 19 February 1934. News of the meeting enraged the Reich Church office in Berlin, especially as Theodor Heckel, on his abortive visit to London just prior to this (see above), had been denied access to the archbishop. Early in March, Heckel peremptorily summoned Bonhoeffer to Berlin to demand an assurance that he would end his ecumenical activity—an assurance that Bonhoeffer unsurprisingly refused to give.

But Bonhoeffer's ecumenical contacts in London quickly widened beyond his World Alliance friends. J. H. Oldham, as already mentioned, was the key person in international ecumenical networking based in Britain. He was also better acquainted with Germany on the inside than any other British ecumenical figure, having studied there before the First World War, acquiring fluency in the language and making close personal acquaintance with leading figures in the German missionary movement. What is more, Germans had special reason to be grateful to him for his skilled and persistent diplomatic work both during and immediately after the war, which ensured the continuance or reestablishment of German missions in British and British-occupied territories. That trust was about to blossom again as the German missionary bodies felt the full force of the Nazi attempts to suppress or abolish them outright, and once again it was to Oldham that they turned for help. Oldham, too, maintained a keen interest in German theology and philosophy and continental thought in general. By the early 1930s he was being inspired by Karl Barth and, intriguingly, had even in 1932 acquired a copy of Bonhoeffer's *Akt und Sein*.[15] Although they had not actually met before Bonhoeffer came to London, when they did the rapport and gratitude were immediate on both sides. In Oldham, Bonhoeffer now had an ally in London who knew German and Germany better than any other British church-related official of the time. They met a number of times, probably both at the Athenaeum club and Oldham's office at Edinburgh House, but equally likely at Oldham's home in Surrey where Oldham and his wife Mary were famously hospitable to guests from all over the world. At the practical level, Oldham was to be especially helpful to Bonhoeffer in finding assistance for refugees from Germany. No less was he important in securing ecumenical support for the church opposition in Germany, though not on such a public level as George Bell. Between them, Bonhoeffer, Oldham, and Bell made a diverse but effective team. They were to be together at the crucial Fanø conference in August 1934.

Friendship with George Bell

This brings us to the most important figure of all, in terms of friendship and collaboration, among Bonhoeffer's new London acquaintances: George Bell.[16] That his full entry into the story has been left till now is not intended to diminish in any way his significance, but simply to ensure that due weight is given to the other actors before he takes centre stage. Although they had been in or around the same meetings in Geneva in 1932 and in Berlin in January and February 1933, and Bonhoeffer had overseen the publication in German of Bell's *A Brief Sketch of the Church of England*, they did not really register personally with each other until shortly after Bonhoeffer's arrival in London, at the meetings of the executive committees of Life and Work and the World Alliance there 2–4 November. Bell had been alerted to Bonhoeffer's arrival in London by Adolf Deissmann and H. L. Henriod. The young German theologian and the English bishop instantly recognized the importance of the other. In Bell, Bonhoeffer saw one who, already showing obvious sympathy with the church opposition in Germany, could do so much to rally opinion on its behalf throughout the world. Indeed, Bell's being chairman of Life and Work, the most inclusive ecumenical body then in existence, was the nearest the ecumenical movement had to an official spokesperson. In Bonhoeffer, Bell, who spoke very little German despite having had dealings with the German churches for over a decade, saw someone uniquely placed to be an informant and interpreter of what was going on in his country.

In 1933 Bell, then aged 48, had been bishop of Chichester for four years after an already distinguished career, including ten years as chaplain to Randall Davidson, archbishop of Canterbury, followed by five years as dean of Canterbury Cathedral. He was now completing his monumental, two-volume biography of Davidson, which virtually constitutes a history of the Church of England in the first quarter of the 20th century.[17] Bell was passionately interested in the performing arts, and had no mean literary gifts, as shown by his winning a major poetry prize while an undergraduate at Oxford. At Canterbury he brought religious drama into the cathedral, commissioning works by contemporary writers such as John Masefield and T. S. Eliot, and was later to encourage the same interests throughout his own diocese. Bell represented the more broad-minded catholic tendency in the Church of England, and from his time as archbishop's chaplain he was deeply committed both to the search for Christian unity and to the reconciling mission of the church in the world. He was not an exceptionally profound scholar or original thinker, but he studied widely and assiduously and had the capacity to see into the heart of an issue and to communicate his convictions cogently and persistently. He was also gifted in developing relationships of patent sincerity with figures from other traditions, and was a superbly firm but gentle diplomat at the conference table. He had attended the first postwar conference of the World Alliance at Oud Wassenaar in 1919, and the 1925 Stockholm Conference on Life and Work. At the latter he spoke powerfully on the need for a strong continuing organization and became a member of the Life and Work Continuation Committee. While dean of Canterbury (1924–1929) he was instrumental in getting the Assembly of the Church of England to set up its own Council on Foreign Relations, and he initiated the conferences between British and German theologians at Canterbury (1927) and Eisenach (1928). In 1932, following the death of Theodore Woods, bishop of Winchester, he was elected president of the Universal Christian Council for Life and Work and so was now at the helm of the most widely representative body of the churches—mostly Western Protestant but with a number of Orthodox—then in existence.

From the time of the Life and Work meeting in Berlin in January that year and Hitler's accession to power, Bell had been deeply concerned about the German scene and the churches' role in it.[18] By the summer it was clear that, with the dramatic development of the Church Struggle, he could play a key role as occupant of one of the leading positions in the ecumenical movement. The stage was thus well set for the first really effective Bell–Bonhoeffer encounter early in November at the afore-mentioned executive committee meetings. Bell had Bonhoeffer to lunch at the Athenaeum Club, and soon after invited him to come to Chichester on 21 November and spend a couple of days there. Never too high minded to despise the enjoyments of gracious living, Bonhoeffer reveled in the relaxed spaciousness of the bishop's palace and the generous hospitality of Bell and his wife, Henrietta, which enabled the further examination of the theological and political issues at stake in Germany to become, if not pleasure, then at least satisfying business.

So began one of the most significant Christian friendships of the 20th century. In some ways Bell and Bonhoeffer were contrasting figures: Bell the sagacious, broad-minded catholic Anglican, Bonhoeffer the Barthian radical. There was also the difference in age—Bell was almost if not quite old enough to be Bonhoeffer's father, but that disparity became a positive factor in the relationship. Bell was soon to be calling Bonhoeffer and his friend Franz Hildebrandt "my boys," and that may indicate a deeper emotional note being rung on his side, for the Bells were childless. Bonhoeffer, for his part, for all his strength of character and independence of mind did at times feel the need for older and wiser counsel. His father, Karl Barth, and now George Bell were to be the only people he really accorded this role. There were other factors that Bell and Bonhoeffer found they had in common: a love of the arts (though Bell evidently was not as passionate about music as Bonhoeffer); they shared the same birthday (4 February); for each, the First World War had taken brothers—in Bell's case, two. In 1942, the friendship was to culminate in a dramatic and poignant venture of ecumenical solidarity in resistance to tyranny.

Bonhoeffer, briefed by Bell, reported fully on the Hossenfelder episode to his friends in Berlin, who understandably had been anxious about its possible consequences. As it happened, there was not much cause to worry about British public opinion at this stage. The press, especially the *Times*, was covering the German church drama on an almost daily basis, and the weekly religious press was even more focused on the scene. Reactions were of alarm and disgust at the overt antisemitism of the German Christians and the heavy-handed police actions employed or condoned by Ludwig Müller. Of course, the precise issues felt to be at stake in Germany itself were not always clearly recognized. Typical was the comment in the *Baptist Times* on 13 December 1933: "Protestantism has won the first round in the conflict with Hitlerism which threatened to destroy it as a Christian Church. All other parties in the Reich, racial, social, and political, have

been destroyed; Protestantism alone has successfully resisted Hitler's
dictatorship and survived in the struggle." But while this description
may have been vastly oversimplistic and unwarrantedly triumphalist,
it clearly expressed where Christian sentiment in Britain lay, and the
article's following sentences describing the German Christian programme of non-Aryan, Nordic religiosity were entirely accurate. For
Bonhoeffer and the other London pastors, to be in this atmosphere
where the gut reaction in all the British churches was so overwhelm-
ingly in sympathy with the German church opposition was a major
factor in encouraging their continuing attack on the Reich Church
leadership.[19] Bell himself was taking a high-level ecumenical initiative
in writing a letter of concern to Reich bishop Müller. Bonhoeffer was
still hoping that the idea floated at Sofia, of an ecumenical delegation to the German church, would bear fruit and it was discussed at
the November executive board meetings.[20] The plan stalled, however,
partly it appears because of hesitancy in Geneva.

At Christmas 1933 Bell and Bonhoeffer exchanged greetings.
These were more than seasonal pleasantries. Bonhoeffer replied to
Bell's thus:

> It means very much to me indeed to know that you are sharing
> all the time the sorrows and the troubles which the last year has
> brought to our church in Germany. So we do not stand alone, and
> whatever may occur to one member of the Church universal, we
> know that all the members suffer with it. This is a great comfort for
> all of us; and if God will turn back to our church sometime now or
> later, then we may be certain, that, if one member be honoured, all
> the members shall rejoice with it."[21]

Bell further showed his solidarity with a letter in the *Times* of
17 January 1934, drawing attention to the significance of the "Muzzling Decree" issued by Reich bishop Müller on 4 January, which was
intended to suppress all public debate by pastors on the state-backed
church policy, and to Müller's patent breaches of faith. Further, he
made direct approaches to Müller himself and even President Hindenburg. When the Pastors' Emergency League issued a proclamation

urging pastors not to obey the Muzzling Decree, the London German pastors sent a telegram to the Reich Church government identifying themselves with the League's statement and declaring the withdrawal of their confidence from the Reich bishop. The "now or later" of which Bonhoeffer had spoken to Bell at Christmas still seemed a long way off during that first month of 1934, which was proving a traumatic one for the church opposition. The first moves began to be made by such as Karl Barth and Gerhard Jacobi to convene independent, free synods. Secession from the Reich Church was a clearly growing possibility. The questions were, How much support there would be for it, how united would the opposition remain, and on what basis? On 25 January Hitler held a long-awaited reception for Protestant church leaders. Many had hoped that this would enable them to expose Müller as untrustworthy and, indeed, untrusted by the church leadership at large, a hopeless candidate for uniting and pacifying the churches. But the reverse happened. Thanks largely to an intervention by Reich Marshal Hermann Göring, who marched into the meeting and portentously announced that there was now evidence of the dissident pastors receiving help—including money—from abroad, Hitler lost his temper and berated the company for their incompetence and disloyalty. When Martin Niemöller tried to mollify Hitler by insisting on their loyalty to the German Reich and people, Hitler snapped back: "Leave the German people to me; you stick to your sermons." The meeting closed with the pastors in disarray, and Müller's position strengthened by default. It emerged that Göring's remarks were based on some incidental remarks made by Niemöller and his secretary on the telephone earlier in the day, a phone that had obviously been tapped.[22] Bonhoeffer himself, when he heard the news from Berlin, clearly regarded the chancellery reception as a disaster—one more disaster in a darkening scene.

Meanwhile, other people in London were taking an in interest in Bonhoeffer, and not just in church circles. At new year 1934, George Bell was approached by Lord Lothian (Philip Kerr), editor of the prestigious journal *The Round Table*, who was wishing to devote the March issue to the struggle for the soul of Protestantism in Germany. Bell gave a warm commendation of Bonhoeffer as just the person to write the kind of article that was wanted, and it was agreed that Lothian, Bell, and Bonhoeffer should meet. They did so over lunch on 16 January. Lothian was extremely interested in Bonhoeffer and all he had to say. But by then Bonhoeffer felt he must decline the invitation to write the piece. There had already been accusations in Berlin linking him with the reports on the Church Struggle in the *Times*, which he had truthfully and strenuously denied. But somehow word had reached Berlin that Bonhoeffer was now assisting Bell with an article for *The Round Table*. Any overt authorship was now politically out of the question. But Bell did consult Bonhoeffer on the article he himself was now to prepare, which was to be an augmented version of an essay by the Swiss pastor and ecumenical worker Alphons Koechlin.

Bell was soon, partly in response to pleas from Bonhoeffer, turning his mind to another exercise for his pen. Through the early months of 1934 Bonhoeffer grew increasingly concerned for a clear word from the ecumenical organizations on where they stood with regard to the German church conflict. This was not simply an issue of principle (though it certainly was that), but a matter of practical urgency. Pastors who were being suspended or even imprisoned, and their parishioners, needed for their own immediate spiritual encouragement and morale an unmistakable signal that the wider Christian world was in solidarity with them. The clearest form of such a message would be for the ecumenical movement to sever completely all contacts with Müller's church as heretical and to deal only with the opposition. That was Bonhoeffer's aim, shared for a time at least by such as H. L. Henriod in Geneva. As chairman of the Universal Christian Council for Life and Work, George Bell was the nearest thing to an official mouthpiece that the ecumenical movement as a whole had at that time. Bonhoeffer pleaded with him to make a definitive declaration. "The question at stake in the German Church," he wrote to Bell on 13 March 1934, "is no longer an internal issue but is the question of the existence of Christianity in Europe; therefore a definite attitude of the ecumenic movement has nothing to do with 'intervention'—but is just a demonstration to the whole world that Church and Christianity as such are at stake. . . . Please do not be silent now! I beg to ask you once more to consider the possibility of an ecumenic delegation and ultimatum."[23] A month later his pleading was even more desperate, as a result of a note from a beleaguered friend in Germany who had stated "in the present moment there depends everything, absolutely everything on the attitude of the Bishop of Chichester."[24] August Jäger, a man with an already ruthless reputation as State Commissar in the Prussian Church, had just been appointed "legal administrator" by Ludwig Müller with the ominous charge to "complete the legal unity of the German Evangelical Church." Müller had himself issued on 13 April a "Message on Peace in the Church," which announced that actions against church officers were to be called off. On the same day, however, a "Church Decree on the Pacification of the Situation in the Church" declared that Müller's amnesty did not apply to "actions with national political implications." The Pastors' Emergency League almost instantly made a declaration in response to these decrees, stating emphatically that the real fault, need, and danger of the church were being overlooked by Müller, who was once again ignoring the whole question of the *confessional* basis of the church. Bonhoeffer soon had a copy of this declaration, and on 25 April made and sent a translation of it in his own hand to Bell.[25]

Bell was thus being kept fully up to the mark with inside information from Bonhoeffer. Two days later, on 27 April, Bell and Bonhoeffer sat down together at the Athenaeum to discuss the idea of a pastoral letter to be sent to all churches involved in Life and Work, calling attention to the significance of what was happening in Germany. This letter would be issued on Ascension Day, 10 May. It was not, however, only Bell and Bonhoeffer who were involved in this venture. Joe Oldham had also been keenly following the German scene, had his own contacts in both Germany and Geneva, was in frequent contact with Bell, and sent Bell his own version of a draft for such a letter in mid-April.[26] Oldham also was in more frequent touch than Bell with the American ecumenicals. On 2 May Bell sent copies of his proposed draft to Bonhoeffer, Oldham, Alphons Koechlin, and Hans Schönfeld in Geneva. Bonhoeffer was greatly appreciative of the text but suggested several small yet significant changes. One especially deserves highlighting because it illustrates how at times even Bell did not quite grasp the sharpness of the theological issue as seen by the confessing opposition itself:

You speak "of the loyalty (of the pastors) to what they believe to be Christian truth." Could you not say perhaps: to what *is* the Christian truth—or "what we believe with them to be the Christian truth"? It sounds as if you want to take distance from their belief. I think even the Reichsbishop would be right in taking disciplinary measures against ministers, if they stand for something else but the truth of the Gospel (even if they believe it to be the truth)—the real issue is that they are under coercion on account of their loyalty to what *is* the true Gospel—namely their opposition against the *racial and political element as constituent for the Church* of Christ.[27]

It was to be a continual complaint by such as Bonhoeffer and Barth that the Anglo-Saxon world was congenitally prone to seeing the Church Struggle as primarily about "religious freedom," whereas in their view it was more than that; it was for the specific truth of Christ, not a general human principle, however lofty: the *binding* of the conscience to the gospel rather than its inherent liberty. But it was a measure of the trust and respect in which each held the other that Bonhoeffer could write so frankly to Bell in this way and that Bell, equally, could accept the substance of Bonhoeffer's criticism. Bell's final text at the point at issue spoke of "the disciplinary measures which have been taken by the Church government against Ministers of the Gospel on account of their loyalty to the fundamental principles of Christian truth . . ."

Bell's pastoral letter in its final form was headed "A Message Regarding the German Evangelical Church to the Representatives of the Universal Christian Council for Life and Work from the Bishop of Chichester."[28] It was put out on Ascension Day and two days later appeared in the *Times*. It is a short document, only about 540 words, but expresses amply enough the concerns felt by many regarding the imposition on the church of state-sponsored coercion and racial categories incompatible with Christian principle. It did not deliver the ultimatum Bonhoeffer had originally been hoping for, but he knew that Bell had gone as far as his official responsibility would allow. He was grateful and delighted: "In its consciousness it strikes at the chief points and leaves no escape for misinterpretation," he wrote to Bell.[29]

The ecumenical movement was beginning to find its voice. Friendship was indeed proving crucial.

Bell's effort, while modest even within his own terms, had come at a most critical point in the Church Struggle. On 22 April, the Confessing opposition had met at Ulm and declared itself the one lawful Evangelical church in Germany before the whole of Christendom. Two weeks after Ascension Day, the free synod so long hoped for by the leaders of the opposition met at Barmen in the Ruhr and there, largely under Karl Barth's inspiration, drew up the famous Barmen Theological Declaration that clearly and unequivocally spelled out for the present context the true basis of Evangelical faith: "Jesus Christ, as he is attested to us in Holy Scripture, is the one Word of God which we have to hear, and which we have to trust and obey in life and in death. We reject the false doctrine that the Church could and should recognize as a source of its proclamation, beyond and besides this one truth of God, yet other events, powers, historic figures, and truths, as God's self-revelation."[30] In six main theses this dichotomy between the affirmation of biblical faith and false teaching to be disowned was repeated in relation to the church's life, ministry, and relation to the state. Thus was laid the foundation of the Confessing Church. Bonhoeffer himself was not at Barmen, being preoccupied in London. But through what was said on Ascension Day, he, Bell, and Oldham had given a great gift to the Barmen synod: the awareness that the ecumenical world was with them, watching and waiting and praying. Nor do we find Bonhoeffer making much comment on Barmen at this stage. For him, it was simply axiomatic that Barmen defined the true church and set its direction.

There was another reason why we find relatively little mention of the Barmen Synod in Bonhoeffer's letters during these days. His most pressing preoccupation was with the ecumenical conference to take place on the Danish island of Fanø in August. That event and Bonhoeffer's role in it merit a chapter on its own and so will not be dealt with further here. Following Fanø, Bonhoeffer was even more determined to maintain the solidarity of the German pastors in Britain with the Confessing Church. As recounted above,[31] they formally broke with the Reich Church on 5 November 1934.

Finally, mention should be made of Bonhoeffer's ecumenical interest in the native British churches, and not just with the Church of England either. Thanks to the interest of Rudolf Weckerling, a German exchange student, he visited Richmond Methodist College, gave a lecture on the German church situation, and was deeply moved by the memorials to the many former students who had died so young of disease on the mission fields.[32] He attended meetings of the local interdenominational ministers' fraternal in Forest Hill, and at the invitation of the Baptist minister Ernest Reeve preached at his church at Perry Rise. It was probably through this contact that he also visited Spurgeon's College, the Baptist theological college in South Norwood. Equally, while on a visit to Birmingham he much enjoyed the Quaker ethos of Woodbrooke College, Selly Oak. But most noteworthy of all were the visits he made in April 1935, facilitated by George Bell, with Julius Rieger to the Anglican religious houses and theological seminaries of the Society of St John the Evangelist (Cowley, Oxford), the Society of the Sacred Mission (Kelham), and the Community of the Resurrection (Mirfield). These visits were to satisfy more than a tourist interest. For Bonhoeffer was about to return to Germany at the call of the Confessing Church to be director of an illegal seminary. He was convinced that seminary training had to be grounded in a definite community life, indeed a "new monasticism," and he was eager to learn from the English examples. As will be seen, the impressions he gained and the personal links he made on these visits, particularly at Kelham and at Mirfield, were to be abiding and important inspirations in his future work with all its problems and, indeed, dangers. He remained an ecumenical learner through ecumenical friendship.

CHAPTER 6

"The Hour Is Late": Fanø 1934 in Context

The conference that took place on the Danish island of Fanø in late August 1934 is rightly regarded as a vital episode in both the modern ecumenical story and the career of Dietrich Bonhoeffer.[1] It was here that the Council of Life and Work, in the words of the official history of the ecumenical movement, "solemnly resolved to throw its weight on the side of the Confessing Church in Germany against the so-called 'German Christians' and by implication against the Nazi regime."[2] It was here, too, that Bonhoeffer made what many regard as one of his most notable statements ever, a decisive and outspoken call for the churches to reject war and declare themselves for peace. Both these views of Fanø's significance require some qualification. Many things apart from these happened at Fanø and there was a complexity in the dynamics of the gathering which has to be acknowledged for a full understanding of what it meant for the ecumenical movement and if Bonhoeffer's distinctive role is to be brought into relief. Above all, this event, which fell almost exactly halfway through Bonhoeffer's time in London, has to be set in historical and biographical context.

The Context: Rising Peril and the Need for Self-Examination

The Free Synod of Barmen at the end of May 1934 had voiced a decisive word. This, however, did not do anything to mitigate the trauma of political developments in the following weeks and the increasing pressure upon the German churches. On 30 June came the shocking news of the "Röhm Putsch" when Hitler moved against the suspect Nazi dissidents of the *Sturmabteilung* (Storm Troopers) and other possible rivals for leadership. Over 200 were shot in cold blood. Hitler managed to portray this as an act of salvation for Germany, and many churches—including some in the Confessing Church—held services of thanksgiving the following Sunday. During July there were coup attempts by the Austrian National Socialists and on 25 July the Austrian chancellor Engelbert Dolfuss was assassinated. Italian troops mobilized on the border with Austria. Then on 2 August the aging president of Germany, Paul von Hindenburg, died. While his presence since Hitler's accession had been little more than nominal and he could hardly be said to have had a moderating influence, he represented the last remaining vestige of the pre-Nazi order of government. Hitler assumed to himself the presidential office as well as the chancellorship, and a plebiscite on 19 August confirmed his new title as "*Führer* and Reich chancellor of the German people." The grip of dictatorship was tightening inexorably—not least on the churches. Early in July a "Church Law for the Evangelical Press" was promulgated, followed soon by a decree from the Reich minister of the interior and public education, Wilhelm Frick, banning all discussion of church disputes in the press and public gatherings. In August the national synod reiterated gratitude for the deliverance wrought by Hitler, ratified the legality of Reich bishop Müller's measures, and resolved that all pastors should swear an oath of service to the *Führer*, the German people, and state. Meanwhile, the tide of militarism was running ever more strongly. Hitler had brought Germany out of the Geneva disarmament conference and the League of Nations the previous autumn. Not until 1935 was it openly declared that Germany was massively rearming, but the planning and first stages had been in operation since

1933. Dietrich Bonhoeffer, briefed by his brother-in-law Hans von Dohnanyi with inside information, was in no doubt that Hitler was bent on war. Although physically apart from Germany during most of his London period, Bonhoeffer clearly felt oppressed by what was happening in his homeland and by its implications for the wider world, as much as if he had been there. His sermons rarely referred directly to the events in Germany but there are evident clues to his state of mind in his preaching at Sydenham and at the St Paul's church. On the Sunday following the Röhm bloodbath, 8 July 1934, he delivered an ominously toned sermon on Luke 13:1-5, Jesus' words in response to the Galileans massacred by Pilate: ". . . unless you repent, you will all likewise perish."[3] The note of judgment was never far from his preaching, not in a negative, moralizing sense but as calling the church to awaken to its real situation, and instead of a complacent self-satisfaction to grasp the true joy offered by the gospel. Later in the year, he preached a series of sermons all based on 1 Corinthians 13, Paul's great hymn on the primacy of love, deliberately culminating on Reformation Sunday (4 November 1934). Throughout the series he urged that the church of the Reformation cannot be content with its foundational doctrine of justification by faith alone if this faith does not lead to a consuming love in God: a message which in the first sermon of the series he also turned into a warning against the temptation of people like himself in the Confessing Church to congratulate themselves on their own orthodoxy, "to be unloving towards one's opponent." On Reformation Sunday, he reached the conclusion with verse 13: ". . . and the greatest of these is love." The message was clearly addressed to both the congregation in London and to all Protestants in Germany:

> And the church that calls a people [*Volk*] to belief in Christ must itself be in the midst of that people, the burning fire of love, the nucleus of reconciliation, the source of the fire in which all hate is smothered and proud, hateful people are transformed into loving people. Our churches of the Reformation have done many mighty deeds, but it seems to me that they have not yet succeeded in this greatest deed, and it is more necessary today than ever.[4]

Such words manifested an underlying ecumenical consciousness, a realization that one's own tradition, be it ever so precious and revered, must be held up to scrutiny like all others, and, indeed, may have to learn from others. But the "others" may not even be of the Christian world. Toward the end of the sermon of 8 July 1934, on repentance, Bonhoeffer tells a story about "A great man of our time—who is not a Christian, but it is tempting to call him a heathen Christian," who, while director of a school, after a punishable incident took place decided not to punish the pupils but to examine his own conscience. Thereby he learned of his own guilt and that "there could be room for the Spirit of God only in the spirit of humble realization of guilt," and that "faith and hope and love could be found only in repentance."[5] The great man was Mahatma Gandhi, by now the focus of Bonhoeffer's wish, growing over at least the past four years, to visit India. It was no longer just a fascination with the orient at large that drew him, but Gandhi's example of nonviolent resistance in particular, and the spirituality of such as Rabindranath Tagore. Bonhoeffer's time in London coincided with Gandhi's growing profile in Britain as the constitutional debate about the future of India, jewel in the crown of the British Empire, intensified and the sessions of the Round Table leading to the India Act of 1935 took place. As well as reading intensively on Gandhi, Bonhoeffer went at least twice to hear his close collaborator Mira Behn (Madeleine Slade) address public meetings in London.

Very revealing of his increasing impatience with his entire Protestant tradition and his wish for its exposure to the East is a passage in a letter to his grandmother Julie Bonhoeffer in May 1934, barely a week before the Barmen Synod took place:

> I'm thinking again of going to India. I've given a great deal of thought lately to the issues there and believe that there could be important things to be learned. In any case it sometimes seems to me that there's more Christianity in their "heathenism" than in the whole of the Reich Church. Christianity did in fact come from the East originally, but it has become so westernized and so permeated with civilized thought that, as we can now see, it is almost lost to us. Unfortunately I have little confidence in the church opposition . . .[6]

It is striking that it was at precisely the time when he was most determinedly christocentric in his theology, a Barthian of the Barthians, that he felt impelled to look *beyond* the Christian world that assumed the ownership of Christ. Christians might have to look to so-called heathens for a truer understanding of Jesus Christ, especially as far as obeying his command to make peace was concerned. This urgent pulse equally runs through his letter to his Swiss friend Erwin Sutz the previous month:

> While I'm working with the church opposition with all my might, it's perfectly clear to me that *this* opposition is only a very temporary transitional phase on the way to an opposition of a very different kind, and that very few of those involved in this preliminary skirmish are going to be there for that second struggle. I believe that all Christendom should be praying with us for the coming of resistance "to the point of shedding blood" and for the finding of people who can suffer it through. Simply suffering is what it will be all about, not parries, blows or thrusts such as may still be allowed and possible in the preliminary battles; the real struggle that perhaps lies ahead must be one of simply suffering through in faith. Then, perhaps, then God will acknowledge his church again with his word . . .[7]

The direction his thought was taking—toward the setting up of his Finkenwalde community and the writing of *Discipleship*—is amply confirmed by a letter several months later to his brother Karl-Friedrich, in which he speaks of the restoration of the church requiring "a new monasticism" in "a life of uncompromising discipleship, following Christ according to the Sermon on the Mount," in which "alone lies the force that can blow all this hocus-pocus sky-high."[8] From early 1934, then, Bonhoeffer was living under an eschatological sense of a *kairos*, a time of unprecedented crisis and opportunity in which European Christianity—Reich Church *and* Confessing opposition *and* ecumenical "Christendom"—were all under judgment and called to hear the word of God afresh. Only if this sense of it being "the time [*kairos*] of your visitation" (Luke 19:44) is appreciated can Bonhoeffer's radical stance at Fanø be fully understood.

The Fanø Conference: Its Nature and Purpose

What is summarily called the Fanø conference comprised two meetings held almost concurrently. The larger one was the regular biennial
meeting of the Universal Christian Council for Life and Work and
met 24–30 August. Alongside this, but beginning two days earlier,
was the study conference organized by the joint Youth Commission of
Life and Work and the World Alliance. A number of devotional sessions were shared by the two conferences, and members of the youth
conference attended several business sessions of the Life and Work
meeting as observers. A main task of the Life and Work meeting was
to agree on plans for the next world conference. It had at first been
hoped that this would take place in 1935, the tenth anniversary of
the founding Life and Work conference at Stockholm. At its 1932
meeting, however, the council decided that this be postponed to 1937
in view of the current economic crisis and the need for fuller preparation. Fanø would see agreement that the theme of the conference,
to be held in Oxford, would be "Church, Community and State,"
and it appointed J. H. Oldham—attending a Life and Work meeting for the first time—to oversee and organize the study programme.[9]
The theme had been in the minds of the Life and Work leadership
for some time. Church–state relationships and the rise of totalitarian regimes were posing questions to the ecumenical family all over
Europe and elsewhere. In the minds of many delegates, however, the
most recent events in Germany would not only lend urgency to the
envisaged theme for Oxford 1937 but would demand a response from
the meeting at Fanø itself. The main theme of the youth conference
was likewise "Church and State."

As a secretary of the Youth Commission, Bonhoeffer's primary
responsibility was for the youth conference. Throughout the preceding
months he carried a heavy load of responsibility, in cooperation with
H. L. Henriod and Theodóre de Félice in Geneva, for the organization of the programme and securing the right composition of delegations from countries in his allotted areas of Europe. He also obtained
the assistance of one of his Berlin students, Jürgen Winterhager. In
addition, however, at the Sofia meeting of the World Alliance executive committee in September the previous year, he had agreed to the

suggestion that he work with others on a "Catechism of Peace" as a main World Alliance contribution to the 1934 Life and Work meeting.[10] This particular idea did not materialize, but the invitation for him to make a plenary presentation to the main Life and Work conference remained and for this he prepared—in his own way, as soon became evident. In his view, the ominous developments in Germany throughout 1934 and the Barmen Synod had drastically changed the significance of Fanø as an ecumenical gathering and charged it with an unprecedented responsibility equal to Barmen itself. This, to his mind, affected every aspect of the two meetings and what would be said and done there. Would Fanø dare to make a decisive declaration about peace in face of the gathering world crisis? And would Fanø take the decisive step of identifying the Confessing Church as founded at Barmen to be the true Evangelical Church of Germany and as such recognized to be *the* German partner in the ecumenical movement? These two issues were of equal urgency in his mind.

The matter of recognition of the Confessing Church presented itself even prior to the meeting in the question of who would be attending from Germany. This provided Bonhoeffer with his most taxing problem in the lead-up to Fanø. The logic of Barmen was that the Confessing Church could recognize as authentic representatives of the German Evangelical Church at ecumenical gatherings only those who identified with it on the basis of the Barmen Declaration. Equally, the Confessing Church required the ecumenical fellowship to make the same recognition. Hitherto, the relations of the Geneva office of Life and Work, including the joint secretariat with the World Alliance, with Germany had been via the Foreign Relations department of the Evangelical Church in Berlin. That office was now a department of the Reich Church under the direction of Theodore Heckel and would hardly be expected to recognize the claim of the Confessing Church in drawing up the list for the German delegation. But equally, what line would the ecumenical office in Geneva take? Here the attitude was far more equivocal than Bonhoeffer had hoped for. Henriod and de Félice, however sympathetic personally to the Confessing cause, felt bound by their constitutional rules, according to which the composition of delegations was a matter for member churches and national organizations. As yet the Confessing Church had not, in their view, formally declared itself a separate church alongside the Evangelical Church in its Reich Church form, and could not expect separate (let alone exclusive) treatment.[11] Thus was emerging the issue which was to vex relations between the Confessing Church and the ecumenical bodies for years to come.

As far as the German delegation to the youth conference was concerned, Bonhoeffer had relatively little trouble since he could assume responsibility for this anyway, and recruited a list drawn mainly from his former Berlin students who were keen supporters of the Confessing Church as well as the World Alliance. "The ten members of our German youth delegation all stand firmly in the Confessing Church," he told de Félice,[12] and objected strongly to any separate approach from Geneva to organizations like the German YMCA, among whose members would be a more ambiguous attitude to the Reich Church. His delegation, he insisted, would not participate in any session at which Reich Church members were present. Far more fraught was the question of the Confessing Church's participation in the main Life and Work conference. Bonhoeffer and the Confessing Church leaders with whom he consulted (Karl Koch, president of the Confessing synod, and Martin Niemöller) were adamant that a recognized and specific presence of Confessing Church representatives at Fanø was essential. Heckel and the Reich Church Foreign-Relations office were determined to prevent this. For Bonhoeffer, the question was a peculiarly personal one since, soon after the Barmen Synod, Hans Schönfeld had renewed the invitation for him to make a plenary presentation to the main conference. But on what basis, now, would he be doing so? He made clear that he refused to be a member of a delegation nominated by the Reich Church, and could only participate if he was recognized as a representative of the Confessing Church. At one point he offered to withdraw his participation altogether. The tortuous arguments with Geneva ran throughout July and much of August.[13] Bonhoeffer solicited the help of George Bell, who consulted with Bishop Ove Ammundsen, who in turn proposed a way forward: that Bell as president of the Council of Life and Work, and using the executive power to which he was entitled in an emergency, invite President Koch to send two people from the Confessing Church as expert advisers. Bell accordingly wrote to Karl Koch inviting him and Friedrich von Bodelschwingh to come to Fanø. In fact, neither was able to. This left Bonhoeffer in a real quandary about his own position. He eventually agreed that he would participate in the main meeting— but as a secretary of the Joint Youth Commission and so ensuring his independence from the Reich Church delegation led by Heckel. At least the existence of the Confessing Church was being recognized by the governing body (if not the staff) of Life and Work, and Bonhoeffer wrote gratefully to Ammundsen, indeed almost apologetically: "please always write to me when you have the feeling that I am doing something wrong. These ecumenical matters are for us Germans something that we only learn if we keep paying attention, gaining experience, and receiving help—and for this I thank you."[14] At the same time, he urged on the bishop the need for a decisive statement from Fanø, anxious lest even among his own supporters there may be too much caution "for fear of seeming unpatriotic." The gathering must speak out openly as *Christians*, come what may.[15]

As if the matter of participation was not trouble enough, Bonhoeffer ran into difficulty with Hans Schönfeld over his proposed presentation to the main conference. On 14 June, Schönfeld wrote to him with the request to submit proposals and suggestions for the second day of the main conference in Fanø when the topic would be "The church and the peoples of the world." Schönfeld asked that he address particular these questions:

1. On what basis, and with what right, does the church have a responsibility to speak on international problems? How is the relationship of ecumenicity to internationalism properly understood?

2. By what means, and within what limits, does the church work to help in solving international problems?[16]

Schönfeld evidently had in mind a generalized, analytical examination of theological principles and ecclesiastical policy, in keeping with the study material already being prepared for such a major conference on church and state. He enclosed copies of the papers from other notable scholars which were to be published shortly before the conference,[17] commending in particular the contribution of W. Menn as an example of the kind of presentation envisaged. Bonhoeffer could certainly have written on the questions suggested in the way requested. He had after all already addressed church, race, nation, and ecumenical responsibility in his lectures in Berlin, Gland, and Ciernorske Kúpele the previous year.[18] But for Bonhoeffer the time for such theological argumentation had long since gone. An authoritative word *from* the church *now* on God's command to peace, not yet another discourse *about* the church and internationalism, was required. This would necessitate his returning to the question of just what the World Alliance believed itself to be, in order to utter such a word. Accordingly, he submitted his theses under the title "The Church and the Peoples of the World: The Fundamental Principles of the World Alliance." Schönfeld, somewhat dismayed at what he received, wrote back begging him "to adopt a more comprehensive approach to the theme 'The Church and the Peoples of the World' or 'Internationalism and Ecumenism.'"[19] Bonhoeffer, however, was not wanting to be "comprehensive" but to be as sharply focused as possible, and thus he ignored Schönfeld's plea. Once again, he was engaging the ecumenical movement on his own terms.

Fanø: 22–30 August 1934

The youth conference comprised 58 delegates from Austria, Belgium, Czechoslovakia, Denmark, France, Germany, Great Britain, Hungary, India, Ireland, Japan, Madagascar, the Netherlands, Norway, and Poland, with an émigré from Russia.[20] The French group included Jean Lasserre, Bonhoeffer's friend from his year at Union Seminary, New York. The programme went largely to plan. Following an opening session on organizational matters on the evening of 22 August, work began next morning with Bonhoeffer leading devotions and then chairing the first session. The Congregationalist E. C. Blackman, one of the British delegates, reported afterward: "We started in the right atmosphere, for at our devotions on the first morning Bonhoeffer reminded us that our primary object was not to commend our own views, national or individual, but to hear what God would say to us."[21] That and subsequent days were occupied in hearing reports on church–state relations in various countries, and the task of the church in relation to society. On 25 August, the conference moved into resolution mode, drafts having been prepared on topics including the right to conscientious objection (a prime issue for this age group) and the distinct role of the church vis-à-vis the state and society. Tensions arose at two points in particular. One German delegate requested that a passage dealing with infringements of the rights of minorities and freedom of expression be withdrawn since this could be interpreted as the meeting giving its support to press attacks on Germany. This was a sensitive issue even for some on the "Confessing" side and, indeed, a serious one since no one knew quite what would await them on return home (prior to the meeting Bonhoeffer had warned the Geneva staff of the extreme anxiety the German delegates would likely be carrying, and even requested that, contrary to the usual practice at such conferences, this time there should be no light-hearted evening entertainment). Then there was considerable debate on the wording of a resolution stating that the church as a universal fellowship, standing within but not "of" the nation, "ought not to give its blessing to any war whatsoever." A Polish delegate, supported by a Hungarian, wished to replace this "any war" by "aggressive war." After debate, the original wording stood but in the vote there were abstentions on the Polish and Hungarian sides on the grounds that the particular political and geographical situations of their countries needed to be recognized and they could not condemn defensive war. It was now late at night, and tempers became frayed when a German woman delegate (according to one account, Hilde Enterlein of Potsdam), evidently seeing anti-German sentiment at work, queried the motivation of these abstentions. The atmosphere was fast becoming explosive and the chairman, Pierre Toureille, proposed a short time of prayer. In its account of what happened next the report is as eloquent as can be imagined, on what Bonhoeffer's theology of the church being Christ existing as community meant in practice and in ecumenical context:

Then Bonhoeffer reminded the Conference that we are one Church in spite of differences of opinion. We will build up the Church [together by] listening to God. The remark that we are divided is not [made] as a reproach, but as a witness to the profound problems confronting] the Church. We are in deep sympathy with our Hungarian [friends]. Strong expression is a good thing to show the real facts, but having said them we join in common prayer, penitence and worship.

A Polish delegate said that they agreed with [this] vision of the Church; no expression of opinions must be so strong as to destroy our real unity as one Church.

The Hungarian delegation then thanked Bonhoeffer on account of his speech and understanding. We have come here to collaborate as far as possible; we will work for the unity of the church.

This moving session concluded at 12:30 A.M. with prayer.[22]

Bonhoeffer was well satisfied with the youth conference overall, not least the way in which, as well as coming down firmly on the peace issue and the rights of conscientious objectors, the discussions leading to the strong resolutions on the sovereignty and universal nature of the church had echoed the witness made at Barmen: "In face of the growing claims of the State the Church should abandon its attitude of passivity and, without fear of consequences, declare the will of God."[23] The resolutions were also presented to the main conference.

The main conference right from the start had to cope with major tensions, especially on the German issue. Here Bonhoeffer's role was necessarily confined to informal conversations, advice, and lobbying, and there is no doubt that he used to the full such opportunities as he had. The official German (Reich Church) delegation led by Heckel naturally wished it not to be dealt with at all, arguing that it was a purely internal German affair in which an international body had no competence to intervene. There was also a measure of support for this view within some other delegations since there was no precedent for such ecumenical intervention. World Alliance delegates from Germany attending independently of the Reich Church group also made clear from the start that they would not take part in public

discussions on "the internal affairs of the German Church."[24] Even
among some of the Confessing leaders back in Germany there was
nervousness about the consequences should Fanø take sides too explicitly and thus prompt an impression of giving way to anti-German
pressures, thereby putting the Confessing Church itself in a yet more
dangerous light before the German state. It was very soon clear, however, that there was no way the issues could be kept off the agenda.
For many delegates, especially from France, Britain, and the USA, it
had become the key issue of the hour. In any case, George Bell had
taken a preemptive initiative with his Ascension Day pastoral letter
on behalf of Life and Work, and at the very least the Council would
have to decide whether or not to endorse that letter. It belongs to
ecumenical history, of which full accounts are to be found elsewhere,
that after three days of plenary debates, closed sessions, and meetings of a working group, the main conference did effectively take sides
with the Confessing Church—despite vigorous protests from Bishop
Heckel. The momentous resolution passed on 30 August covered a
lot of ground.[25] It stated the concern for church–state relations as a
fundamental worldwide concern of Christian faith. It expressed the
"grave anxiety" by many representatives "lest vital principles of Christian liberty should be endangered or compromised at the present time
in the life of the German Evangelical Church." It stated the belief
of the Council in "the special task of the ecumenical movement to
express and deepen the essence of mutual responsibility in all parts
of the Christian Church." It recognized "the peculiar difficulties of
a situation of revolution" but went on to declare autocratic church
rule, use of force, and the suppression of free discussion as "incompatible with the true nature of the Christian Church," and asked "in
the name of the Gospel" for proper freedom of teaching and life on
the German Evangelical Church. It endorsed the action taken by the
bishop of Chichester. And most decisively: "The Council desires to
assure its brethren in the Confessional Synod of the German Evangelical Church of its prayers and heartfelt sympathy in their witness to the
principles of the Gospel, and of its resolve to maintain close fellowship with them." This represented a major triumph for the ecumenical
support of the Confessing Church—as may be measured by Theodor

Heckel's lengthy and vigorous protest (alleging that the Council had exceeded its competence, and denying many of the alleged infringements of liberties in Germany)—and had considerable impact among the churches at large.

It was not, however, a flawless success. At the request of Heckel, a short additional clause was inserted into the resolution, conveying the sympathy of the Council "to all its fellow Christians in Germany" in their present difficulties, and its wish "to remain in friendly contact with all groups in the Evangelical Church." Seen at the time as an innocent gesture of goodwill, it was in due course to generate serious difficulties in relations between the Confessing Church and the ecumenical movement.[26] For the moment, for such as Bonhoeffer there was sheer relief and gratitude that the Confessing Church was recognized and supported. What is more, on the very same day the resolution was passed the Council took an even more definitive step in support by co-opting both Bonhoeffer and Karl Koch, president of the Confessing Synod, onto the Council as consultative members—again notwithstanding objections by Heckel. Soon after Fanø, Bonhoeffer wrote to George Bell thanking him for his great help to the Confessing cause at Fanø. The resolution, he said, "has become a true expression of a brotherly spirit, of justice and truthfulness."[27]

For most of the time in the main conference at Fanø Bonhoeffer was relatively hidden from sight and sound, being involved in the oversight of the youth conference, or walking the corridors in quiet advocacy of the Confessing Church cause. On 28 August, however, he made his two presentations. For only one of these is the full text extant, and this is what has become known as Bonhoeffer's "Peace Sermon."[28] It was evidently delivered in the opening devotional session in the morning and it has justly become famous as Bonhoeffer's most outspoken and most oft-quoted public utterance on the church's responsibility for peace. It is based on the text Psalm 85:9: "I will hear what God the Lord will speak: for he will speak peace unto his people, and to his saints." Caught between the "twin crags" of nationalism and internationalism, he begins, the ecumenical church does not concern itself with possibilities but with obedience to the command of peace, a binding commandment not open to discussion. The church is part of this commandment: "There shall be peace because of the Church of Christ, for the sake of which the world exists. And this Church of Christ lives at one and the same time in all peoples, yet beyond all boundaries, whether national, political, social or racial." The members of this church are bound through the commandment of God more inseparably than by any other tie, however revered. There is no escape for them from the command of Christ. He asks rhetorically, How does peace come about? Through banks, through money, universal rearmament? He continues: "Through none of these, for the single reason that in all of them peace is confused with safety. There is no way to peace along the way of safety. For peace must be dared. It is the great venture. It can never be made safe. Peace is the opposite of security. To demand guarantees is to mistrust, and this mistrust in turn brings forth war."[29]

It is the church itself that must call the world to peace—the whole church, not just the individual Christian or the individual church, for whom the powers of hate prove too strong: "Only the one great Ecumenical Council of the Holy Church of Christ over all the world can speak out so that the world, though it gnash its teeth, will have to hear, so that the peoples will rejoice because the Church of Christ in the name of Christ has taken the weapons from the hands of their sons, forbidden war, and proclaimed the peace of Christ against the raging world."[30] The Ecumenical Council *is* in session now, Bonhoeffer insists. "We can still do it today. . . . The nations are waiting for it in the East and in the West. Must we be put to shame by non-Christian peoples in the East? . . . The hour is late. . . . The world is choked with weapons. . . . The trumpets of war may blow tomorrow? For what are we waiting? . . . Who knows whether we shall see each other again in another year?"

His Berlin (and later Finkenwalde) student Otto Dudzus recalls that morning: "From the first moment the assembly was breathless with tension. Many may have felt that they would never forget what they had just heard. . . . Bonhoeffer had charged so far ahead that the conference could not follow him. Did that surprise anybody? But on the other hand: could anybody have a good conscience about it?"[31] Later that day Bonhoeffer gave his paper based on his "Theses for the

Fanø Conference" on "The Church and the Peoples of the World. The Fundamental Principles of the World Alliance." The full text has not survived but presumably Bonhoeffer followed the summary theses he had earlier presented to Hans Schönfeld.[32] Here again is the insistence that war cannot be treated either as a political necessity (conventional politics) or as a problem to be solved by rational means (secular pacifism), but only by obeying God's command "Thou shalt not kill." The power of evil will not be broken by means of organizations, but by prayer and fasting, and the power of Christ. Nor is it pacifism which overcomes the world but faith which hopes in the coming of Christ. But most striking of all is the initial thrust of the paper, reiterating the demand that the World Alliance face the question whether it is a church or a society with a definite purpose. "It is only as Church that the World Alliance can preach the Word of Christ in full authority to the Churches and nations. As a society it stands without authority with innumerable other societies of the same kind."[33] The paper received a somewhat mixed reception in the following discussion, the Oxford scholar and socialist politician Richard Crossman in particular being alarmed at what he saw as an unthinking slide toward sheer pacifism in the meeting.[34]

From the perspective of Bonhoeffer's understanding of ecumenism, however, certain observations should be made on the two presentations. First, much of what is said in both papers is a much sharpened concentration of his arguments at ecumenical gatherings the previous year: that an acceptance of the givenness of war as a political necessity (which he had earlier seen as fruit of the "orders of creation" nationalist theology), on the one hand, and secular pacifism (which he had earlier identified with "Anglo-Saxon liberalism"), on the other hand, were alike to be rejected in light of the divine command. Second, there is his insistence that the World Alliance (and by implication, presumably, the Universal Council on Life and Work) should view itself as *church*, since it is placing itself under the word of God. It is not surprising that Bonhoeffer's theses had so alarmed Hans Schönfeld, whose own paper prepared not long after on the same topic "The Universal Church and the World of Nations" was couched in general principles making major concessions to the limitations imposed on the churches by the realities of the world. Schönfeld argued:

But the Church of Christ lives *within History*. This means that she enters into a fallen world, is involved in the existence of a fallen world, is involved in the sinfulness of the fallen world. The Church of Christ never appears in any other form than in that of individual Churches belonging to different separate confessions, and she is only able to know and confess the divine truth in a fragmentary manner, and indeed mingled with error which strives against the truth.[35]

By contrast, for Bonhoeffer everything is sharpened into an immediacy recognizing that *now* is the time to speak and act *as* this church in the name of Christ, and in so doing *realize itself* as the one universal church of Christ, casting aside all the confessional and national limitations that Schönfeld wished to have acknowledged as conditioning factors. In this regard, the "Peace Sermon" has often been misinterpreted[36] as a call to summon the great "Ecumenical Council" of the church of Christ in order that such a Council might speak authoritatively to the world. But Bonhoeffer is not making such a call: he is daring to claim that that Ecumenical Council is *actually here and now* meeting in Fanø and should behave accordingly. This was his most radical declaration yet on how the ecumenical movement should see itself, and the most radical challenge the ecumenical movement had itself received, from any quarter, to assess its own significance. But it was evidently the rights and wrongs of pacifism in the abstract which still drew most participants' attention in response. Finally, there is the almost throwaway remark toward the end of the "Peace Sermon," where Bonhoeffer asks whether he and his hearers should be "put to shame by non-Christian peoples in the East?" This clearly is echoing his growing interest in India and Gandhi's practice of nonviolence. Bonhoeffer was wishing to bring to the conference the sense, noted earlier, that Western Christianity and the ecumenical movement itself were under judgment and in need of education from outside the Christian part of the *oikoumene*, such was the eschatological crisis of the hour.

Recollections and Perspectives on Fanø

Many issues were dealt with at Fanø in addition to the German situation and peace questions, not least in importance being the plans agreed in preparations for the 1937 Oxford Conference. No doubt, as so often with large international conferences, there were almost as many opinions on what were the highlights as there were participants. An interest in Bonhoeffer, fed with hindsight on the later dramas of his career, is apt to make for a distorted slant on the event overall, and on how he was viewed at the time. For a number of participants it was not Bonhoeffer in isolation (indeed if at all) but the German participants as a whole who were of most interest. E. C. Blackman wrote in his report on the youth conference:

> The difficult position of our German friends became more and more apparent. Naturally their very presence, the situation in their country being what it is, considerably heightened the interest of the Conference. They were very careful in stating their case and in defending themselves against misrepresentation. A casual observer might have received the impression that the German delegation had set itself to oppose every statement coming from the French and English parties. The falseness of such an impression became obvious as time went on, however. As might have been expected, the German delegation seemed more deeply concerned with the whole problem of the relation of the Church to the State.[37]

George Bell, even before he arrived home, penned a full report for the London *Times*.[38] In it he stresses how the German situation dominated so much of the proceedings yet in a largely irenic spirit, and cites the key paragraphs on the resolution expressing support for the Confessing Synod while sympathetic to all Christians in Germany. He makes clear the particular concern of the conference for the Confessing Christians, notwithstanding the protests of the official German delegation, while being remarkably fulsome in praise of Theodore Heckel personally. The measures taken were in no way politically inclined, nor religiously factional, the whole conference having taken place in a "brotherly spirit." Yet he concludes with a warning: "But [the resolution] does not conceal the deep anxiety, however kindly expressed, which all the Churches of Christendom now feel about the German Church. Nor does it hide the fact that the wrongs which it so gravely sets forth are doing deep injury to the German Church and imperil its whole future." Bell cites in confirmation of the Council's solidarity with the Confessing Church Karl Koch's co-optation onto the Council, but, interestingly, does not mention Bonhoeffer's like appointment. Perhaps this was because Bonhoeffer, unlike Koch, had not an official position as a leader of the Confessing Church. For the purpose of measuring the profile of Bonhoeffer against that overall stance of Fanø, however, Bell's article is very revealing. It will have been noted that the Fanø resolution nowhere mentions the key issue in the Church Struggle, of the Aryan paragraph, nor any of the theological content of the Barmen Declaration. The weight of its concern lies on the anxiety that "vital principles of Christian liberty should be endangered or compromised," and it was the use of coercive measures and restrictions on "freedom to preach the Gospel of our Lord Jesus Christ" that was condemned. In his Ascension Day message, Bell himself, under Bonhoeffer's persuasion, had spoken of measures taken against ministers of the gospel "on account of their loyalty to the fundamental principles of Christian truth" and remarked on Christian opinion abroad "disturbed by the introduction of racial distinctions in the universal fellowship of the Christian Church" (i.e., the Aryan paragraph, for example). It would not be fair to say that Fanø represented a retreat back to the spirit of Bell's first draft of his Ascension Day message which, as Bonhoeffer had argued, was an appeal to the rights of conscience as distinct from adherence to Christian *truth*. The Fanø paragraph of support for the Confessing Church does speak of sympathy for the Confessing synod's "witness to the principles of the Gospel," and Bell's report cleverly keeps a reference to the Aryan paragraph as implicitly included in the Council's endorsement of his Ascension Day message: "The Council also desired, while endorsing all that had been said about the Aryan paragraph, to concentrate its whole weight on maintaining the principle of Christian liberty. It speaks plainly and strongly about the dictatorship of the Reichbishop and the proposed oath . . ." Bell, as this statement makes clear, felt duty bound to reflect the weight of sentiment at Fanø: sympathy with the suffering, rather than affirmation of the content of the witness of the Confessing Church. Nevertheless, as Bonhoeffer's letter to Bell showed, this was more than enough for his gratitude. The Confessing Church had significant friends in the *oikoumene*.

An obvious factor in Bonhoeffer's relatively inconspicuous place in the firsthand reports applied to all German participants belonging to the opposition: the desire to preserve their personal anonymity in face of possible police actions at home. Henry Smith Leiper, American Presbyterian and ecumenical secretary of the Federal Council of Churches in the USA, attended Fanø as part of an extended European itinerary and wrote a travel diary in the form of letters to family and friends at home.[39] At Fanø he was a member of the group that drafted the crucial resolution on Germany and the Confessing Church. His whole account of Fanø is fascinating, indeed, at times entertaining, with some observations that may surprise those who view Fanø only as an episode of critical encounters. In a similar vein to Bell he recounts: "Considering the depth of the feelings aroused, and the sharp differences of opinion which existed among the delegates, it really was wonderful that there was not a single point during the discussions when all the participants were not perfectly courteous and Christian in their dealings with one another. There were lots of frank statements made, but no harsh words, no threats, no indignant personal attacks"[40] (perhaps he had not known of the late-night contretemps in the youth meeting). Leiper had known Bonhoeffer from his time at Union Seminary, and in 1939 was to be involved with Bonhoeffer's short-lived visit to America and fateful return to Germany. Many years later he recalled how, at Fanø, "I was not surprised to have Dietrich come to my room, soon after the meetings had started, to talk about his problem"—the problem being Heckel's wish to remove him from London.[41] Bonhoeffer made clear to him fearlessly that, regardless of consequences, he had to fight the regime of Ludwig Müller and "to oppose openly the whole effort of Hitlerism to take over the control of the Church in Germany." In his 1934 travel letters, however, Leiper does not mention Bonhoeffer by name nor any such interview with anyone from the opposition except for one person with whom Leiper and George Bell talked about the Confessing movement. But the impression is that this person was a visitor to the conference rather than a participant. Leiper had numerous contacts in Germany, and earlier on his travels among other things had attended the Barmen Synod, spent time in Berlin attending the Congress of the Baptist World Alliance, and also had meetings with Reich bishop Müller, Heckel, other Reich Church figures, and members of the Confessing Church. He was therefore under no illusions about what was happening and his sympathies were wholly with the Confessing Church. It is a tribute both to his generosity of spirit as well as a caution about rushing to a final judgment that he comments after conversations with Heckel at the Fanø meeting:

> You see, he was chosen from the opposition by Müller as a sort of conciliatory step and we have reason to believe that his heart is more with the opposition than with the official Church government. Yet in representing the latter he has to be exceedingly careful as to what he says and does. His old friends distrust his motives and his new associates feel uncertain as well. He feels that if he gets out a worse man would be put in, and I think there is no doubt about that, for he is the ablest man in the Church government. If he can carry through I think it will be better for all concerned than that he should resign at the present moment.[42]

It would be wrong to suggest either that Leiper or, for that matter, Bell, with his cautionary, nonjudgmental attitude, was being naïve about Heckel or that Bonhoeffer was blindly prejudiced against him. Their respective attitudes reflected the different perspectives of the concerned and fair-minded observer from outside—and probably their concern with a broader picture of the world at that time—and the passionately involved insider. Bonhoeffer personally had good reason to be dismissive of Heckel's claim to credibility following his attempts to cajole and browbeat the London German pastors, and Bonhoeffer personally in Berlin, earlier in the year. Equally, Leiper was a highly intelligent monitor who (like George Bell) knew much of the truth of what was happening yet, like many a concerned ecumenist, was prepared to keep hoping for greater unity in the German churches' response to the crisis before hard and fast battle lines were irrevocably drawn. That Bonhoeffer's mind was already made up should not lead us—with the benefit of hindsight—to disparage those who were following in the same direction if more slowly. Of course, with the clarity of the prophet Bonhoeffer's mind *was* already decided. The reports we have cited throw into even sharper relief just how radically far ahead he was on his own journey of resistance. As previously mentioned, he had even insisted that no Confessing representative could even sit in a session where Reich Church members were present. *His* lines were already clearly drawn. It may not be incidental, therefore, that in the official group photograph of the Fanø conference, in which Heckel appears seated on the front row close to George Bell, there is no trace of Bonhoeffer at all.[43]

Almost immediately after Fanø, on 3 September, Bonhoeffer reported on the outcome to a meeting of the Reich Council of Brethren in Würzburg, and then proceeded to Bruay-in-Artois in France for a small conference of younger British and German theologians who had been at Fanø. These in their different ways were to show that Fanø, having met one great challenge, was spawning new questions both for the Confessing Church and the ecumenical fellowship.

The young Bonhoeffer at Gland

Max Diestel, Bonhoeffer's superintendent and mentor in Berlin

Ecumenical Youth Conference in Gland, 1932

On the beach at Fanø, 1934

Dietrich Bonhoeffer's Fanø registration papers

Bishop George Bell

Willem Visser 't Hooft

Henry Smith Leiper, director of the Federal Council of Churches

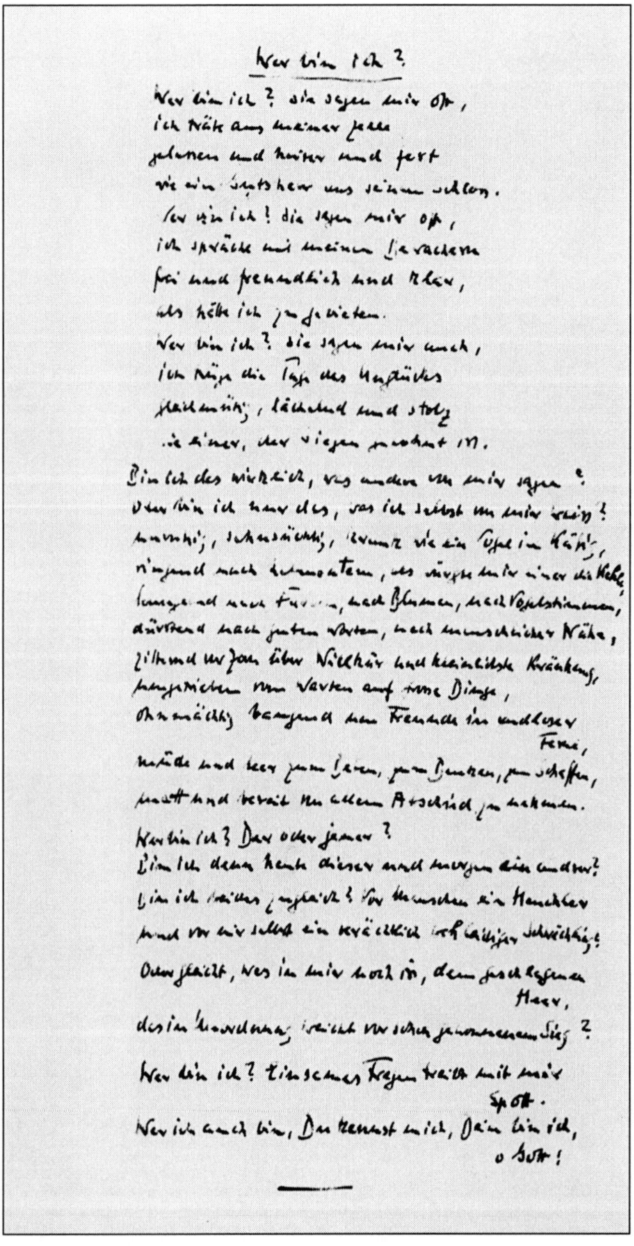
Wer bin ich?

Wer bin ich? Sie sagen mir oft,
ich träte aus meiner Zelle
gelassen und heiter und fest
wie ein Gutsherr aus seinem Schloss.
Wer bin ich? Sie sagen mir oft,
ich spräche mit meinen Bewachern
frei und freundlich und klar,
als hätte ich zu gebieten.
Wer bin ich? Sie sagen mir auch,
ich trüge die Tage des Unglücks
gleichmütig, lächelnd und stolz,
wie einer, der Siegen gewohnt ist.

Bin ich das wirklich, was andere von mir sagen?
Oder bin ich nur das, was ich selbst von mir weiß?
unruhig, sehnsüchtig, krank, wie ein Vogel im Käfig,
ringend nach Lebensatem, als würgte mir einer die Kehle,
hungernd nach Farben, nach Blumen, nach Vogelstimmen,
dürstend nach guten Worten, nach menschlicher Nähe,
zitternd vor Zorn über Willkür und kleinlichste Kränkung,
umgetrieben vom Warten auf große Dinge,
ohnmächtig bangend um Freunde in endloser Ferne,
müde und leer zum Beten, zum Denken, zum Schaffen,
matt und bereit von allem Abschied zu nehmen.

Wer bin ich? Der oder jener?
Bin ich denn heute dieser und morgen ein andrer?
Bin ich beides zugleich? Vor Menschen ein Heuchler
und vor mir selbst ein verächtlich wehleidiger Schwächling?
Oder gleicht, was in mir noch ist, dem geschlagenen Heer,
das in Unordnung weicht vor schon gewonnenem Sieg?

Wer bin ich? Einsames Fragen treibt mit mir Spott.
Wer ich auch bin, Du kennst mich, Dein bin ich, o Gott!

Bonhoeffer's "Who am I?" handwritten original, June 1944

Bonhoeffer in Tegal Prison

The concentration camp at Flossenberg, where Bonhoeffer was hanged

CHAPTER 7

"The Question Has Been Posed": Is the Ecumenical Movement Church?

Both to Bonhoeffer and to many others involved, the Fanø conference of August 1934 marked a new phase in the ecumenical movement. It was a transition from conversation, debate, and dialogue toward decision and commitment; from generalized considerations about Christian truth to a firm grasp of *where* the truth, here and now, lay and was to be affirmed—in this case with the Confessing Church as founded on the Barmen Theological Declaration. None of the ambiguities that lurked at Fanø, nor any of the misgivings Bonhoeffer himself had felt there, could withstand the overwhelming relief and gratitude he felt that the ecumenical movement had now ventured beyond hesitations in fundamentally identifying with the Confessing Church. It was now in historically uncharted territory but the momentum was undeniable.

Bonhoeffer's immediate actions after Fanø[1] were relatively undramatic but presaged much of his future ecumenical path. First, on 3

September, he attended a meeting of the Confessing Church leadership, the Reich Council of Brethren, in Würzburg and reported on what had happened at Fanø. He urged that gratitude be expressed, to George Bell above all. Nevertheless, he stated, there had been puzzlement on why the Confessing Church had not as such been represented at the conference, and confusion had become evident in the clause which committed Life and Work to remain "in friendly contact" with all church groups in Germany. This, in his view, resulted from a failure by the Confessing leaders to make their position absolutely clear: that the Confessing Church was not a group within the German Evangelical Church but was authentically itself *that church* in contradiction of the claims of the Reich Church. Bonhoeffer was thus laying down a marker from which there could be no retreat. The Confessing Church could not, except by denying everything it claimed to be and to stand for, sit at the same ecumenical table with those from Germany it deemed to be representing heresy. So crucial was the need for this case to be presented, Bonhoeffer argued now and later, that the Confessing Church should appoint a representative solely for ecumenical affairs.

Next, Bonhoeffer went to Bruay-en-Artois, in northern France, for the small conference of young British and German theologians, all of whom had been at Fanø, organized under the auspices of the Youth Commission, on the theme "A Theological Word from Ecumenical Youth on the Task of the Church Today."[2] Although smaller than intended,[3] it was significant as an attempt at transposing the dramas of Fanø into the seemingly more mundane questions being faced by churches and Christians at local level. It was also illuminating as an encounter between the post-Barmen confessional stance of the Germans and the more pragmatically ethical Anglo-Saxon approach to the role of the church in society. As his report on Bruay makes clear, Bonhoeffer was no longer dismissing the latter approach as nontheological liberalism and therefore of no account. Neither stance was to be played off one against the other. The Confessing Church now had friends who knew where heresy lay, and regardless of difference on some theological matters the fostering of such friendship now had primacy.

Back in London, Bonhoeffer fulfilled his remaining eight months' pastoral ministry there. Here were continuing dramas, in particular in November when Bonhoeffer's and other German congregations in England rejected the authority of the Reich Church and formally identified with the Confessing Church.[4] His plans for visiting India got as far as receiving an invitation from Mahatma Ghandi but finally proved abortive, for one particular reason. On 19–20 October a Second Confessing Synod, in its way as decisive as Barmen, took place at Dahlem in Berlin. After Barmen, the simple claim that the Confessing Church alone represented the German Evangelical Church had proved insufficient. A structural and administrative alternative to that of the Reich Church was required, and this is what the Dahlem Synod called into being. Its remit included supervision of ordinations and theological training. Special seminaries would be needed and, by late 1934, Bonhoeffer knew that from the next spring forward his own future would be as director of one of these. Having preached his final sermon to the Sydenham congregation on 10 March 1935, he made his tour of English religious houses and seminaries and in mid-April returned to Germany.

Paradoxically, it was during the next two years, while his energies were so intensely focused on one specific responsibility within his church in his native land, that his mind was exercised as never before on the ecumenical issue in its broadest range. It was while stationed at his one particular post in the ongoing Church Struggle that he was to issue his weightiest challenge to the whole ecumenical movement. In autumn 1933 Karl Barth had castigated Bonhoeffer for allegedly fleeing the conflict for the more tranquil ecumenical world abroad. He was wrong. Now, there were doubtless some in ecumenical circles who feared they were losing a powerful advocate due to his disappearing into the remote, rustic hinterland of eastern Germany and having to work underground amid the ever-tighter restrictions of the Nazi state. They, too, were to be proved mistaken.

Political and Ecumenical Developments to May 1938

The nearly four years from the Fanø conference to the Utrecht conference of May 1938, at which the constitution for a World Council of Churches (WCC) was agreed, were hardly likely to foster optimism on the German and international scene. On 1 May 1935 Hitler announced the implementation of his earlier decree reintroducing full military conscription. On 15 September, to thunderous applause at a Nazi rally in Nuremberg, he announced the "Reich Citizens' Law" which distinguished Reich citizens "of German blood" from a second class of nationals without political rights, and forbade mixed marriages between "Aryans" and "non-Aryans." In March 1936, German troops reoccupied the Rhineland where under the terms of the Versailles Treaty Allied forces had been stationed until 1930. In March 1938 came the most overtly expansionist of Hitler's moves to date: the *Anschluss*, by which Austria was (willingly) incorporated into the German Reich.

Together with the civil war in Spain, the Italian assault on Ethiopia, and the ever deepening entrenchment of Soviet totalitarianism, this context made all the more critical the attempts to strengthen the ecumenical fellowship in order to provide a coherent Christian witness to the whole world. Following the Fanø conference, for Life and Work all attention was now focused on the conference "Church, Community, and State," scheduled for Oxford in July 1937. The preparatory study work for this, and much of the content of the conference programme itself, was under the guiding genius of J. H. Oldham.[5] The executive meetings of Life and Work (accompanied by the Youth Commission) at Chamby, Switzerland, in August 1935 and August 1936 were crucial staging posts in this process. Faith and Order was similarly engaged with its next world conference, scheduled to take place almost immediately after the Oxford Conference, in Edinburgh, in August 1937. This close conjunction had more than incidental significance. Since the preliminary informal meeting of ecumenical leaders at York in May 1933,[6] the moves were gathering apace toward drawing the main strands of the ecumenical movement—Life and Work, Faith and Order, International Missionary Council, World

Student Christian Federation, and so forth—into one inclusive body. Steering was provided by a consultative group in which the main actors were J. H. Oldham, William Temple, William Adams Brown, and Samuel McCrea Cavert. At Westfield College, London, 8–10 July 1937 (i.e., just before the Oxford Conference) a Committee of Thirty-Five met to consider the proposals to form a World Council of Churches. The plans were put in turn to the Oxford and Edinburgh conferences, each of which appointed seven persons to a Committee of Fourteen that met in London immediately after Edinburgh, with William Temple in the chair. This meeting issued invitations to the churches to send representatives to a provisional conference in May 1938. This would draw up a constitution for the proposed new body, which would be submitted to the churches together with proposals for maintaining the work of Life and Work and Faith and Order. This meeting duly took place in Utrecht, 9–13 May 1938. As a result, the World Council of Churches (WCC) came into being, though it was not formally constituted, thanks to the intervention of war, until its first assembly at Amsterdam in 1948.

This process was one from which, notwithstanding the crucial importance of the ecumenical movement and the German situation to each other, the Confessing Church, as eventually virtually all German church bodies, found itself excluded due to a set of intractable circumstances. The ecumenical developments, however, involved not only organizations and structures, but personalities and relationships. A new generation of leadership was arising, and one name in particular must be highlighted: W. A. ("Wim") Visser't Hooft (1900–1985). This Dutch Protestant, still in his thirties at the time of the Oxford and Edinburgh conferences, had risen to prominence in the ecumenical world through the YMCA and World Student Christian Federation (WSCF), becoming secretary of the latter in 1932. He had, in equal measure, proven organizational skills and theological competence (he was a committed disciple of Karl Barth), and at the 1938 Utrecht meeting was appointed general secretary of the embryo WCC. He had long been deeply concerned about the German Church Struggle, mobilizing WSCF interest in it, and had made clear where his sympathies lay.[7] The Confessing Church leaders might hitherto have found the Geneva ecumenical staff rather equivocal in their attitudes, and would still experience problems getting access to the ecumenical bodies, but now they had a clear supporter and advocate at the very heart of ecumenical leadership. Visser't Hooft and Bonhoeffer were to become very important to each other.

The Seminary: An Intense Life, but Still Ecumenical

Bonhoeffer's seminary, one of five set up by the Confessing Church, enabled him to fulfill his longstanding ambition of creating a community of study where the experience of community living would itself be at the core of learning. Deliberately choosing isolated sites—less likely to attract attention from the authorities—on the Baltic coast east of Stettin,[8] for a short time it was housed in beach cabins at the small resort of Zingst but soon moved to the village of Finkenwalde and took up residence in a former school. There it remained until closed by the Gestapo in September 1937, after which the work of ordination training continued in a yet more clandestine, dispersed way in "collective pastorates." In all, 113 students passed through Finkenwalde.[9] Some became members of the House of Brethren, a community attached to the seminary and supplying a core of pastors available to assist Confessing congregations in emergency. Among the earliest intake of students to Finkenwalde was Eberhard Bethge, soon to become Bonhoeffer's closest friend. These ordinands who had opted for the Confessing Church rather than the apparent security of the Reich Church, as well as taking on all the inherent risks and loss of privileges, now faced spartan living conditions and unusually concentrated study, with a major focus on confessional writings of the Reformation tradition, biblical exegesis, homiletics, and pastoralia. But Finkenwalde, for all its focus on maintaining the truly Lutheran and Reformed tradition in face of its perversion by the German Christians and the acquiescent Reich Church, breathed a decidedly *ecumenical* air. This was intentional. In fact, while still in London, in a memorandum to the Youth Commission, Bonhoeffer asked:

Would you be willing to help me find some young students or pastor for the Seminary which I am supposed to start in the near future for the Confessional Synod. I should like to have the ecumenic aspect of it made clear from the beginning. We are now thinking if we could combine the idea of a Christian community . . . with the new Seminary. At any rate would support from the ecumenic movements be most valuable for the carrying out of our plans.[10]

Such internationalizing plans were never fulfilled, but the students entering Finkenwalde did at times wonder if they really were at a German Protestant seminary. For one thing, they were surprised at the amount of time spent each day both at corporate prayer and in silent private meditation on scripture. Bonhoeffer's experiences at the Anglo-Catholic seminaries and religious houses in England were being reflected here, especially the daily offices at the Community of the Resurrection in Mirfield where the whole of Psalm 119 was recited in the course of each day.[11] Still more unexpected was the introduction of the practice of personal confession to another brother, although Bonhoeffer was quick to point out that it was Martin Luther, no less, who had commended the spiritual benefit of the discipline. Nor did he have inhibitions about commending the spirituality of Roman Catholic writers such as Georges Bernanos, whose *Diary of a Country Priest* deeply impressed him.[12] Not surprisingly, rumours went abroad about the "Catholic" tendencies of Finkenwalde, these even reaching the ears of Karl Barth who responded with some alarm. But equally Bonhoeffer drew upon and advocated some venerable Protestant forms of spirituality that not all his ordinands would have known, for example the *Losungen*, the daily "Watchword" Bible texts produced by the Moravian Brethren of Herrnhut.

If this community regime was rigorous—and some students indeed chafed at it—it also induced in these future pastors a stamina for resistance to the ever-increasing pressures from the state and the official church authorities. The period 1935–37 saw a relentless process of measures against the Confessing Church. No longer was it Reich bishop Müller (now largely discredited by all parties) and the German Christians who were the main threats but the state itself, working both directly and through the Reich Church, which by 1937 it controlled completely. In July 1935 Hitler instituted a Ministry of Church Affairs under the Nazi lawyer Hans Kerrl, who in September introduced a wide-ranging "Law for the Protection of the German Evangelical Church." This became the basis for a succession of measures aimed at complete legal and financial control of all church activities. In October 1935 Kerrl set up a Reich Church Committee led by a hitherto respected Lutheran pastor, Wilhelm Zoellner, to regulate church affairs including ordinations. Provincial committees dealt with the individual churches. Here lay the greatest danger for the Confessing Church's ministry, for recognition by the church committees offered a measure of status, security, and financial support to a pastor, denied to those who stayed "outside" with the Confessing Church, loyal not only to the Barmen Declaration but to the Dahlem Synod's church administration. But could one not, asked some of Bonhoeffer's students, hold to the theology of Barmen while accepting the authority of the committees and the practical benefits this would bring? To Bonhoeffer, this was no small compromise but a great betrayal of all that the Confessing Church meant, and it pained him that several students took this course. By the end of 1935, it had become illegal to make appointments, financial collections, proclamations, theological examinations, and ordinations outside the authority of the committees. To serve the Confessing Church was ipso facto to be outlawed by the Nazi state. Zoellner, at length seeing that his committee was but a state puppet, resigned in February 1937. The precedence of the National Socialist Party over the church was solemnly pronounced by Kerrl, who now appointed Friedrich Werner, a German Christian, as director of the church chancellery. State control was now complete.

The summer of that year saw a huge wave of arrests of pastors, most notably, on 1 July, that of Martin Niemöller, whose incarceration was to last until the end of the war in 1945. From now on the Church Struggle meant a struggle to survive. It was in this context, where at Finkenwalde the pressures were felt so acutely by young pastors-to-be, that Bonhoeffer wrote two of his most celebrated works: *Discipleship*,[13] which was based on his lectures given at Finkenwalde (and in Berlin where he continued to lecture until banned in August 1936), and *Life Together*,[14] an exposition of life in community drawing on the whole Finkenwalde experience and its theological basis.

Confessing Church and Ecumenical Movement: The Mutual Challenge

Finkenwalde may have been in a remote location, and its life sharply focused on the pressing issues of what it meant to be church in Germany, but physical distance counted for little as far as Bonhoeffer and the ecumenical movement were concerned. The ecumenical issues followed him there, and he in turn continually knocked on the ecumenical door. Indeed, it was very soon after his arrival at Finkenwalde that the question of what the Confessing Church and the ecumenical movement signified to each other detonated a sharp exchange with a leading ecumenist.

Bonhoeffer hitherto had had few dealings with the Faith and Order movement, the organization of which had suffered greatly since the late 1920s due to the world financial crisis, causing it to lose its fulltime staff. Despite being unable to meet as regularly as before, however, its continuation committee continued in being, and by 1935 its secretary was the Anglican Leonard Hodgson (1889–1969). Hodgson was at that time a canon of Winchester Cathedral, with a reputation already established as one of the ablest theological minds in the Church of England. He had been both fellow of an Oxford college and a professor of Christian apologetics in the USA. Soon after arriving in Finkenwalde, in the summer of 1935, Bonhoeffer received from Hodgson an invitation to attend the next meeting of the continuation committee in Hindsgaul, Denmark, a major item on the agenda being plans for the next World Conference on Faith and Order.[15] The committee, Hodgson had said, was "extremely anxious to have the advice of all branches of the Christian Church" in deciding on its programme for 1937. Bonhoeffer, on learning that Bishop Heckel was also expected to attend the meeting, replied in a lengthy and trenchant letter that it would be impossible for him to attend if any representative of the Reich Church was present.[16]

Doubtless Hodgson thought that on behalf of the committee he was being fair-minded, generous even, toward the Confessing Church, with the desire "to be guided in our deliberations by all sections of Christian thought" and the anxiety "that Germany should not be represented exclusively by the Reichskirche." He went on: "I think you will understand our position when I say that we cannot, as a Movement, exclude the representatives of any Church which 'accepts our Lord Jesus Christ as God and Saviour.' Right from the start there has been a general invitation to all such churches, and we cannot arrogate to ourselves the right to discriminate between them." But Bonhoeffer was adamant. What greater privilege could a theologian and pastor receive, he asks rhetorically, than an invitation to a great ecumenical synod gathered to hear the word of our Lord Jesus Christ, of praying for the Holy Spirit to lead to the unity of all Christendom? In face of Christ there could be no pharisaical self-righteous pretensions or accusations against others but only repentance and mutual, brotherly respect. But, he proceeds, the Confessing Church takes a fundamentally different position toward the Reich Church as compared with its attitude toward all other churches in the world and wholly contradicts the claim of the Reich Church to accept the Lord Jesus Christ as God and Savior. The teaching as well as the action of the Reich Church leaders clearly show that it no longer serves Christ but the Antichrist: "Obedience to the only heavenly Lord Jesus Christ continues to be coordinated, nay, subordinated to obedience towards worldly masters and powers. The Reich Church thereby continues to betray the only Lord Jesus Christ . . ." In the light of Barmen, the Reich Church government can no longer claim to compose the Church of Christ in Germany nor any part of it. The core paragraph of the whole letter reads:

> No member of the Confessional Church . . . can thus recognize in the Reich Church a church which pays homage to our Lord Jesus Christ as God and Saviour; he must rather beseech God that He may confound the Reich Church Government as an instrument of the Antichrist.—Being a minister of the Confessional Church I cannot attend an oecumenical conference unless it either excludes the Reich Church or ventures openly to charge both the Reich Church and the Confessional Church with responsibility. This, however, means actually to interfere in their conflict and effectively to pronounce a judgment based upon allegiance to the Word of God and duly established in the name of God's whole communion.[17]

The fight being conducted in Germany, Bonhoeffer states, is on behalf of Christianity everywhere—a call of ultimate warning to churches all over the world that may be attacked by the very same powers. If the ecumenical movement and Faith and Order in particular were to face up to this challenge and make a judgment, however painful and disruptive it might be, it could prove to be the regeneration of the whole ecumenical movement and all Christendom.

Hodgson replied with an even longer letter[18] seeking to explain patiently and reasonably that the constitution and rules of Faith and Order would not permit it to venture any such judgment as Bonhoeffer was asking for, and that, moreover, this would prove impracticable. It would require a full hearing of both sides, and an unduly prolonged meeting of the continuation committee. Furthermore, the Reich c\ hurch leaders themselves would refute the claim that they denied Christ as God and Savior. Moreover, Faith and Order, unlike Life and Work, did not seek to commit the churches to joint action, but only to face each other in deliberation on an equal basis and without questioning each other's right to be at the table, facing differences honestly and "speaking the truth in love."

Bonhoeffer saw no point in replying further. Hodgson had a fair point as far as the aims and rules of Faith and Order were concerned. But Bonhoeffer was speaking from within a context where those very aims and rules seemed manifestly inadequate to the situation. Hodgson had a clear view of the nature of that part of the ecumenical movement in which he held responsibility. From Bonhoeffer's standpoint, the integrity of the ecumenical movement required that understanding to be questioned or at least widened. Hodgson saw his ecumenical organization as essentially a seminar for theological discussion where everyone was equal before the moderator's chair. For Bonhoeffer there could be no equality where one party had forfeited its right to be called church—and, moreover, was enjoying privileges while the other party was being persecuted, harassed, and imprisoned, often with the actual connivance of the other side.

It was no doubt spurred by this particular exchange, as well as in response to the issues of German representation at ecumenical gatherings that had repeatedly come to the fore since the preparations for the Fanø conference in 1934, that Bonhoeffer now penned an essay "The Confessing Church and the Ecumenical Movement."[19] This substantial piece, some 6,500 words in length, stands as the great *summa* of Bonhoeffer's contribution to ecumenical thought. It includes but goes beyond the challenges he had issued before: as long ago as 1932 in his lectures at Gland and Ciernohorské Kúpele on the need for a theology of the ecumenical movement;[20] the critique in his Berlin lectures of 1932–33 of the ecumenical movement for evading the questions of truth and heresy;[21] and his call at Fanø for the ecumenical gathering there and then to believe in itself, and act as the church of Christ among the nations.[22] But now all was focused with extraordinary sharpness by the specific, urgent need of the hour—and in a manner which opened up a quite new way of viewing the ecumenical movement.

Almost at the beginning, Bonhoeffer dares to claim: "The German church struggle is the second great stage in the history of the ecumenical movement and will be decisive for its future."[23] He speaks gratefully of the interest and concern taken by the evangelical ecumenical world in the German conflict, for the outspoken calls on behalf of the Confessing Church by George Bell and Bishop Ammundsen, and for the actions taken at Fanø including the election of Karl Koch to the Council of Life and Work (in passing, it may be noted that neither here nor anywhere else does Bonhoeffer refer to his own appointment). The ecumenical movement worldwide has shown its recognition of and oneness of spirit with the Confessing Church through countless instances of prayer and supportive messages. This has been recognition of a common cause in which the struggle of the Confessing Church has been wrought "on behalf of all Christendom, particularly for Western Christendom."[24] This encounter is, admittedly, offensive to the nationalist who views external ecumenical interest as an unwarrantable interference in internal German affairs, "since no one wants to show their sores to a stranger."[25] But concern at such a level as this is to indulge only in political tactics, whereas the real crisis is at a much deeper and fundamental level: "The ecumenical movement and the Confessing Church have encountered each other"[26]—and in this encounter each must ask the other the reason for their existence.

On the one hand, the Confessing Church puts a genuine question to the ecumenical movement, insofar as this church stakes all its identity and existence on its *confession*. Nothing else, nothing but the confession. "There is only a yes or a no to this confession as articulated *in a binding fashion* in the Barmen and Dahlem synodal resolutions."[27] This is the only basis on which the Confessing Church can enter ecumenical conversations. If the ecumenical movement also admits as partners those churches which the Confessing Church accuses of heresy, the conversation must be broken off. If this prompts crisis in the ecumenical movement, says Bonhoeffer in effect, so be it. For the question cannot be suppressed indefinitely, as to just what the ecumenical movement is: "Is the ecumenical movement in its visible form church? Or conversely: Has the real ecumenicity of the church as attested in the New Testament come to visible and appropriate expression in ecumenical organizations?"[28] It should be noted that Bonhoeffer is not asking if the ecumenical movement is *a* church but, rather, a body of churchly quality.[29] By "church," Bonhoeffer is here not meaning an organization satisfying the usual definition of doctrinal basis, order of ministry, sacraments, and so forth but simply a community of faith placing itself under the word of God and therewith coming to an authoritative *decision* on where its obedience to Christ lies. This would be in contrast to "an association of Christians, all of whom are rooted in their own churches, an association that now comes together for common tactical-practical action or for non-binding dialogue with other Christians. In that case, they leave open the question of the result and the theological possibility of such practical action and of these activities."[30]

Bonhoeffer pays sincere tribute to the progress made in fostering ecumenical study and cooperation led by such as J. H. Oldham and the Research Department in Geneva. Far from dismissing this, he welcomes such work but recognizes that it is precisely this recent process which raises the fundamental theological questions: To what end, and on what basis, will *decision* be made for committed action? Or is there to be endless discussion of possibilities, forever evading a division of the spirits, which seems to be the presupposition of many German, English, and American theologians and is widely accepted in ecumenical working groups? There is fear that if questions of truth, authority, and obedience were to be put then the ecumenical movement would collapse. By contrast, "There is only one way for ecumenical work to be rescued, namely, that it courageously take up this question, as it has been posed and obediently leave the rest to the Lord of the church. Who can say that the ecumenical movement will not emerge more strongly from the struggle prompted more strongly and more authoritatively precisely by this disruptive challenge? . . . Historical speculation ends at God's commandment."[31]

The essay proceeds with a severe critique of that liberal view of ecumenism which regards the unity of the one church as comprising the sum total of all the branches of the Christian tradition, each of which can claim a partial apprehension of the truth but limited by the inherent insufficiency of human knowledge: the one-sided view that fullness of truth will only be found in unity. But with a mask of supposed humility such an understanding betrays a disregard for *truth* as the basis for unity, and this leads back to the significance of the confession. The Confessing Church by its very nature—and its refusal to sit with the German Christians—thrusts the question of truth into the ecumenical ring. Not, Bonhoeffer is careful to state, that the Confessing Church, in confessing against the German Christians, is thereby also confessing against all other churches in Christendom, some of whose theologies may also appear questionable to the signatories of Barmen. It is rather that *here and now*, in face of pseudo-Christian heresy, in Germany in 1935, *this* and not *that* is what affirmation of the evangelical faith requires. The Confessing Church is doing no more than inviting other churches in the world to recognize its confession as the valid affirmation of the gospel of Christ—and to reflect on the implications of this for the witness of all churches everywhere. Still less is the Confessing Church setting itself up as the sole, pure standard-bearer of truth and righteousness. Rather, in the ecumenical encounter "it enters into such contacts bearing its own share of the guilt for the inner turmoil of Christendom, enters into that guilt, and, amid all false theologies it may encounter along the way, acknowledges first of all its own guilt and the inadequate power of its own proclamation."[32] Its first confession is of its *own sin*.

In turn, then, the Confessing Church is questioned on its own existence by the ecumenical movement. The Confessing Church, like any other church, enters the ecumenical movement with no other claim of right to be there except in the forgiveness of its sins, by grace alone. The ecumenical movement, simply because it is not the Confessing Church nor created by that church, is not to be denied its reality but is to be taken with due seriousness. Then, in a passage laden with deep and permanent significance for an understanding of the ecumenical movement, Bonhoeffer states:

> It is a fact that a divided Christendom is coming together in a unanimous confession of its own distress and in unanimous prayer for the promised unity of the church of Jesus Christ; indeed that common worship services, common sermons, even common celebrations of the Eucharist are being shared and ecumenical Christendom is still or once again a possibility, and all these things are happening in the name of Jesus Christ and with a prayer for the support of the Holy Spirit. In view of this fact, is countering it with a pathetic "impossible," really the first and only appropriate response? Does one really have the right to summon the anathema over all such activity from the very outset? Is not this witness of all Christian churches at the very least something that must prompt a moment's pause and reflection? We must openly and unequivocally acknowledge that the concrete existence of the ecumenical movement does not in and of itself represent a proof of its truth and Christian legitimacy. But if it cannot represent a proof, cannot it be at least an indication of the promise that God wishes to bestow on this activity?[33]

It is likely that here Bonhoeffer was not only targeting tendencies toward self-sufficiency, not to mention self-righteousness, within the Confessing Church. At that time Karl Barth was still locked in a skeptical view, bordering on dismissive, of the ecumenical movement as a vain and willfully human endeavour to construct what only God could create. Bonhoeffer's bestowal of the notion of *promise* on the enterprise is brilliant in its simplicity, allowing recognition of what may indeed be a frail, earthen vessel yet one which is to be affirmed for what it might yield under grace. This could even be said to be a Barthian critique of Barth's attitude.[34] The Confessing Church will therefore "*never be ashamed of the voices of its brothers* and will instead gratefully grant and try to provide them a hearing."[35] Bonhoeffer's final paragraph captures what he said at Fanø and lifts it up as a charter for the ecumenical future:

> Whether the hope for the Ecumenical Council of Protestant Chris-tendom will be fulfilled, whether such a council will not only wit-ness for the truth and unity of the church of Christ authoritatively but also be able to bear witness against the enemies of Christian-ity throughout the world, whether it will pronounce judgment on war, racial hatred and social exploitation, whether through such true ecumenical unity among all Protestant churches in all nations war itself might one day become impossible, whether the witness of such a council will fall on receptive ears—that depends on our own obedience to the question now posed to us and on how God chooses to use our obedience. It is not an ideal which is set up but a commandment and a promise—it is not high-handed implementa-tion of one's own goals that is required but obedience. The question has been posed.[36]

The question was raised, but was it heard either in Germany or elsewhere? The article appeared just a month after it was written, in August 1935, in the journal *Evangelische Theologie* (vol. 7). The immediate impact seems unclear. Within Germany, in any case, it was before long overshadowed by Bonhoeffer's 1936 paper "On the Ques-tion of Church Communion,"[37] which proved highly controversial on account of a single sentence taken in isolation: "Whoever knowingly separates himself from the Confessing Church in Germany separates himself from salvation."[38] But it must be accounted something of a tragedy for the ecumenical movement that in Bonhoeffer's lifetime the 1935 paper appeared only once, in German and in Germany, for it is one of the most outstanding pieces of ecumenical theology in the twentieth century, unsurpassed as an example of a theology mediating between one church and the ecumenical fellowship and demonstrating the inherent importance of each to the other. This can be acknowledged without claiming that it is in all respects a satisfactory paper, in that it raises more questions than it answers. The point is that, like Barth's *Romans* commentary, it did actually put those questions which others were either not seeing or were evading. Among the most perceptive studies in English on this and other writings by Bonhoeffer in the years 1932–35 is an article by the Jesuit theologian John Wilcken that appeared in 1969.[39] Wilcken is deeply sympathetic to Bonhoeffer's project of making the ecumenical movement face the question of truth versus heresy but is not uncritical:

> There can be no doubt that Bonhoeffer was too optimistic in his attitude to the ecumenical movement. He was eager that something should be achieved, and achieved quickly. After all, it was clear that the world was in a dangerous state, and, in particular, Bonhoeffer was deeply aware of the desperate state of affairs in Germany at the time. It was his hope that the Ecumenical Church, by speaking the authoritative Word of God to the world, would provide the solution to the world's problems. Clearly he was expecting too much.[40]

Moreover, Wilcken suggests, Bonhoeffer leaves open the fundamental question of how one knows what is true and what is heretical. But Wilcken also recognizes that for Bonhoeffer the "confession" was not an abstract matter of doctrinal disagreement with the heretics. The issue "is thus not primarily a doctrinal one, but rather one of the Church's struggle for survival despite the attacks of its enemies."[41]

Bonhoeffer's ecumenical theology, we might say, was less theoretical than a call to arms; it was *performative* theology, inviting the ecumenical movement, like the Confessing Church, to experiment with what it recognized the gospel of Christ to be, and to learn from the actions it undertook and whatever consequences flowed from them. This was quite new for most ecumenical thought at the time. As we shall see later in this chapter, one reader, Wim Visser't Hooft, did take Bonhoeffer's paper seriously and made use of it, so that two years later the article, almost incognito, directly contributed to the preparation of one of the most important ecumenical events of the time. Its challenging question on whether the ecumenical movement is indeed a church is no less pertinent today.

Maintaining the Links

Bonhoeffer's paper on the Confessing Church and the ecumenical movement states with absolute clarity the rationale for the ecumenical policy pursued by Bonhoeffer and much of the leadership of the Confessing Church during 1935–38, years which saw the consolidation of the ecumenical movement and the initiating of the World Council of Churches. In the first place, Bonhoeffer made every effort to maintain links with trusted ecumenical circles outside Germany, both on his own behalf and on that of the Confessing Church. Even before leaving London at the end of January 1935, his report to the Youth Commission on follow-up work to the Fanø conference also looked forward to continuing projects such as an international youth conference with conscientious objection as a major question for discussion; and, as has been mentioned, he also hoped that the ecumenical movement could recruit students from abroad to attend his seminary.[42] In February 1937 he was still hoping for a student-exchange programme between Finkenwalde and seminaries in Britain and Scandinavia.[43] The one notable success in this direction was the much-publicized visit of the Finkenwalde seminarians to Sweden that Bonhoeffer arranged and led in March 1936.[44] This visit—which included a reception by Archbishop Eidem and meetings with theological faculties in Stockholm, Uppsala, and Sigtuna—acquired the status of an official invitation from the Church of Sweden and so was a notable coup for the Confessing Church. By the same token, it was a severe embarrassment and cause of anger to Theodor Heckel and the Reich Church Foreign Office. Bonhoeffer was acting true to the argument in his 1935 paper that the Confessing Church needed both the solidarity and the questioning of the ecumenical movement. His good personal relations with church leaders such as George Bell, Erling Eidem, and Ove Valdemar Ammundsen were vital here.[45]

Equally, when it came to the matter of representation of the Confessing Church at official ecumenical meetings, he was resolute in rejecting any possibility of the Reich Church being admitted on equal terms—as he had made clear to Leonard Hodgson with regard to Faith and Order. But the matter proved scarcely less problematic with Life and Work, where the clause in the Fanø resolution affirming the wish to remain "in friendly contact" with all church groups in Germany was exploited to the full by the Reich Church, and by Theodor Heckel in particular. The issue became ever more fraught as preparations got under way for the 1937 Oxford Conference, which, with its highly charged subject matter of church, community, and state, was set to be the most significant ecumenical gathering of the decade and at which, together with the Edinburgh Faith and Order conference, crucial steps would be taken toward forming a World Council of Churches. As early as 13–14 May 1935 Confessing Church representatives met in Hannover with J. H. Oldham, chief engineer of the Oxford study programme. This meeting, and Oldham's presence at it, had been summoned in view of the increasingly intimidating situation faced by the Confessing Church, with new waves of arrests of pastors and raids by the Gestapo on church offices. Bonhoeffer, still in process of setting up his seminary, was summoned by telegram to attend and urged the Germans to deliver a forthright demand that ecumenical representatives abroad stop expecting the Confessing Church and Reich Church to cooperate in preparing for Oxford—and equally that the Research Department in Geneva be less equivocal in its attitude to the claims of the Confessing Church. Oldham reported this fully to Bell. But almost immediately and again later that summer, Bonhoeffer himself was dispatched by Karl Koch to fly to England in order to keep Bell and others fully informed of the critical situation. Bonhoeffer might be a relatively junior figure in the counsels of the Confessing Church but its leaders knew that he—almost unique among them in his fluency in English—was a most vital instrument for mediating with the ecumenical world.

It is a long, complex, and sometimes tedious story, but the nub of the issue between the Confessing Church and the ecumenical organizations was that of who from Germany should be invited to the international meetings.[46] This was a far from purely administrative matter. Life and Work was now, largely under J. H. Oldham's skillful direction, organizing the major conference to take place in Oxford in 1937. But there was a reluctance, especially by the Geneva staff, to follow radically the decision taken at Fanø of identifying with the Confessing Church as the true representative of German Protestantism and to exclude the Reich Church as represented by Bishop Heckel and others. The Confessing Church, and Bonhoeffer above all, felt that to compromise here would be to betray all that the Barmen Declaration had stood for, and all the risks and costly actions it had prompted in faithfulness to the gospel. There is no doubt that Bell and Oldham strongly sympathized with the Confessing Church at this point, while in Geneva Hans Schönfeld and H. L. Henriod wavered—as if Fanø's decision also to "maintain friendly contact with all groups in Germany" now outweighed the prime resolve to support the Confessing Church. Oldham in particular made known his deep distrust of Heckel and his ability to manipulate the reasonable people in Geneva.[47] But the ecumenicals were faced with a genuine problem: if only Confessing representatives were invited to Oxford, there was the strong likelihood of their being refused travel visas by the German authorities. Better, then, to ensure a Confessing presence at the cost of one or two Reich Church people also being present—even Heckel. For their part, the Confessing leaders were also faced with a very real dilemma by their uncompromising stand: with their repeated absence at ecumenical meetings they risked cutting themselves off completely from the very movement and people whose solidarity they sought. It was not wholly surprising, therefore, that some Confessing leaders felt that the possibility should at least be discussed of some cooperation with Zoellner's committee in preparation for Oxford. For his part, Bonhoeffer felt that with such as George Bell and J. H. Oldham he had trustworthy and sympathetic friends who were fundamentally allied with the Confessing Church and were doing their best to implement that solidarity and commitment within the constraints of rules and circumstances not of their own devising. With Faith and Order it was quite another matter. In this case there was little or no prior stance of sympathy with the Confessing Church, and the "impartial" application of the rules on inclusivity of representation obviated from the start any serious consideration of the claim of that church: constitutional procedures, not theology, were paramount. And, in practice, the Geneva staff of Life and Work, too, were inclined to follow the constitutional rather than theological way, to Bonhoeffer's increasing frustration.

The outcome of these maneuverings was that no Confessing Church representatives were present at the meetings of the Youth Commission and the council of Life and Work in Chamby, Switzerland, in 1935, but in August the following year, also at Chamby, Bonhoeffer, Karl Koch, and two other Confessing Church representatives did attend. Final plans for the programme of the Oxford Conference were agreed. The Confessing Church delegates kept their distance from Heckel and the Reich Church group. Bonhoeffer did not speak in the plenary sessions (his name never appears in the minutes) but worked intensively behind the scenes in informal discussion with Bell and others. He was especially grieved at the way in which a resolution prepared by Oldham, Henry Leiper (USA), and Marc Boegner (France) on the Jewish question was eviscerated by the other German representatives. Over the following months, the arguments about German representation at Oxford dragged on. As late as February 1937 Bonhoeffer attended meetings of the Youth Commission and preparatory study groups in London. This, however, marked the end of his formal responsibilities within the Youth Commission, since a serious dispute emerged between himself and H. L. Henriod over the composition of the German youth delegation to Oxford. At Chamby, in 1936, an agreement had apparently been reached that the German *church* delegation should consist of 21 persons, seven each from the Confessing Church, the Lutheran Council, and the Reich Church. At the London meetings, 16–24 February, it transpired that Henriod was insisting that the same formula be applied to the youth delegation, whereas Bonhoeffer maintained that this was a matter for the Germans on the Youth Commission itself to determine. Bonhoeffer claimed the support of George Bell (whom he twice visited that month) for his interpretation. The meeting was heated at times, and the ensuing Bonhoeffer–Henriod correspondence was uncompromising if diplomatic in tone.[48] The outcome was Bonhoeffer's resignation from the Youth

Commission, and he recommended Udo Smidt to replace him. It was the culmination of the growing disillusion with Henriod, as with Hans Schönfeld, that had begun even prior to Fanø 1934. In fact, the Genevan policy was now beginning to make Heckel and the Reich Church, not the Confessing Church, seem the real victors of Fanø after all. Had there been a deliberate attempt by Geneva to sideline Bonhoeffer? Or was he simply part of the collateral damage caused by Geneva staff's prioritizing of maintaining the links with Germany that Heckel's office could apparently ensure? The answer to such questions requires much more to be known about the tensions building up in ecumenical leadership as the Oxford and Edinburgh conferences drew near and the plans for a World Council began to take shape. As it was, Bonhoeffer's resignation marked the end of his formal involvement with the ecumenical organization to which he had been officially attached since 1931—but not a severance with the ecumenical movement as a whole in which he sought to continue involvement in other ways.[49]

Eventually, the Confessing Church withdrew its intention to attend Oxford as it appeared that one German group under Reich Church leadership would be required. But, in any case, the dispute became academic when Kerrl's ministry for church affairs refused permission for any Germans to attend Oxford, with the exception of a small and quiescent group from the free churches. Nor were any Germans present at the Utrecht meeting of May 1938, when the constitution of the new World Council of Churches was agreed upon and its first secretariat appointed. Before that happened, however, work on the theme of the Oxford Conference continued in the Confessing Church. In April, the Confessing Church committee preparing contributions for Oxford, chaired by Hans Böhm, accepted a short report, "War and Peace," which bears many of the hallmarks of Bonhoeffer's thinking.[50]

Bonhoeffer at Oxford?

Paradoxically, for many participants at the 1937 Oxford Conference, the absence of the leading Germans made the issues of "Church, Community, and State" still more present and pressing, and the witness of the Confessing Church yet more poignantly relevant, even if the German issues could not receive substantial treatment in the conference itself. At least, "We are greatly moved by the afflictions of many pastors and laymen who have stood from the first in the Confessional Church for the sovereignty of Christ, and for the freedom of the Church of Christ to preach His Gospel,"[51] stated the conference in its message to the German Evangelical Church. It is tempting to speculate on what might have happened if Bonhoeffer himself had been there. In a material way he was, for his 1935 paper "The Confessing Church and the Ecumenical Movement" had not lain completely unnoticed. One person who had read and been impressed by it was W.A. Visser't Hooft, at that time still general secretary of the World Student Christian Federation and collaborating with J. H. Oldham on the preparatory material for Oxford. Their volume *The Church and Its Function in Society*[52] provided a thorough and wide-ranging survey of the current doctrinal understandings of the churches, their histories, the forms of Christian action and the witness of the church in society. Visser't Hooft's contribution included a chapter on "The Church as an Oecumenical Society" and raised the question, "Is there a church in the churches?" Forty years later, he recalled the importance for him of Bonhoeffer's essay in tackling this issue:

> Now one does not need a deep knowledge of the technique of *Formgeschichte* or *Redaktionsgeschichte* to discover that the point of view which I developed in this chapter was deeply influenced by Bonhoeffer's article of the year before. I echoed what he had said about the two ways of looking at the ecumenical movement as an association of a utilitarian character or as in a certain sense an embodiment of the Church of Christ. And I stated in conformity with Bonhoeffer's conviction: "Representatives of churches can never meet without at least attempting to live up to their main obligation, which is to *be the Church*, and to announce the Lordship of Jesus Christ over the world."[53]

Visser't Hooft does not wish to exalt Bonhoeffer as the only significant influence in developing a deeper church-consciousness in the ecumenical movement from that time (he cites Karl Barth, New Testament studies, and Eastern Orthodox influence also). "But," he continues, "it seems to me quite clear that Bonhoeffer's thought made a very real contribution to the creation of that theological climate in which it became possible to propose the formation of a World Council of Churches which would demand from the churches a more definite commitment than the previous ecumenical bodies had done."[54] Although Visser't Hooft does not deal with the issue of *confession* as such, substantial sections of his pre-Oxford chapter read like a paraphrase of Bonhoeffer's article. For example, closely similar to Bonhoeffer's is Visser't Hooft's desire to move beyond "cooperation" of the churches together with his criticism of the branch theory of the church; and throughout Visser't Hooft echoes Bonhoeffer's refusal, in the interests of the search for truth, to seek a position or understanding of the church above and beyond the present encounters in disagreement. The alternative is not, however, sheer paralysis:

> It is impossible for the Oxford Conference to claim that its voice is the voice of the Church; but it is equally impossible for it to *deny* that it is such a voice. The *positive claim* is impossible because it can be made only when the Churches are ready to be re-united into one body in which all members accept each other as full members of the Church, and in which there is a basic agreement on the faith and order of the Church. The *denial* is impossible, because it would deny in advance that at the Oxford Conference (where more than two or three will be gathered in the name of Christ) Christ himself may be present, and that the Oxford Conference may illustrate the truth: *Ubi Christus, ibi ecclesia.*[55]

This was not to be the last time that Bonhoeffer's influence was to find an ecumenical channel via Visser't Hooft, soon to be appointed first general secretary of the WCC. Yet one could hardly imagine a more Bonhoefferian plea being put to Oxford. Did the conference itself echo it? At certain levels there were resonances. Afterward, in his introduction to the conference reports, J. H. Oldham stated: "Nothing stood out more clearly . . . than the recognition that the Church in its essential nature is a universal society, united in its one Lord and that in Him there can be neither Jew nor Greek, Barbarian nor Scythian, bond nor free."[56] Oxford gave rise to an oft-quoted slogan, "Let the Church be the Church!" This phrase does not actually appear in any of the official reports,[57] but it clearly expresses much of their repeated affirmations that in face of totalitarianism, militarism, racism, and economic injustices the church must itself be a true community exemplifying the reign of God, and is called to declare prophetically the will of God for the whole range of human life and society. Moreover, speaking of "The Oecumenical Church," the report of Section V, "The Universal Church and the World of Nations," recognizes the problem of the divided church which nevertheless believes in its given unity: "True oecumenicity therefore must be the goal of all our efforts. Churches must not simply be tolerant one towards another but concerned about unity one with the other."[58] But the question of unity in the truth is not addressed full square, as Bonhoeffer wished. "Let the Church be the Church!" was indeed an apt rallying cry as the world slid once again toward war—and how different was this from the mood with which the churches were swept in the tides of nationalism a quarter of a century earlier. But one cannot help believing that Bonhoeffer would have wanted to say, "Let the ecumenical movement itself be church!"

CHAPTER 8

Christian, Ecumenical, German: Shifting Priorities, 1938–1939

In May 1938, the month when the constitution of the World Council of Churches was laid down, Dietrich Bonhoeffer could unequivocally be described as an ecumenical Christian: unreservedly identified with the suffering Confessing Church; serving as director of its illegal and clandestine training of ordinands in the remote east of Further Pomerania; and equally asserting the claim of the Confessing Church to be the sole rightful representation of the German Evangelical Church in the ecumenical movement. Thirty months later, in the autumn of 1940, his paramount concerns and engagements could not be so simply described. His relationship both to his church and to the ecumenical movement had become problematic, not through any disloyalty to either but on account of dramatically changed circumstances which meant that neither his being a Confessing pastor nor an ecumenical theologian could be manifest as had previously been the case. Occurring at the midpoint of this period, the outbreak of war at the beginning of September 1939 was certainly the great pivotal event. But Bonhoeffer had long foreseen its coming, and it was but one of several critical developments which were impelling him to shift his priorities in order to maintain his foundational commitments to being Christian and ecumenical. Hitherto, his loyalty had been to the Confessing Church as belonging to the church of the *oikoumene* and thus serving the *oikoumene*. Now, however, it was first a matter of being a citizen of that particular part of the *oikoumene*, Germany, which was in the grip of a malaise about to threaten the wider world. He was moving in a direction which would lead to quite new perspectives on what it meant to be Christian and to be ecumenical. This chapter examines the shifting ecumenical scene and Bonhoeffer's role within it during the two years from May 1938 to May 1940.

The Slide to War

On the European scene, following the Austrian *Anschluss* in March,[1] the year 1938 was dominated by the Czechoslovakian crisis, with Hitler demanding "protection" for Germans living in the Sudetenland. This led to the Munich agreement of 29–30 September 1938, signed by France, Britain, Italy, and Germany, which ceded the Sudetenland to Germany as the price of peace—but was soon regarded as only a postponement of war in face of Hitler's continuing expansionism. Meanwhile, Germany's internal policy against the Jews became ever more threatening. Early in October 1938 all Jewish passports were recalled and new ones had to be stamped with "J." On 9–10 November occurred *Kristallnacht* ("Crystal Night"), when synagogues and Jewish-owned shops throughout Germany were attacked and burned, and some 35,000 Jews arrested. Hitler was by now secretly ordering the German press to prepare the people psychologically for war. Publicly, on 30 January 1939, he addressed the Reichstag, justifying his aggressive foreign policy and threatening the "destruction of the Jewish race in Europe." In March, German troops occupied the whole of Czechoslovakia. At the end of April Hitler renounced the 1934 German–Polish Non-Aggression Pact and the Anglo–German Naval Treaty of 1935.

Within these developments, however, were concealed the first plans to overthrow Hitler. From as early as 1937, the *Führer's* enthusiasm for a war was not, to say the least, shared throughout the highest ranks of the *Wehrmacht*, the German regular army.[2] General Werner von Fritsch, head of the General Staff, made known his objections and was dismissed by Hitler in January 1938. Hitler assumed to himself the supreme command of all the armed forces. Subsequent to this, a small group of officers formed, including the head of the central Office of Military Intelligence, Colonel Hans Oster, and chief of the Army General Staff, General Ludwig Beck. Their concern to stop Hitler from leading Germany into a disastrous war advanced to the point where Beck prepared a memorandum for the head of the General Staff, General von Brauchitsch, to hand to Hitler. But Brauchitsch hesitated and refused. Beck resigned in disgust. If Hitler were to persist in his demands on Czechoslovakia in September 1938, and if France and Britain were to call his bluff and declare war, then those generals still opposed to Hitler were prepared to mount a *Putsch* on behalf of the better interests of the nation. But the Munich agreement removed the case for revolt, which remained buried when war did break out in September 1939, while Hitler's spectacular success in the west in 1940 seemed in most German eyes to more than confirm his strategic genius. Nevertheless, resistance cells persisted. Their main military leadership was located in the office of the Head of Military Intelligence (the *Abwehr*), Admiral Wilhelm Canaris. His assistant was a lawyer who coordinated the liaison between the military and civilian arms of the movement: Hans von Dohnanyi, Dietrich Bonhoeffer's brother-in-law.

The Ecumenical Scene

For the ecumenical movement, this period was both the best and the worst of times.[3] Thanks to the Utrecht meeting of May 1938,[4] it was now possible to speak of a World Council of Churches (WCC) "in formation," its basis being "a fellowship of Churches which accept our Lord Jesus Christ as God and Saviour." Utrecht appointed a Provisional Committee, with William Temple as chairman, together with an administrative committee. W. A. Visser't Hooft[5] was appointed general secretary. Two part-time associate general secretaries were appointed: William Paton of Great Britain, longtime associate secretary of the International Missionary Council (IMC) and soon to be general secretary of the IMC on J. H. Oldham's retirement in September 1938; and an American, Henry Smith Leiper.[6] Paton and Leiper would continue to work from London and New York respectively, while the main office of the WCC under Visser't Hooft would be in Geneva. In fact, the Geneva secretariat was essentially formed out of the already existing Life and Work office and its Research Department. But the designation of Paton and Leiper as associate general secretaries of the WCC meant a displacement of H. L. Henriod, who had been secretary of Life and Work (and the World Alliance) since 1931. Henriod relinquished the Life and Work secretaryship in 1938 but remained with the World Alliance until its demise in 1951. He had not been as stalwart as Visser't Hooft and others wished in his responses to the Church Struggle, being more tolerant of the Reich Church's claim to be the inclusive representative of the German Evangelical Church.[7] The same was true of Hans Schönfeld, head of the Research Department, with whom Visser't Hooft was in clear disagreement as regarded support for the Confessing Church, and this situation was made no easier by the fact of Schönfeld's salary being paid by Heckel's office in the German Reich Church.[8] Visser't Hooft, however, was able to stamp his own authority on Genevan policy and he signalled a new orientation toward the Confessing Church. But in addition, he recognized that Schönfeld's gifts and experience in other areas—especially his wide range of contacts throughout Europe—could be to the great advantage of the WCC in the coming crisis, and so they proved.[9] At a crucial point there would even be a measure of reconvergence between Bonhoeffer and Schönfeld. A most significant and foresighted strengthening of the Geneva staff came with the appointment in 1939 of Adolf Freudenberg, a Confessing Church pastor who had emigrated to London, as secretary for refugee relief work. That the headquarters of the WCC was being established in the relative security of neutral Switzerland was, of course, a natural advantage in the context of war, both potential and actual.[10]

The infant WCC may have been cradled in the structure of Life and Work, but other players were major stakeholders, two in particular: Faith and Order, and the International Missionary Council (IMC). Following the Oxford and Edinburgh conferences of 1937, Faith and Order had been coequal with Life and Work in convening the Utrecht meeting. But its organizational base was much weaker and it had never had an administrative centre or staffing comparable to that of Life and Work. Its secretariat effectively comprised the Anglican theologian Leonard Hodgson,[11] now an Oxford professor. There were misgivings in some Faith and Order circles about whether the WCC, given the heavy role of Life and Work, would prove too oriented toward socioeconomic issues at the expense of theological and doctrinal work (a tension which continues to this day) and that the distinctive work of Faith and Order would simply be swallowed up in this new and (as it seemed to some) not wholly sympathetic body. At the Faith and Order meeting in Clarens, Switzerland, in August 1938, such fears were mostly allayed by William Temple and others. The WCC scheme was approved, and Faith and Order would continue as a quasi-autonomous commission within the WCC. A not dissimilar solution transpired for the IMC, which, as child of the Edinburgh Missionary Conference of 1910, could be considered the senior body in the whole ecumenical enterprise. At an enlarged meeting of the IMC held in Tambaram, India, in late 1938, the formation of the WCC was welcomed; the need for close cooperation with the WCC was affirmed, especially as a means of enabling the so-called younger churches of the world to access the ecumenical movement; and a joint body was set up to work out means of cooperation. The fact that William Paton was now both secretary of the IMC and an associate secretary of the WCC was obviously significant here. Indeed, a major factor in all the new developments was the mutual regard, trust, and friendship (if not always agreement) that marked the network—often overlapping the boundaries of the various organizations—of ecumenical leaders at this stage.

By 1939, therefore, the ecumenical movement had a lot to show for itself in terms of consolidation, organization, and energy. In material terms its resources might be slender and the darkening world scene lent no comfort externally, but there was no doubting the vision and determination of its leaders. The Provisional Committee of the WCC met in St. Germain, France, in January 1939 and heard of the substantial number of churches that to date had accepted the principles and basis of membership issued by the Utrecht conference. It set August 1941 as the date for the first assembly. Developing relationships with the IMC were affirmed. Information on the committee's decisions was sent to the Vatican. Moreover, it was more than "committee ecumenism" that was being serviced. Six months later, 24 July–2 August, there met in Amsterdam the World Conference of Christian Youth, bringing together 1,500 delegates from 71 countries, under the aegis of the main ecumenical youth bodies (YMCA, YWCA, WSCF), the Ecumenical Youth Commission of the WCC, and the World Alliance for Friendship through the Churches. With just weeks to go before the world went to war it was a remarkable witness. Its final message rang out: "The nations and peoples of the world are drifting apart, the churches are coming together. There is a growing conviction of the essential togetherness of all Christians."[12]

For their part, the general secretary and the provisional governing body of the WCC were showing their mettle in dealing with Germany. Visser't Hooft himself happened to be in Germany in November 1938 and witnessed firsthand the demonic violence of *Kristallnacht*. With Henriod of the World Alliance and Adolf Keller of Inter-Church Aid, he issued a strong protest, calling for concerted action by the churches of the ecumenical fellowship to assist Jewish refugees, and this bore fruit in WCC Provisional Committee's establishment in January 1939 of the secretariat for refugees, under Adolf Freudenberg, mentioned earlier. Meanwhile, Visser't Hooft was determinedly countering Theodor Heckel's ambitions to control German access to the WCC. In April 1939 relations between the Reich Church and WCC became explosive when eleven German church leaders, headed by Friedrich Werner, minister for church affairs, issued a declaration based on the German Christian "Godesberg Declaration" condemning all "supranational or international churchliness," whether Roman Catholic or "World Protestant," and declaring Christian faith to be "the unbridgeable opposite to Judaism."[13] Visser't Hooft, as did George Bell and Karl

Barth, wished for an immediate response. The upshot was a declaration published in the international press, including the London *Times*, reaffirming the oneness of the church of Christ irrespective of nation, race, or sex, and the closeness of the church to the Jewish people as recipients of the promises of God. It was signed by William Temple, Marc Boegner, Visser't Hooft, and William Paton. Heckel reacted angrily, demanding the statement's withdrawal on the grounds that that the WCC had exceeded its competence and had made an "intolerable intervention in domestic German affairs."[14] The arguments on this and on German representation on the WCC Provisional Committee ran on into the summer, by correspondence and by meetings between Visser't Hooft and Heckel in Berlin, without resolution. But the WCC leadership had made clear where it stood on the basic issues.

In the account thus far, the ecumenical movement had shown what it could be at its best. But in face of war, both leading up to and following the actual outbreak, there emerged some serious weaknesses which at root were a compound of problems within the constituent churches themselves. The churches, at and after the 1937 Oxford Conference, had clearly affirmed that their fellowship could not and must not be sundered by war, and this represented a huge difference from their stance in 1914–18. But their capacity actually to prevent war, or help bring the conflict to a just resolution once it had started, was another matter. During 1939 there was a rush of initiatives by church leaders in the European democracies, with calls for prayer[15] and joint public statements against nationalism and the use of force, together with proposals for conferences or procedures for arbitration. George Bell, for instance, suggested a meeting of theologians in Rome to "discuss fundamental principles in a true international order and in social justice."[16] But the pope could not see the utility of such a proposal when he had already, so it was argued, made the church's position on these matters totally clear. It was even more difficult to conceive how German theologians could be expected to participate in international discussions which would have to address, if not publicly declare on, political questions that could not even be raised at home. Visser't Hooft was warned by German friends that in the present situation even those who inwardly felt sympathetic to such initiatives would feel the dice loaded against them if they so much as attended a conference held effectively under Western democratic auspices. The Scandinavian churches were inherently disposed toward inclusive mediation, but even the Norwegian bishop Eivind Berggrav, a member of the WCC Provisional Committee and president of the World Alliance, warned Bell of the danger of creating "a Maginot line" between churches in the democracies and those on the other side.[17] But did this then mean that the churches in the democracies should stay silent? From Switzerland, Karl Barth had no inhibitions and in April urged that, when war broke out, a message be sent to the German people on behalf of all the churches, declaring that the war was not against them as such but against their criminal rulers, and that the German people should ask themselves whether it was not their duty to do everything they could to end it and prevent a victory by their false leaders. From the USA came yet another proposal, this time for a small conference of experts in international affairs with theologians and church leaders. This met in Geneva in July under the auspices of the WCC and the World Alliance and even included two Germans, Wilhelm Menn and O. H. von der Gablenz. But there was no consensus. Even among the Westerners who attended there were strong disagreements on the attitude to be taken toward Nazi Germany. Nothing could be collectively addressed to the immediate situation. What did emerge was a document reflecting on the discussions, "The Churches and the International Crisis," which was sent out to the churches and served as a useful discussion paper for the longer term.[18] But the lack of ecumenical consensus before 1 September 1939 was to become even more apparent once war started.

Bonhoeffer's Path to War

For Dietrich Bonhoeffer during this period, the overarching political and ecclesiastical issues of the hour became enmeshed with his personal existence to an unprecedented degree,[19] demanding of him the most difficult and fateful decisions he ever had to make. For the time being, the training of ordinands continued underground in the remote, far-eastern collective pastorates of Köslin and Gross-Schlönwitz, but still under surveillance and pressure from the Reich authorities and beset by the vexed question of the demand on pastors (later rescinded) of an oath of loyalty to the Führer. The anti-Jewish measures of summer and autumn 1938 suddenly bore heavily on the Bonhoeffer family. Gerhard Leibholz, husband of Dietrich's twin sister Sabine and a so-called non-Aryan, was now extremely vulnerable in his post at Göttingen University and even their children were suffering harassment. Early in September the Leibholzes, assisted by Dietrich Bonhoeffer and Eberhard Bethge, made it over the border into Switzerland and emigrated to London as refugees. Then came *Kristallnacht* on 9 November. Bonhoeffer was deeply troubled by the crime,[20] although there is no record of his making any public protest. On top of all this loomed the most personally pressing question of all: the likelihood of military call-up for men of Bonhoeffer's age group. Consistent with his earlier statements of near-pacifist beliefs, he could not in conscience serve in Hitler's army. But as a pastor, to refuse military service would implicate the Confessing Church in a stance the vast majority of its members did not share or even understand, and could precipitate from the regime a response deadly for the whole church. On 3 November 1938 came the first intimation of his call-up with the requirement (enjoined on all his age group) to enter his place of residence with the police "Military Registration Record" and to report on any change of address or extended holiday travel. The moral impasse seemed total. Given these pressingly immediate, local, and personal issues, any consideration of ecumenical affairs might well have seemed an irrelevant luxury if not a dangerous distraction. Indeed, from the spring of 1938 to March 1939 we find Bonhoeffer taking no evident interest in any of the ecumenical developments, even those aimed at preserving or rebuilding peace, that were engaging the churches internationally. In March 1939, however, the ecumenical sphere suddenly reemerged as offering a possible route through the personal dilemma: Might it be in order for him to leave Germany and work abroad, at least for a time?

The context of this development was the increasingly fraught competition between the sections of German Protestantism for recognition within the WCC, and particularly for representation on its Provisional Committee. No Germans had been officially present at the Utrecht meeting of May 1938 or at any of the subsequent meetings of the Provisional and Administrative committees. The ecumenical movement was developing and consolidating itself beyond the reach of Germany, to the disquiet of the leaderships of both the Confessing Church and the Reich Church. Theodor Heckel, as head of the Reich Church's Foreign Office, was claiming the right to be the sole German channel of representation, and was finding in Hans Schönfeld a sympathetic ear on the WCC side. For the ecumenical officials it was indeed a tempting possibility to accept the promises of funding, communication, and travel permissions that Heckel could obtain. Meanwhile, the Confessing Church—in accordance with Bonhoeffer's wish in 1934 following the Fanø conference—now had its own secretary responsible for ecumenical and foreign relations, Hans Böhm, in Berlin. In 1936, Böhm had become a member of the Provisional Administration (the governing body) of the Confessing Church. For his part, W. A. Visser't Hooft was determined to resist the Heckel-Schönfeld line of working only through the official Reich Church channels, and during March and April 1939 was visiting Germany and developing his own direct contacts with Böhm and the Confessing Church leaders, who were opposed to having Heckel on the Provisional Committee unless the Confessing Church also had a place. This was, in truth, a significantly more moderate demand than the hard-line approach they had advocated and Bonhoeffer had most strongly pressed during 1934–37, which asserted the Confessing Church's *sole* right to be recognized as the German Evangelical Church. Events were moving on and a judgment had to be made on whether total exclusion from the ecumenical table was too high a price to pay for a theological principle however valid. By April 1939 the ecumenical leadership under Visser't Hooft was wholly supportive of the Confessing Church's current approach. Visser't Hooft proposed to George Bell and Marc Boegner[21] that the WCC wait until Heckel demanded a place on the committee and then consult with the Confessing Church leaders, which would effectively put the ball back in Heckel's court. But very soon afterward, Heckel became embroiled with Visser't Hooft over the WCC's response to the extreme nationalist declaration of German theologians,[22] which left Heckel in bad odour in ecumenical circles. Heckel went on to make even more unrealistic demands for yet more Reich Church representation on the Provisional Committee. In late July, the Administrative Committee met in Zeist, Netherlands, and agreed on a proposal that Germany should have three places on the Provisional Committee, one of which should go to a person fully backed by the Confessing Church. Visser't Hooft and Bishop Yngve Brillioth of Sweden were deputed to go to Berlin to put this to Heckel, but before they could go the outbreak of war intervened. Visser't Hooft later commented: "For the next six years the relations between the World Council and the German Evangelical Church would remain undefined. This had at least the advantage that we were free to maintain personal contacts with all who were true friends of the ecumenical movement."[23]

During 1939, however, the Confessing Church was also ready to explore other avenues into the ecumenical movement, and early in the year Bonhoeffer discussed with Hans Böhm in Berlin how, with his many ecumenical contacts abroad, he might help in this. This was the point at which the ecumenical calling and the personal situation neatly coincided for Bonhoeffer, who by now was desperate (as in 1933) to step for a time outside of Germany in order to recollect himself and ponder his future. The prospect of visiting London particularly appealed to him, since it would enable him to see his sister Sabine and family again, and he was eager for the chance of a heart-to-heart conversation with George Bell about the dilemma posed by military call-up and where his responsibility really lay, inside or outside Germany. For his part, Böhm proposed that Bonhoeffer explore what kind of position might be given to, or created for, a Confessing Church person in one of the ecumenical bodies such as Faith and Order. "He was to explore the possibilities for making the ecumenical associations more aware of the Confessing Church's interests, discuss proposals for this, and possibly bring in one of the colleagues who had emigrated, such as Hildebrandt."[24] The official purpose of his visit would therefore be under mandate from the Confessing Church, but as Eberhard Bethge (who accompanied Bonhoeffer to London) notes, it was, rather, his agonizing personal situation that dominated his mind.[25]

Bonhoeffer and Bethge arrived in London via Ostend on 12 March, and remained five weeks. There was an immediate reunion with Sabine and Gerhard Leibholz. The day after arrival he wrote to George Bell, requesting a meeting with him. This could not be arranged until early April, in Chichester. Meanwhile, there were meetings with Julius Rieger and several of the other London pastors and members of his former congregations to whom he preached at least once. He also spoke to a meeting in Bloomsbury of "non-Aryan" Christians. On 25 March, Bonhoeffer wrote at some length to Bell, explaining in advance both his official mission on behalf of the Confessing Church and his personal quandary. On the former, he stated openly that the relationship of the Confessing Church to churches abroad was, "mainly owing to travelling difficulties," unsatisfactory. Continual exchange of opinion and the advice of other churches were necessary. He continued:

> We are fully aware of and gratefully appreciate what is continuously being done for us from individuals to individuals. But, I think, we must try to go a step further and to come to some sort of regular cooperation with and to a better representation of the Confessional Church in the oecumenic movements. If we are not going to make a decisive step forward in this direction, I am afraid, we shall very soon be cut off entirely from our brethren abroad, and that would at any rate mean a tremendous loss to us. What I think we should therefore try to get, is a man, who could devote all his time to establish the necessary contacts, to cooperate in the oecumenic meetings and conferences, learning and contributing.[26]

A failure similar to that which had marked outside support for the Russian Christians must be avoided, he urged. Most frankly of all, he declared that "the German representatives in Geneva simply cannot represent the cause of the Confessional Church."[27] So there was "a real vacancy" which must be filled—and, moreover, Bonhoeffer even hinted that he had an idea for meeting the eventual financial difficulties.

At about the same time, Bonhoeffer wrote in similar terms to Leonard Hodgson,[28] secretary of Faith and Order, who was now professor of moral and pastoral theology at Oxford. Bonhoeffer sought an interview with him, to which Hodgson agreed for 29 March. Bonhoeffer's letter prepared the ground for their meeting, their first-ever direct contact, and mentioned only in passing their unfruitful correspondence four years' earlier in which Bonhoeffer had stiffly declined the invitation to attend the preparatory meeting for the 1937 Edinburgh Faith and Order conference, in view of the Reich Church also being represented at it. As in his letter to Bell, Bonhoeffer stressed the urgency of improving relationships with the ecumenical bodies but was even more specific than in his address to the bishop: "we [in the Confessing Church] feel it to be necessary to find a way of a permanent representation in the oecumenic movement and particularly in the department concerning 'Faith and Order.'" This was far from being a one-sided begging for help, however:

> We need the theological help of other churches in order to be able to bear the burden of responsibilities which God has laid upon us, *and we wish to give you a witness of the Christian insights, which God has given us* anew during the last years. I feel strongly that something has to be done quickly practically and effectively in order to establish new relations between you and us. Would it, for instance, not be possible to have a permanent German secretary of the Confessional Church in Geneva or in London, and if not permanent then perhaps for one year or two?[29]

Bonhoeffer's previous self-distancing from Faith and Order as compared with Life and Work owed nothing to any instinctive theological preference for the latter at the expense of the former. He had never lent his voice to the slick slogan popular in some Life and Work and World Alliance circles during the 1920s, "doctrine divides, service unites." In 1932 he had argued that these two socially oriented bodies needed more, not less, theology, that they were suffering from a lack of theological basis, and they should *not* leave doctrine to Faith and Order.[30] His quarrel with Faith and Order in 1935 had not been with its doctrinal emphasis at the expense of ethics, but with the way in which, in his view, it had not been doctrinally acute enough, as shown by its refusal to countenance a contemporary decision between truth and heresy.[31] It should also be noted that approaches to both Bell and Hodgson, stressing the mutual need of the Confessing Church and the ecumenical fellowship, were entirely consistent with the assertion in his 1935 essay "The Confessing Church and the Ecumenical Movement" that the Confessing Church and the ecumenical movement had made an encounter and must question each other.[32]

The meeting took place in Hodgson's college rooms in Christ Church, Oxford. It was long, involved, at times heated, and as unproductive as their 1935 correspondence had been. This time, Bonhoeffer, in contrast to four years earlier, was not asking for *exclusive* recognition of the Confessing Church over against the Reich Church but simply—as with the Confessing Church's arguments for representation on the WCC Provisional Committee—for *a* recognition of its rightful existence as a church and for help in making its distinctive voice known. But once again Hodgson held fast to the rules of Faith and Order, as he made clear to Bonhoeffer in his *résumé* written next day. In the first place, he stated, no church had direct representation on the continuation committee, which was appointed by the World Conference. The German Evangelical Church, not having been present at the 1937 Edinburgh Conference, was not in a position to have a representative on the continuation committee. That committee could *co-opt* representatives of those churches wishing to be represented on it. "For this purpose it is necessary to be able to have communication in each case with a central body having full confidence of the whole church, and be able to invite representatives in its name. We are advised that at the present time there is no such church, and that we must not attempt to treat the different groups as if they were separate churches."[33] The most he would offer was for Confessing Church representatives to be invited as guests to the continuation committee or to work on the different commissions, for which some finance might be available. This was far from what Bonhoeffer had hoped for, which was a recognition that the witness of the Confessing Church was of peculiar and positive importance for the ecumenical movement while the stance of the Reich Church (or the "Evangelical Church," for which Heckel claimed overall responsibility) was rather different. He left Oxford with further disappointment and disillusionment. Precisely who was advising Faith and Order that the German scene should not be regarded as one where "separate" churches existed? At root the basic problem remained, that Faith and Order was not prepared to make any theological judgment whatever about the status of a church or group, provided it had made a formal declaration of belief in "the Lord Jesus Christ as God and Saviour." Within the terms of the constitution of Faith and Order, Hodgson was acting properly. In the context of the apocalyptic scale of what was happening in Germany and was soon to engulf Europe, Bonhoeffer felt equally justified in implicitly questioning the adequacy of that constitution if it meant that—as he had maintained in his Berlin lectures of 1932[34]—the ecumenical movement was sidestepping the question of truth versus heresy and denial of the gospel.[35] William Temple, chairman of the WCC Provisional Committee and of Faith and Order, was strongly supportive of Hodgson's line when the latter reported to him on the meeting with Bonhoeffer.[36] Bonhoeffer was bound to feel that such official ecumenical leadership, for all its claims to impartiality, was playing into the hands of the Reich Church, due to its refusal even to consider the terms of the struggle as seen by the Confessing Christians. Nor did it appear that such ecumenical figures saw the real point of what Bonhoeffer was proposing: not just a Confessing Church representative on an ecumenical committee, but a quasi-staff person based outside Germany who would thus be spared the almost certain refusal of travel permission by the Reich authorities. Bonhoeffer evidently would not be averse to being so appointed himself.

Just before or after the meeting with Hodgson came an encounter of a very different kind. Bonhoeffer had heard from Julius Rieger that Visser't Hooft was coming to England and would be seeing George Bell. Thus he was spurred to begin his letter to the bishop of 25 March by asking if he could arrange a meeting for him with Visser't Hooft: "I am very anxious to see him during his stay in London."[37] This proved—just—possible, the only time and venue they found mutually convenient being an hour or so at Paddington station. It was their first-ever

meeting, despite Bonhoeffer's previous ecumenical work and Visser't
Hooft's grateful use of his essay "The Confessing Church and the Ecumenical Movement" in writing the preparatory material for the 1937
Oxford Conference.[38] Visser't Hooft, for his part, was surprised that
instead of beginning with the relations about the Confessing Church
and the WCC, Bonhoeffer launched into his personal dilemma about
military service, as if the Dutchman had been his lifelong friend. He
went on to talk openly about the coming war: "Hitler would surely
attack Poland in the summer or autumn and . . . this would lead to
war on a large scale."[39] Visser't Hooft sensed he had private information (this was, as is now known, indeed the case and was provided by
Hans von Dohnanyi) and found the whole conversation deeply moving. In contrast with his fruitless meeting with Hodgson, Bonhoeffer, for his part, experienced new hope and encouragement. He and
Visser't Hooft knew that in war communication between those within
and those outside Germany, however risky, would be an ecumenical
imperative. So began and was instantly sealed a friendship springing
from instinctive mutual trust and regard, which was to prove vital during the coming conflict.

At their eventual meeting in Chichester, early in April, Bonhoeffer
privately poured out his heart to Bell on the personal dilemma facing him. The only alternative to conscription or conscientious protest
would be service somewhere outside Germany, perhaps on behalf both
of the ecumenical movement and the Confessing Church, or maybe
with one of the British missionary societies. But would not this be
flight rather than fight? It seems that Bell gently invited him to relax
his scruples on this point and, as a good counselor, simply let Bonhoeffer talk and talk, while he listened. Certainly, afterward Bonhoeffer wrote gratefully to the bishop, thanking him "for the great help
you gave me in our talk at Chichester. I do not know what will be the
outcome of it all, but it means much to me to realize that you see the
great conscientious difficulties with which we are faced."[40]

Then, early in April, with Gerhard Leibholz and Julius Rieger he
went to the south coast of England again, this time to Bexhill-on-Sea,
where Reinhold Niebuhr was taking a holiday just prior to starting his
first series of Gifford Lectures to be given at Edinburgh University on

The Nature and Destiny of Man. It was eight years since he and Bonhoeffer had been together at Union Seminary, New York, though they had corresponded at least once, and they had much news to catch up on and thoughts to share. Learning from Bonhoeffer about his situation, Niebuhr immediately promised to get invitations for him to make a prolonged trip to the USA to visit his friends in the National Council of Churches and to lecture in one or more colleges. That at least would postpone the danger of military call-up and obviate the danger completely if war should come while he was away.

Bonhoeffer and Eberhard Bethge returned to Germany on 18 April. Five days later, Bonhoeffer applied at the military enlistment office in Schlawe for twelve months' leave of absence from 1 May 1939 to be spent in the USA. A door was indeed being opened out of the impending danger. There was the promise that, at one stroke, he could solve his conscription dilemma, safeguard the Confessing Church from the charge of fostering treasonable pacifism, and fulfill his calling as a theologian of and in the worldwide ecumenical movement. How this promise actually transpired proved to be rather different both for Bonhoeffer and for the ecumenical movement, because in all this formulation of what it meant to be Christian and ecumenical one factor was being left out of the equation: what it meant to be *German* here and now. If up till now Bonhoeffer had been foremost among ecumenists in asserting that the local and particular is not an end in itself but finds its true value within the universality of the *oikoumene*, he was about to discover and demonstrate that, in turn, the particular has a special responsibility if it is from there that the whole *oikoumene* is most imperilled.

Transatlantic Ecumenism: The American Episode

On 12 June 1939 Bonhoeffer arrived in New York. Reinhold Niebuhr's promise to secure an invitation from the Federal Council of Churches in the USA had borne fruit. For an indefinite period, he would be free of the danger of the military call-up. He went with the blessing of the leadership of the Confessing Church. Henry Smith Leiper, ecumenical secretary of the Federal Council and well known to Bonhoeffer through meetings of the World Alliance and Life and Work,[41] in his formal letter of invitation outlined Bonhoeffer's forthcoming duties as "a combination of pastoral service, preaching and lecturing in the theological summer school at Columbia and Union Seminary, to begin with, and later in the Seminary in the usual term."[42] The colleges would clearly regard it as a great coup to have a leading theologian of the Confessing Church on the podium. This arrangement, then, grew out of a clear conjunction of needs: Bonhoeffer's need for protection from the Reich authorities, and America's need for theological strengthening. It was, moreover, a classic instance of ecumenical responsibility and solidarity. The worldwide church as represented in America—and Leiper, it should be noted, was now also an associate secretary of the nascent World Council of Churches—was coming to the aid of the valiant but suffering Confessing Church whose voice would now be amplified across the Atlantic. Here, it could truly be said, was international ecumenism in action.

Yet Bonhoeffer had come with misgivings. The basic uncertainty, which months earlier he had confessed to George Bell and Visser't Hooft, about where his prime duty lay had not been resolved. Very soon after arrival in New York, beset by worries over the state of the collective pastorate training he had left behind, together with sheer unaccustomed homesickness, he decided he had made a mistake in coming. Nevertheless, it took some agonizing days to make a final decision. A clinching point came when he discovered that among his duties he would be expected to lecture to German refugees, which if known back in Germany would certainly make him *persona non grata* with the authorities there. He therefore felt he had come on a misunderstanding, and on 20 June he met with Henry Leiper and told him as much. His travel diary records: "Visit with Leiper. With that the decision has been made. I turned it down. He was visibly disappointed and indeed somewhat put out. For me it may mean something more than I am able to foresee at the moment. God alone knows."[43] Leiper had good cause to be dismayed, and, indeed, to feel badly treated. He and colleagues had gone to considerable trouble in arranging their visitor's programme, his hospitality, indeed, his funding, too. All their goodwill and brotherly Christian solidarity seemed to count for nothing in Bonhoeffer's inexplicable decision. Some 25 years later, Leiper wrote of this meeting:

> What was my surprise and dismay to learn from my guest that he had just received an urgent appeal from his colleagues in Germany to return at once for important tasks which they felt he alone could perform in the resistance movement he had already served so effectively. I did not press him for details of what that work might be. Yet it was abundantly clear from his manner and his tenseness that he felt it something he could not refuse to undertake. It was soon clear to me that he had already determined his course of action . . .[44]

Leiper's impression of Bonhoeffer's having suddenly received an urgent summons from Germany is at odds with Bonhoeffer's own testimony to his constant wrestling with the *inner* summons from his heart and conscience. It may be that Leiper's account is somewhat embellished by the wish to downplay how offended he actually felt at the time, and that he has retrospectively read into the episode the later narrative of the hero and martyr; it is unlikely that Bonhoeffer would at that time have spoken directly about "resistance" and his role within it. Certainly, for his part, Bonhoeffer was aware that he had caused dismay, offense, and incredulity. Other American friends like Paul and Marion Lehmann were also puzzled and anxious for him, and whatever admiration may be felt for Bonhoeffer's decision and its courage, the hurt caused to his would-be helpers should not be minimized.

Within the ecumenical fellowship the accepted canons of behaviour had been violated. Not only so, but Bonhoeffer's decision could be seen as quite contradictory to his efforts in London three months earlier, to seek a post for a Confessing Church representative—maybe even himself—within the ecumenical organizations now being drawn together with the formation of the WCC. The door to that possibility, at least as far as Faith and Order was concerned, had been shut. Now a door had been opened to a situation where Bonhoeffer in New York would only be a few minutes' walk away from Leiper's desk as associate general secretary of the WCC—and Bonhoeffer was walking away from it. By his own honest account, Bonhoeffer was not entirely sure of his motives at this point. Intuition, if not instinct, was in play as much as rationality. Was he reneging on his ecumenical commitment? Or was he, perhaps, finding his way toward a new understanding of what ecumenism meant in a world now on the edge of war? Here we must turn to Bonhoeffer's most famous and oft-quoted justification of his decision, in a letter written to Reinhold Niebuhr, whose advocacy had issued in the invitation to America and who therefore was most entitled to an explanation:

> I have made a mistake in coming to America. I must live through this difficult period of our national history with the Christian people of Germany. I will have no right to participate in the reconstruction of Christian life in Germany after the war if I do not share the trials of this time with my people. . . . Christians in Germany will face the terrible alternative of either willing the defeat of their nation in order that Christian civilization may survive, or willing the victory of their nation and thereby destroying our civilization. I know which of these alternatives I must choose but I cannot make that choice in security.[45]

The admiration rightly prompted by these lines typically focuses on the writer's clear-sighted courage, his wish for solidarity with his people despite all the dangers he would face, and the long-term view of what would be needed in Germany after the war. But no less remarkably, solidarity with his people and church in Germany is not the only solidarity on view here. In speaking as he does of the peril facing "Christian civilization" or "our civilization," a wider commitment is apparent. It is not just Germany nor his church there which is imperilled by a Nazi military victory, but the wider *oikoumene* that recognizes Christ as formative for its life and values, or what might be termed "the Christian West." The threat to the *oikoumene* lies in Germany, and as a responsible German that is where he must now go and engage with the threat. In a way which he cannot fully explain nor even wholly foresee for himself at present, he will be living out his own choice under the "terrible alternative"—a path, an engagement, and a fate undertaken ultimately for the sake of the *oikoumene*. It will be, in short, a case of vicarious representative action, *Stellvertretung*,[46] on the widest ecumenical plane. His American hosts might be disappointed, perplexed, and annoyed; they cannot yet comprehend that in the longer view it is as much for their sakes as anyone else's that he is sailing home to danger. Bonhoeffer is not abnegating his ecumenical responsibility, but the form of this responsibility which had brought him to America, and which was awaiting his contribution there, now had to cede priority to a yet-more-demanding expression of it. One can agree with Eberhard Bethge that "when at last, in 1939, the ecumenical movement could have saved him, he turned his back on it," provided we read his next sentence also: "Paradoxically, it is his final entrance into German particularism which has made him ecumenically so alive and effective today."[47] He was temporarily forsaking one expression of ecumenism in order to discover another.

A further perspective on this commitment is gained from the single substantial piece of writing that Bonhoeffer undertook during these few weeks in New York. He was not totally captive to his agonized decision making, but used his time in Union Seminary to read widely in American church history, contemporary theology, and church life, and had extensive conversations with a variety of academics and clergy including Henry Sloane Coffin, Henry P. van Dusen, and H. Richard Niebuhr. His reading and observations bore fruit in the extensive essay on the American Protestant scene, "Protestantism without Reformation."[48] This essay is perhaps most often quoted for its sharp observations on the American understanding of freedom: "America calls itself the land of freedom. Today this means the right of the individual to think, speak, and act independently. In this framework, religious freedom is a self-evident possession for the American. The church's proclamation, organization and congregational life can flourish in complete independence and without interference. "[49] This unconditional "Protestantism," Bonhoeffer argues, is more a tribute to the world and the state than an affirmation about the essential nature of the church which, in authentic Reformation tradition, exists under the word of God and only in obedience to and confession of that word

finds its true freedom. Hence the plethora in the USA of denominations in all their variety, where the liberty to be so diverse seems to
matter more than the question of the truth of what they believe and
proclaim—hence the deliberate irony of the essay's title. But to see the
essay as essentially or wholly critical would be a serious misreading.
Rather than a censorious lecture to Americans from the continent,
it is intended as an exercise in *encounter* between the continental and
the "Anglo-Saxon" churches and in identifying their significance for
each other.[50] Bonhoeffer is desperate to get beyond superficial mutual
caricatures or, equally, touristic interest in each other's historical and
cultural peculiarities:

> Why should a Christian in Germany be concerned with something
> typically American, and why should a Christian in America be inter-
> ested in the typical Continental Reformation? At most it may be
> possible to take a certain aesthetic joy in the variety of appearances
> and forms of Christianity; it is also possible to welcome the other
> church as a complement to one's own church. But in this way it is
> impossible to come to a genuine encounter or to have an exchange
> that leads to commitment. As long as we are interested in Ameri-
> can peculiarities, we are merely operating in the realm of detached
> observations. It is a different question what God does to and with
> his church, in America, how God reveals himself to the church and
> whether and how we may recognize God in that church.[51]

The tone thus strongly recalls Bonhoeffer's 1935 essay "The
Confessing Church and the Ecumenical Movement."[52] Ecumenical
encounter is born out of a common need to apprehend the truth of
God in Christ. Therefore, it has to be asked: "What is God doing to
and with his church in America? What is he doing through this church
to us and, through us, to it?"[53] Here it is striking how the writer has
moved beyond the kind of assumed sense of continental superiority
that he manifested in his American visit of 1930–31, and also beyond
the judgments of his early ecumenical involvement which had posited
an almost unbridgeable gulf between the theologies of the continental legatees of the Reformation and their Western liberal Protestant

counterparts.[54] Despite all the marked differences and disagreements across the Atlantic divide, this 1939 essay concludes: "The decisive task today is the conversation between the Protestantism without Reformation and the churches of the Reformation."[55] For all their singularities, these respective groupings are bound together in a mutual obligation to the truth. It is one *oikoumene* in which they are set and to which they have a common witness.

Bonhoeffer was not, therefore, turning his back on America in distaste. Indeed, he was at pains to complete the essay *after* his return to Germany in late July. He could have had every reason to drop it amid all the preoccupations that now weighed on him as he took up his work again and as the crisis of war rolled in. That he did not do so testifies to how real was his sense of the wider *oikoumene* to which he belonged, and of the continuing importance of the ecumenical church within it.

Bonhoeffer was back in Berlin on 27 July. From now on, his context was to be determined by war—imminent, then actual, then increasingly destructive, and finally genocidal. On 23 August came the potent warning of the signing of the Non-Aggression Treaty between Germany and the Soviet Union. On 1 September Germany invaded Poland, and two days later Britain and France declared war on Germany. The German onslaught on Poland was massive, effective, and completed by early October. It included the first mass killings of Jews as well as a virtually genocidal policy against all Poland with the elimination of leading sections of Polish society, and the incorporation of conquered Polish land into the Reich. Meanwhile, in the West life remained relatively quiet until April 1940, when Hitler invaded Denmark and Norway, followed in May by the *Blitzkrieg* strikes against Belgium, Holland, Luxembourg, and France, culminating in the British evacuation from Dunkirk and the fall of France in mid-June. After formally accepting the French surrender at Compiègne near Paris, Hitler the all-conquering leader was greeted back in Berlin by huge and ecstatic crowds, marking the apogee of his popularity. Soon after, the daylight air attacks on Britain began as a preliminary to invasion, but in face of strong resistance by the Royal Air Force these largely ended by early autumn and were replaced by nighttime bombing, by which time Hitler was in any case starting to contemplate a much bigger and eastward undertaking—against the Soviet Union.

For the ecumenical movement, as was noted in the previous chapter, apart from an overall rejection of nationalistic feeling (in marked contrast to 1914) the approach of war had not resulted in a real consensus among the churches. From the onset of hostilities, divergences grew still wider even among the churches of the allied and neutral countries. During the early months of the war Visser't Hooft was growingly troubled by an apparent moral relativism in British, French, and Dutch circles: "There was such a fear of national self-righteousness and such a sense of the failure of all nations that very many refused to make up their minds about the basic issues of this war."[56] He laid some of the blame for this on the ecumenical movement itself and on the ambiguity of some of its achievements: "We had placed such an emphasis on the duty for the church to remain the truly ecumenical church that there was a danger that the church would be looked upon as a haven of refuge above the world and not give guidance to its members for their decisions in this world."[57] The basic divide lay between those who considered a negotiated peace with Nazi Germany as still the best option, and those who believed the removal of the Nazi regime to be the prerequisite of a credible peace. The Scandinavian churches remained the most committed to mediation. Alongside the meeting of the WCC Administrative Committee in Apeldoorn, Netherlands, in January 1940, Bishop Berggrav of Oslo brought a group from the Scandinavian churches who requested ecumenical consideration of the proposals he had already shared with church and political figures in London and Berlin. William Temple and the four British participants at Apeldoorn produced a statement on the conditions for peace. It stated the need for guaranteed sovereignty for the Czech, Slovak, and Polish peoples and for a definitive peace to be negotiated at a European congress including these peoples.[58] It was not intended for publication but gradually leaked out to the press in a number of countries. It had no effect whatsoever. The Administrative Committee itself tried to address the issues of the war, but the Scandinavian initiative had effectively stymied any further ecumenical action—the Scandinavians were reluctant to conceive any move without German involvement. Visser't Hooft wanted a clear protest, at least, against such violations of humanity and freedom as were taking place. Marc Boegner of France and Alfons Koechlin of Switzerland supported him, but even such a word would be tantamount, in the view of others, to aggravating the present conflict even further.[59] William Temple proposed another statement of basic moral principles, but Boegner and Koechlin felt that at such a critical moment such generalities would be worse than silence. The outcome, frustrating to all, was just one surviving paragraph of Temple's statement.

Visser't Hooft did not give up his efforts to induce the ecumenical movement to utter a clear word of guidance, and in April wrote a long discussion paper on "The Ecumenical Church and the International Situation," which he circulated to a wide circle of colleagues. There was appreciation but also criticism, and of the latter none was more decisive than William Temple's. Evidently chastened by the experience at Apeldoorn in January, Temple now regarded any collective ecumenical voice as an unreal possibility. There was "a plethora of counsels" among the churches but no consensus, and on a practical level the ecumenical movement itself did not at present exist in a form that could speak together. Instead: "I want us all to prophesy individually, and to do this in contact with one another through your office, so the same message will be given ecumenically with a variety of emphasis."[60] While Temple was writing (20 May), his words were given brutal weight as Hitler's forces—already occupying Denmark and Norway—stormed across Holland and Belgium and into France. North of the Alps, apart from Switzerland and Sweden, little was left of neutral Europe. War had torn through the very fabric of travel, communications, and meetings on which ecumenical life had largely been woven since 1918. Plans for an inaugural WCC assembly in 1941 had, of course, to be abandoned. Following Apeldoorn, even the WCC Administrative Committee could not meet again until January 1946. Visser't Hooft later commented: "The provisional structure of the Council, which had not yet been authorised by the Churches, seemed altogether too shaky to stand the strain. It appeared for a time as though hardly any contacts could be maintained with the Churches."[61] Temple had actually pointed to the way in which, remarkably, the ecumenical movement was to continue and in certain respects deepen during the next six years. It did so largely through personal, and necessarily often surreptitious, contacts for which the Geneva office was the vital nexus.

Ecumenism, its organizational expression now virtually paralyzed for the time being, was to discover in unexpected ways its innermost nature as mutuality and community. It was in this new scenario, devoid of so much infrastructure, that Dietrich Bonhoeffer and the ecumenical movement were also to rediscover each other.

In a Germany at War: Entry into the Resistance

Bonhoeffer's return from the USA in late July 1939 for a time—even after the outbreak of war—saw not any marked disruption but a steady continuation of his previous activities with the collective pastorates in the countryside of Further Pomerania. A stream, albeit reduced, of ordinands still came for training. Bonhoeffer carried out inspections of parishes for the Confessing Church. Restrictions grew, however. In March 1940 the collective pastorates' work was closed on orders from the Gestapo. From September he was forbidden to speak in public and had to report regularly to the police. Even his inspectorate work was now forbidden. It was in this situation that the Old Prussian Council of Brethren agreed to second him for specialized theological work, which in effect meant that in one or more suitably quiet environments he could now concentrate on the long-awaited task of writing his *Ethics*.

There was, however, always still the looming threat of his military call-up. The way through this dilemma was not, as in the previous year, to be sought through migration out of Germany but, strangely, through entry into one of the central instruments of the German war machine, the *Abwehr* (Military Intelligence), within which lay camouflaged a main centre of the resistance to Hitler. The official role of the *Abwehr* was to gather from countries abroad, whether enemy or neutral, information pertinent to German military strategy and operational planning, as well as espionage, to carry out acts of sabotage.

No less, for some years it had also harboured dissidents against the Nazi regime. From 1935 its head was Admiral Wilhelm Canaris, a career naval officer of conservative political disposition who had become disillusioned with the Nazis and repelled by the depravity of the regime. His chief of staff was Colonel (from December 1941, Major-General) Hans Oster. In the *Abwehr* it was Oster who was the main driving force in resistance matters, while Canaris was protective rather than proactive. Almost on the eve of war, in late August 1939, Oster recruited as his special deputy Hans von Dohnanyi, husband of Dietrich Bonhoeffer's older sister Christine. A lawyer by training, Dohnanyi had worked in the Ministry of Justice from before the time of the Nazi regime. Continuing there after Hitler came to power, he was privy to much that was happening in the new order and compiled a "chronicle of shame," a catalogue of Nazi crimes that would provide clear moral grounds for action against the regime. Under Oster a key role of Dohnanyi would be the recruiting of agents ostensibly for official *Abwehr* work but, in actuality, by sympathy and background, highly suitable for resistance purposes.

Dietrich Bonhoeffer enjoyed good relations with his brother-in-law. From well before the war Dohnanyi had several times in conversation shared with him highly confidential information on what was going on both in the higher reaches of the regime, and in military and civilian dissident circles. There is no doubt that Bonhoeffer was both well informed about, and sympathetic to, the political opposition. It was not until August 1940, however, that Dohnanyi in his relation to Bonhoeffer moved from being confidential informant to recruiting agent for the active resistance. That month, Dohnanyi and Oster discussed with Bonhoeffer the possibility of his serving as an unpaid agent of the *Abwehr*, ostensibly for intelligence-gathering purposes, but in fact acting as an emissary of the resistance to circles abroad. The fact that *Abwehr* service would qualify him for military exemption brought mutual advantage. The anomaly of a pastor, and moreover one known to be out of favour with the regime, being asked to work in a department of the Military Intelligence Office of the Armed Forces High Command, would be dealt with by pointing out that in the very nature of its work, especially at a time of national crisis, the *Abwehr* had to draw on the services of persons of all kinds of backgrounds and opinions. Bonhoeffer, with his wealth of contacts abroad thanks to a near-decade of international ecumenical activity, fitted admirably the *Abwehr* agent profile.

CHAPTER 9

In Ecumenical Conspiracy: 1939–1943

The two-and-a-half years from Bonhoeffer's entry into active political resistance in the autumn of 1940 to his arrest in April 1943 form a period which, though relatively short, is one of the most intensely studied and discussed periods of his whole life and is still the subject of ongoing research. This reflects the complexity and controversial nature of much of his activity, which in turn is reflected in this chapter being the longest in this whole work. Not that his activities will be more than sketched here. Our main object is to highlight how Bonhoeffer's decisions and involvements were related to a certain developing *ecumenical* consciousness, understanding, and commitment on his part. Amid the heroic excitements of the conspiracy and the ethical challenges it posed, this dimension is liable to be overlooked if Bonhoeffer's acquired ecumenical experience is regarded only as background to his role in the conspiracy or significant merely as a useful tool in its service. It certainly was such, but it was also more, in these drastically changed circumstances of war and resistance. By the time of his arrest Bonhoeffer had become even more of an ecumenist—and, in more than one sense, a conspiratorial one.

Bonhoeffer and the Changing Ecumenical Scene

At this point, some further observations must be made about Bonhoeffer's relationship to the ecumenical movement and his entry into the political resistance. First, we have seen how Bonhoeffer had already distanced himself from the ecumenical peace initiatives immediately prior to the outbreak of hostilities and during the first months of the war. This was in part because much of the contact between the ecumenical figures abroad and Germany was now increasingly reliant upon the Reich Church Foreign Office, and Bishop Theodor Heckel in particular, lending greater weight also to Hans Schönfeld—already somewhat compromised in Bonhoeffer's eyes—in Geneva. During 8–15 July 1940 both Schönfeld and Nils Ehrenström from Geneva were in Berlin, but Bonhoeffer was away speaking at gatherings of pastors and attending Council of Brethren meetings in the regions of Königsberg and Stettin. But there was a more fundamental reason for this apparent indifference on Bonhoeffer's part. As Eberhard Bethge comments: "Of course, ecumenical conferences and synods had to advocate peace at all costs before the war broke out in full fury in May 1940. Bonhoeffer, however, had already taken his stand on the one condition for peace that could not be discussed in any church body inside Germany—the removal of Hitler."[1]

Second, Bonhoeffer's value to the active resistance movement (and also his ostensible qualification for official *Abwehr* service) certainly lay in his contacts abroad which he had gained through his ecumenical involvement. It is therefore tempting to view Bonhoeffer's ecumenical experience and commitment as now simply proving of practical utility to the resistance and conspiracy. Having trusted and well-placed friends in Geneva, London, Stockholm, Oslo, and elsewhere, he could be a most effective courier. The Bonhoeffer narrative then, however, too easily becomes read as one of a journeying away from specifically church-related commitments, whether of the Confessing Church or of the ecumenical movement and its organizations, to a largely secular political engagement. This can then be easily viewed as the contextual preparation for what Bonhoeffer was to write of in prison as "religionless Christianity." This, however, is not only a gross oversimplification of Bonhoeffer's thought processes; it is based on a quite erroneous assumption that, in entering the political conspiracy, Bonhoeffer was leaving behind the substance of ecumenism and concern for Christian unity, in favour of merely exploiting the advantageous contacts ecumenical life had given him. In truth, far from divorcing him from his earlier ecumenical concern, the entry into political resistance brought Bonhoeffer into a reengagement with ecumenism and to new expressions of it at several levels. To understand this fully, some account must now be given of the overall nature of the German resistance itself.

The Nature of the German Resistance

The "German resistance" was not a single organization or movement but comprised several distinct groups and circles, of which the opposition group within the *Abwehr* was just one, albeit of central importance. [2] The *Abwehr*-related group was crucial in that, under Hans Oster and more specifically through Hans von Dohnanyi's desk, much of the coordination between the civilian and military wings of the resistance was effected. On the strategic political level, the most senior military and civilian opposition circle was that led by General Ludwig Beck, chief of the Army General Staff from 1935 to 1938,[3] and Carl Friedrich Goerdeler, lawyer, government official, and former mayor of Leipzig. There was a tacit understanding in resistance circles that, in the event of a successful *Putsch*, Beck would be the new head of state and Goederler the chancellor. The Beck-Goerdeler group included other senior governmental figures such as the foreign policy expert Ulrich von Hassell, diplomat and ambassador to Rome from 1932 to 1938 and a member of the Central European Economic Council. Next, within the very establishment of government itself, specifically the Foreign Ministry (*Auswärtiges Amt*), there was an active group of mainly younger officials and career diplomats bitterly opposed to Nazism, and not only on account of Hitler's contemptuous attitude toward the traditional diplomatic approach to international affairs.

Here the senior figure was Ernst Freiherr von Weizsäcker, State Secretary of the Foreign Ministry from 1938. In a way parallel to Wilhelm Canaris's role in the *Abwehr*, Weizsäcker (who also had a naval background) acted as a cautious, protective father figure to his younger and more actively engaged staff, and furthermore contrived to place some of them in significant posts abroad. His assistants included names later to be made illustrious by the resistance, and tragically by their fate, such as Hans-Bernd von Haeften and Adam von Trott.

Whether in the army, the *Abwehr*, or the Foreign Ministry, Hitler's opponents had to operate clandestinely as small networks of friends, *Freundeskreise*, invisible to those not of the circle. There were, however, also *Freundeskreise* not located within any institution but free standing and drawn together by shared interests and convictions. Notable here was the group that coalesced around Count Helmut James von Moltke, the "Kreisau Circle," so-named after his estate in Silesia where the group sometimes gathered.[4] Moltke, great-grandnephew of one of Prussia's most celebrated 19th-century generals of the same name, was a jurist adviser to the Armed Forces High Command on questions of international law. The circle comprised intellectuals of varying political outlook including socialists and, rather than action oriented, was mainly occupied with thinking out an order for a post-Nazi Germany and a new Europe. Its ethos was a remarkable blend of aristocratic bearing (Count Paul Yorck von Wartenburg, another Silesian landowner, was a member) and free-thinking mentality. Some members such as von Trott and von Haeften belonged also to other circles of resistance, and even for a time Hans Schönfeld of Geneva attended. Other groups not dissimilar to the Kreisau Circle included the "Freiburg Group" of academics from the Albert-Ludwig University, which formed after *Kristallnacht* in 1938, and which had close ties with the Confessing Church,[5] and the "Stuttgart Circle," which formed around the industrialist Robert Bosch. Then there were left-wing groups of much more decidedly political affiliation such as the *Rote Kapelle* ("Red Orchestra"), which existed as cells within the German army on the eastern front and were suspected of being largely supported and used by the Russians for Soviet military and political purposes. Finally, there were small-scale actions such as the "Beer

Cellar" attempt on Hitler's life by Johann Georg Elser in Munich in November 1939, and the outstandingly courageous White Rose leaflet protest movement by students in Munich in 1942–43.

Bonhoeffer, in joining the *Abwehr* operation, was thus taking on a comparatively small role within one organization which was a key part of a much wider and variegated resistance movement throughout Germany. Politically, the resistance embraced a wide spectrum, from monarchists (like Beck and Goerdeler) to liberals and socialists. Equally, while the resistance included figures whose motivation was ambiguous and whose attitudes reflected elements of National Socialism, there were many, whether in the *Abwehr*, the army itself, the foreign Ministry, the Kreisau Circle, or similar groups, who were strongly imbued with Christian conviction and ethical values, both Protestant and Catholic. Goerdeler was devoutly Protestant. Adam von Trott sat loose to the institutional church but identified himself as Christian and believed passionately in the Christian ethic. Hans-Bernd von Haeften was a highly theologically aware Protestant layperson who had been close to Bonhoeffer since they attended school together in Berlin and were confirmed as teenagers. Moltke, shaken by the turmoil under Hitler, had turned from Christian Science to firm Protestant belief during the 1930s. Yorck von Wartenburg, on active military service from 1939 to 1941 until seriously wounded on the eastern front, was a lay member of the Silesian Confessing Synod and of the Old Prussian Council of Brethren. Bonhoeffer's closest associate in the Munich office of the *Abwehr* was the Roman Catholic lawyer Josef Müller, legal adviser and attorney for Catholic institutions. What made Bonhoeffer almost unique as an active member of the resistance was that he was an ordained Protestant minister. In joining the resistance he was, in the circles with which he was most immediately involved, joining what in effect was a lay ecumenical venture.

To describe the German resistance as "ecumenical" may be thought hyberbolic, since, while the leading figures were indeed marked by a common Christianity, they were not actively and essentially related to one another on that basis but, rather, on their shared overall political objectives. Such a view, however, not only downplays the role that common Christian values played in creating the mutual trust that underlay the dangerous, underground discussions of those political objectives. It also ignores a crucial dimension to the resistance whereby conscious Christian commitment, interchurch relations, and specific ecumenical bodies played a vital role: *international* links were essential to the main German resistance, for the fundamental reason that an overthrow of Hitler would not only need to be carried out within Germany itself but, to be successful, would require recognition by the allied governments that a credible non-Nazi government had been brought into being, with which a negotiated peace would be possible.[6] Allied encouragement before, and recognition and support following, the coup would therefore be vital. As Klemens von Klemperer, the leading historian of this aspect of the resistance, points out, of all the resistance movements in Nazi-dominated Europe, the German *Widerstand*, unlike those of for example occupied France, the Netherlands, Denmark, and Norway, had no foreign government-in-exile from which it could assume moral and material support. It was dependent on *winning* sympathy—from the erstwhile enemies of Germany.[7] Moreover, this necessarily outward-looking feature of the German resistance went beyond merely tactical considerations: "The *Widerstand* . . . in its particular predicament of witnessing its own nation degraded at home, and having to turn against its own government, had reason to detect in the war the dimension of a 'world civil war' in which it could make common cause and discuss 'common plans' with the powers fighting its own country."[8] This meant arguing common cause with the Allies on the basis of the fundamental human values of freedom, justice, and dignity, in which all of the churches represented in the ecumenical movement (and especially, for example, at the 1937 Oxford Conference) had a deep investment. Klemperer may be slightly guilty of overstatement but he expresses well a wider and longer historical significance of the resistance: "Transcending as it did, national interest in the realm of human rights, the foreign policy of the resistance may stand as a model for the human-rights policy which has evolved since the Second World War in a world still plagued by dictatorships."[9]

Before the war, elements in the German opposition such as the Beck-Goerdeler group had already been in contact with the British

Foreign Office and with other European capitals. With the onset of war such contacts could only be very indirect, and via neutral governments or consulates and other significant institutions in neutral countries. Of major significance was the Vatican.[10] Pope Pius XII and Germany were well known to each other, he having been papal nuncio in Berlin from 1920 to 1929, and then cardinal state secretary from 1930 to 1939, during which time the concordat between the Vatican and the Nazi regime was signed. With the pope's approval, during the first six months of the war the *Abwehr* circle, using Joseph Müller as mediator, conducted clandestine discussions with British diplomatic representatives at the Vatican on a possible peace settlement. On both sides there were hopes of a positive outcome, but at the end there was confusion on the exact terms of the agreement that had supposedly been reached, and the launch of Hitler's major western offensive in April 1940 was the final blow.[11] The Vatican nevertheless continued to be an important point of contact throughout the war. In the opposite direction lay neutral Sweden, alone of the Nordic countries to remain unoccupied for the war. Following the tradition begun by Nathan Söderblom, founder of the Life and Work movement who died in 1931, the (Lutheran) Church of Sweden remained in the forefront of ecumenical life thanks to leaders like Erling Eidem, bishop of Uppsala from 1931 to 1950, and Manfred Björkquist, director of the famous educational Sigtuna Foundation and bishop of Stockholm from 1942. As a state church it had ready access to diplomatic channels, and this added to its importance for the German resistance, although there was caution on the Swedish side lest its political neutrality be seen to be violated.

For the resistance, however, the most important neutral territory lay immediately adjacent: Switzerland. In the first place, there was no lack of foreign consulates there, of both belligerent and neutral countries, including, of course, Germany itself. The opposition in the Foreign Ministry in Berlin used its opportunities to plant a number of its own circle as eyes and ears in its Swiss outposts. Closest to Ernst von Weizsäcker in the Berlin Foreign Ministry was Erich Kordt, a Roman Catholic from the Rhineland who acted as liaison with other resistance groups and especially worked at establishing outposts abroad to facilitate contacts with foreign governments. Soon after the outbreak of war he dispatched his brother Theo (who had worked at the London embassy) to Berne, ostensibly to safeguard German interests on humanitarian matters such as the treatment of prisoners of war (Switzerland was a protective neutral power), but actually to act as an intermediary for the German opposition and to reestablish ties with the British Foreign Office emissary there, T. Philip Crowell-Evans.[12] The significance of Berne was further heightened by the presence there of the legation of the USA and especially, after the USA entered the war, by the arrival there of the diplomat Allen Dulles who served as director of the Office of Strategic Services (OSS) in Switzerland. Dulles, who knew well both Germany and Austria from before the war, oversaw a major intelligence-gathering operation on Germany and Nazi-dominated Europe. It is now clear that Dulles received a steady stream of information both from and about the German resistance and reported regularly on it to Washington.[13]

But along with Berne there was Geneva, in international terms of equal importance to the capital of the Swiss Federation on account of the major organizations that had been located there since the end of the 1914–18 war. By 1939, the League of Nations was largely defunct, and one of its main children, the International Labour Organization, was transferred from Geneva to Canada in 1940, but there was still a significant concentration of diplomatic missions there, together with international bodies such as the International Committee of the Red Cross (ICRC). There was, moreover, the headquarters of the World Council of Churches "in formation" and associated international Christian organizations such as the YMCA and World Student Christian Federation. Still in its infancy, at the same time the WCC was already shouldering a huge burden of care for refugees, prisoners of war, and other victims of the conflict, and by its very nature and purpose had a wide range of contacts with churches in many countries. It was, more than anything else, the presence of the WCC which made Geneva, of all places in Switzerland, especially important to the German resistance. Crucial here was the personal role played by its general secretary W. A. Visser't Hooft. Not only was he a stalwart champion of the cause of the Confessing Church, but his increasing dissatisfaction with what he saw as the overly neutralist stance to the conflict taken in the early months of the war by many of the Western churches soon became vindicated. After Hitler's military triumphs in the West, the case for such neutralism largely vanished, as France, Belgium, Holland, Denmark, and Norway and their churches felt the full and brutal weight of occupation, and as Britain for a time stood under threat of invasion and then experienced months of bombing. Even Sweden, while militarily neutral, was left in no doubt about what was at stake for Europe as a whole. As a Dutchman, Visser't Hooft in the first place felt the pain of his own country's plight, and on behalf of the Dutch resistance turned to good account the privileged place of his office in a neutral country. His memoirs give what is probably an understated account of his role in setting up the "Swiss Road," whereby he was able to facilitate contacts between the underground in the Netherlands and the Dutch government in exile in London, on one occasion in 1941 actually being able to travel to London via unoccupied France and Lisbon.[14] But there were wider contacts with resistance movements. These especially included Germany, and here some of the initiative came from within Germany itself. Ernst von Weizsäcker in the Foreign Ministry not only placed Theo Kordt in the Berne consulate. Being aware that the Gestapo also had agents in Switzerland (it probably tried to infiltrate even the WCC), in January 1940 he worked out a secret ordinance with the Genevan consul-general to facilitate travel to Germany by WCC staff without Nazi Party interference, and likewise to forward ecumenical reports to Germany and later also to occupied countries. In May 1940 Weizsäcker managed to get another young and highly active member of the diplomatic opposition circle, Gottfried von Nostiz, appointed as consul in Geneva and yet another, Albrecht von Kessel, posted there in 1941. Klemperer comments on these two:

> Highly educated, sensitive, and idealistic, they fed on a common sense of mission for which their Swiss assignment promised to offer the proper outlet. And if they did not see themselves exactly as proponents of "democracy," their mission, as Kessel put it, was that of "an era of European cooperation" and of "social justice." . . . As

attested by William A. Visser't Hooft, . . . their primary concern was the establishment and maintenance of connections with his organization and against determined opposition from the Nazi Party and the Gestapo, to enable it to pursue its task of caring for prisoners of war and internees and to maintain contact with the Churches in Germany as well as in the occupied countries. At the same time they formed a link with the so-called "Swiss Road" which Visser't Hooft, residing in Geneva, had carefully devised in order to reach the Dutch Resistance Movement.[15]

The WCC became, therefore, a vital nerve centre for the international dimension of the German resistance and its links with the outside world. Members of the resistance who could travel to Switzerland on diplomatic passes had ready access to its staff. Adam von Trott visited several times. Hans Bernd Gisevius and Eugen Gerstenmaier also appeared and, in due course, Dietrich Bomhoeffer. In turn, Hans Schönfeld was able to travel into Germany, his travel facilities also being helped by his continuing connection with Theodor Heckel in the Reich Church Foreign Office. If that was a source of concern to Visser't Hooft and others who regarded Heckel with deep suspicion, and Schönfeld himself with some uncertainty due to his less than forthright support for the Confessing Church, this had to be set against Schönfeld's undeniably useful range of German contacts, including members of the Kreisau Circle. The same applied to Gerstenmaier who had been one of Heckel's officials but became a member of the Kreisau Circle. Under the unprecedented pressures of facing wartime tyranny, the lines of alliance were shifting somewhat. But as well as specific events, visits, plans, and discussions that took place in Geneva, a most vital element in the whole picture of resistance was the reception and transmission of information about what was happening in Germany and the occupied lands, which made the need for resistance and an overthrow of the Nazi regime—if not actual military defeat for Hitler—a moral necessity. The historian Victoria Barnett comments: "It is clear from the archives in Geneva that ecumenical leaders were receiving detailed information from the onset of the war—including information that could only have come from

German military and intelligence sources—and that the significance of this information was clear to them. Conclusive documentation of the [Jewish] genocide didn't come till 1942, but they interpreted the ominous early signs accurately."[16] The information was coming from a variety of church and other sources, including Gerhart Riegner at the World Jewish Council in Geneva, who was in close and almost daily touch with Adolf Freudenberg, secretary for refugee relief work in the WCC. Barnett suggests that much of the information came from Hans von Dohnanyi's desk in the *Abwehr* and his wider network of contacts.

In actively entering the conspiracy as an *Abwehr* agent, Bonhoeffer was therefore becoming part of a wide movement both in Germany and internationally, with strong (though not exclusively) Christian and church impulses and in which the ecumenical centre in Geneva was a vital nexus of communication. Seeing it as such may appear to reduce Bonhoeffer's status in the resistance. He was indeed neither an originator nor a leader of it; his role was as a modest bit player. Or rather, in terms of the actual conspiracy, his role was very specific: at the request of senior figures in the *Abwehr*, to act on particular occasions as an intermediary with church and ecumenical contacts abroad. In terms of commitment, however, he invested as much of himself as any other conspirator, with all the risks incurred in what was in legal terms treason against his country's leadership, and with that, the willingness to pay the ultimate price. Even this, however, does not exhaust what the community of resistance meant to Bonhoeffer. Having joined the movement, he became almost by default a pastoral and ethical theologian to it. Eberhard Bethge recalls:

> I remember an evening in Sakrow, where the Dohnanyi family lived, early in the war. We were just sitting together at the fireside, and Hans von Dohnanyi, who had certain elements of piety even then, asked Dietrich, "What about Jesus' saying, "Whoever takes up the sword will perish by the sword"? What about us—we are taking up the sword." And Dietrich answered, "Yes, that's true. And Jesus' word about whoever takes up the sword will die by the sword is valid. It's still valid for us now. The time needs exactly those people

who do that, and let Jesus' saying be true. We take the sword and are prepared to perish by it. So, of course, taking up guilt means accepting the consequences of it. Maybe God will save us but first of all you must be prepared to accept the consequences." He meant of course it needs exactly those people who accept Jesus' word—the truth of it and so the consequences of it, of perishing. That Germany needs at this moment of its history these kinds of Christians, and that is what being Christian means.[17]

This was exactly the kind of issue with which he was dealing at that very time in the writing of his *Ethics*. But we can go further. In identifying so completely with the resistance to the extent of putting his ecumenical contacts at its service he was, in effect, claiming the international community of resistance as part of the ecumenical movement and, indeed, in itself a form of ecumenism. This meant that as an agent of the conspiracy he was also habitually building new ecumenical relationships and working on new ecumenical understanding, whether directly related to the resistance or not. He had put his ecumenical connections at the service of the resistance, and in turn the resistance enabled him to develop his ecumenical activity which took on a new and invigorated life in the years 1940 through 1943. This becomes clear as we examine how he operated both on his specific *Abwehr* missions abroad, and in his continual relationships with conspiratorial colleagues. These missions during 1941 and 1942 comprised three visits to Switzerland, one to Norway, one to Sweden, and, finally, one to Italy.

The Three Swiss Visits

Bonhoeffer's three visits to Switzerland on behalf of Hans Oster and Hans von Dohnanyi in the *Abwehr* circle are fully narrated and documented elsewhere.[18] This account therefore simply highlights how, as well as conveying information to his ecumenical contacts about the state of the resistance and other conditions inside Germany, and inquiring what possibilities of negotiation there might arise with allied governments, Bonhoeffer used every opportunity to restore and develop ecumenical links between the churches. His first visit to Switzerland was from 24 February to 24 March 1941. In addition to his main goal of visiting Geneva and the WCC, he spent time with his significant former acquaintances Karl Barth and Alphons Koechlin in Basel, Erwin Sutz in Rapperswil near Zurich, and the exiled Friedrich Siegmund-Schultze. These visits and lengthy conversations constituted a reestablishing of ecumenical relations at the most personal level of friendship. His hosts were as eager to hear as he was to share his firsthand accounts of the situation of the Confessing Church and the political scene at large in Germany. Naturally, he did not disclose to them the full nature of what he was now involved in. Barth, it has to be said, was somewhat puzzled and dubious about Bonhoeffer's evident willingness to journey abroad on a pass validated by the Gestapo. He was able to write to both George Bell and to the Leibholz family in England. In Geneva, as well as Visser't Hooft, he met with Nils Ehrenström and with Adolf Freudenberg at the WCC refugee desk, from whom he sought information on internees at the Gurs refugee camp in southern France, in particular his friend Herbert Jehle. Another important contact in Geneva was Jacques Courvoisier, professor of church history and chair of the WCC ecumenical relief organization for prisoners of war. For an insight into all that was on Bonhoeffer's mind during this visit, Courvoisier's account of a morning's discussion with him and Visser't Hooft is revealing:

> We talked about the life of the churches in the world, of the ecumenical reality which was taking shape right across the different events of the time, of the policy the Church was best advised to follow in these circumstances; we also touched upon politics and even strategy, for one just could not ignore that, and Bonhoeffer impressed us as being extremely well informed concerning these problems, which, some people think, have nothing to do with the message of the Church. At the end of our conversation Bonhoeffer declared that everything we had dealt with was certainly very interesting, but he would prefer to discuss more important and more basic matters. He asked if in the afternoon we might not meet with

some theologians in order 'to theologize seriously'. This was done, and in the afternoon we spent several hours at the lake-side with some Geneva pastors and discussed baptism. I do not remember what we said . . . but I do remember this man who was involved in the struggle of the Church and in the political struggle at the risk of his life, for whom the essential thing, even under the most threatening circumstances, remained what Karl Barth some years before had called theological existence, and for whom the meaning of political engagement was given in theological engagement.[19]

Ehrenström also records meetings that included H. L. Henriod, with whom Bonhoeffer had collaborated in the World Alliance and the Ecumenical Youth Commission until their dispute in 1937,[20] and with Charles Guillon, French ecumenist and leader in the YMCA central office in Geneva. Guillon was able to use his double residence to travel frequently into France and maintain contact with groups such as CIMADE (*Comité Inter-Mouvement auprès des Èvacués*) which worked with internment camps in the south of France and was increasingly involved with resistance networks helping Jews and other victims of Nazism escape into Switzerland. Ehrenström notes on 8 March an evening meeting and supper in his home with Visser't Hooft, Bonhoeffer, Henriod, and Guillon: "the situation in France and Switzerland; W. Alliance; peace aims."[21] It was evidently at this or a meeting earlier that day that, according to Guillon, in a remark he made a week later to the French Protestant leader and ecumenist Marc Boegner, that Guillon was told by Bonhoeffer, "our churches are for the collaboration and have thus betrayed the cause."[22] It is intriguing to speculate whether by "our churches" Guillon was indicating the French churches; or whether this was Bonhoeffer referring to his own German churches, or the churches in belligerent Europe as a whole. It is also clear from Ehrenström's notes that he and Bonhoeffer discussed Roman Catholic–Protestant problems.

Visser't Hooft noted in Bonhoeffer a hunger for the kind of ecumenical theological existence denied him since his return from America and the onset of war. As well as with these meetings and conversations, that hunger was agreeably met to some extent by reading, in the WCC library, the ecumenical and church literature published in Britain and America since the start of the war but denied entry to Germany. It was, however, with Visser't Hooft himself that the primary purpose of his mission was fulfilled. During his week in Geneva Bonhoeffer gave him a full picture of life in Germany, including the ever-increasing pressure upon the Confessing Church, differing attitudes within the church to the state and the war, further arrests of pastors, the Nazi euthanasia programmes—and the reality of an underground yet determined opposition. Bonhoeffer was not the only visitor to arrive in wartime Geneva on behalf of the resistance, but as someone of unimpeachable integrity in ecumenical circles his was a vital corroborative report. Visser't Hooft wrote a full account which he sent to George Bell via Bill Paton in London.[23] He also sent to Bell and William Temple a longer document arising out of discussions with Bonhoeffer, Nils Ehrenström, and the Scotsman Denzil Kirkpatrick on the conditions for peace, and enquired of Temple what for Britain would be the minimum conditions of peace if Germany changed its regime.[24] The basic question was whether the allied powers would ever be convinced about the reality of the German opposition or would be prepared to take it on trust. Trust was something that perhaps only the ecumenical community could foster.

Bonhoeffer's second Swiss visit took place six months later, 29 August through 26 September 1941. By now German forces were invading deep into Russia. The Lend-Lease Act, by which the USA was giving material aid to Britain, was in operation, and the Atlantic Charter stating the postwar aims of the USA and the Allies had just been signed. The question of "peace aims" was becoming more critical—especially for the German resistance. In Geneva, Bonhoeffer was presented by Visser't Hooft with recent books of major importance by British Christians on the major issues of the war and a just postwar settlement. The first was George Bell's *Christianity and World Order* (1940), in which Bonhoeffer's closest English friend reiterated his demand that a distinction be made between "Germany" and "National Socialism," and that efforts should be made via neutral channels to discover "what terms of peace would be likely to create a lasting peace and not lead to a further poisoning of international relationships."[25]

Bonhoeffer read this gratefully and responded warmly to Bell by letter from Switzerland: "The certainty of our ecumenical fellowship is growing and is a great comfort and encouragement. I have had the great pleasure and satisfaction to read your newest book and I am sharing your hope for a strong stand of the churches after the war."[26]

The second book was William Paton's *The Church and the New Order* (1941).[27] Paton, as well as being as J. H. Oldham's successor as secretary of the International Missionary Council, and associate secretary of the WCC in London, was also leader of the London-based Peace Aims Group that had been formed by the WCC and the World Alliance before the outbreak of war, and which was seeking to maintain communication with opposition circles in Germany, especially via Geneva. Paton's book was but one manifestation of the intense interest in and debate on peace aims taking place in British church circles just then. Other expressions were the positive response by British church leaders of all main denominations to the five Peace Points issued by Pope Pius XII in December 1940; the Malvern Conference in January chaired by William Temple; and J. H. Oldham's weekly *Christian Newsletter* and its associated series of books.[28] Bonhoeffer in Geneva was immensely encouraged in reading all such material, which revealed a British approach to the war and a postwar world rather different from that conveyed by either Germany's propaganda machine or the British government's own public voice as heard on the BBC Overseas Service.

Paton's book, however, demanded special attention because it proposed in some detail what an acceptable postwar Germany and Europe should look like, and so Bonhoeffer set out his response in a paper which he wrote with Visser't Hooft.[29] Immensely grateful for Paton's perception of the difficulties that would face a reconstruction of Germany in every sense, and also for Paton's appreciation of the value of the Confessing Church and its potential role in rebuilding relations after the war, he nevertheless warned that a non-Nazi government would need "to get such terms of peace that it has some chance to survive"[30] and not be discredited in the eyes of its own people. This would need to be known in advance by the opposition. Furthermore, Bonhoeffer argued that Paton was displaying too many Anglo-Saxon assumptions about the evident and immediate desirability of human "rights and liberties" in face of the omnipotent state, in a situation (as in Nazi Germany) "where *all* order has been destroyed." Questions of legitimate *authority* will need to be faced, if the mistakes of "liberalism" are not to be repeated. Bonhoeffer was engaging in a remarkable kind of ecumenical encounter with his British counterparts, at once open, generous, and yet not uncritical. This exchange should be seen as consistent with the line he had pursued in his 1935 paper "The Confessing Church and the Ecumenical Movement"[31] and his 1939 essay on American Christianity, "Protestantism Without Reformation."[32] It was a further manifestation of his belief that the churches of the world *needed* each other for their own self-understanding and theological renewal as they took up their common tasks in the world.

It was in this spirit that he had left Germany on this Swiss visit, as he wrote to Eberhard Bethge for his birthday, reminiscing about journeys they had undertaken together, "of horizons we discovered together in connection with these trips, of European hopes and tasks, of the mission of the church in the future—and all of this in the hope that you and I and many, many others who are of the same mind, that all of us may one day work together toward this future."[33] Among those "many, many others" were his British ecumenical friends and contacts with whom his inquiries and thoughts on a negotiated peace and postwar settlement were communicated by Visser't Hooft from Geneva. In Switzerland they included, as well as Visser't Hooft himself, Karl Barth, Friedrich Siegmund-Schultze, and Erwin Sutz, each of whom he visited again on this visit, and Adolf Freudenberg in whose house on Lake Champaix he stayed for a time. It was evidently during a meeting in Freudenberg's home in Geneva that, so Visser't Hooft recalls, Bonhoeffer was asked what he prayed for in the present situation, to which he replied, "The defeat of my country, for I believe that this is the only way in which it can pay for the suffering which it has caused in the world."[34] Freudenberg himself remarks: "As a matter of course I too discussed with Bonhoeffer extensively, and with deep interest, questions concerning Church and politics. But in retrospect I am inclined to think that for him the essential party of our meetings was the friendly companionship where he found relaxation, ease and a much-needed chance to get his breath."[35] Visser't Hooft also recalls a long discussion in a lakeside restaurant with Genevan friends, when Bonhoeffer shared the thoughts he was setting out in his *Ethics*, and his attempt to overcome the dualistic separation between sacred and secular, church and world.[36] Bonhoeffer's primary efforts in Geneva were on behalf of the resistance. But Geneva produced only doubtful results for his mission, in that his paper as mediated by Paton and his British colleagues prompted little response in British and American political circles where skepticism about the reality of a competent German resistance still prevailed. But these encounters and discussions were high compensation in the practice and strengthening of ecumenical life.

Bonhoeffer's third Swiss visit was in May 1942. Since the second visit, the situation of Jews in Germany had dramatically deteriorated. In the autumn of 1941 wearing of the Yellow Star became compulsory, Jewish homes were being forcibly evacuated, and the first eastward deportations from Berlin and elsewhere had begun. Bonhoeffer had been drawn by Hans von Dohnanyi into an audacious plan, so-called Operation 7, to enable a number of people affected by the Nazi racial laws to escape into Switzerland, ostensibly as *Abwehr* agents—but, of course, never to return to Germany. This visit was therefore was intended to include some planning for the reception of these "agents." From one point of view, however, the visit was deeply frustrating, in that Visser't Hooft proved not to be in Geneva but on his way to London. Bonhoeffer was nevertheless able to see Freudenberg, in whose apartment there was an informal evening with Jacques Courvoisier, Henry d'Espine (pastor and professor of practical theology), and other pastors. "In a lively and sober way he told us of Germany, mainly of church affairs, and was keen to hear what we knew and thought."[37] But this Genevan visit was dramatically curtailed when Bonhoeffer learned that, of all surprising things, George Bell was on an extended visit to neutral Sweden. Bonhoeffer immediately hurried back to Berlin to set up the most momentous journey of his whole life. Before that is dealt with, however, mention must be made of another foreign visit that had taken place a few weeks earlier, in April.

The Norwegian Visit

Since the German invasion and occupation of Norway in April 1940, the (Lutheran) Church of Norway and other churches had been closely identified with the patriotic spirit of resistance. But the church itself came to the forefront of public opposition from February 1942, when the newly appointed pro-Nazi prime minister Vidkun Quisling banned a service in Trondheim Cathedral, sparking off a wave of protests and arrests, culminating in a refusal by all the bishops to undertake offices connected to state church duties, then resignations by pastors of all their offices, and the resignations of 1,000 teachers. Eivind Berggrav, bishop of Oslo[38] and inspiring leader of the church resistance, was arrested. His long association with the ecumenical movement (he was now chair of the executive of the World Alliance) did him no favours in National Socialist eyes and his visits to Britain in early 1940 made him highly vulnerable to charges of sedition. But, equally, military circles in Berlin were alarmed by the prospect of widespread disturbances in the Norwegian population, and it was a legitimate official concern of the *Abwehr* both to find out more of what was going on and, if possible, to defuse civilian unrest.

In fact, the German resistance had members serving in Norway, including Theodor Steltzer, a Wehrmacht transport officer who belonged to the Kreisau Circle and was thus known to Helmut von Moltke. He had agreed with Moltke that he would send a telegram to Berlin if Berggrav was arrested. When this happened the *Abwehr* dispatched two emissaries, Moltke and Bonhoeffer. Their stated object was to warn the authorities in Norway that the policy of occupation would be imperilled if Berggrav was removed, so inflaming the Norwegian population. Moltke and Bonhoeffer travelled to Norway via Sweden, being in the country 12–16 April, and returned via Sweden and Denmark. They were not able to visit the imprisoned Berggrav— on the last day of their visit he was released from prison but transferred to house arrest in a forest chalet—but they did meet with other senior figures and friends of the bishop. If in official *Abwehr* terms the visit was to observe and convey to the authorities the dangers of their church policy, what Bonhoeffer and Moltke actually did was to encourage the church leaders to hold fast to the path of resistance. This was a striking instance of returned brotherly ecumenical solidarity. For nearly a decade the Confessing Church had been encouraged in its stance by the support and sympathy of the ecumenical fellowship abroad. Now, in turn, through Bonhoeffer it was standing alongside another church under totalitarian pressure, admittedly a church imbued with the patriotism animated by foreign occupation, but nevertheless, as Bonhoeffer could but note, was offering more overt resistance by its pastors' resignations than even the Confessing Church had achieved. Some years later, Berggrav told how impressive Bonhoeffer had appeared to those who had met with him: "Bonhoeffer insisted on bitter resistance—even as far as martyrdom."[39] While travelling through Sweden, Bonhoeffer took the opportunity to write to his ecumenical friend Erling Eidem, archbishop of Uppsala. Noting that it was six years since they had last been together: "Terrible things have taken place in the meantime. But the more hopeless the ruptures in the world become, the more strikingly Christians must maintain the bond of peace that unites them in Jesus Christ. Only in this way can the peoples someday find their way back to one another."[40]

The Meeting with George Bell: Sigtuna, May 1942

We come now to the most dramatic intervention by Bonhoeffer in the resistance—his visit to meet with George Bell on discovering, during his third visit to Geneva in May 1942, that Bell was just then in Sweden. A great deal is known and has been written on this journey and encounter,[41] first of all that Bell was in Sweden on an extended visit under the auspices of the British Ministry of Information, which was seeking to foster links between different departments of British and Swedish cultural life. It is also known that Bonhoeffer's visit was enabled at short notice by Hans Oster and Hans von Dohnanyi, with the approval of General Beck, who provided travel permits and funding. On behalf of the resistance Bonhoeffer informed Bell in fullest possible detail of the conspiracy: who was involved in terms of its leading figures and their wish to know in advance if the Allies would negotiate a peace with a non-Nazi government, given that in the event of an overthrow of Hitler it would implement a complete demolition of the Nazi apparatus of terror and occupation. Bell was asked to convey this confidential information to the British government in the hope that the reality of a German resistance would at last be acknowledged and a coded message of encouragement then be sent via Geneva. That all this happened in the lakeside town of Sigtuna, that Bell was astonished but delighted to see his closest German friend so unexpectedly, that Bell did on his return to London convey the information in a personal meeting with the foreign secretary Anthony Eden, and that the hoped-for positive response was not forthcoming—all this is well known. At the same time, certain things are not clear, and the unclarity mainly concerns what has been termed "the riddle of the two messengers." For Bonhoeffer was not the only emissary to Bell on behalf of the resistance, for Hans Schönfeld, accompanied by Nils Ehrenström, also appeared. It is not entirely clear whether Bonhoeffer and Schönfeld—who was not in Geneva at the time of Bonhoeffer's visit there—knew of each other's intentions to visit. Certainly Bell was given no inkling from Schönfeld, who was the first to meet with the bishop, that Bonhoeffer was also on his way. The details and possible explanations need not detain us here, and indeed the information about the resistance conveyed by the two Germans was essentially the same. Bell's own accounts of the meetings, however, reveal a significant difference of approach between Bonhoeffer and Schönfeld.

According to Bell,[42] he himself arrived in Stockholm on 13 May and visited many different parts of Sweden while staying for most of the time in the British legation. On the evening of 26 May he was visited by Nils Ehrenström, who took him to the Student Movement House where, to his surprise, Hans Schönfeld was waiting to see him and proceeded to supply him with much information on conditions in Germany, the position of the churches, the nature and aims of the resistance, and their plans for an overthrow. Three days later he saw Schönfeld again. Bell continues:

That evening I went to Uppsala to stay with Archbishop Eidem. I told him of our talks. He had no doubt of Schönfeld's sincerity, or of the great strain from which he was suffering. But when we talked together next morning, 30 May, he said that he thought Schönfeld was too wishful in his thinking, and found a relief in pouring out to sympathetic ears.

But the next day, Sunday 31 May, was crucial. I went that morning to Sigtuna, where I was met by Mr Harry Johansson,[43] Director of the Nordic Ecumenical Institute. I lunched with Dr Manfred Björquist, head of the Sigtuna Foundation, and his wife. Then, to my astonishment, after tea, arrived a second German pastor, Dietrich Bonhoeffer. He had known nothing of Schönfeld's visit (nor Schönfeld of his) . . .[44]

They talked for a time in private about Bonhoeffer's recent experiences and his difficult personal situation: "Turning then to my conversations with Schönfeld, I emphasized the suspicion with which my report would be met by the British Government when I got home. And I said that, while I understood the immense danger in which he stood, it would undoubtedly be a great help if he were willing to give me any names of leaders in the movement."[45]

This Bonhoeffer proceeded to do, at length, listing names of crucial leaders on both the military and civilian wings of the movement— a very significant amplification of the more general information that Schönfeld had shared. The private talk then ended, for Schönfeld arrived, and he, Björquist, Johannson, Ehrenström, Bonhoeffer, and Bell joined in general conversation. Schönfeld spoke of the conspiracy in tactical and strategic terms: numbers; key positions held by resistance figures in radio, industries, the police, and the like; guarantees that should be given to the Soviet Union on the question of borders after the war; and the likelihood of officers in the German High Command respecting the concerns of the Soviet government. Schönfeld, evidently, was proceeding on the basis of what peace settlement, involving an equitable "understanding," might be least painful to Germans as a whole. But, Bell continues:

Here Bonhoeffer broke in. His Christian conscience, he said, was not quite at ease with Schönfeld's ideas. There must be punishment by God. We should not be worthy of such a solution. Our action must be such as the world will understand as an act of repentance. 'Christians do not wish to escape repentance, or chaos, if it is God's will to bring it upon us. We must take this judgement as Christians.' When Bonhoeffer spoke of the importance of the Germans declaring their repentance, I expressed very strong agreement with him.[46]

Three years later, in his address at the memorial service for Dietrich and Klaus Bonhoeffer held in London on 27 July 1945, Bell expressed himself in similar and no less heart-stirring terms:

Of these solemn last talks I had with Dietrich I will say nothing further but this: deeply committed as he was to the plan for elimination, he was not altogether at ease as a Christian about such a solution. "There must be punishment by God," he said. "We do not want to escape repentance. Oh we have to be punished. Christians do not wish to escape repentance or chaos, if God wills to bring it on us. We must endure this judgement as Christians." Very moving was our talk: very moving our last farewell. And the last letter I had from him, just before he returned to Berlin, knowing what might well await him there, I shall treasure for the whole of my life.[47]

Bonhoeffer and Bell met again briefly in Stockholm on 1 June. Both Schönfeld and Bonhoeffer wrote to Bell of their profound gratitude for his manifest solidarity. Bonhoeffer's letter ran:

Let me express my deep and sincere gratitude for the hours you have spent with me. It still seems like a dream to have seen you, to have spoken to you, to have heard your voice. I think these days will remain in my memory as some of the greatest of my life. This spirit of fellowship and of Christian brotherliness will carry me through the darkest hours, and even if things go worse than we hope and expect, the light of these few days will never extinguish in my heart. The impressions of these days were so overwhelming that I cannot

express them in words. I feel shamed when I think of all your good-
ness and at the time I feel full of hope for the future.

God be with you on your way home, in your work and always
I shall think of you on Wednesday. Please pray for us. We need it.[48]

In a later recollection in 1956, Bell said of the Sigtuna meeting:
". . . and we pledged one another again in unfailing Christian brotherhood. I shall never forget him."[49]

Clearly something was happening in these encounters between
Bonhoeffer and Bell which went well beyond the impartation of confidential information, beyond exchanges on the practicability of an
overthrow, beyond political planning and the weighing of possibilities for a successful outcome. Bonhoeffer's interjection, interrupting
Schönfeld's measured presentation on what might be acceptable to
German opinion as well as to the allies, was tantamount to a *confession*. Germany was guilty of crimes beyond those of any other nation
at that moment, there was Christian complicity in those crimes, there
had to be a facing of judgment and punishment no less by—indeed,
especially by—Christians and even those in the conspiracy.[50] Bonhoeffer's words to Bell on the need for repentance were an instance of
Stellvertretung, that "vicarious representative action" of which he was
writing in his *Ethics* as the core of all human responsibility in society,
and which had been central to his thinking on the community of
the church from the time of his writing *Sanctorum Communio*.[51] In
Sigtuna, *Stellvertretung* was revealed as the basal truth of Christ existing as ecumenical community, no less than of Christ existing as local
congregational community. Bell was the confessor on behalf of the
ecumenical community, both then and in the years to come.

The Italian Visit

What proved to be Bonhoeffer's final visit abroad was to Italy and
took place, not long after the Sigtuna meeting, 26 June through 10
July 1942. Throughout the war the Vatican remained an important
means of communication between the German resistance and possible

contacts in allied circles. On this occasion Hans von Dohnanyi was keen to employ as emissary not only himself and the Roman Catholic Josef Müller of the Munich *Abwehr* office, but Dietrich Bonhoeffer also. On 26 June Dohnanyi and Bonhoeffer flew together to Venice, where they were joined by another member of the Munich *Abwehr* resistance circle, the economist, brewery owner, and honorary Portuguese consul in Munich Wilhelm Schmidhuber. In Rome they hoped to find an answer from London to George Bell's approach to the Foreign Office. None came. But, as well as what no doubt was the pleasure of being in the city Bonhoeffer had loved since his first and transformative visit there in 1923, there was opportunity of meeting with clerics from Josef Müller's circle, including Johannes Schönhöffer of the *Propaganda Fidei*, whom he had already met at the Ettal monastery near Munich, and the Jesuit Father Robert Leiber, secretary and close adviser of Eugenio Pacelli before he became Pope Pius XII. He also talked with the German Jesuit Ivo Zeiger, professor of church law and history at the papal Gregorian University and an adviser to the pope, though he was not of Müller's conspiratorial circle, being in some sympathy with the Nazi regime.

A New Catholic Encounter

Bonhoeffer's months of study in Rome during 1923 had provided his first experience of life abroad and it had been transformative at many levels. A kind of poignancy therefore attaches to his visit to Italy and the Vatican nearly two decades later in June 1942, in that this proved to be his last foreign journey ever. But whereas his 1923 visit had been his first eye-opener to the Roman Catholic world and to the fundamental reality of the *church*, this last visit was just one manifestation of a most remarkable feature of his life while a resister: a growing engagement with Roman Catholic life and thought, more serious and profound than ever before in his career. This came about through the particular circumstances of his *Abwehr* involvement. From the onset of his recruitment into Military Intelligence, Hans Oster and Hans von Dohnanyi decided that Bonhoeffer should be attached to the Munich *Abwehr* office and to work alongside Josef Müller, reserve first lieutenant in that office and effectively Bonhoeffer's senior there, and where he would also be mentored by Wilhelm Schmidhuber and Captain Wilhelm Ickradt (secretary in the Portuguese consulate and head of the Aviation office in Military Intelligence). There were two main advantages in his being assigned to Munich. First, *Abwehr* activities there were less likely to be under as close surveillance by the Reich Security Police as in Berlin and so a relative amateur like Bonhoeffer would be less of a risk there than if he were based permanently in the capital. Second, Munich's geographical location close to the borders with Switzerland and Italy made it sensible to have Bonhoeffer attached there in view of his likely international excursions. Not that he would be there all the time. He set up a study bedroom in his parents' home in Berlin. He was a frequent and welcome guest at the estate of his friends, the Kleist-Restov family, in remote Klein-Krössin, and it was there that he had come to know Maria von Wedemeyer, to whom he became engaged in January 1943. It was just as well if he conveyed the impression of being a courier, despite the discomforts of long-distance train journeys in wartime. In Munich, he could and did sometimes stay with his aunt, Countess Christine Kalckreuth, an artist. But Josef Müller made another arrangement which was to have peculiar benefits.

As a Catholic attorney and the legal adviser to Catholic institutions in Bavaria, Müller had good relations with a wide range of senior Catholic figures and introduced Bonhoeffer to Angelus Kupfer, the abbot of the Benedictine monastery at Ettal, a village to the south of Munich (and close to Oberammergau, famous for its passion play). Founded in the 14th century, undergoing many vicissitudes in its history, impressively rebuilt in the 18th century in the extravert baroque style, the Ettal monastery was now one of the largest Benedictine houses in Germany. It would be an ideal temporary home for someone needing to live unobtrusively yet within reach of Munich, and it would provide a scholarly retreat where he could write in peace. So Bonhoeffer was invited into Ettal and lived there from November 1940 to February 1941, staying overnight in the monastery's nearby guest house, working on his *Ethics* in the library by day, eating with the brothers of the community, and enjoying the times and places of silence. So here he was able to taste again the ordered communal life that had long appealed to him and in which in his own way he had led and taught at Finkenwalde. He was made warmly welcome in Ettal. Indeed, his welcome had preceded him, for he discovered that *Discipleship* and *Life Together* were prescribed reading in the community. Soon after his arrival, he wrote to Eberhard Bethge: "The apparently characteristic Benedictine hospitality, which comes so naturally to them, the truly Christian deference shown to the stranger for Christ's sake, is almost embarrassing. You should really visit sometime! It is a rich blessing."[52] The practical day-to-day arrangements for Bonhoeffer's stay were seen to by Father Johannes Albrecht, who became a kind of guardian angel and a good friend. As the liaison between the monastery and higher officials in Berlin, Albrecht often had to visit the capital and on at least one occasion was entertained in the Bonhoeffer parents' home.[53]

Ettal, however, was not just a scholarly retreat. One of Müller's evident reasons for getting Bonhoeffer placed there was that the monastery itself played a role as a meeting point in his resistance circle. As well as acting in his own right as a link between Hans von Dohnanyi's office and the Vatican, Müller had around him a network of oppositional Roman Catholics, clergy and lay. Several of these would come to Ettal for confidential meetings with Father Johannes, including Father Alexander Hofmeister, abbot of another nearby Benedictine house at Metten which Bonhoeffer also visited on occasion, and who accompanied Müller on some of his travels. In December 1940 Hans von Dohnanyi brought his family to spend Christmas in the area—and with another objective conveniently in mind, since one evening in the monastery a group met through much of the night: Abbots Kupfer and Hofmeister; Müller, Bonhoeffer, and Dohnanyi; Wilhelm Schmidhuber and Ickradt from Munich; and the three clergy from the Vatican whom Bonhoeffer would later meet on his visit to Rome with Dohnanyi in 1942—Robert Leiber, Ivo Zeiger, and Johannes Schönhöffer. Of those who met that night, Bonhoeffer and Dohnanyi would die as resisters, while Hofmeister would suffer in Dachau concentration camp, and Schmidhuber, Ickradt, and Müller would be imprisoned. Bonhoeffer had also been introduced by Müller to Father Johannes Neuhäusler, political adviser to Cardinal Michael Faulhaber, archbishop of Munich. While Bonhoeffer was still at Ettal, Neuhäusler was arrested and began four years' captivity in Dachau and Sachsenhausen. Bonhoeffer must have reflected ruefully that it would have been difficult to imagine himself having conversations about an overthrow, a negotiated peace, and a new order with a like number of Protestant pastors, even in the Confessing Church. As Victoria Barnett points out, Bonhoeffer's stay at Ettal remains a topic of particular importance for further research.[54]

One thing is clear, however, and that is the renewed attention Bonhoeffer gave to Roman Catholicism, and therewith to wider ecumenical issues, as a result of the Ettal experience. He writes to Eberhard Bethge from Ettal: "I have come from quite a wonderful mass. With the Schott book [a lay missal] in hand one can pray along with and readily affirm it. It is indeed not simply idol worship, even if the way the Mass proceeds from our sacrifice for God to God's sacrifice for us is difficult for me and seems to be going in the wrong direction. But I need to understand it better. I am still a guest there, after all. The ordered life is again very good for me . . ."[55] In the same letter he confesses a "longing for the Lord's Supper" but found quite unacceptable the atmosphere of a Lutheran service of confession in Munich where "the questions being asked were so dreadfully legalistic that I was quite glad not to be invited to Communion. That was not much better than the sacrifice of the Mass!" To his parents he writes of the value of the ordered communal life for his work: "It would certainly be a loss (and indeed was a loss in the Reformation!) if this form of communal life preserved for fifteen hundred years were destroyed, something those here consider entirely possible."[56]

In Munich he met with a leading priest in the Redemptorist missionary order and wrote to Bethge commending it for its practical work and new ideas on mission among the poor.[57] Moreover, it is evident that Bonhoeffer was having serious conversations with his new Catholic friends on theological and ethical topics, and these bore pertinently on what he was writing in his *Ethics*, not least on the question of euthanasia: "The more I am able to write, the more the material engages me. I find Catholic ethics in many ways very instructive and more practical than ours. Up to now we have always dismissed it as 'casuistry.' Today we are grateful for much—precisely on the topic of my present theme."[58] He is less positive about the Catholic teaching on marriage and associated questions of free choice of spouse, sterilization, and birth control. "In all these matters the Catholic moral code is in fact almost unbearably legalistic. I spoke a long time with the abbot and Johannes about this. They believe that the church's position on birth control is the main reason why most men do not come to confession anymore. On this point the practice of confession seems to me truly to be extremely dangerous."[59] Not necessarily to be ascribed specifically to the influence of the Ettal period, but nevertheless reflecting a wish to remedy what he felt to be a deficit incurred by Protestantism's reaction to Catholic "natural law" teaching, is the importance that Bonhoeffer gives in his *Ethics* to the whole area of "natural life."[60]

As had happened much earlier in Bonhoeffer's life,[61] close encounter with the Roman Catholics prompted questions about unity and the reunion of the churches. In fact, the new prompting began even before he had actually taken up residence in Ettal, as shown in a fascinating letter to Eberhard Bethge written on the train to Munich in mid-November 1940.[62] Bonhoeffer had just met with Wolfgang Staemmler, leading Confessing Church figure and now president of the Old Prussian Council of Brethren. "We discussed Catholicism—very reasonable." Staemmler reported that the prominent Confessing pastor Hans Asmussen had recently preached at a service held by the *Una Sancta* movement of Catholics and high-church Lutherans, which Bonhoeffer felt was going "too far," but then a paragraph later he returns with "One more word on the catholic question: How did we Lutherans come together with the Reformed?" The reference is to the way in which the Confessing Church brought together churches of both Lutheran and Reformed traditions on the basis of the Barmen Theological Declaration. But any marriage between the two traditions, given their long history of theological differences, especially over the nature of Holy Communion, was suspect in many eyes on both sides, and there was a widespread anxiety that underlying matters of theology were left unresolved. The Fourth Confessing Synod of the Old Prussian Union in Halle in 1937 ratified a declaration on the theological question, reached after long and arduous discussion, formulated jointly by Lutheran, Reformed, and United Church leaders as a final step toward sacramental (table) fellowship. Bonhoeffer answers his own question:

> Actually quite untheologically (for the theological formulation of Halle is, of course, more of a determination of facts than a theological solution—which it by no means is!!); by two things: by the "guidance" of God (Union, Confessing Church), and by the recognition of what is objectively given in the sacrament—Christ is more important than our thoughts about him and about his presence. Both are theologically questionable foundations, and yet the church made a decision for fellowship of the altar—that is, for church fellowship. It made a decision to recognize the Union as God's guidance; it made a decision to subordinate its thinking and doctrine of Christ to the objectivity of Christ's presence (even in the Reformed Lord's Supper). But it came to no sort of theological unity (apart from Halle!). Would not both of these things also be possible in relation to the Catholic Church: recognition of the "guidance" of God in recent years and recognition of the presence of Christ (for traditional Lutherans, even easier with Catholics than with Calvinists!). It seems to me as if churches unite not primarily theologically but rather through faith-based decisions, in the sense above. That is a dangerous sentence, I know! One could make anything of it! But isn't this how we have acted, practically speaking, in the Confessing Church? Of course, the guidance was more visible then. I am not suggesting all this could take place tomorrow or the next day, but I would like to keep my eyes open in this direction![63]

Bonhoeffer's "dangerous sentence" foreshadows a good deal of subsequent ecumenical development, and remains no less challenging whenever "theological difficulties" are cited as obstacles to unity as distinct from unresolved differences which can be held together within a unity believed to be willed by God and accepted in faith. What is indisputable is that, for Bonhoeffer, the goal of unity remained clear and imperative, and for him the "guidance" of God was manifest in the common dangers which the churches were facing in the contemporary scene.

The Wider Ecumenical Dialogue: Preparing for Peace

In his 1941 visits to Geneva, Bonhoeffer had discovered just how intense, already, was the discussion in ecumenical circles abroad on the outcome of the war and a just peace. In Britain it was being pursued in J. H. Oldham's *Christian Newsletter* circle and associated publications, in the Peace Aims Group led by William Paton and chaired by William Temple, by the Malvern Conference and its follow-up, and the Political and Economic Planning (PEP) group, also chaired by Temple. In the USA, the Federal Council of Churches was busy with its Commission on a Just and Durable Peace. Both George Bell in his *Christianity and World Order* and Paton in his *The Church and the New Order* were calling for the Confessing Church, thanks to its integrity in steadfast witness to the gospel, to be recognized as the essential partner in reconstructing a new Germany. Bonhoeffer was gratified to find so much hope invested in his church, but equally was aware how meagre were the available resources to meet those hopes. The end of the war would find it perilously weakened in leadership (so many of its pastors, for example, on conscription into the army were sent to the deadly eastern front as a convenient way of having them eliminated), and moreover still suffering from its effective isolation from the wider ecumenical scene since the mid-1930s, an isolation most painfully apparent at the 1937 Oxford Conference. From Oxford onward, the Confessing Church was completely outside the process leading to the setting up the World Council of Churches.

Geneva was the vital communications link between the wider ecumenical discussions and the churches of continental Europe. Visser't Hooft saw to it that as much as possible of the material coming from Britain and America was reproduced and distributed wherever possible. In 1943, he himself produced a discussion paper, "Analysis of agreements and disagreements concerning the message of the church about the creation of a just and durable peace," which was used in a number of countries to stimulate discussion about the future. Visser't Hooft, in retrospect, saw this wider discussion as a foundational step toward identifying the tasks that the WCC would in due course take up.[64] Nor was all this ecumenical talk mere theory. The WCC already had in place its active refugee service headed by Adolf Freudenberg. In 1943 plans were laid for a Reconstruction Department of the WCC, which went into action in 1944, co-ordinating the interchurch service agencies of the churches in the USA, Britain, Sweden, Switzerland, and—soon—in liberated France, Belgium, and the Netherlands. But Visser't Hooft was naturally also concerned with the shape to be taken by the WCC itself, still in its infancy and still awaiting its constitutive assembly. In 1943 he wrote a lengthy memorandum covering the future shape and responsibilities of the council in a chaotic postwar world in need of reconciliation, and the basic talks of evangelism and the fostering of the unity of the churches. This, too, was discussed in the USA, Britain, Sweden, and Switzerland. Nor was this the only ball rolling. Already in 1940 George Bell had called for preparations to be made now for "a conference of Christian leaders, protestant and Catholic, from amongst the belligerent and neutral countries to meet together as soon as possible after the Armistice,"[65] and for this to include both clergy and laity, "meeting as a symbol of the Universal Church." In fact, Visser't Hooft tried to set up an ecumenical meeting in Sweden of American, British, Scandinavian, and Swiss church leaders in 1943 or 1944, but this proved impossible because of refusal of visas by the allied authorities.[66]

Aware of so much that was happening on the wider scene, Bonhoeffer was concerned that the Confessing Church should not be locked in self-pitying isolation but should consider its proper role in any new ecumenical order. Not that there were no proper preoccupations at home. The resistance circles in Germany, including both the Beck-Goerdeler group and the Kreisau Circle, were increasingly attending to a post-Nazi constitution and political order. This had to include the matter of church–state relations. At the request of Hans von Dohnanyi, Bonhoeffer consulted with the Confessing Church lawyer Friedrich Justus Perels and together they produced a draft document,[67] the proposals of which included abolition of the Ministry for Church Affairs, a repeal of all the state measures that had prompted the Church Struggle and had led to the oppression of the Confessing Church, and a law for the "freedom of belief in the German Evangelical Church." The document is unequivocal in demanding that the new church order must be consistent with the stand taken by the Confessing Church and its leadership must be provided by those who had proved their integrity in the Church Struggle. There is also, however, an interesting comment on the need for what amounts to an intra-Protestant ecumenism, which resonates with Bonhoeffer's November 1941 remarks to Eberhard Bethge on unity being a matter of faith but not necessarily full theological agreement: "The special interests of the regional churches, still rooted in certain traditional historical and confessional scruples, would certainly be overcome in the near future by means of a strong church leadership."[68] Characteristically, Bonhoeffer was not satisfied with legal arrangements and safeguards. He also produced a strong confession of guilt by the church to be read from all pulpits after a successful overthrow, which found a place in his *Ethics*,[69] and was also drafting a pulpit proclamation calling for repentance and renewed Christian commitment.[70]

Bonhoeffer's strong affirmation of the claims of the Confessing Church—the Church Struggle, he states, will not be over until all encroachments of the state on the church have ceased—has extra significance when it is seen in the context of war and political resistance. For among those Protestants active in the resistance were a number who had not identified fully, if at all, with the Confessing Church. These included some attached to the Kreisau Circle such as Hans Schönfeld and Eugen Gerstenmaier. Equally, there were many pastors in the Confessing Church who had not ventured into the active resistance. Was there now as clear a line as formerly between the followers of Christ and the anti-Christ? There are signs that Bonhoeffer was cautious about relating too closely to those in the resistance who had consciously not taken the Confessing stance, which is why he had no problems with working with an individual such as Helmut von Moltke, for example, but kept a certain distance from the Kreisau Circle collectively. His draft on the reorganization of the church does not go further than stating the need for a reorganized church to conform confessionally and in spirit to the Confessing Church. Who would choose to belong to it, or separate from it, in a post-Nazi Germany, was not for him the issue, which was rather what that church would *be*.

If Bonhoeffer had reservations about the Kreisau Circle, he was much more positive about the other body of intellectual resisters within his knowledge, the Freiburg Group, and it was in collaboration with this group that, following his discussions in Geneva, he became most directly involved in the international ecumenical discussion. This group, which largely comprised academics from the Albert-Ludwig University, was formed after *Kristallnacht* in 1938, and had strong ties with the Confessing Church. Its core members were Walter Eucken, professor of economics; Constantin von Dietze, economist with speciality in agriculture and trade sciences; Adolf Lampe, economist and adviser to Carl Goerdeler; Gerhard Ritter, professor of history; and Erik Wolf, professor of church law and legal philosophy. All these were active members of the Confessing Church—Ritter had actually been present at the Barmen Synod in 1934, and Dietze had been arrested in 1937 for his church activities.

By late 1942 the danger of the Confessing Church facing stagnation and isolation from the burgeoning ecumenical discussions on social order was weighing heavily on Bonhoeffer. At his meeting with George Bell in Sweden in May that year, he and the bishop had pledged their mutual support and prayer on behalf of their respective churches. But this could not be only one-way traffic from the "free" world to the beleaguered Germans. Germany, and the Confessing Church above all, should be contributing substantially to the thinking of the ecumenical fellowship. The danger came not only from the particular isolating circumstances of the hour. German Lutheranism always had an innate tendency to defeatism on matters of world order and the political realm: intractable problems would remain insoluble until "the end" and the coming of the reign of God in its final glory. This negative eschatology cut the nerve of any real engagement with the realities of the world. When, as likely as not, the war ended in chaos, what would be needed was not anaesthesia but a cordial for drooping spirits. In Berlin, Bonhoeffer found his concerns resonating with Oskar Hammelsbeck, theologian and religious educationalist in the Confessing Church, and discussed further with Justus Perels, Hans Böhm, and Superintendent Otto Dibelius. The matter was placed on the agenda of the Confessing Church Provisional Administration, which recommended that Bonhoeffer contact the Freiburg Group on its behalf. In effect, the Freiburg Group was being asked to act as a commission of the Confessing Church on social ethics. This suited the Freiburg thinkers well, for they were already in process of formulating responses to the works of Bell and Paton, which they had received from Geneva. Bonhoeffer visited Dietze and Wolf and secured their cooperation. Early in November, Dietze came to Berlin and met with Bonhoeffer, Dibelius, Hans Asmussen, Böhm, Perels, and probably the Berlin industrialist and Confessing Church member Walter Bauer also. A further meeting to take place in Freiburg later that month was agreed upon. Bonhoeffer did not attend this Freiburg meeting but provided notes for it, and discussions on a "Freiburg memorandum" continued in Berlin with Dietze, including one in early 1943 in the Bonhoeffer home.

The exact nature of Bonhoeffer's input into the Freiburg memorandum is not known. Bethge cites notes thought to have been made for the November 1942 Freiburg meeting, which list topics in the areas of economics, state law, justice and human rights, the Jews, education, and "The Church's proclamation to the world."[71] There is probably at least strong affinity between Bonhoeffer's eventual contribution to the memorandum and the two essays "A Theological Position Paper on State and Church"[72] and "On the Possibility of the Church's Message to the World."[73] But the dating of these papers may precede the contact with the Freiburg Group by a year or more. It is possible, for example, that the second, which has been included as a chapter in *Ethics*, arose in response to the discussions which Bonhoeffer had with Visser't Hooft and Ehrenström in Geneva in 1941. Whatever their exact provenance, it is clear that Bonhoeffer was engaged with these topics over a period of at least two years, during which time he was both working on *Ethics* and engaging with the wider ecumenical discussion, and that therefore what we have from this period is a collection of drafts and redrafts of papers on related topics not necessarily all destined for the same readership, some intended for *Ethics*, others not so intended but of very similar content. Victoria Barnett has raised the question of whether there may also have been links between the Freiburg Group and the resistance contacts in the Vatican, and whether as early as their Rome visit of June 1942 Bonhoeffer and Dohnanyi may have had discussions there on the possibility of such collaboration.[74]

The Freiburg memorandum, finished in January 1943, covered a future legal system, church policy, social and economic policy, foreign policy, and the future peace. Its discovery by the Gestapo in 1944 led to the arrest of nearly all the Freiburg members, the torture and death of Perels, and, of course, both Bonhoeffer and Goerdeler were executed, too. Gerhard Ritter not only survived but ensured that the document also was salvaged, and it was fed into the preparatory material for the first assembly of the WCC in Amsterdam in 1948.

Conspiratorial Ecumenist

In the light of all the foregoing in this chapter, a certain image of Bonhoeffer during his conspiratorial years—late 1940 to his arrest in April 1943—must be abandoned: a lone if not lonely man, writing hidden away in a monastic cell or on a remote Junker estate during long intervals between secretive courier work for the political conspiracy, in a life far removed from his earlier immersion in church and ecumenical activity. So, too, must be cast aside the simplistic notion that because Bonhoeffer was brought into the conspiracy on account of his ecumenical contacts abroad, his ecumenical experience was now just of utilitarian value to the political conspiracy, a pretext, a shell to provide a means of communication but no longer a pearl of great price for its own sake. As has been amply demonstrated, if his ecumenism provided Bonhoeffer with utility for the resistance, it is equally the case that his involvement in the conspiracy provided him with the means of fulfilling still further his ecumenical vocation which he now pursued with at least as much commitment and vigour as when active in the World Alliance and when presenting the claims of the Confessing Church to the ecumenical fellowship and vice versa.

By way of underlining this still further, we conclude this chapter with a glance at the theological work on which Bonhoeffer was focussed throughout this period and which, if events had allowed him to complete it, he would have regarded as his life's main achievement. *Ethics* is rightly regarded as a reflection on involvement in the conspiracy. It is not hard to see just below the surface the kinds of ethical decisions and risks that Bonhoeffer felt compelled to take, in passages such as those on the structure of responsible life[75] and the willingness to bear guilt.[76] Equally apparent is the contemporary background to the sections on guilt, justification, and renewal, including the church's need to confess its own guilt of silence and inaction in face of state oppression and mass murder; and to the section on the rights of natural life in face of the Nazi policies of elimination of "unworthy life." This is all very evident. But *Ethics* is a work of well-nigh universal significance because it is shot through with an *ecumenical* perspective, that is, a vision of Christian responsibility in and for the whole *oikoumene*, the inhabited earth. At an earlier stage, 1933–37, the period of the Berlin Christology lectures and *Discipleship*, there had been a focus on Jesus Christ as the centre of human existence. Now, the eye is on the whole human realm of which Christ is the centre, and on what it means for humanity to take the form of Christ in the world, anywhere and everywhere.

"What is behind the desire, which is awakening in Christendom everywhere throughout the world, to hear a message from the church to the world that offers solutions? . . . The strength of the church's spirit is not yet exhausted. Christians throughout the world have grown closer to one another than ever before. Jointly they must tackle the task of proclaiming a message from the church."[77] These opening sentences in Bonhoeffer's essay "On the Possibility of the Church's Message to the World" are an ironic recitation of a commonly held view which he is about to question as to its basis—yet which he wishes to affirm on certain conditions. The church's word to the world must be a *concrete* directive, not abstract principle. Here he returns to precisely the same point as he reiterated tirelessly to the ecumenical peace movement a decade earlier.[78] As before, he shows a keen awareness of different Christian approaches—Roman Catholic, Anglican, Protestant, free church, American, European. But here there is a new wholeness and inclusivity about the address. There is to be no double morality, one for the world and another for the church community. "God's entire law and entire gospel belong to all people in the same way."[79] *Ethics* is set within the total, overall biblical perspective of the Pauline vision, of all things having been created through Christ and for Christ, in whom "all things hold together." (Col. 1:16f.). In Christ God has reconciled the universe to Godself. In Christ God and reality are conjoined, God and world cannot be known apart from each other in Christ. Set within this universal perspective, previous boundaries, separations, dichotomies are relativized if not abolished. He is concerned not just with Germany, but with "the West"—and also further afield (the imperialist scarring of the East is not overlooked). Bonhoeffer writes at his desk with Luther looking over his shoulder, but writes neither to reassure fellow Lutherans on the veracity of what they believe to be the Lutheran tradition, nor to evangelize other traditions with it. He writes to critique it as much as to commend it, and he does so in such a way that his exposition can readily be received and recognized by those of other traditions as questions and new insights pertinent to them, too. Thus in his arguments for overcoming "thinking in two realms," and for taking seriously "the things before the last" as well as "the last things" he is writing for the whole Christian community, everywhere. Finally, what holds it all together is, yet again, *Stellvertretung*, vicarious representative action. Only now, this is not only the unitive bond of the Christian community, in which members of the body of Christ are Christ to each other—though it is. Nor is it only the bond of ecumenical fellowship as epitomized by Bonhoeffer and Bell at Sigtuna. It is also, now, seen as the basis of human responsibility in society as such, the form in which Christ takes shape in the world, the *oikoumene*.

CHAPTER 10

Ecumenism from Prison

Dietrich Bonhoeffer was arrested and placed in Tegel Military Detention Centre, Berlin, on 5 April 1943. On the same day, Hans von Dohnanyi and his wife, Dietrich's sister Christine, were arrested together with certain others in the *Abwehr* circle, including Hans Oster. In a life marked by a successive changes and upheavals, the shutting and locking of the cell door signified the last and most drastic break in Bonhoeffer's career. He was now brutally separated from his wider world of relationships, community, and active responsibilities. Fifteen months later, in one of his poems, he was to write of suffering as one of the "Stages on the Way to Freedom":

Wondrous transformation. Your hands, strong and active, are fettered.
Powerless, alone, you see that an end is put to your action.
Yet now you breathe a sigh of relief and lay what is righteous
calmly and fearlessly into a mightier hand, contented.
Just for one blissful moment you could feel the sweet touch of freedom,
Then you gave it to God, that God might perfect it in glory.[1]

This was probably penned about the time of the failure of the 20 July 1944 plot, which signalled what Bonhoeffer's eventual fate, and that of so many others in the resistance, would be. Up until that time, however, it was not absolutely the case that "an end had been put to his action." As demonstrated by his remarkable prison writings (and the immense amount of commentary they have stimulated) for most of his year and a half in Tegel Bonhoeffer was able still to find means of "action" even behind the locked cell door.[2] From soon after his arrest, letters to and from family members and his fiancée Maria von Wedemeyer were permitted, and also visits from them. The secret correspondence with Eberhard Bethge began in November 1943. Two main phases of the period in Tegel are usually identified. The first was from the time of his arrest until late April 1944. During this time he was under interrogation by the Reich Military Prosecutors on suspicion of using his *Abwehr* service as a means of evading conscription, and also on account of questions surrounding "Operation 7."[3] He had genuine hopes that, with good legal defense counsel, he could face trial in the spring of 1944 and be cleared of the charges. The investigations dragged on, however, with further delays caused by the heavy Allied bombing during the winter of 1943–44, and by April 1944 it became apparent that his confinement was to remain indefinite, with or without charges.

It was at the end of April 1944 that the second phase began, it by now having become clear that it was futile to expend further hopes and mental energy on preparing his defense case. This proved a stimulus to renewed intellectual effort, his letters to Bethge taking on a fresh burst of life with his radical questioning of what Christianity means in the contemporary world, and his explorations of a "religionless Christianity" for a "world come of age." It was not until October, three months after the July plot failure, that the threat from the Gestapo became much more real with their discovery of files deeply incriminating to the whole Dohnanyi circle. Bonhoeffer was transferred to the Gestapo cells in the centre of Berlin, then early in 1945 to Buchenwald concentration camp, and finally to the execution yard at Flossenbürg on 9 April 1945.

In all this it has to be asked, Did imprisonment mean an end to his ecumenical life and interests? The answer, however surprising, is: not at all.

Continuing Contacts

Threads of communication to the ecumenical community, albeit of the most fragile kind, remained thanks to the contacts in Switzerland. It took only three days for George Bell to receive word on 7 April of Bonhoeffer's arrest.[4] From two months before his arrest, against the advice of some in the *Abwehr*, Bonhoeffer had been preparing for another visit to Switzerland. But in July, Eberhard Bethge was dispatched there by the *Abwehr*, ostensibly to gather information from Swiss-based mission organizations about developments in the Far East, but in reality to inform the ecumenical circles of what exactly had happened to Bonhoeffer, Dohnanyi, and others. During 8–10 July he met with W. A. Visser't Hooft in Geneva and with Karl Barth in Basel. As a truly tangible as well as comforting sign of his continuing concern and friendship, Barth handed Bethge a cigar to be passed to Bonhoeffer at an opportune moment, which came when Bethge was able to visit Tegel for the first time, with Bonhoeffer's parents and fiancée, on 26 November. That visit was only brief and obviously, under those conditions, Bethge could hardly report anything of importance. But just what it meant for Bonhoeffer to know that his ecumenical friends in Switzerland were in continuing solidarity with him is well conveyed in his letter to Bethge soon after: "Now Karl's cigar is here before me, a truly improbable reality so—was he nice? And understanding? And V[isser't Hooft]? It is simply marvellous that you saw them!"[5] Bethge himself had been drafted into the military in August, and from early in 1944 until his own arrest at the end of October that year served with a unit in Italy.

The continuous relationship that Bonhoeffer reestablished with his friend, sustained all the time Bethge was on active service in Italy, was vital and not only as the source of strength and intellectual stimulus manifest in their correspondence. It provided Bonhoeffer with a living link, even if only in imagination, to the wider world of his ecumenical career. "If you do get to Rome," he writes before Bethge's posting to Italy begins, "do visit Schönhöffer in the 'Propaganda Fidei'."[6] Schönhöffer, it will be recalled, was one of the priests in the circle of resisters whom Bonhoeffer had met in the Ettal monastery and also in Rome on the visit made with Dohnanyi in July 1942.[7] A few days later, another thought occurs to him:

> A "World Alliance" man with whom I have attended many conferences, I believe, a professor and a Protestant, lives in Florence. Unfortunately I have forgotten his name, but you can find him in the World Alliance Annual Book that is among my books, under "Italy" and can write to him without hesitation using my name. He knows me well. Perhaps he can be of some use to you. It is always good to have someone like that available. If you can't find the handbook, Renate [Bethge] might telephone Diestel and ask him: he will know immediately and perhaps several other addresses. I would not neglect this but take all these addresses along just in case. You can gain very useful connections in this way.[8]

The Italian in question may well have been Dr Cesare Gay, a member of the Ecumenical Youth Commission when Bonhoeffer was a youth secretary of the World Alliance;[9] or possibly Professor Ernesto Comba.[10] Bonhoeffer was doubtless keen to ensure that in Italy Bethge should not be bereft of all friendly support in case of need. It might also well be that he was so emphatic about following up this possible contact in order that his own plight should be communicated as widely as possible in the ecumenical circles that knew him. What is most apparent, however, is just how real this ecumenical community still was to him, and how a much part of it he felt, whether Max Diestel, his Berlin mentor since his student days,[11] or this Italian whose name he could not recall but whose face he could see. Bethge's whole Italian itinerary provided a source of both nostalgic and imagined contemporary delights, as Bonhoeffer recalled his own student experiences in Rome where the Catholic Church had made such an impression upon him, and the visit he and Bethge had both made in the summer heat of 1936. The thought that Rome might be destroyed in the war was a "nightmare" to him.[12] He urges Bethge to use any opportunity to attend the Holy Week services in Rome, especially in St Peter's and the Lateran, which he describes in well-remembered and graphic detail: "Somewhere in Rome I also saw a Greek Orthodox Easter service which impressed me very much at the time—that's twenty years ago now!"[13] The world of the *oikoumene* remained very present to him.

A Continuing Ecumenical Formation

Bonhoeffer's ecumenical perspectives continued to evolve during his first year in prison, and did so in ways that have an important bearing on the new theological note he was to sound in his letters from the end of April 1944. Signs of this continuing evolution are evident in three major interests that recur in his writings.

First, there is *a spirituality rooted in the centre of church tradition yet universal in its embrace.* A little more than a month after his arrest he writes to his parents of how he misses conversation:

> Despite all my sympathies for the *vita contemplativa*, I am nevertheless not a born Trappist monk. Anyhow, a time of enforced silence may be a good thing. After all, Catholics claim that the most effective scriptural expositions come from the strictly contemplative orders. By the way, I am reading the Bible straight through from the beginning and am just coming to Job, whom I specially love. I am also still reading the Psalms daily as I have done for years. There is no other book that I know and love so much.[14]

He continues also to use the Moravian *Losungen*, the "Daily Watchwords," for biblical meditation. Three weeks later he writes on Ascension Day, "a great day of joy for all those who are able to believe that Christ rules the world and our lives,"[15] and his thoughts travel "to all of you, to the church and the worship services from which I have been separated for so long now," and also to the many people who move through the prison building "bearing their fate in silence." In the same spirit he celebrates Pentecost, "the church festival that is in a special way a celebration of community."[16] The sound of church bells prompted a great longing to be in a worship service, but like John of Patmos "in the Spirit on the Lord's Day" (Rev. 1:9f.), he celebrated such a good worship service on his own "that I didn't feel the loneliness at all, for each and every one of you was a part of it, as well as the congregations in which I have celebrated Pentecost in the past." He recites over and over again Paul Gerhardt's Pentecost hymn *"Zieh ein du deinen Toren"* ("O Enter Lord, Thy Temple," and especially its verse *"Du bist ein Geist der Freude . . ."* ("You Are a Spirit of Joy . . ."). This leads to a brief but profound reflection on the "miracle of tongues":

> The Babylonian confusion of languages, through which people are no longer able to understand one another because each speaks his own language, is to end and be overcome by the language of God, which each human being understands and through which alone people are also able to understand one another again, and that the church is where this is to take place—these are indeed very deep and important thoughts. Leibniz wrestled all his life with the idea of a universal script that was to represent all concepts, not by words but with clear and obvious signs—an expression of his desire to heal the fractured world of his day—a philosophical reflection of the Pentecost story.[17]

Advent and Christmas are likewise observed in the cell—or, rather, their observance in the cell enables him to travel mentally both in space and time out into the world whose renewal is signalled by these festivals.[18] Once again it is to the hymnody of Paul Gerhardt that Bonhoeffer turns. Gerhardt's Christmas hymn *"Fröhlich soll mein Herze springen"* ("All My Heart This Night Rejoices"), with its thought that Christ will "restore" whatever is dear but has been lost, inspires him, deriving as it does from the doctrine of *anacephalaiosis* or "recapitulation" propounded by the second-century father Ireneaus[19] (and which Bonhoeffer also sees as a fulfillment of Ecclesiastes 3:15, "God seeks out what has gone by"). Later on in prison, Bonhoeffer sought to come to terms not just with items lost, but fragments of life left *incomplete*, an anxiety which he felt typical of his generation, faced as it was by the disruption brought by social upheaval and war—not to mention the grave doubts about his own future. "What matters . . . is whether one still sees, in this fragment of life that we have, what the whole was intended and designed to be, and of what material it is made."[20] Bonhoeffer was thus through biblical study, meditation, personal devotion, all the while continuing in inward participation in the great liturgical life of the church. This was nourishing a faith which was at once deeply personal yet identified with the entire *oikoumene* embraced by the gospel. Confined to a fragment of life in a cell, he was nevertheless conscious of the whole scene in which, by God's grace, his life took part and in which it found its true worth and meaning.

Second, Bonhoeffer *in his thinking and reading is grappling with the concept of humanity as a wider historical whole*. His earlier reference to not being a Trappist monk notwithstanding, Bonhoeffer's prison existence did take on something of the ethos of the monastic. In September 1943, he refers to the "stormy world events in recent days" (probably meaning the accelerating war in Italy) which "race through one's body here like electricity, and one wishes to be able to accomplish something useful someplace."[21] Frustrated by his confinement which separates him from the wider world to which he belongs, he sees a likeness between himself and the monk in Karl Gottfried von Leiter's poem *Der Kreuzzug* ("The Crusade") as set to music by Franz Schubert.[22] For his reading, Bonhoeffer eagerly devours historical subjects, the more extensive their treatment the better. Hans Delbrück's *Weltgeschichte* ("World History") "reads just beautifully. But I find it more a German history."[23] He asks his parents to get him a copy of Ortega y Gasset's recent *The Nature of Historical Crises* and his *History as a System and Other Essays toward a Philosophy of History*, together with Heinz Pfeffer's book on the British Empire and the USA.[24] By the early summer of 1944, he is also reading Wilhelm Dilthey, the 19th-century philosopher of history who envisaged historical method as an exercise in unitive understanding, working toward a grasp of human history as a single, living whole.[25] Bonhoeffer is wrestling with the concept of history as a continuum, which he sees as deriving from

Hegel but admits to being less than sure about what actually gives history its unity, even in Europe.[26]

Such a communal understanding of the human historical enterprise carries a certain ethical implication. This is clear in the novel, one of the several literary exercises that Bonhoeffer attempted in prison. Here Major von Bremer, a conservative but generous-minded Junker cast by Bonhoeffer as the voice of wisdom, comments to his audience of earnest and high-minded young people at his meal table:

> For me the main issue for individuals and for peoples [*Völker*] and nations is whether or not they have learned to live with other human beings and peoples. That's more important to me than all their ideas, thoughts, and convictions . . .
>
> But I would not agree . . . that what we learn from history and life is the need for compromise. People who speak that way are still focussed only on ideas and therefore are continually resigning themselves to discovering that no idea prevails in life in pure form. They then call that compromise and see it as a sign of the imperfection and wickedness of the world.
>
> I look only at people and their task of living with other people and I view succeeding at this very task as the fulfilment of human life and history.[27]

During these months Bonhoeffer's mental and ethical horizon was therefore increasingly that of the whole human community in its need of finding a *modus vivendi* of just and peaceable relationships. This was determinative of all other concerns. Not surprisingly, therefore, in reviewing the roots of European culture he asks:

> Isn't a knowledge of other countries and a deeper encounter with them a much more important element of education for us today than knowing the classics? Of course there can be philistinism either way. But perhaps it's one of our tasks to make encounters with other people and countries a real cultural experience that goes beyond politics or business, beyond snobbery. This would be a fruitful use of cultural and educational currents that to date have been

neglected and it would also bring us back in touch with an old European tradition.[28]

Here, of course, he was paying tribute to his own formative experiences during his younger days.

Third, along with a spirituality focused on the tradition of Christian prayer and biblical reflection yet set within an interest in the widest reach of human community, *Bonhoeffer distances himself ever further from traditional confessionalism.* He does not disown his Lutheran heritage, but views it with a cool objectivity and at times a quite critical detachment. On Reformation Sunday, 31 October 1943, he writes to his parents about this day "that can evoke a great deal of reflection again, precisely in our time"[29] in view of the consequences of Luther's action "that were exactly the opposite of those he intended, and that overshadowed his own last years and at times even made him question his life's work." Instead of the unity of all Christian peoples had come new division and collapse of the church and Europe; instead of the "freedom of the Christian" had come degeneracy, chaos, the peasants' revolt—and so forth. Kierkegaard had said that Luther today would say the opposite of what he had said back then. "I think that is true—*cum grano salis.*"[30] Writing to Eberhard Bethge, he admits that his arguments (already well rehearsed in his *Ethics*) for taking seriously the penultimate realm as where one lives while believing in the ultimate, and of not rushing too quickly to the New Testament at the expense of the Old, "would give Lutherans (so-called!) and pietists goose bumps, but nevertheless it's true."[31] Having confessed to Bethge just how important he finds the material gifts he receives from him, and all his family and friends, which compensate for the lack of "table fellowship," he goes on, again anticipating that Bethge may be surprised: "I have quite spontaneously experienced Luther's instruction to 'bless oneself with the cross' at morning and evening prayer as a help. There is something objective about it for which a person here particularly longs. Don't be alarmed! I will definitely not come out of here as a 'homo religiosus.' Quite the opposite: my suspicion and fear of 'religiosity' have become greater than ever."[32] Then, evidently feeling that he has burned his boats as far as any chauvinistic Protestantism is concerned, he makes a further disclosure: "I am presently reading a great deal in Tertullian, Cyprian, and other church fathers, with much interest. To some extent they are much more contemporaneous than the Reformers and simultaneously a basis for Protestant–Catholic conversation."[33]

In some respects, he is already conducting a conversation with Roman Catholics. In March 1944, as his second Passiontide in prison approaches, he reflects on whether "we've made too much of this question of suffering and been too solemn about it." He used to wonder, he says, how Catholics seem to pass by and say little about difficult circumstances. "But doesn't that show greater strength? Perhaps, with all their history, they know better what suffering and martyrdom really are, so they remain silent about minor harassments and hindrances."[34] A positive appreciation, indeed, from the author of *Discipleship*.

Moreover, Holy Week 1944 provided Bonhoeffer with a particular occasion to distinguish conviction from partisanship, as emerged in his correspondence with his fiancée, Maria von Wedemeyer. The issue arose out of the longstanding tension between the Berneuchen movement, which had emerged in the 1920s as a sacramental and liturgical reform movement within German Lutheranism, and the Confessing Church. Bonhoeffer himself had over time expressed deep unease with the "Berneucheners" and what appeared to be their preoccupation with the niceties of ritual and church music at the expense of public and costly witness in the spirit of the Barmen Declaration. It is possible that the saying often attributed to Bonhoeffer, "Only those who cry out for the Jews may sing Gregorian chant," was aimed at the Berneucheners. Maria's father, Hans von Wedemeyer, who had been killed in 1942 while serving as a major near Stalingrad, had been devoted to the Berneuchen movement. In late April 1944, Maria reported to Dietrich a rather uncomfortable episode during the recent Holy Week which she had spent at Bundorf in northern Bavaria, acting as governess for the children of her cousin Hedwig von Truchsess. At Bundorf, the Holy Week services and devotions were led by no less than the co-founder of the Berneuchen movement, Professor Wilhelm Stählin, who was a close friend of the Wedemeyer family. According to Maria, Stählin had suggested she be sent away from Bundorf for the week so as to spare her, effectively, having to choose between loyalty to her late father and her fiancé. Maria herself was angry at this: "The fact that I'm Father's daughter and your fiancée is an indivisible whole."[35] Membership cards or pledges were abhorrent to her, she declared. She wished to familiarize herself with all the various routes and decide on her own path. Dietrich was even more incensed than she was, and strongly supported her stance, both out of respect for her right to personal decision and on account of what he saw as a false stereotyping of the Confessing Church by Stählin:

> Where lies the fanaticism for which we [in the Confessing Church] are so fiercely vilified, on his side or mine? I'm very sorry that he should have strayed so far from the Christian spirit, though the [Confessing Church] may itself be partly to blame, albeit only where its more immature representatives are concerned. . . . I firmly believe that Father and I would always have regarded ourselves as brothers in Christ, even if we had differed on this point or that and may even have thought each other mistaken in some respects. We would always have been quite prepared to learn from each other, certainly, and would only have wished to assist each other in the knowledge of Christ and in his love—especially at a time like the present, when all that matters is whether or not one opts for Christ, not Christian 'opinions.'[36]

Dietrich's quarrel with the Berneucheners, he tells Maria, is that they were saddling faith with an unnecessary *style*. Maria should feel free to follow whatever leads her to freedom under Christ: "We want to obey and belong to Christ, no one else!" This was, of course, virtually word for word the voice of the Barmen Declaration.[37] We may be sure that it would have been a wholly different matter if Holy Week at Bundorf had been in the hands of the German Christians.

It is significant that these remarks were penned to Maria at almost the same time as the first of Bonhoeffer's "radical" theological letters to Eberhard Bethge (30 April 1944). It reveals something of the wider cast of mind which was leading him in that letter to state: "What keeps gnawing at me is the question, what Christianity is, or who

Christ is actually for us today?"[38] In the light of that central question, other issues were becoming relativized and new questions presenting themselves—including the ecumenical ones. If the most important question for humanity was now, for Bonhoeffer as for Major von Bremer, how people and nations could actually live together, then the most important question for the church was how it could serve *that* quest and goal. This provides the framework for the radical thoughts on "religionless Christianity."

Ecumenism in the World Come of Age

> What does a church, a congregation, a sermon, a liturgy, a Christian life, mean in a religionless world? How do we talk about God— without religion, that is, without the temporally conditioned presuppositions of metaphysics, the inner life, and so on?[39]

The torrent of questions that poured into Bonhoeffer's letter of 30 April 1944 to Eberhard Bethge, together with his own first attempts to answer them over the next three months, was to ignite a theological debate that continues today. For our immediate purposes here, the main lines of Bonhoeffer's thinking can be are summarized as follows. In these "radical" letters it is quite clear what Bonhoeffer is criticizing as "religion." It is to think "metaphysically," by which he means to locate reality in a sphere beyond this world, and to see this world as inferior in status to that reality: in other words, to see life on earth as only a preliminary to heaven.[40] Further, "religion" means to think individualistically: its main concern is with one's own salvation, fulfilled on the far side of death.[41] Religion in these senses is becoming less and less central in the (Western) world which no longer sees need of it. Over the last five centuries or more, "God" as the answer to unsolved mysteries has become less and less necessary in face of the advances of the natural and human sciences. As the unsolved questions shrink in number, so God is progressively exiled to the fringes of everyday human life. Humankind has "come of age," manifesting a new maturity and autonomy. In such a situation, Christianity has tried to maintain a rear-guard action, still insisting that God is necessary to people's "inward" lives in the recesses of their souls, or answering the "ultimate" questions of life and death. Such apologetics seeks to demonstrate that people are not as autonomous, secure, successful, and happy as they claim to be. Human weaknesses must still be found to which "religion" provides the answers.

Bonhoeffer rejects this dubious and increasingly desperate approach which seeks to deny the maturity of contemporary humankind in order only *then* to demonstrate the relevance of the gospel. More worthy of Christ, and truer to Christ's own attitude to people as seen in the gospels, is to allow people to be claimed by the gospel in all their strength and maturity. We should seek God in what we know, not in what we do not.[42] Jesus Christ calls not to religion but to life, and claims for the kingdom of God not the "religious" sector in life, but the whole of human life in all its dimensions.[43] We might paraphrase Bonhoeffer's thoughts by saying that a "religionless" Christianity is simply the obverse of a fully human Christianity.

Bonhoeffer's phrase "religionless Christianity" can be misunderstood to mean that he was envisaging a form of Christianity not only doing without all traditional creedal formulae but totally shorn of all cultic and institutional elements: in effect a churchless Christianity, amounting to little more than an ethical movement for the betterment of humankind inspired by the example of Jesus "the man for others." If, indeed, he was now regarding the question of the church as irrelevant, then obviously he would now also be discarding the ecumenical commitment which he had followed for almost his entire career since his student days. But, in fact, the question of the church becomes ever more urgent for him in these writings. He certainly regards the traditional formulae and life of the church as deeply problematic for the expression of Christian faith in the present world. His aim, however, is not to jettison but to reinterpret and reorientate them for authentic life and witness in the world of today and tomorrow. His key question, as phrased in his letter to Bethge of 30 April 1944, is: "How do we go about being 'religionless-worldly' Christians, how can we be *ek-klesia*, those who are called out, without understanding ourselves *religiously as privileged*, but instead seeing ourselves *as belonging wholly to the world?*"[44] These key phrases "religiously as privileged" and "belonging wholly to the world" merit further examination in their significance for ecumenical Christianity in the "world come of age," but meanwhile some of Bonhoeffer's other comments pertinent to the ecumenical context must be noted.

First, the crisis of "religion" in the contemporary world is seen by Bonhoeffer as itself an ecumenical crisis. All Christian traditions, without exception, are caught up in this crisis and none of them have yet seen its implications, let alone thought out a constructive response:

> As in the scientific domain, so in human affairs generally, "God" is being pushed further and further out of our life, losing ground. The historical views of both Catholics and Protestants agree that this development must be seen as the great falling-away from God, from Christ, and the more they lay claim to God and Christ in opposing this, and play them off against it, the more this development considers itself anti-Christian. The world, now that it has become conscious of itself and the laws of its existence, is sure of itself in a way that is becoming uncanny for us.[45]

Later, in his "Outline for a Book," Bonhoeffer's notes include:

> Outdated controversies. Especially the interconfessional ones; the differences between Lutheran and Reformed (and to some extent Roman Catholic) are no longer real. Of course, they can be revived with passion at any time, but they are no longer convincing. One must simply be bold enough to start from this. The only thing we can prove is that the Christian-biblical faith does not live or depend on such differences.[46]

Bonhoeffer has therefore taken further his view expressed to Bethge in 1940 that interchurch union or agreement is a matter of a decision of faith, not theology.[47] Now, his suspicion about the significance of theologically defined confessional differences and distinctives has been triggered into a full-scale rejection of their relevance. How *any* church or particular tradition can speak of the most fundamental

Christian matter, Jesus Christ, to a world whose autonomy makes obsolete the previously held "religious" assumption about its need—this question transcends everything else in significance. That means a new learning experience for all churches without exception, a return to the most basic starting point for understanding the faith anew. This is most strikingly expressed in the baptismal sermon Bonhoeffer wrote in prison for his infant godson, Dietrich Bethge, in May 1944:

> You're being baptized today as a Christen. All those great and ancient words of the Christian proclamation will be pronounced over you, and the command of Jesus Christ to baptize will be carried out, without your understanding any of it. But we too are being thrown back all the way to the beginnings of our understanding. What reconciliation and redemption mean, rebirth and Holy Spirit, love for one's enemies, cross and resurrection, what it means to live in Christ and follow Christ, all that is so difficult and remote that we hardly dare speak of it anymore. In these words and actions handed down to us, we sense something totally new and revolutionary, but we cannot yet grasp it and express it. This is our own fault.[48]

There is, then, for Bonhoeffer a new ecumenicity born first out of a common ignorance which can nevertheless instill a necessary humility, a return by all Christians and churches to the nursery where everything is to be seen and explored as if for the first time. This prompts Bonhoeffer to expound his view of the need for the *disciplina arcana*, the "discipline of the secrets" as practiced, so some scholars have believed, in the early church where the mysteries of the faith were not bandied abroad before they could be completely understood. The discipline would comprise "prayer and doing justice among human beings,"[49] whereby eventually a new language would be learned in which to proclaim the faith with transforming power in the world.

Bonhoeffer, however, while cautious about rushing into new prescriptions, is by no means totally agnostic about the future shape and priorities of a church in a world come of age. This becomes very evident in his "Outline for a Book,"[50] written in August 1944, well after the failure of the plot against Hitler, and therefore one of his latest writings to have survived—indeed, it might almost be termed his last will and testament for the church. Here he rehearses again his observations on the coming of age of humankind, the essentially rear-guard actions of the churches against the maturity of the world, and even the eventual failure of the Confessing Church to do more than stand up for "the cause" rather than exemplifying personal faith in Christ and taking risks for others. There follows his concentrated and pithy rejection of a "religious" concept of transcendence as a relation to a superior, all-powerful deity, arguing instead for participation in the being of Jesus and his "being there for others" as the true experience of transcendence. Then, as has been noted, arguing that interconfessional issues—even in relation to Roman Catholics—are increasingly unreal, comes his proposal for a concluding chapter, on *the church*. "The church is church only when it is there for others." This is no mere theorizing—first of all, it must give away its property to those in need and the clergy must either live on the freewill offering of their congregations or take a secular job. The church must participate in the worldly tasks of life in the community" and "must tell people of every calling what a life with Christ is, what it means 'to be there for others.'"

There can be no doubt that Bonhoeffer envisaged this as the crucial point to which his book was heading and, we may well imagine, the direction his interests would have followed had he survived Hitler's revenge. He was imagining the context, postwar, post-Nazi, when the challenge would no longer be whether the church would be persecuted but whether it would be noticed any longer; and equally when the maturity of the nonreligious world could no longer be doubted, but how it would *use* its maturity would be the question. A church which confined itself to the ever-diminishing "religious" areas of life, outside the realm of everyday cares, responsibilities, and joys, would be locking itself into a false kind of transcendence, the transcendence of God's assumed distance from humanity rather than the more truly biblical transcendence of otherness. By default the church would be indicating a God who is beyond the reach of the world, when instead its calling is to reveal the God who transforms the world by the way God is present in it in Christ, confronting it—even at its strongest and most mature—in the suffering love of the crucified. And it would have to witness to God not so much by words as by example.

Contradiction or Fulfillment of Earlier Thinking on Church and Ecumenism?

If Bonhoeffer had certain definite ideas on the shape and direction of the future church, by the same token he must have had a vision for the ecumenical movement as well. As we have seen, Bonhoeffer throughout his imprisonment was writing out of a continued ecumenical consciousness and commitment, maintained literally to the very end. That is confirmed by his last recorded words before being taken to Flossenbürg on 8 April 1945, and his death the next day: "Tell [Bishop George Bell] . . . .With him I believe in the principle of our universal Christian brotherhood which rises above all national interests, and that our victory is certain."[51] But what implications for such an ecumenical commitment arise out of his radical theological letters, on religionless Christianity and the world come of age, and his compelling statement that the church is church only when it exists for others? At this point we may return to his question posed to Eberhard Bethge on 30 April 1944: "How do we go about being 'religionless-worldly' Christians, how can we be *ek-klesia*, those who are called out, without understanding ourselves *religiously as privileged*, but instead seeing ourselves *as belonging wholly to the world*?"[52] His final message for George Bell is explicitly ecumenical in nature; his question to Bethge is implicitly no less so. Bonhoeffer is averse to any notion of privilege in religion and nothing speaks more loudly—even if unconsciously—of privilege than do confessional differences and the self-justifying pride and the largely fictional identities they generate to sustain and reproduce themselves, a dynamic which constantly vitiates ecumenical commitment.

What is clear is that Bonhoeffer sees the new situation of a world come of age as itself encouraging a new ecumenism, if only because the old (and more recent) interconfessional questions are losing significance and reality. The end of religion and the coming of age of humankind pose questions to which no single confession or church tradition has any better answers than any of the others. Persistence in separate confessional identities which demand repeated (and ever more sophisticated) self-justifications simply distracts from the need to face the mature world. This does not by itself legitimate all ecumenical activity. A wholly united church, would not, of itself, automatically be in a better position. The question remains, what *kind* of church is required? Bonhoeffer's reference to the church being those in some sense "called out" indicates his affirmation of a distinctive identity and role for the church. But, immediately going on to reject this as meaning a possession of the "religiously privileged," he denies that this entitles the church to claim a special relationship to God denied to the rest of humanity. The church does not set itself over against the world but, rather, identifies with and belongs wholly to it, before God.

Bonhoeffer's key theological motif, we have seen, right from his student time has been *Stellvertretung*, "vicarious representative action." This is at the heart of his doctoral thesis on the church, *Sanctorum Communio*.[53] The church, "Christ existing as church-community," is founded on, grounded in, and sustained by the vicarious representative action of Jesus Christ, the bearer of sins in his forgiving grace, reflected in in the vicarious representative action of its members for one another. Identified on this basis, the church is decidedly not a "religious association": it is the new humanity before God. The theme is heard again in his 1932 Berlin lectures on the nature of the church and his 1933 course on Christology.[54] It reappears powerfully in *Ethics*, where vicarious representative action is seen as the form of all truly responsible human action in society.[55] Now, without diminishing the significance of any of its previous roles in his theology, and without actually being named as such, vicarious representative action is what defines the relationship of the church to the world. The church takes upon itself the need of the world before God. This had been powerfully expounded in the conclusion to *Discipleship*, where the community of follows of Jesus Christ are those who allow the image of Christ to be formed in themselves:

Christ has taken on this *human form*. He became a human being like us. In his humanity and lowliness we recognize our own form. He has become like human beings, so that we would be like him. Whoever from now on attacks the least of the people attacks Christ, who took on human form and who in himself has restored the image of God for all who bear a human countenance. . . . The form of the incarnate one transforms the church-community into the body of Christ upon which all of humanity's sin and trouble fall, and by which alone these troubles and sins are borne.[56]

Both in his letters to Bethge and in his "Outline for a Book," Bonhoeffer was critical of his own Confessing Church which, despite its courageous stand for the Christian faith against the nationalistic heresy, had not really ventured beyond into "taking risks for others." Its voice on behalf of the voiceless, above all the Jews, was muted. Yet it is also clear that by exemplifying an "existence for others" in the manner of Christ, "the man for others," Bonhoeffer is calling not just for a church of social and charitable action or even political campaigning. He is asking for a deep, incarnational identification of the church with the human community in which it is set, which must be the first stage of vicarious representative action. What this entails can perhaps be best illustrated by Bonhoeffer's own actions of responsibility while in Tegel, in relation to his fellow prisoners. These were not limited just to his many acts of kindness and generosity, which included helping those injured in the air raids, and writing a report on how prisoners should better be treated in such emergencies,[57] together with a long report intended for his uncle Paul von Hase on conditions generally in the prison.[58] He writes prayers for use by prisoners, and is generous in sharing his own presents of food from friends and family. Alongside all these actions must be laid the signs of a deeper journey of identification with all around him, seen most profoundly and movingly in his long poem "Night Voices."[59] Here he sets out what he hears, actually and in imagination, of the thoughts and anxieties and protests of prisoners trapped in fear, longing, and guilt in the dark hours:

Mute is their chorus,
Wide open my ear:
"We, the old, we the young,
we the sons of every tongue, we the strong, we the weak,
we the watchful, we who sleep,
we the rich and we the poor,
all alike in calamity's hour,
we the bad, we the good,
wheresover we have stood,
we whose blood was often shed,
we witnesses of the dead;
we the defiant and we the resigned,
we the innocent and we the maligned,
tormented by long loneliness in heart and mind.
Brother, searching and calling are we!
Brother, can you hear me?"

The poem continues hauntingly, through painful expressions of guilt, of sinning and being sinned against, of all kinds of deceit and betrayal: "We saw the Lie raise its head/and failed to pay homage to Truth." Bonhoeffer is in effect praying with them and on their behalf, and in doing so, with all of wayward, fearful, sinning, and soon-to-be-defeated Germany. It is an act of vicarious representative action, involving the giving up of religious privileges, at the deepest spiritual level—as was, indeed, the action of himself and his fellow conspirators in the resistance. Almost at the end comes the most poignant verse of all. A nearby cell is door is opened and an unknown prisoner is led away for the ultimate punishment. He, too, is heard:

I go with you, Brother, to that place
And I hear your last word:
"Brother, when the sunlight I no longer see,
Do live for me!"

Bonhoeffer, we have seen, had repeatedly challenged the ecumenical movement to act as the church—for instance, when, in international sessions, he called it to recognize itself *as* the universal church of the nations. From the standpoint of his prison theology, we may imagine him now calling for the churches, as before, under the word of Christ to act vicariously toward each other but also, now, to identify with their world in the deepest possible way; to confess that they do not have special privileges but themselves belong to the sinful world in its longing for justice, forgiveness, reconciliation, and peace, and that they are simply the first hearers of the gospel. That means a fundamental reorientation away from themselves to the world, the *oikoumene*—and through vicarious representative action in the *oikoumene* finding themselves more truly as the body of Christ, and thereby finding their unity. Religionless Christianity is the ultimate logic of ecumenism.

CHAPTER 11

Still Ahead of Us?
The Continuing Quest

"Bonhoeffer had charged so far ahead that the conference could not follow him." So Otto Dudzus recalls the electrifying effect of Bonhoeffer's morning address to the ecumenical conference at Fanø in 1934.[1] Eighty years on from that event, has the ecumenical movement moved beyond Bonhoeffer or is he still ahead of it in important respects? That is the main question for us as we conclude this study.

The Making of an Ecumenical Saint

The process of Bonhoeffer's recognition as, in Victoria Barnett's apt term, an "ecumenical saint"[2] began very soon after his death, especially in the English-speaking world. "The story of Bonhoeffer belongs to the modern Acts of the Apostles," declared Reinhold Niebuhr in June 1945, in the American journal *Christianity and Crisis*.[3] A month later, on 27 July, in London, the memorial service for Dietrich and Klaus Bonhoeffer was held in Holy Trinity Church, Holborn, and broadcast on the BBC Overseas Service. Julius Rieger conducted the service, George Bell preached in English, followed by Franz Hildebrandt in German. Bell surveyed Bonhoeffer's life and service both to the Christian resistance in Germany and to the wider church, and spoke movingly of his final meeting with him in Sweden in 1942. His concluding remarks were prophetic in their anticipation of what now awaited his friend's reception in the ecumenical world:

> And now Dietrich has gone. He died, with his brother, as a hostage. Our debt to them, and to all others similarly murdered, is immense. His death is a death for Germany—indeed for Europe too. He made the sacrifice of human prospects, of home, friends and career because he believed in God's vocation for his country, and refused to follow those false leaders, who were the servants of the devil. He was inspired by his faith in the living God, and by his devotion to truth and honour. And so his death, like his life, marks a fact of the deepest value in the witness of the Confessing Church. As one of a noble army of martyrs of differing traditions, he represents both the resistance of the believing soul, in the name of God, to the assault of evil, and also the moral and political revolt of the human conscience against injustice and cruelty. He and his fellows are indeed built upon the foundation of the Apostles and the prophets.
>
> Our Lord said, "Except a grain of wheat fall into the ground and die, it abideth alone; but if it die, it bringeth forth much fruit. He that loveth his life shall lose it, and he that hateth his life in this world shall keep it unto life eternal." To our earthly view Dietrich is dead. Deep and unfathomable as our sorrow seems, let us comfort one another with these words. For him and Klaus, and for the countless multitudes of their fellow victims through these terrible years of war, there is the resurrection from the dead: for Germany redemption and resurrection, if God please to lead the nation through men animated by his spirit, holy and humble and brave like him: for the Church, not only in that Germany which he loved, but the Church Universal which was greater to him than nations, the hope of a new life. "The blood of the martyrs is the seed of the Church."[4]

In the immediate postwar years, Bell himself through his writing and public speaking was foremost in calling attention to Bonhoeffer and his significance as a Christian martyr for truth and justice, and thereby a representative of that "other Germany" whose cause the bishop had taken up so assertively throughout the war. Bell's own ecumenical stature increased still further following the inauguration of the World Council of Churches (WCC) at its first assembly in Amsterdam in 1948 and his appointment as moderator of its central committee, a position he held until the second assembly in 1954. He was made an honorary president and continued as such until his death in 1958. Just how closely Bonhoeffer continued to accompany him in his ecumenical concerns may be seen in his book 1954 book *The Kingship of Christ*, a neat *summa* of his ecumenical experience and mature thinking. Here he not only further recounts his personal dealings with Bonhoeffer, but cites and echoes the attack on "religion" in Bonhoeffer's prison writings.[5]

Indeed, by the early 1950s Bonhoeffer's major works were not only being published—or, indeed (in the case of his prewar writings), republished—in German, but in English, too, and in due course other languages as well. His theology became a subject of intense academic study, and his life was of no less interest. Biographies became plentiful, none as authoritative as Eberhard Bethge's massive and definitive opus which was published in Germany in 1967, with an abridged English edition in 1970, and a revised unabridged English version in 2000.[6] Films, radio and television documentaries, and dramatized treatments on stage and screen followed and continue to this day. The International Bonhoeffer Society holds a congress every four years and draws participants from every continent. The marking of each decade's anniversaries of Bonhoeffer's birth and death are now almost routine in many countries. The "Bonhoeffer industry," as cynics were dubbing it as far back as the 1960s, and whose demise has been regularly and confidently predicted, shows no sign of slowing down.

Just by being who he was, Bonhoeffer has been an ecumenical influence. His appeal and interest transcend all confessional and religious boundaries. He has become a common reference point for Christians of all traditions, an embodiment of faith, integrity, truthfulness, and courage to the point of martyrdom. In many churches around the world he is a literally iconic figure. Above the west door of Westminster Abbey in London, Bonhoeffer's statue, next to that of Oscar Romero, stands centrally among the nine other 20th-century martyrs commemorated there. To many Roman Catholics (and increasingly, Orthodox, too) he is a respected and intriguing face of Protestantism. To non-Germans he is the welcome assurance that there really was another Germany, just as for many Germans themselves he provides an acceptable link with their national past. Non-Christians, including secular humanists, confess their real respect for him. He has provided a meeting place for Christian–Jewish dialogue, notwithstanding the fact that in the post-Holocaust world even a Bonhoeffer cannot presume to escape suspicion of complicity in overall Christian antisemitism. Simply by being a figure with whom so many people from diverse traditions wish to identify, he has been of immense influence on an ecumenical scale.

His posthumous influence on the ecumenical movement as such, however, requires much more to be said, and much more than can be set down here. We shall therefore just note certain trails through ecumenical life since 1945 where his explicit footprints can clearly be seen, as well as where his influence is more diffuse but nonetheless apparent.

The Ecumenical Movement: Tracking Bonhoeffer's Influence

Both within and beyond the formal bounds of the World Council of Churches, Bonhoeffer's influence on the ecumenical story since 1945 can be clearly traced at specific points.

1. *Postwar repentance and reconciliation.* Bonhoeffer's call for Christian confessing of Christ to begin with the confession of Christian guilt was strongly echoed in the first postwar meeting of German Protestant leaders with ecumenical representatives, at Stuttgart, in October 1945.

This issued in a notable and public acknowledgment by the Germans (including even such as Martin Niemöller who had suffered as Hitler's special prisoner) of their failures of witness under Nazism. W. A. Visser't Hooft, who was present at the meeting along with George Bell, specifically recalls that he had already received a copy of Bonhoeffer's poem "Night Voices"[7] and Bishop Otto Dibelius had expressed his hope that the German church should speak as Bonhoeffer had done: "Thus Bonhoeffer was not absent at Stuttgart. . . . At the very beginning of the meeting I spoke of the great encouragement which Bonhoeffer's witness had given us."[8] George Bell spoke similarly. The Stuttgart Declaration was bitterly resented by some circles in a defeated Germany still feeling more sinned against than sinning, and has, from other quarters, including Eberhard Bethge, been criticized for not speaking specifically enough (it has no mention of the fate of the Jews, for example).[9] But there is no doubt that in its immediate context it was a positive factor in healing the wounds at the international level, and in setting the tone for ecumenical encounter in the new era. Visser't Hooft comments: "It is perhaps not sufficiently wellknown that the response from a number of other churches to the Stuttgart Declaration took the form of concrete statements concerning their share of guilt for the great catastrophe and that in this way something of Bonhoeffer's vision concerning the church as a fraternity of mutual correction and forgiveness became reality."[10]

2. *Ecumenical movement as "confessing."* At Amsterdam in 1948, the inaugural assembly declared the WCC to be "a fellowship of churches which accept our Lord Jesus Christ as God and Saviour." At the third assembly, New Delhi 1961, a revised basis was adopted which included the replacement of "accept" by "confess." How much weight should be accorded this linguistic change may be debatable, but it is certainly the case that to "confess"

implies more than do terms such as "accept," and still more than "regard."[11] To *confess* Christ as Lord, God and Saviour means much more than a formal creedal statement about the status of Jesus Christ, even of his divinity. It is to affirm belief that *Christ* is Lord, as distinct from other claimants to ultimate sovereignty and obedience, be they political, ideological, or religious. It is to prepare the community of faith for combat with the false powers of the world in any area of life. Thus the WCC is not only claiming to be a confessing movement itself, but is expecting that all its member churches will be confessing churches. That means that the ecumenical movement should continually be exposed to Bonhoeffer's question of truth versus heresy—and therefore be prepared to risk debate about the truth. Certainly, the German Church Struggle has been a potent case study for the postwar ecumenical movement, with the witness of the Confessing Church an inspirational example. Of course, for a number of years there were actual survivors from the Christian opposition under Hitler who became inspirational ecumenical leaders, including Martin Niemöller and Hans Lilje, but Dietrich Bonhoeffer wearing the martyr's crown remained the most potent embodiment of confessing resistance. There was no guarantee, however, that Bonhoeffer's translation into postwar ecumenical life would have happened automatically. The prime mover in ensuring that the Confessing Church legacy and Bonhoeffer's role in it were transmitted into the heart of WCC consciousness was Visser't Hooft. As I have argued elsewhere,[12] of all the ecumenical bodies in the 1930s it was the World Student Christian Federation (WSCF), under Visser't Hooft's leadership as secretary, which had made closest alliance with the Confessing Church and took the greatest sustained interest in the import of the Barmen Declaration. In 1938, Visser't Hooft took that commitment to his desk at the infant WCC, and it was primarily through him that "confessing" infused the consciousness of the new ecumenical body in the postwar years. Successive general secretaries of the WCC have used particular occasions in its life to remind its governing bodies of his significance for its contemporary witness. Thus Philip Potter, in his report "Costly Ecumenism" to the central committee meeting in Berlin in August 1974, paid tribute to Martin Niemöller and Hans Lilje who were present there, and spoke at some length on Bonhoeffer's ecumenical witness, emphasizing his search for a true fusion of faith in sacramental unity and the struggle for peace and justice: "He exemplified this in his writings and his untiring witness in the fateful 1930s and 1940s and paid the penalty of martyrdom for his ecumenical conviction." Potter described the WCC as inheriting the tradition of such as J. H. Oldham and of Bonhoeffer, who said "We shall only know what we do." A quarter-century later, in February 2001, the WCC central committee met in Potsdam and on 4 February—Bonhoeffer's birthdate—gathered in Berlin for the launch of the programme "Decade to Overcome Violence: Churches Seeking Reconciliation and Peace." At a torchlight rally at the Brandenburg Gate, general secretary Konrad Raiser reminded the gathering that Bonhoeffer would have been 95 on that day, and named him among the great "cloud of witnesses," along with such as Oscar Romero, Martin Luther King, and Mahatma Gandhi.[13]

3. *The "Missionary Structure of the Congregation" (MSC) programme.* This was instigated by the third WCC assembly at New Delhi, in 1961, and comprised a wide-ranging series of studies on how local congregations could be renewed to witness effectively at a time of rapid social change, engaging in secular society with transformative patterns of mission centred on the world instead of the church. It engaged many churches at all levels, mainly in Europe and North America, and has been described as

"the most important WCC study on the theology of mission" in the years between New Delhi and the Uppsala assembly (1968).[14] Bonhoeffer's prison theology, identifying the church as church when it "exists for others" and calling for the church to take its responsibility in the secular life of the world, was a powerful impulse in the programme, as signalled in the very title of the major report *The Church for Others and the Church for the World: A Quest for Structures for Missionary Congregations*.[15]

4. *Instances of a "status confessionis."* As well as invoking in general the spirit of a confessing church, the fellowship of churches in the WCC has since the 1960s seen specific cases where one or more churches have declared a *status confessionis* to have arisen; that is, a situation where actions of the state or other secular forces, or religious authorities, are so evil that obedience to or acquiescence in them by the church and Christians would constitute a denial of the very gospel itself, and thereby commit the church to heresy. That requires a decisive "no" from the church with appropriate declarations of opposition in word and deed. In virtually every known instance where this has occurred since the 1960s, the example of the German Church Struggle has been cited and Dietrich Bonhoeffer seen as role model and theological mentor. This was very clearly seen in the Christian opposition to apartheid in South Africa from the early 1960s where, as in 1930s Germany, churches were challenged in the very fundamentals of their faith and practice by the imposition of racist policies. Those opposing racial discrimination and oppression, which ran through both society and the churches, declared apartheid to be not just morally wrong and politically misguided, but theologically a *heresy*. The German Confessing Church, and Bonhoeffer in particular, became inspirational for this stance.[16] It was under direct inspiration from Bonhoeffer that the Dutch Reformed pastor Beyers Naudé, foremost among

white Christian opponents of apartheid, founded the Christian Institute in 1963 as the instrument of a confessing church against apartheid, a move for which he suffered expulsion from his church and, in due course, trial and years of house arrest by the authorities.[17] The Dutch Reformed Church meanwhile withdrew from the WCC in response to the statement drawn up at the pivotal Cottesloe Conference in 1960, at which concerned South African church representatives and a WCC delegation had met in the wake of the infamous Sharpeville massacre. The conference declared, among other things, that exclusion of anyone from any church on the grounds of race or colour was inimical to faith in Jesus Christ. The solidarity of the WCC and many of its member churches with the Christian opposition to apartheid was to be a prime feature, at times controversial, of ecumenical life for the next 30 years. Moreover, in 1964, Visser't Hooft specifically connected apartheid with a *status confessionis*. The Lutheran World Federation and the World Alliance of Reformed Churches, both of which have significant member churches throughout southern Africa, declared apartheid a heresy in 1982 and actually suspended those churches supporting the system, pending confession of their guilt. The WCC Programme to Combat Racism (PCR), which was set up in 1969, including the creation of its Special Fund to assist liberation movements in southern Africa and elsewhere, can be seen as a practical extension of this confessing stance. It is not surprising that those who, especially in the churches of the North, expressed alarm at this policy were made to face the example of Bonhoeffer's involvement in the conspiracy for liberation in *his* own country. In fact, within Germany, and no less controversially, the Evangelical Church had in 1957–58 entered a lively and potentially divisive debate on whether nuclear armament and nuclear deterrence were compatible with Christian faith and so constituted a *status confessionis*, although here the initial challenge was provided by Karl Barth. In addition to the issues of race and peace in a nuclear age, the *status confessionis* has notably been raised as an ecumenical issue posed by the global economic system. Here the most vigorously prophetic voice has been the German theologian Ulrich Duchrow, who draws much upon Bonhoeffer, insisting that, no less than militarism and racism in Hitler's Germany, the inhumanity and destructiveness of the global market economy—in which the churches themselves are deeply implicated—is a confessing issue.[18] The body which has taken up this call most decidedly is the World Alliance of Reformed Churches,[19] which at its assembly in Debrecen, Hungary, in 1977 embarked on a *processus confessionis* with the programme "Break the Chains of Injustice."

5. *Justice, Peace, and the Integrity of Creation (JPIC)*. The JPIC process was initiated as a programme priority by the WCC at its sixth assembly, in Vancouver, in 1983. It was an attempt to link and treat holistically the issues of peace, systems of injustice, and the imperilling of the environment and of all life on the planet. This was to be more than yet another effort in applying Christian ethics, nothing less than a *confessing* of the faith and thus a new vision of the missionary task of the church. JPIC was truly worldwide in its reach, and its single biggest expression was the convocation held in Seoul, Korea, in 1990, and it was given further prominence at the next WCC assembly, Canberra 1991. While not all the early hopes of JPIC were fulfilled (the notion of the churches "covenanting" together on responding to the issues created some difficulties in understanding), the aims and language of JPIC continue to infuse the life of the churches more widely, and at more levels, than any other ecumenical project from the late 20th century. Again, Bonhoeffer was a significant inspiration in its genesis, especially his

speech at Fanø in 1934[20] calling on "the one great Ecumenical Council of the Holy Church of Christ over all
the world" to speak out against war and weaponry. This
recollection was especially pertinent in a Europe divided
by the Cold War and laden with nuclear arsenals, and
above all in the two Germanies, East and West. At the
ninth assembly of the Conference of European Churches
in 1986, it was the Protestant churches from both sides of
the Berlin Wall who called for the convening of an assembly of churches in all countries that were signatories to
the Helsinki Final Act. Thus the First European Ecumenical Assembly of churches of all traditions from every part
of the continent took place in Basel, Switzerland, in May
1989, under the theme "Peace with Justice." Embracing
the whole JPIC agenda, Basel anticipated the dramatic
changes about to sweep across Europe, and its outcomes
enabled people and churches to engage creatively with
those changes.

These cases by no means exhaust Bonhoeffer's persistent influence
on ecumenical and church life generally. Instances of lesser indebt-
edness, explicit or diffuse but nonetheless significant, are readily
detectable. Whenever, for example, the adjective "costly" appears, as
it regularly does in titles or themes of publications, it is hard not to
believe the author of *Discipleship* to be standing near with his warn-
ings against "cheap grace" and his call for costly discipleship.[21] One
instance is the WCC 1993 report *Costly Unity*, which, as part of the
JPIC Process, sought to bring together the concerns for the unity
of the church (Faith and Order) and the social ethics agenda (Life
and Work).[22] Much of the debate during the 1970s, especially in the
wake of the Programme to Combat Racism, about violence and social
change, evidently took cognisance of Bonhoeffer.[23] In April 1973 the
Commission on Social Responsibility of the Evangelical Church of
Germany published 12 theses on "Violence and the Use of Violence
in Society." The 11th thesis, "Violent action as involvement in guilt,"
is highly redolent of Bonhoeffer's *Ethics*: "The task of Christian ethics

is not to justify the use of violence and condone it without reserve, but to make the Christian understand that his attitude must always include the recognition of his own unavoidable involvement in the guilt of others, and the willingness to take that guilt on himself."[24] For their part, a number of Latin American liberation theologians, while not seeing Bonhoeffer as their primary inspiration, express a sense of resonance with elements in his theology, especially on religion as a corrupting force, and on the insights gained from what Bonhoeffer called "the view from below."[25]

The posthumous Bonhoeffer has thus certainly been a major and powerful ecumenical influence. But has he still more to offer? Do the major influences we have just noted reflect his profile in its entirety and its bearing on the ecumenical movement today and tomorrow?[26] Or, drawing on our study as a whole, what further impacts from Bonhoeffer should be expected? As we conclude this study, three main features of the ecumenical Bonhoeffer and his theology that emerge from the preceding chapters must be highlighted.

1. The Ecumenical Role Model

Right at the start of this study it was remarked that those passionately interested in Bonhoeffer do not always rate his ecumenical work as of first importance, while many ecumenists do not instinctively turn to Bonhoeffer as a major source of inspiration or guidance for their commitment to the cause of Christian unity. By now it should have been amply demonstrated why both these kinds of readings are seriously inadequate to who Bonhoeffer was and to what he said, did, and thought from the start of his theological career to the very end. But it was also remarked that ecumenical circles are sometimes prone to claim the heroic martyr figure too easily as a kind of figurehead or mascot for the cause without heeding just how challenging, restless, and often critical a figure he was on the scene. We have shown that once induced into ecumenical work as a youth secretary of the World Alliance for Friendship through the Churches he entered into it very much on his own terms, with his own theology and with his own vision of what the ecumenical movement should be, and followed his own path through it. Hence we may justly speak of Bonhoeffer's own ecumenical quest. He brought to the movement extraordinarily high expectations of how it should speak and act for peace, and of how it should respond to the question of *truth* versus *heresy* posed by the German Church Struggle. That led to him making demands upon it, not all of which could be met. He was often an uncomfortable person to deal with, especially as far as the ecumenical office in Geneva was concerned and eventually, in 1937, his patience with the Youth Commission office, and with H. L. Henriod in particular, ran out. In 1939 he was felt to have let down his ecumenical friends in the USA with his decision to forgo their generous hospitality and return to Germany. But his criticisms, and sometimes severe frustrations, in regard to the ecumenical movement were simply the reverse side of his loyalty to it. Even when his hopes for the clearest word were not quite as fully met as he would have wished—as in George Bell's Ascension Day message of 1934 or at the Fanø conference soon after—he was genuinely and generously full of gratitude when it was clear that his trusted friends like Bell, Oldham, and Visser't Hooft had done their utmost to move in the desired direction.

Furthermore, it was to the totality of the ecumenical movement that Bonhoeffer was committed. The fact that from 1931 his immediate responsibility lay within the World Alliance and that he was thereby drawn closely into the larger Life and Work movement—being co-opted onto its executive committee at Fanø in 1934—did not imply a basic preference in principle for Life and Work at the expense of Faith and Order. His dispute with Faith and Order, as shown in his sharp exchanges with Leonard Hodgson in 1935, was not about the priority given by Faith and Order to doctrine as distinct from social ethics, but about Faith and Order's mistaken view of the German Church Struggle and its refusal to see the Reich Church as mired in the German Christian heresy and therefore not meriting a place at the ecumenical table. By 1939, moreover, Bonhoeffer and his colleagues in the leadership of the Confessing Church were so desperate to overcome their isolation from the fast-developing ecumenical scene and the advent of the World Council of Churches, that Bonhoeffer made his ill-fated attempt with Leonard Hodgson for a permanent Confessing Church attachment to Faith and Order. It is a fact of ecumenical life that from the very formation of the WCC there has been a somewhat uneasy relationship between its two main streams of Life and Work and Faith and Order. This tension in one way or another has persisted to this day in terms of competing programmes (and funding), and perhaps will always be a necessary dynamic within all ecumenical bodies. But Bonhoeffer himself cannot be used to justify a sectarian stance within the ecumenical movement. He saw it whole and, as we have learned, his interest in interconfessional issues and his hopes for their eventual resolution did not wane but, if anything, increased during his time in the political resistance and even during his imprisonment.

What is more, there was his sheer diligence and industry. Despite all his other commitments, whether academic or pastoral, at every stage of his adult career—as a youth secretary of the World Alliance, as an executive committee member of Life and Work, as correspondent and counsellor on ecumenical matters whether at Finkenwalde or Berlin or when visiting Geneva during the war—he was assiduous in fulfilling his responsibilities. He was no status seeker or mere passenger on the ecumenical gravy train (not that there was much gravy in the financially straitened 1930s). He took his full share of the hard graft and grind: the taxingly detailed work of organizing meetings nationally and internationally, the endless writing of letters and reports, the papers and conference lectures, not to mention the extensive travelling and the committee work itself—all took their due of his time and energy. Such industry could only have been the expression of a deep and wholehearted commitment, paralleled by his unremitting devotion to the day-to-day needs of the congregations which he pastored. How does this make Bonhoeffer different from any other truly committed servant of the ecumenical movement? What is outstanding about him? The answer is: nothing, and that is the whole point. What Bonhoeffer says in *Life Together* about the community of service, he would surely wish to apply to every level of community, including the ecumenical: "The community of faith does not need brilliant personalities but faithful servants of Jesus and of one another. It does not lack the former but the latter."[27] For Bonhoeffer such work, precisely in its lack of glamour, was a form of *Stellvertretung*, vicarious representative action. To wish to admire Bonhoeffer the brilliant theologian, the heroic resister, and the courageous martyr without also seeing him as the servant dutiful in the necessary humdrum tasks, is to misunderstand both him and the movement which was so important to him. Today, in a time and a culture where excitement is valued above reality and celebrity more than genuine community, for this reason alone Bonhoeffer is a significant role model for ecumenists.

We have also drawn attention to the way Bonhoeffer himself did not arrive on the scene a ready-made ecumenist, but was by stages formed into one. His formation was grafted onto an innate curiosity and interest in the wider world and a respect for what is other, inculcated by his family and upbringing. It was fostered by a combination of foreign travel, the experiencing of other cultures and encountering other confessions, and, above all, the *personal encouragement and mentoring* by such senior figures as Adolf Deissmann, Friedrich Siegmund-Schultze, and—especially—Max Diestel. "The ecumenical movement needs a new generation of leaders," observed the American ecumenist Michael Kinnamon, listing contemporary challenges at the tenth assembly of the WCC at Busan, South Korea, in November 2013.[28] But leaders do not arrive from nowhere or automatically. Bonhoeffer's own formation as an ecumenist and his role in the ecumenical mentoring of his own students in turn offer an instructive case study for use here.

2. Is the Ecumenical Movement Church?

"There is still no theology of the ecumenical movement";[29] "Is the ecumenical movement, in its visible form, church? Or conversely: Has the real ecumenicity of the church as attested in the New Testament come to visible and appropriate expression in ecumenical organizations?"[30] Taken together, Bonhoeffer's opening statement to the 1933 youth conference in Ciernohorské Kúpele[31] and the question posed in his 1935 paper "The Confessing Church and the Ecumenical Movement"[32] crystallize his insights into the ecumenical movement of the

1930s, its problems and its potential. The challenge he laid down was barely answered in his own lifetime, although Visser't Hooft, as we have seen, registered Bonhoeffer's concern in his preparatory essay for the 1937 Oxford Conference.[33] But the questions Bonhoeffer asked still await a full response today, for they engage with a major issue which the infant WCC had face within two years of its inauguration in 1948, which has repeatedly (and divisively) raised its head at intervals down to the present and still shows no sign of resolution given the assumed terms of the debate. This issue is the theological status of the WCC and, indeed, all ecumenical bodies at whatever level. Do they have ecclesial status? If so, of what kind? If not, are they purely functional organizations, a platform for dialogue between the churches and for joint action on certain matters?

In 1950 the WCC Central Committee, meeting in Toronto, after lengthy and at times heated discussion, produced an agreed statement, "The Church, the Churches and the World Council of Churches."[34] It was intended to clarify and answer concerns that were already being raised in some member churches, in particular the anxiety that the WCC might become a kind of "superchurch" claiming an authority over the constituent churches. The Toronto Statement declared unequivocally: "The World Council of Churches is not and must never become a superchurch." It has no legislative authority over its member churches; it is not designed to negotiate unions between churches since these can only be conducted by the churches themselves; it is not based on any one doctrine of the church (ecclesiology), nor does membership in it "imply the acceptance of a specific doctrine concerning the nature of Church unity." On the positive side, members of the WCC were held to believe that the church is one, Christ being its one Lord. They believe that the membership of Christ's church is wider than their own church. They are committed to serious conversation, even in disagreement, and to solidarity and mutual service when in need. The Toronto Statement prompted much relief with these clarifications, allaying fears of an ecumenical monster being created, and down the years it has remained a touchstone of ecumenical understanding. There was and are still, however, a range of possible interpretations of its meaning—or perhaps, one should say, its orientation.

Was Toronto, for example, a final and definitive statement on what might be expected of the WCC, that is, essentially a means of dialogue and cooperation? The Orthodox representatives had fought hard to ensure acceptance of the principle that membership of the WCC did not commit any church to regard another member as a church in the full and proper sense, and they achieved that aim. Thus the statement remained studiously neutral on ecclesiological understandings, and thereby also kept open the way to dialogue with the Roman Catholic Church.[35] But others were uneasy with what appeared to be an overconcern with neutrality as the ecumenical ideal at the expense of growth toward more visible unity. Lesslie Newbigin, missionary and bishop in the recently formed Church of South India, commented: "clearly a provisional neutrality is necessarily required of the Council on matters about which its member Churches are divided. But must it not be made clear that this neutrality is provisional?" He continued: "It must be made clear that the [Toronto] statement defines the starting-point, and not the way or the goal. . . . To be committed to neutrality as a permanent principle would be to reduce the Council to the position of a debating-society . . ."[36]

To say that the WCC, or any ecumenical body, must be neutral (even if only provisionally so) on ecclesiological issues is one thing. To interpret this as meaning that the Council as such *has no ecclesial reality or is of no ecclesiological significance*, is quite another. This issue has arisen repeatedly, for example, as recently as during the work of the Special Commission on Orthodox Participation in the WCC, which was set up following the eighth assembly of the WCC in 1998. Indeed, it was not only Orthodox concerns that were emerging here. One way out of the impasse between claiming too much for the Council, on the one hand, and, on the other hand, not allowing it any ecclesial significance whatsoever, is to make a distinction between the ecumenical organization and the ecumenical *movement*, of which the organization is an expression and instrument. One of the earliest commentators on the Toronto Statement, the Anglican William Nicholls, in 1951, argued that "The churches as a whole have not been penetrated by the ecumenical movement. The leaders of the churches who come together officially in the World Council have not in all cases experienced the revolution in theological thought that participation in the unofficial ecumenical movement brings to those who are open to it."[37] The language used here is quite intriguing: the *movement* is "unofficial" while the organization or institution, sanctioned by the churches' leaders or governing bodies, is evidently "official." But if the movement is the dynamic and, indeed, revolutionary impulse which is challenging the churches and calling the organization into being, it is hardly theologically adequate to describe it simply as "unofficial." It surely calls for recognition, if not of ecclesial, then at least of *pneumatological* significance, and the organization as deriving *its* significance *from that*. If Bonhoeffer's question is not liked, then the question, "Is the Holy Spirit at work, and if so what is the Spirit actually doing?," has to be asked and is no less challenging.

An enrichment of language and conceptuality is required to cope with the ecumenical movement and its instruments in their diverse forms. In one of the most creative writings on Christian Councils as instruments of ecclesial communion, Lukas Vischer, sometime director of the WCC Commission on Faith and Order, distinguished between the structure of a council and the actual communion between churches established as a result of the council's work.[38] Councils, he states, do have ecclesiological significance in the promotion of this communion. Such communion can never be enforced or imposed, but must be enabled to grow or be brought to birth. "If the Christian Councils are really to act as midwives to assist at the birth of new fellowship . . . they must become places where the strains and tensions of our time can really be dealt with. Movements and groups must be able to feel themselves to be an integral part of the Christian Councils and even those who feel that they no longer belong to any confessional group must be able to feel that they belong to the Councils."[39] A similar note was sounded by the Dominican ecumenist Jean-Marc Tillard—though with a rather stern rider attached:

> The councils of churches must be seen by their members themselves as a crucible in which, with the grace of the Spirit, God prepares in one place or another the visible and canonical communion of all those communities which are faithful to his Son Jesus Christ. But

that requires the churches involved to have a common will to look for much more in their unity than support that allows them to be content with a situation that does violence to the gospel.[40]

A council, says Tillard, has as its main task *to receive the gospel afresh*. If so, it carries huge pneumatological and indeed ecclesial significance. Vischer describes councils as, if not manifestations of actual communion, *living in anticipation* of the goal to be attained. Such theologians, including more recently Alan Falconer,[41] therefore are prepared to give much fuller and more positive theological significance to ecumenical bodies than did the Toronto Statement. This is very much in line with Bonhoeffer's insistence in 1935 that the Confessing Church would be wrong to deny the significance or even the possibility that "a shattered Christianity is coming together in unanimous acknowledgment of its needs and in unanimous prayer for the promised unity of Jesus Christ."[42] But Bonhoeffer goes still further. Again and again, it is the *promise* that attaches to the ecumenical movement, not its humanly perceived strengths and weaknesses, achievements, and failures, which he highlights. Thus when Bonhoeffer asks, "Is the ecumenical movement church?," this is only partly a rhetorical device. Bonhoeffer knew very well that those gathering at Gland or Fanø would never think that they literally constituted a church in the manner of their own respectively defined traditions, confessional bases, and systems of government. But Bonhoeffer, as we have seen repeatedly, had a definite theology of the church which was at the same time his ecumenical theology: the church is Christ existing as church-community, founded on Christ and his vicarious representative action and manifest in the vicarious representative service of its members to one another. For Bonhoeffer, this was where the church, the body of Christ, appeared; and where it appeared in the international context this was the ecumenical movement. What he was hoping for was a recognition by those present at such ecumenical meetings that if they were indeed gathered under the word of Jesus Christ and seeking obedience to him, engaging in mutual prayer and service and intercessory prayer for the world, they were at least a foretaste of the visibly one church of Christ *and should speak and act accordingly*. Above all, being drawn from all over the world, the *oikoumene*, they were the clearest manifestation possible, there and then, of a cardinal mark of the true church, its ecumenicity: "The range of the one church of Jesus Christ is the entire world."[43] The meeting at Fanø *is* the ecumenical council of the church of Christ for *that* moment, in *that* hour of world crisis ("Who knows if we shall see each other again another year?").[44] What is to stop it daring to act as such and sending to all believers the radical call to peace?

Bonhoeffer's call, resounding throughout the years 1932–34, for the ecumenical movement really to believe in itself and to anticipate as much as possible what it means to be the one church of Christ in and for the whole world, is a call to risk taking, which is what confessing always involves. The risk even of error can be faced, because it knows that its final security lies not in its own wisdom and righteousness but in the forgiveness of sins, its own sins first of all. There is therefore in Bonhoeffer a holy restlessness which can never be satisfied with a minimizing ecumenism basically content with cooperation, dialogue, and lazy theories of "reconciled diversity." These reduce the church to a religious association and the ecumenical movement to a federalizing of such religious bodies. But the church for Bonhoeffer is not a religious body; it is nothing less than the *new humanity* created in Christ.[45] In a world of conflict, it is at the international level that community in Christ, the new humanity, must be most decidedly revealed. That is what the ecumenical movement is for. To take it seriously means attaching incredibly high expectations to it. For this reason, Bonhoeffer will ever be a challenge to the ecumenical movement, or at any rate he will be well ahead of it for as long as we can see at present. At the very least, a move toward a genuinely *conciliar* fellowship in which the churches are accountable to one another, a move which the churches in the past forty years have periodically considered and then moved nervously away from, would be a step in Bonhoeffer's direction. Much is heard today of the need for the churches to "own" the ecumenical movement. But by "owning" is often meant controlling. So long as churches are unwilling to be pulled out of their isolation and self-sufficiency into a wider movement of belonging, to be caught up into and owned by rather than owning the movement of the Spirit, they can never be signs of the new humanity in Christ. At root is the question of whether the churches themselves really wish to be truly one. Behind this claim to ownership lies some questionable theology, and even more questionable historical amnesia. Justice needs to be done to the fact that vital to the ecumenical movement has been the witness and activity of parachurch movements, especially among the youth and laity. Indeed, it was largely out of the Christian youth and student movements of the late 19th century that the modern ecumenical movement was born. Bonhoeffer's point remains: we need a theology which recognizes as *significantly church* any place wherever and however the catholicity, the universality, of community in Christ is emerging and being confessed, as a sign of the new humanity in the midst of the old order of division and death.

Writing of the continuing significance of the Confessing Church and Bonhoeffer for the ecumenical movement, the German theologian Ulrich Duchrow succinctly summarizes the position: "Until the final coming of the Kingdom of God, this fellowship [of the WCC] will always be an imperfect yet visible sign of the one holy church. It is vitally important, nevertheless, that the suppressed question of the ecclesial authority of the ecumenical movement be looked at again and clarified, otherwise the universal Church of Jesus Christ lacks visible concrete form."[46] Duchrow draws heavily on the Confessing Church and Bonhoeffer's theology in his trenchant analysis of the effects of a new kind of confessionalism among the churches themselves, his criticism being particularly aimed at bodies like the Lutheran World Federation which unwittingly or otherwise can be seen as subverting the wider ecumenism represented by the WCC and the need for a true solidarity between the global North and South. The way to a true confessing of Christ today, argues Duchrow, cannot be by first returning to the confessions of the 16th-century Reformation, however revered, but by discerning what confessing means *today* and then drawing on such wisdom as the past may offer. Instead of a world-confessional consciousness and membership as the primary loyalty, Duchrow calls for an ecumenism based on unity at the local level linked with other contexts at the global level. "Unless people are ready and equipped for holistic Christian confession with an ecumenical dimension at the local level . . . there is little prospect of a universal confessing church appearing on the ecumenical horizon."[47] This was written in 1981, but the issues are still very much alive and unresolved. The issues also go much wider than the Lutheran communion. We live in a time of obsession with "identities" at the confessional and denominational level, only partly justifiable on the argument that it is only when individuals and communities know who they are that they can relate meaningfully with others.[48] It has to be asked how much a search for identity involves fictional creations, myths designed to *prevent* new relationships with others. Bonhoeffer, who realized that the assumed traditional confessional identities were losing significance in a world come of age, insists on resisting such distractions from the ecumenical way.

In his prison letter to Eberhard Bethge of 22 April 1944, Bonhoeffer makes one of his most significant autobiographical asides: "I don't think I've ever changed much, except perhaps at the time of my first impressions abroad, and under the first conscious influence of Papa's personality. It was then that a turning from the phraseological to the real ensued."[49] We noted early in this study the importance of Bonhoeffer's family ethos in forming an attitude of deep interest in and respect for what is other, and avoiding superficial chatter.[50] We have had even more cause to take account of Bonhoeffer's widening experience of the world and other confessions in his ecumenical formation. Now, in retrospect, he describes this as "a turning from the phraseological to the real." He was from that point forever searching for the *concrete* expression of faith in the self-revealing God of Jesus Christ. For him, the concrete meant actual community, not theological or philosophical abstractions. To an extent this was realized in the life together at Finkenwalde. But he no less looked for it at the international level, the *oikoumene*. The ecumenical movement for him was the church taking shape, Christ as community taking shape visibly, the *new humanity* appearing and witnessing in the midst of the old world, across all divisions and conflicts. What is at stake in the ecumenical movement is nothing less than letting this community, the new humanity, take shape as an experienced reality. Because this is the will and purpose of God in Christ, it is this ecumenical impulse, not the churches in their assumed self-sufficiency, which receives God's promise. Conversely, it is not the ecumenical movement which is "provisional" (though its transient forms may be), but the churches wherever they are deaf to their calling to catholicity, content with their confessional so-called identities, locked in their nationalized (and thereby heretical) structures and mistaking their assumed social roles for genuine enculturation. Bonhoeffer was a disturber of the ecumenical peace precisely because he believed in the true ecumenical calling so passionately and thus took the ecumenical bodies far more seriously than they did themselves. The ecumenical movement today should likewise stop implicitly apologizing to the churches for questioning their status quo and instead call them ever more urgently to account in fulfillment of their calling to be one, holy, catholic, and apostolic in confessing Christ as Lord of the world. The ecumenical quest is indeed a journey from the phraseological to the real.

3. Belonging "Wholly to the World"

The shift from a church-centred to a world-oriented understanding of mission that took place from about 1960 has remained a major feature of ecumenical life as manifest in the WCC. Since the 1974 Lausanne Conference it has also been marked in the increasingly prominent place of social justice and peace concerns in the global evangelical community. Further, the relationship between the unity of the church and the renewal of the whole human community has been a major preoccupation of ecumenical study since the 1980s. Bonhoeffer has played a significant role in this overall redirection, but he is still ahead of it in important respects.

In 1944, Bonhoeffer had asked: "How can we be *ek-klesia*, those who are called out, without understanding ourselves religiously as privileged, but instead seeing ourselves as belonging wholly to the world?"[51] His question has not been adequately answered thus far, even in the ecumenical community. There can be much talk about a "worldly" or "world-oriented" or "secular" understanding of mission but Bonhoeffer was asking first not about what Christians and churches should *do* but what, or who, they *are*, and to what or where they belong. As of 2013, the most recent ecumenical statement on the church, *The Church: Towards a Common Vision*,[52] building on earlier studies, states well in its final chapter, "The Church: In and for the World," the biblical vision of the inclusive purpose of God's love for all people and all creation: "The Church was intended by God, not for its own sake, but to serve the divine plan for the transformation of the world."[53] Moreover, "The Church does not stand in isolation from the moral struggles of humankind as a whole. Together with the adherents of other religions as well as with all persons of good will, Christians must promote . . ."[54] Christian communities cannot "stand idly by" in face of human suffering and the plight of creation: "The world that 'God so loved' is scarred with problems and tragedies which cry out for the compassionate engagement of Christians."[55] Prophetic engagement with the abuse of power, if necessary to the point of persecution and even martyrdom, is called for.

All this is well and very clearly stated as the conclusion to the whole document, which is set in the perspective of God's purpose being to establish *koinonia* between Godself and all that God has made. Perhaps, however, it is the very fact of this being the final chapter of the document that lends a sense that such statements are mostly being made for the sake of good form and to give an impression of theological correctness. The presupposition of the document seems to be not just that church and world are to be distinguished (which, of course, they have to be) but that they are related only from one side, that of the church. It is a one-way bridge from church to world. The world is the object of the church's action, it is the world that has to be actively transformed by the church's witness, and it is the world's plight that calls for Christian compassion. In all this still lurks the tendency to what Bonhoeffer calls "privilege" on the part of Christians. It is the church that rides to the rescue of the imperilled world. One recalls the popular ecumenical slogan of the 1960s, "Let the world write the agenda!," which sounds very world oriented but in fact implies that once the agenda is set out, it will be the church that graciously deals with it and, moreover, always *knows* in advance what is to be done.

Allied to this is the tendency of the statements of churches and ecumenical bodies to paint the plight of the world in ever more luridly apocalyptic colours, inducing a state of utter helplessness and despair unrelieved save for the "hope of the gospel" of which the church is privileged bearer. This is apt to be not so much an exercise in responsible realism about the state of the world as a ploy by the church to secure for itself a superior vantage point over against the world. It is an assault on the world born out of insecurity (as aggression often is), a prime example of what Bonhoeffer calls an attack on the adulthood of the world. It is a simplistic view of the world that ignores the genuine ability of individuals and communities to make a positive difference— in other words, under certain conditions to be justifiably optimistic. Writing in the winter of 1942–43, shortly before his arrest, Bonhoeffer defends optimism (all optimism, not just "Christian") as "a power of life, a power of hope when others resign," never to be despised however often it is mistaken:

> It is the health of life that the ill dare not infect. There are people who think it frivolous and Christians who think it impious to hope for a better future on earth and to prepare for it. They believe in chaos, disorder, and catastrophe, perceiving it in what is happening now. They withdraw in resignation or pious flight from the world, from the responsibility for ongoing life, for building anew, for the coming generations. It may be that the day of judgment will dawn tomorrow; only then, and no earlier, will we readily lay down our work for a better future.[56]

Bonhoeffer's question, about how followers of Christ can see themselves not only as "called out" but "belonging wholly to the world" is hardly answered by the constant reiteration of calls for Christians and churches to witness prophetically for justice and peace, to respond compassionately to human need and the plight of the creation. These are right and just so far as they go, but left to themselves they do not reach to that point of "belonging wholly" to the world for which Bonhoeffer is searching. They do not reach to that point of profound identification with the world in its strengths as well as weaknesses, its hopes as well as its fears, which Bonhoeffer sees as the logic demanded by discipleship of the incarnate one and which alone enables effective and sustained engagement of the world. On the pastoral level, it also ignores the need for the spiritual resources required to energize and guide such witness and engagement, and to deal with the consequences for those who undertake them, and so they tend to lapse into cheap statements and fruitless gestures. The result of all authentic witness and engagement is not—one hopes—just the transformation of the world but the transformation of the church and believers, too. At the end of *Discipleship*[57] and again in *Ethics*,[58] Bonhoeffer teaches that it is not as though Christians and the church somehow bear the image of God and *then* take it into the world and bring it to bear on the lives of others. In Christ, God and world are united and neither God nor the world can be met without the other. It is in that engagement of faith with the world that the image of God in Christ is created in us. It is in sharing the sufferings of God in the world that one *becomes* "a human being, a Christian."[59] This is an invitation to be transformed, as much as to transform.

"Belonging wholly to the world" requires, first, a deep identification with the human world of which one is a part yet which often wishes one were not so. It is an identification with the world before God, in all its light and darkness, heights and depths. This is as much a spiritual exercise as one of political and social analysis (which is certainly required). It means that deep, daring, and patient solidarity which makes its own the sighs of hope and fear, faith and doubt, of that part of the *oikoumene* whose life it shares. Rather than trying to make people pretend that they are the ones who can put the world right—a way that leads either to fantasy or disappointment—it is a truly *intercessory* identification of the kind Bonhoeffer himself had exemplified in his prison poem "Night Voices,"[60] out of which true witness and engagement is born.[61] Prayer and righteous action together are the form of faith in the world come of age. Recalling what was learned in the struggle against apartheid, the South African theologian Nico Koopman believes that "Bonhoeffer challenges us to a spirituality and a life of prayer that enhance the dawning of a life of human dignity and human rights,"[62] and sums up all that Bonhoeffer offers us in inspiration and guidance for responsible living in society: "He shows the way to a threefold action of firstly prayer, which includes spiritual and moral formation, secondly concrete obedience, and lastly active hoping and waiting upon God."[63] "He shows the way to . . ." This is a journey the ecumenical community still has to make in earnest, that is, the discovery and teaching of the spirituality which must undergird and sustain effective social and political engagement as distinct from cheap statements and easy posturing.

It is also in the context of his remarks about belonging wholly to the world that some assessment can be begun of Bonhoeffer's contribution to the discussion of Christianity's relation to other world religions, which is now such an ecumenical priority. In this study, Bonhoeffer's understanding of non-Christian faiths and their theological significance has made relatively little appearance. This should not be assumed to mean that Bonhoeffer had little interest in the subject nor anything to offer for interreligious dialogue today.[64] For one thing, he was clearly foreseeing that Christian–Jewish relationships were bound to need reassessment and reforming in the wake of the Holocaust and of Christian silence and complicity in that evil. For another, we know how open he was to learning about the Islamic reality in North Africa[65] and the Muslim perspective on Europe.[66] Third, there is his highly significant interest in Gandhi and his unfulfilled wish to visit him in India during 1934–35. His motivation there was to learn about nonviolent methods of resistance, and therewith to discover from the so-called pagan world of the East more of what it meant to be Christian in terms of actual obedience to the Sermon on the Mount.[67] Bonhoeffer offers his own perspective on the issue of dialogue with other faiths, namely, his emphasis that in the incarnate Christ, God in human form, God has bound Godself to all humanity, and disciples of Christ are made brothers and sisters of all human persons irrespective of their religion or nonreligion.[68]

Dialogue with people of other faiths (and of no faith) thus takes place within a vision of the inclusivity of God's embrace of all humankind in Christ, the whole *oikoumene*. Here a new acknowledgment should be made of the important WCC Faith and Order study programme "The Unity of the Church and the Renewal of Human

Community," which was launched in 1982 and reported to the WCC assembly at Canberra in 1991, and which was a creative attempt to explore the relationship of the search for Christian unity to a divided and conflictual world. A remarkable contribution to this study was the presentation made to the Faith and Order Plenary Commission at its meeting in Stavanger, Norway, in 1985 by Frieda Haddad, a Lebanese lay theologian of the Greek Orthodox Patriarchate of Antioch. Haddad was not herself able to be present in Stavanger; Lebanon was still enmeshed in the terrible civil war, and her paper was read on her behalf. It is entitled "The Christian Community as Sign and Instrument for the Renewal of Human Community: A Lebanese Perspective." She describes how Lebanon inherited from both Ottoman and French rule a system of government which preserved the *millet* system, whereby limitations and rights of each religious community were carefully set out, including the proportions to which they were entitled in representative government. This sought to provide checks and balances against any one community becoming either too dominant or too marginalized and oppressed—a precarious balance, as Lebanon's history shows all too well. But Haddad argues that, from her faith perspective, this was inadequate for an understanding either of how she understood her church, or what it meant to be a member of Lebanese society. It reduces human community to legally defined association. So she asks, What does it mean to be "church" in Lebanon, and what does it mean to be Christian in Lebanon? In a powerful and moving way, given the fearful nature of her context there and then, she protests against all thinking in primarily legal and institutional terms, whether of church, society, or nation. She goes on:

> He who takes his citizenship seriously works earnestly for the advent of a renewed human community where the "other" lives, for he cannot legitimately share in the communal reality of the body politic without sharing in the reality of the other, he cannot conceive of himself as answerable to state laws without answering at the same time for the other. In simple and direct terms this means, for instance, that the unbearable living conditions of the displaced, no matter what their religious affiliations are, are unbearable to me

personally. Their uprooting from their villages and towns is my personal uprooting. This involvement with the other rules out any theological formulations that would consider the other as "unholy," or as incapable of being hallowed. I cannot look at him as being part of the *human* community whereas I am part of the "Christian" community. My life and his life are interwoven in the body politic. My hope of salvation, my way to the infinite passes through the other, through our fulfilled finitude. [69]

For Frieda Haddad, then, being church in the perilous context of Lebanon meant an unconditional identification with the *whole* of her society as a human community and its crying needs, a commitment transcending all demarcations and assumed tribal loyalties. She wants to speak not so much about "Christian witness and mission" in a majority Muslim society but about social education for the elimination of authoritarian legal structures, a revolution in the understanding of what it means to be human in community. So her conclusion is: "The Christian community is not a minority group seeking to elaborate for itself a defensive standpoint over and against the yearnings of the human community in which it is called to live. It rather seeks to nurture in its bosom a genuine openness to the common heritage that binds Christians and Muslims together."[70] It takes as its point of reference the whole life of the *polis*, the body politic, the human community, or, as we might say, the *oikoumene*, and seeks to discern the signs of hope for its future. She recognizes the danger that this might drift just into ethical pragmatism, but she maintains the Godward dimension to the Christian's responsibility, a responsibility that may include suffering, perhaps a suffering with the body politic but not abandoning oneself blindly to any of its movements or ideologies. Without mentioning Bonhoeffer, Haddad is here exemplifying superbly what Bonhoeffer was looking for: a church without privileges, existing for and belonging to the whole of its context in the *oikoumene*. That is the truly ecumenical way now and for the future.

". . . And That Our Victory Is Certain"

So we hear again Bonhoeffer's final message, which is one of hope. If any single overriding feature of Bonhoeffer's ecumenism has emerged from this study, it is surely that, while totally committed to the ecumenical quest, Bonhoeffer cannot finally be claimed for any particular structural or organizational expression of it. The ecumenical movement was for him the community of Jesus Christ, the new humanity, becoming manifest throughout the *oikoumene* in a world of conflict. In keeping with his basic doctrine of the church, Christ-existing-as-community, the birth of a community of relationships, relationships of *Stellvertretung*—vicarious representative action—maintained to the very end. He remained, as shown in his final message to George Bell, unswervingly loyal to that reality. It is a reality which not only transcends international divisions and conflicts, it also is greater than any one temporal organizational expression of it. In the coming years, ecumenical structures at any level may well change, perhaps hardly recognizable to those of us who have inhabited the forms established since 1948. That, of course, will not mean the end of ecumenism but merely that its living reality has to be rediscovered and reembodied again and again. Dietrich Bonhoeffer, precisely because he sits loose to particular ecumenical forms while utterly committed to their theological purpose, will remain ahead of us for a very long time to come. "It is not an ideal that has been set up but a commandment and a promise—it is not high-handed implementation of one's own goals that is required but obedience."[71]

Notes

Introduction

1. For the Schönberg story, see Payne S. Best, *The Venlo Incident* (London: Hutchinson & Co., 1950), 200; Eberhard Bethge, *Dietrich Bonhoeffer: A Biography* (Minneapolis: Fortress Press, 2000), 926f.; and Keith Clements, *Bonhoeffer and Britain* (London: CTBI, 2006), 131.

2. Martin E. Marty, the preeminent American writer on religion and society, who has for over 60 years been a most effective promoter of serious Bonhoeffer study, in 2012 published an article sounding the "death-knell of committee ecumenism" as "the task of bureaus, task forces, commissions." Martin E. Marty, "The Death Knell of 'Committee Ecumenism?'" *Sightings* 3 (April 2012), published in *Ecclesia Daily Email Bulletin*, 3 April 2012.

3. See, e.g., Eric Metaxas, *Bonhoeffer: Pastor, Martyr, Prophet, Spy* (Nashville: Thomas Nelson, 2000). Metaxas, an American evangelical, notes well Bonhoeffer's appreciation of "the universal church." But the author's references to "the ecumenical movement" tend to simplistic generalizations, and rarely in his account is there any differentiation between the different strands and organizations. Astonishingly, there is not even mention of the 1931 Cambridge conference of the World Alliance for Promoting International Friendship Through the Churches at which Bonhoeffer made his decisive entry into ecumenical work, and which was by his own account one of the most pivotal events in his whole life; nor of his actual labours as a youth secretary of the Alliance. Even Metaxas's account of the crucial 1934 Fanø conference gets lost in a fog of confusion as to which bodies were actually responsible for the conference and who was involved there. No less seriously, there are huge gaps in his treatment of the relations between the Confessing Church and the ecumenical bodies such as Life and Work, on the one hand, and Faith and Order, on the other—matters in which Bonhoeffer was passionately involved. All too evidently, the ecumenical story is of no real interest for the author, merely a sideshow to what is assumed to be the real Bonhoeffer drama.

4. See n.1, above. Also very helpful are Ferdinand Schlingensiepen, *Dietrich Bonhoeffer 1906–1945: Martyr, Thinker, Man of Resistance* (London: T & T Clark, 2010); and Charles Marsh, *Strange Glory: A Life of Dietrich Bonhoeffer* (New York: Knopf, 2014).

5. Victoria J. Barnett, "Dietrich Bonhoeffer's Ecumenical Vision," *Christian Century* 112, no. 14 (26 April 1995): 454–57.

6. Christine Ledger, "WSCF," in Nicholas Lossky, et al., *Dictionary of the Ecumenical Movement*, 1st ed. (Geneva: WCC, 1991). Cf. Robin Boyd, *The Witness of the Student Christian Movement: Church ahead of the Church* (London: SPCK, 2007), 51. Bonhoeffer's personal engagement with the WSCF as a body was at most tangential.

7. Eberhard Bethge, "True Ecumenism," in idem, *Bonhoeffer: Exile and Martyr*, ed. John de Gruchy (London: Collins, 1975), 79.

8. Dietrich Bonhoeffer, "On the Theological Foundation of the Work of the World Alliance," Lecture in Ciernohorské Kúpele, DBWE 11:356.

9. Konrad Raiser, "Bonhoeffer and the Ecumenical Movement," in John W. de Gruchy, ed., *Bonhoeffer for a New Day: Theology in a Time of Transition* (Grand Rapids: Eerdmans, 1997), 319.

10. Jørgen Glenthøj, "Bonhoeffer und die Ökumene," in *Die Mündige Welt II.1* (Munich: Chr. Kaiser, 1956), 116–203; Armin Boyens, *Kirchenkampf und Ökumene. Darstellung und Dokumentation, vol. 1 1933–39* (Munich: Chr. Kaiser, 1973).

11. See citations list in this volume.

12. W. A. Visser't Hooft, "Dietrich Bonhoeffer and the Self-Understanding of the Ecumenical Movement," *Ecumenical Review* 28 (1976): PAGE NOS?.

13. Ulrich Duchrow, *Conflict Over the Ecumenical Movement: Confessing Christ Today in the Universal Church*, trans. David Lewis (Geneva: WCC, 1981); idem, "The Confessing Church and the Ecumenical Movement," *Ecumenical Review* 33 (1981): 212-231.

14. Barnett, "Dietrich Bonhoeffer's Ecumenical Vision."

15. John A. Moses, "Dietrich Bonhoeffer's Prioritization of Church Unity (*Oekumene*)," *Journal of Religious History* 24, no. 2 (June 2000): 196–212.

16. Raiser, "Bonhoeffer and the Ecumenical Movement," 319.

17. See Ernst Feil, ed., *International Bibliography on Dietrich Bonhoeffer* (Gütersloh: Chr. Kaiser Gütersloh Verlagshaus, 1998); Christian Gremmels, Hans Pfeifer, and Christiane Tietz, eds., *Dietrich Bonhoeffer Jahrbuch/Yearbook 2* (Gütersloh: Gütersloher Verlagshaus, 2005). Subsequent issues of *Bonhoeffer Jahrbuch/Yearbook* published by Gütersloher Verlagshaus.

18. While reserving my judgment on their overall thesis, Mark Thiessen Nation, Anthony G. Siegrist, and Daniel P. Umbel, in their recent work *Bonhoeffer the Assassin? Challenging the Myth, Recovering His Call to Peacemaking* (Grand Rapids: Baker Academic, 2013), deserve credit for emphasizing how important ecumenical relationships remained for Bonhoeffer even during his participation in the wartime resistance. See esp. 77.

19. Keith Clements, *Ecumenical Dynamic: Living in More than One Place at Once* (Geneva: WCC, 2013), 197f.

20. DBWE 6:128f.

21. Rowan Williams, *Lost Icons: Reflections on Cultural Bereavement* (London: Continuum, 2003), 59.

22. The Whigs were a liberalizing, reformist English parliamentary party originating in the late 17th century, opposing absolutist monarchy and supporting the extension of tolerance and political rights.

23. Andrew Chandler, "The Quest for the Historical Dietrich Bonhoeffer," *Journal of Ecclesiastical History* 54, no. 1 (2003): 89–97.

24. For a highly critical view of ecumenical history writing, see John H. S. Kent, *The Unacceptable Face: The Modern Church in the Eyes of the Historian* (London: SCM Press, 1987), 203f.

Ibid., 203.
25. See, for example, the 2000 film *Agent of Grace*, directed by Eric Till.
26. See particularly Mary Glazener, *The Cup of Wrath: The Story of Dietrich Bonhoeffer's Resistance to Hitler* (Savannah, GA: Bell, 1991); and Paul Barz, *I Am Bonhoeffer: A Credible Life* (Minneapolis: Fortress Press, 2008).
27. The phrase "daring, trusting spirit" occurs in Bonhoeffer's poem "The Friend," written in Tegel prison in August 1944 and sent to Eberhard Bethge, DBWE 8:527. On the Bonhoeffer–Bethge friendship, see John W. de Gruchy, *Daring, Trusting Spirit: Bonhoeffer's Friend Eberhard Bethge* (Minneapolis: Fortress Press, 2005).
28. See esp. Dietrich Bonhoeffer, *Creation and Fall*, DBWE 3:62.
29. Dietrich Bonhoeffer, *Discipleship*, DBWE 4:92.
30. Ibid., 4:285.
31. DBWE 8:52.
32. Ibid., 8:460.

Chapter 1: Young Bonhoeffer
1. DBWE 12:253.
2. See Ulrich Becker, "Ecumenical Learning," in Nicholas Lossky, et al., *Dictionary of the Ecumenical Movement* (Geneva: WCC, 2002), 379f.
3. Cf. Simon Oxley, *Creative Ecumenical Education* (Geneva: WCC, 2002), 9–16.
4. Becker, "Ecumenical Learning."
5. Thus I bear in mind the reasons given by Oxley against "formation," but am also influenced by the Pauline phrase ". . . until Christ is formed in you" (Gal. 4:19).
6. For example, the Ecumenical Institute at Bossey near Geneva was founded in 1946, a year after Bonhoeffer's death.
7. The main sources for this section are DBWE 9; Eberhard Bethge, *Dietrich Bonhoeffer: A Biography* (Minneapolis: Fortress Press, 2000); Ferdinand Schlingensiepen, *Dietrich Bonhoeffer 1906–1945: Martyr, Thinker, Man of Resistance* (London: T & T Clark, 2010).
8. Bethge, *Bonhoeffer*, 13.
9. Sabine Leibholz-Bonhoeffer, *The Bonhoeffers: Portrait of a Family* (Chicago: Covenant Publications, 1994), 10.
10. DBWE 9:35f.
11. Ibid., 9:59.
12. Ibid., 9:83.
13. Ibid., 9:88.
14. Ibid., 9:89.
15. Ibid.
16. Ibid., 9:90.
17. Ibid., 9:111.
18. See below, p. 000.
19. DBWE 9:107.
20. A letter in April 1929 from D. Albers, a teacher in Barcelona, to Bonhoeffer implies this. DBWE 10:181.
21. Interestingly, however, Bonhoeffer does not appear to mention anywhere the large and impressive Waldensian Cavour Church, standing prominently in the Piazza Cavour and which he must have seen many times.
22. DBWE 9:106.
23. Italian Baptist newspaper *Il Testimonio* 41 (1924): 246; research by F. Ferrario and M. Kromer. See *Bonhoeffer Jahrbuch 5* (Gütersloh: Gütersloher Verlagshaus 2011/2012), 207–210.

24. DBWE 9:106.

25. Ibid., 118.

26. Adolf von Harnack, *What Is Christianity?* [*Das Wesen des Christentums*] (New York: Harper, 1957).

27. See Ernst Troeltsch, *The Social Teaching of the Christian Churches* [*Die Soziallehren der Christlichen Kirchen und Gruppen*], 2 vols., trans. Olive Wyon (London: Allen & Unwin, 1930 [1912]).

28. The first edition of Barth's *Römerbrief* was published in 1919 but went through several revisions. It was the 1922 edition which made greatest impact. For the English version, see E. C. Hoskyns, trans., *The Epistle to the Romans* (Oxford: Oxford University Press, 1933).

29. Karl Barth, *The Word of God and the Word of Man*, trans. S. A. Weston (London: Hodder and Stoughton, 1928), 43.

30. Bethge, *Bonhoeffer*, 72.

31. See John D. Godsey, *The Theology of Dietrich Bonhoeffer* (London: SCM Press, 1960), 21 n.6.

32. DBWE 1:21.

33. Ibid., 1:34 (emphases Bonhoeffer's).

34. Bonhoeffer draws upon E. Grisebach, P. Natorp, and O. Spann.

35. DBWE 1:71.

36. Ibid., 1:121.

37. See the editorial preface by Clifford Green, ibid., 1:14–17.

38. Ibid., 1:120 n.29.

39. Ibid., 1:180.

40. Ibid., 1:182.

41. Troeltsch, *Social Teaching*, esp. 2:462–65.

42. DBWE 1:268.

43. Ibid., 1:183.

44. Ibid., 1:268f.

45. Ibid., 1:269.

46. Ibid.

47. Ibid., 1:219–23.

48. Ibid., 1:203.

49. Ibid., 1:281.

50. Ibid.

51. DBWE 10:114.

52. Ibid., 10:59.

53. Ibid., 10:76. By war and revolution, of course, Bonhoeffer means the events of 1914–1918 and their immediate aftermath, which had so deeply affected Germany. Spain was staunchly neutral during 1914–1918, and in 1928–1929 the traumas of civil war and dictatorship were still years away.

54. Ibid., 10:104.

55. Ibid., 10:373.

56. Ibid., 10:507.

57. Ibid., 10:170f.

58. Ibid., 10;632.

59. Ibid., 10:265.

60. Ibid., 10:267, 314.

61. Ibid., 10:317.

62. Ibid., 10:315.

63. Ibid., 10:314. Emphases mine.

64. While in America, Bonhoeffer noted with appreciation the passing of a resolution by the Federal Council of Churches against the war-guilt clause in the Versailles Treaty.

65. Ibid., 10:417.

66. Ibid., 10:320.

67. See also his Armistice Day sermon, in ibid., 10:581.

68. DBWE 16:367.

69. DBWE 8:358.

70. See Bethge, *Bonhoeffer*, 174; DBWE 14:112f; Schlingensiepen, *Dietrich Bonhoeffer*, 95.

Chapter 2: Enter a New Recruit

1. Erika Tysoe-Dülken, "World Alliance of Young Men's Christian Associations," in Nicholas Lossky, et al., eds., *Dictionary of the Ecumenical Movement* (Geneva: WCC, 2002), 1219f.

2. Its German name was *Ökumenischer Rat für Praktisches Christentum* ["Ecumenical Council for Practical Christianity"].

3. Originally "World Alliance for Promoting International Friendship Through the Churches"; the slightly shortened title was adopted in 1931.

4. In fact, a joint subcommittee of Life and Work and Faith and Order was considering the mutual relationship of the two bodies, but came to no specific proposals. See Tissington Tatlow, "The World Conference on Faith and Order," in Ruth Rouse and Stephen Neill, eds., *A History of the Ecumenical Movement 1517–1948* (London: SPCK, 1967), 426.

5. Nils Ehrenström, "Movements for International Friendship and Life and Work 1925-1948," in ibid., 567.

6. DBWE 11:118. Deissmann did, however, also warmly commend Bonhoeffer to George Bell as "one of our best young theologians." See DBWE 13:72.

7. See Eberhard Bethge, *Dietrich Bonhoeffer: A Biography* (Minneapolis: Fortress Press, 2000), 43.

8. DBWE 9:53.

9. DBWE 10:281f.

10. DBWE 10:302.

11. DBWE 16:368.

12. Bethge, *Bonhoeffer*, 195.

13. Ibid., 193.

14. DBWE 11:37.

15. See above ch. 1, 000.

16. DBWE 11:38.

17. The Bonhoeffer–Hildebrandt friendship was to prove important to both. A so-called non-Aryan, Hildebrandt found refuge in Bonhoeffer's London parsonage in 1934 before returning to Berlin to serve as assistant to Pastor Martin Niemöller in his Berlin-Dahlem parish. In 1937, after brief imprisonment, he emigrated permanently to Britain, with some years also in the USA after the war.

18. "Draft for a Catechism: As You Believe, So You Receive," DBWE 11:265.

19. Bethge, *Bonhoeffer*, 200.

20. Report in *Cambridge Daily News*, 2 September 1931.

21. "Message on Disarmament," *Record of Proceedings of the Eighth International Conference of the World Alliance for International Friendship Through the Churches*, 12f. The statement cited in quotation marks verbatim here closely resembles the

resolution passed by the Council of Life and Work at Eisenach in 1928 and endorsed by the World Alliance at Avignon in 1929. See Nils Karlström, "Movements for International Friendship and Life and Work, 1919-2925" in Rouse and Neil, eds., *A History*, 564.

22. See Bethge, *Bonhoeffer*, 201.
23. Ibid.
24. Ibid., 200.
25. See below, ch. 6.
26. Report in *Cambridge Daily News*, 5 September 1931.
27. DBWE 11:165–69. According to Bethge, *Bonhoeffer*, 201, he also wrote a shorter piece for a newspaper.
28. DBWE 11:165.
29. Ibid., 11:166.
30. Ibid.
31. Ibid., 11:169.
32. DBWE 11:54.
33. Ibid., 11:135.
34. Ibid., 11:137.
35. Ibid., 11:388.
36. Ibid., 11:316.
37. Ibid., 11:44f.
38. DBWE 1:192.

Chapter 3: Ecumenism and Peace

1. The Church Peace Union was chiefly financed by the American millionaire philanthropist Andrew Carnegie.
2. "Guiding Principles of the 'German Christians' May 1932," in Peter Matheson, *The Third Reich and the Christian Churches* (Edinburgh: T & T Clark, 1981), 5.
3. Ibid.
4. Ibid., 6.
5. Ibid.
6. See ch. 12, "The German Christians (1930–1933)," in Klaus Scholder, *The Churches and the Third Reich*, vol. 1: *1918–1934* (London: SCM Press, 1987), 189–216.
7. *Deutsche Ökumenische Arbeitsgemeinschaft.*
8. *Studentkreis für ökumenische Jugendarbeit.*
9. *Überbundischer evangelischer Jugendkreis für ökumenische Freundschaftsarbeit.* The English version of title used here follows DBWE 11:505, instead of as given in Eberhard Bethge, *Dietrich Bonhoeffer: A Biography* (Minneapolis: Fortress Press, 2000), 238 ("National Evangelical Youth Circle for Promoting Ecumenical Friendship").
10. *Mittelstelle für ökumenische. Jugendarbeit.* The English version of title used here follows DBWE 11:505, instead of as given in Bethge, *Bonhoeffer*, 239 ("German Central Office for Ecumenical Youth Work").
11. Bethge, *Bonhoeffer*, 238f.
12. Ibid., 233.
13. *Arbeitsgemeinschaft der Theologen und Nationalökonomen.*
14. See Bonhoeffer's reply to Reinhold Krause's letter of invitation, 13 November 1931, DBWE 11:66f. Krause became an active Nazi and leading member of the German Christians, and achieved notoriety for his virulently nationalistic and antisemitic speech at a rally of the German Christians in the Berlin Sports Palace in November 1933.

15. Bethge, *Bonhoeffer*, 238.
16. DBWE 11:59.
17. Ibid., 11:343–45.
18. Ibid., 344.
19. Ibid.
20. Ibid., 11:120.
21. Ibid., 11:345–55.
22. Ibid., 11:381f.
23. See below, 000.
24. See DBWE 11:146.
25. Cf. letter of 6 August 1932 to Werner Koch, DBWE 11:135f.
26. See Bethge, *Bonhoeffer*, 242. Nor does any report appear in DBWE 12.
27. Cf. Karl Barth's 1928–29 lectures in Münster, in *Ethics,* trans. G. W. Bromiley (Edinburgh: T & T Clark, 1981), esp. ch. 2, section 9, "Order," 208–46.
28. DBWE 3.
29. See DBWE 11:267f.
30. See Bonhoeffer's own "Primary Report on the Conference of the Provisional Bureau" (published in *Die Eiche*), DBWE 11:346–55.
31. Ibid., 11:351.
32. Ibid., 11:352f.
33. Ibid., 11:353.
34. DBWE 11:365.
35. Ibid., 11:366.
36. Ibid., 11:367.
37. Ibid.
38. Ibid., 11:356.
39. Bonhoeffer also gave a welcoming address at Ciernohorské Kúpele, reconstructed from hearers' notes in DBWE 11:372–74, in which he warned of the growing nationalism and crisis in Germany.
40. DBWE 11:350.
41. Ibid., 11:356.
42. Ibid., 11:356f.
43. Ibid., 11:357.
44. At the Provisional Bureau conference in April, the nationalist Friedrich Peter had defended the concept of geographically and ethnically bounded churches. Cf. DBWE 11:319f.
45. DBWE 11:358.
46. Ibid., 11:359.
47. Ibid.
48. Ibid., 11:361.
49. Ibid., 11:369.
50. Ibid.
51. Ibid.
52. Bethge, *Bonhoeffer*, 251.
53. Ibid.
54. Ibid.
55. "Address in Gland," DBWE 11:377.
56. Ibid., 11:375.
57. Ibid., 11:377.
58. Ibid., 11:378.
59. Ibid., 11:381.

60. Bethge, *Bonhoeffer*, 253, cites Burroughs's report on Bonhoeffer slightly differently: "Europe has to be conquered a second time by *and for* Christ. Are we ready?" (emphasis mine), and states that this exaggerates the crusading note in Bonhoeffer to a degree untypical of him.
61. For 23 September 1932.
62. For 27 September 1932.
63. Ibid.
64. "The World Alliance for Promoting International Friendship through the Churches. Constitution and International Committee as agreed August 1920," in G. K. A. Bell, ed., *Documents on Christian Unity 1920–4* (Oxford: Oxford University Press, 1924), 366f.
65. From Constitution of the Council of Life and Work, cited in Ruth Rouse and Stephen Neill, *A History of the Ecumenical Movement 1517–1948* (London: SPCK, 1967), 553.
66. Tissington Tatlow, "The World Conference on Faith and Order," in ibid., 423.
67. "International Missionary Council Constitution, 1925," in Bell, *Documents*, 372.
68. This did not inhibit the founding conferences of the main ecumenical streams recording the experience of their meetings in highly exalted theological, indeed pneumatological, terms. Thus Faith and Order at Lausanne 1927: "*God's Spirit has been in the midst of us.* It was He who called us hither. His presence has been manifest in our worship, or deliberations and our whole fellowship. He has discovered us to one another. He has enlarged our horizons, quickened our understanding, and enlivened our hope. We have dared and God has justified our daring. We can never be the same again" (emphases mine). See "The Call to Unity," in G. K. A. Bell, ed., *Documents on Christian Unity*, series 2 (Oxford: Oxford University Press, 1930), 2.
69. *Der Weg der dialektischen Theologie durch die kirchliche Welt. Eine kleine Kirchenkunde der Gegenwart* (Munich: Chr. Kaiser Verlag, 1931).
70. Adolf Keller, *Karl Barth and Christian Unity: The Influence of the Barthian Movement Upon the Churches of the World* (London: Lutterworth, 1933).
71. Ibid., 294.
72. Ibid., 305f.
73. Ibid., 314f.
74. On Keller, see Marianne Jehle-Wildberger, *Adolf Keller: Ecumenist, World Citizen, Philanthropist* (Eugene, OR: Cascade Books, 2013). Keller was a member of the Council of Life and Work and was a strong advocate of the Confessing Church. He was present at the 1934 Fanø conference (see below, ch. 6) and played a significant role in its resolution on behalf of the Confessing Church (see Jehle-Wildberger, 179–81). He certainly encountered Bonhoeffer there, but the extent of his other contacts with Bonhoeffer is not clear.

Chapter 4: Crisis 1933: Church, Nation, and Oikoumene
1. Bonhoeffer had evidently been invited to speak some days if not weeks beforehand, and read from a carefully prepared text. The actual broadcast was cut before he reached the end, and it has never been resolved whether this was an act of censorship or merely a technical mishap. See Eberhard Bethge, *Dietrich Bonhoeffer: A Biography* (Minneapolis: Fortress Press, 2000), 259f.
2. Ibid., 258.
3. See ibid., ch. 7; Ferdinand Schlingensiepen, *Dietrich Bonhoeffer 1906–1945: Martyr, Thinker, Man of Resistance* (London: T & T Clark, 2010), ch. 5.

4. DBWE 12:361–70.
5. Bethge, *Bonhoeffer*, 267.
6. Ibid., 266.
7. See Klaus Scholder, *The Churches and the Third Reich*, vol. 1: *1918–1934* (London: SCM Press, 1987), 257f.
8. It is not clear if this is a reference to a speech made by Hitler before the Geneva delegation's visit in April or (more likely) his famous "peace speech" to the Reichstag of 17 May 1933, in which he insisted that Germany did not want war and sounded a ringing endorsement of US President Roosevelt's proposals for disarmament, though with a warning that if Germany did not obtain equal treatment with other nations she would withdraw both from the Geneva Disarmament Conference and the League of Nations. The moderate tone of the speech, for a while, allayed the fears of many in the world at large.
9. *The Churches in Action Newsletter*, no. 2 (June 1933): 1f.
10. Minutes of Life and Work Administrative Committee, London, May 1933 (Geneva Archive), Item VI, "Concerning the German Situation, 2–4.
11. Ibid.
12. Ibid.
13. Ibid.
14. See Bethge, *Bonhoeffer*, 278.
15. DBWE 11:269–332. The text is reconstructed from students' notes.
16. See above, ch. 1, 28-35.
17. "The Nature of the Church," DBWE 11:292.
18. Ibid., 11:319f.
19. Ibid., 11: 330.
20. DBWE 12:164–72.
21. DBWE 12:163.
22. See Bethge, *Bonhoeffer*, 312.
23. This was the venue according to Bonhoeffer's own account in his letter of 6 November to Friedrich Siegmund-Schultze (DBWE 13:31). Bethge, *Bonhoeffer*, 314, suggests (based on Henriod's record?) that it was in André Bouvier's room.
24. Not only was Julius Richter not invited to this discussion, but Bonhoeffer took pains to keep him uninformed about it subsequently. See his letter to Siegmund-Schultze, DBWE 13:31.
25. Ibid.
26. Bethge, *Bonhoeffer*, 314.
27. DBWE 12:174f.
28. See the comment of Ove Ammundsen in a letter to Bell, DBWE 12:174 n.1.
29. See Bonhoeffer to Siegmund-Schultze, DBWE 13:31. Precisely how far Atkinson's amendment changed Bonhoeffer's text is not known but it was clearly acceptable to Bonhoeffer.
30. Ammundsen to Siegmund-Schultze, DBWE 12:174 n.1.
31. See DBWE 12:177–79 for a report on the visit by Bonhoeffer and Richter, from the German Legation to the Ministry of Foreign Affairs, downplaying the significance of the World Alliance meeting and portraying Bonhoeffer and Richter as having done their best to counter attacks on Germany.
32. DBWE 12:174 n.1; Bethge, *Bonhoeffer*, 316f.
33. See above, ch. 3, 000.
34. Bethge, *Bonhoeffer*, 317f.
35. This was originally planned for Budapest, but took place at Fanø, Denmark (see below, ch. 6).

Chapter 5: Ecumenical Friendship: 1933–1935
1. Letter from Barth to Bonhoeffer, 20 November 1933, DBWE 13:39–41.
2. Letter from Burroughs to Bonhoeffer, DBWE 12:145.
3. DBWE 12:154f. Lütgert diplomatically also stated that developing his knowledge of the churches and theology of England would stand Bonhoeffer in good stead in his future academic career and that he was anxious to secure advance approval by the government of an eventual return to academic life in Berlin.
4. DBWE 12:160.
5. On this whole September 1933 episode, see Eberhard Bethge, *Dietrich Bonhoeffer: A Biography* (Minneapolis: Fortress Press, 2000), 321; and DBWE 12:184–86 (Bonhoeffer-Heckel correspondence).
6. In 1933 there were in all six German Protestant congregations in London (not including a Methodist one) plus several in other cities. Julius Rieger, who became a close friend and ally of Bonhoeffer in London, was already pastor of the St George's Church, Whitechapel.
7. See Keith Clements, *Bonhoeffer and Britain* (London: CCBI, 2006), ch. 3, "The London Pastor."
8. Deissmann letter to Bell, DBWE 13:72.
9. See Bethge, *Bonhoeffer*, 356.
10. Burroughs, however, died in 1934.
11. See Keith Clements, *Faith on the Frontier: A Life of J. H. Oldham* (Edinburgh: T & T Clark/Geneva: WCC, 1999).
12. Ten persons attended the York meeting: J. H. Oldham and W. Paton for the IMC; William Temple and Samuel H. Bate for Faith and Order; William Adams Brown and Samuel McCrea Cavert for Life and Work; Valdemar Ammundsen and H. L. Henriod for the World Alliance; W.A. Visser't Hooft and C. Guillon for the YMCA and WSCF.
13. In passing, it may be remarked that, to this writer's knowledge, Bonhoeffer never met William Temple.
14. It has to be said that Headlam's continued sympathy for Nazi Germany, his withering dismissal of the claims of the Confessing Church, and—even during his imprisonment—of Martin Niemöller, were an embarrassment to majority Anglican opinion.
15. See Clements, *Faith on the Frontier*, 272.
16. On Bell, see R. C. D. Jasper, *George Bell: Bishop of Chichester* (London: Oxford University Press, 1967); Andrew Chandler, ed., *The Church and Humanity: The Life and Work of George Bell* (Farnham: Ashgate, 2012); and Edwin Robertson, *Unshakeable Friend: George Bell and the German Churches* (London: CCBI, 1995).
17. G. K. A. Bell, *Randall Davidson*, vols. 1 and 2 (Oxford: Oxford University Press, 1935).
18. See above, ch. 4.
19. At the meeting of pastors and elders of the German congregations in England held on 5 November 1934, at which the decision was made to identify with the Confessing Church, Julius Rieger reported: "It is no secret that all the Protestant churches in England are opposed to the German Evangelical Church. There is no local or national church in England that has not reported the events with abhorrence, protest, mockery and derision" (DBWE 13:234). Note also what Bethge says of the German congregations: "These congregations had also been influenced by the free church environment in England, and had developed a need for independence that now helped them" (Bethge, *Bonhoeffer*, 405).
20. Bonhoeffer letter to Friedrich Siegmund-Schultze, 6 November 1933, DBWE 13:31.

21. DBWE 13:64.
22. For a full account of the meeting and its aftermath, see Klaus Scholder, *The Churches and the Third Reich*, vol. 2, *The Year of Disillusionment: 1934 Barmen and Rome* (London: SCM Press, 1988), 35–46.
23. DBWE 13:118f.
24. Ibid., 13:128.
25. Ibid., 13:132f.
26. See Clements, *Faith on the Frontier*, 292.
27. Letter to Bell, 3 March 1933, DBWE 13:140.
28. Full text in DBWE 13:144–46.
29. Letter to Bell, DBWE 13:147f.
30. The most widely used English full version of the Declaration to date is found in Arthur C. Cochrane, *The Church's Confession Under Hitler* (Philadelphia: Westminster Press, 1962), 237–42.
31. See n.19, above.
32. See DBWE 13:314f.; Bethge, *Bonhoeffer*, 412; Clements, *Bonhoeffer and Britain*, 78–81.

Chapter 6: "The Hour Is Late"

1. For a comprehensive account of Fanø, see Klaus Scholder, *The Churches and the Third Reich*, vol. 2: *The Year of Disillusionment: 1934 Barmen and Rome* (London: SCM Press, 1988), 234–43.
2. Nils Ehrenström, in Ruth Rouse and Stephen Neill, eds., *A History of the Ecumenical Movement 1517–1948* (London: SPCK, 1967), 583.
3. DBWE 13:376.
4. Ibid., 13:392f.
5. Ibid., 13:370. Bonhoeffer's source for the anecdote was Gandhi's autobiography *His Own Story* (London: George Allen and Unwin, 1930), 186–88.
6. DBWE 13:152.
7. Letter, 28 April 1934, DBWE 13:135.
8. Letter, 14 January 1935, DBWE 13:284f.
9. On this aspect of Fanø and Oldham's role, see ch. 12 in Keith Clements, *Faith on the Frontier: A Life of J. H. Oldham* (Edinburgh: T & T Clark/Geneva: WCC, 1999).
10. See ch. 4 above, 000. At the time of the Sofia meeting it was envisaged that the 1934 conference would in fact be in Budapest, the venue subsequently being changed to Fanø.
11. See Henriod letter to Bonhoeffer, 7 July 1934, DBWE 13:176ff.
12. Letter, 12 August 1934, DBWE 13:194f.
13. See Eberhard Bethge, *Dietrich Bonhoeffer: A Biography* (Minneapolis: Fortress Press, 2000), 377–81; and DBWE 13:146–98.
14. Letter, 8 August 1934, DBWE 13:191.
15. Letter, 18 August 1934, DBWE 13:198.
16. DBWE 13:157.
17. Not published until later, as *Die Kirche und das Staatsproblem in der Gegenwart* (Geneva: Forschungsabteilung des Ökumenisches Rates für Praktisches Christentum, 1935).
18. See ch. 3, above.
19. Letter to Bonhoeffer, 13 August 1934, DBWE 13:196.
20. The fully minuted report of the Youth Conference is the mimeographed document *Fanø Fellowship* no. 1 (October 1934), WCC Archives (Geneva) Box 4232.022. Sections of this are cited in DBWE 13:201–210.

21. E. C. Blackman, "The Youth Conference at Fanø," *The Churches in Action* newsletter no. 6 (November 1934) (Geneva: Universal Christian Council for Life and Work and the World Alliance for Friendship through the Churches), 7. Cited also in DBWE 13:201 n.2, where a similar observation from an Austrian delegate, Margarete Hoffer, is likewise recorded.

22. *Fanø Fellowship* 11f.; DBWE 13:208.

23. *Fanø Fellowship* 11; DBWE 13:207.

24. Bethge, *Bonhoeffer*, 383.

25. Universal Christian Council for Life and Work, "Resolutions on the German Church," Minutes of the Meeting of the Council Fanø, August 24th–30th 1934 (Geneva 1934), 50–52.

26. It should be noted that while this clause was evidently requested by Heckel and inserted following the discussion and vote on the resolution supporting the Confessing Church, in the published minutes it appears as paragraph V, *before* the paragraph (VI) on the Confessing Church. Thus it could later be argued, by those who so wished, that Fanø's primary concern was to remain in "friendly contact" with all in the German church rather than making support for the Confessing Church paramount.

27. Letter of 7 September 1934, DBWE 13:213f.

28. "The Church and the Peoples of the World," DBWE 13:307–310.

29. Ibid., 13:308f.

30. Ibid., 13:309.

31. Otto Dudzus, "Arresting the Wheel," in Wolf-Dieter Zimmermann and Robert Gregor Smith, eds., *I Knew Dietrich Bonhoeffer* (London: Collins, 1966), 91.

32. DBWE 13:304–306.

33. Ibid., 13:304f. While Bonhoeffer in the theses submitted several weeks earlier speaks specifically of the World Alliance, it may be presumed that in his actual presentation to the main conference (for which the full text has not survived) he was implicitly also addressing Life and Work, in which of course he did not as yet carry any recognized responsibility beyond that of a secretary of the joint Youth Commission.

34. Bethge, *Bonhoeffer*, 387.

35. Hans Schönfeld, para. 2 of "The Universal Church and the World of Nations," 1936 mimeographed paper, WCC Archives (Geneva) Box 212.008.

36. Including by the present writer.

37. Blackman, "Youth Conference," 7.

38. "Christians in Council—The German Conflict—A Warning from Fano. By the Bishop of Chichester President of the Council," London *Times*, 7 September 1934.

39. Letters written by Henry Smith Leiper during European travels addressed to "Dear Homelanders" (his characteristic form of address to his family), 18 August, 22 August, 4 September 1934. Held in Presbyterian Archive, Philadelphia.

40. Letter of 4 September 1934.

41. H. S. Leiper, "The Acts of the Apostle—Dietrich Bonhoeffer," in Zimmermann and Gregor Smith, eds., *I Knew*, 92.

42. Leiper letter, 4 September 1934.

43. Nor to the writer's knowledge does Bonhoeffer appear on any other photograph of ecumenical meetings where Heckel is visible (e.g., the Life and Work Executive, Chamby 1936).

Chapter 7: "The Question Has Been Posed"

1. See Eberhard Bethge, *Dietrich Bonhoeffer: A Biography* (Minneapolis: Fortress Press, 2000), 391f.

2. For Bonhoeffer's report on Bruay, see DBWE 13:310–13. See also Keith Clements, "Between a Confessing Church and Contextual Ethics: Bonhoeffer, the Bruay Conference and the Continuing Ecumenical Quest for a Public Theology," in Kirsten Busch Nielsen, Ralf K. Wüstenberg, and Jens Zimmermann, eds., *A Spoke in the Wheel: The Political in the Theology of Dietrich Bonhoeffer* (Gütersloh: Gütersloher Verlagshaus, 2013), 109–19.

3. French participants had been expected but, for unaccountable reasons, apart from Jean Lasserre, who hosted the meeting in his parish, none appeared.

4. See DBWE 13:260–63.

5. See Keith Clements, *Faith on the Frontier: A Life of J. H. Oldham* (Edinburgh: T & T Clark/Geneva: WCC, 1999), esp. chs. 12–14.

6. See above, ch. 6 (MSp4).

7. The WSCF leadership, perhaps more than any other ecumenical organization of the time, made explicit its support for the Confessing Church. See Keith Clements, "Barmen and the Ecumenical Movement," *Ecumenical Review* 61, no. 1 (March 2009): 6–16.

8. Present-day Szczecin, Poland.

9. See lists in DBWE 14:1022–26. A further 59 students attended the "collective pastorates," 1937–40 (see lists in DBWE 15:592–94).

10. Memorandum of 29 January 1935, DBWE 13:290.

11. For some time Bonhoeffer maintained contact with Father Paul Bull of Mirfield, who sent him a package of books in May 1936, and in turn asked him how to obtain a copy of *The Way of Holiness*, the exposition of Psalm 119 by R. M. Benson, founder of the Cowley Fathers. He also sought Julius Rieger's help in getting copies of the lectures of Father Herbert Kelley, founder of the Kelham community, who had so impressed him on his visit there. See Keith Clements, *Bonhoeffer and Britain* (London: CTBI, 2006), 83–86, 89. See also DBWE 14:184.

12. See Bethge, *Bonhoeffer*, 562f. Cf. also remarks by Julius Rieger (date and place not stated): "Once we were told that Roman Catholic congregations prayed for the imprisoned and persecuted members of the Confessing Church; when some of us did not see anything remarkable in this, Bonhoeffer reacted sharply, saying: 'I am not indifferent to somebody praying for me.'" See Julius Rieger, "Contacts with London," in Wolf-Dieter Zimmermann and Robert Gregor Smith, eds., *I Knew Dietrich Bonhoeffer* (London: Collins, 1966), 96.

See Bethge, *Bonhoeffer*, 562f.

13. First published in German in 1937 as *Nachfolge* by Christian Kaiser Verlag. The first English editions were titled *The Cost of Discipleship* (London: SCM Press, 1949). The present English edition is *Discipleship*, DBWE 4.

14. *Gemeinsames Leben* was published in 1939 by Christian Kaiser Verlag. For English, *Life Together*, see DBWE 5.

15. Letter of Hodgson, 9 July 1935, DBWE 14:68f.

16. Letter of 18 July 1935, DBWE 14:71–73.

17. Ibid., 72.

18. Letter, 26 July 1935, DBWE 14:76–80.

19. DBWE 14:393–412.

20. See above, ch. 3, 78-83.

21. See above, ch. 4, 97-100.

22. See above, ch. 5, 140-142.

23. DBWE 14:394. Presumably Bonhoeffer recognizes the "first" stage of the ecumenical movement as comprising all those cooperative ventures beginning with the Edinburgh World Missionary Conference of 1910, the formation of the World Alliance, Life and Work, Faith and Order, etc.

24. Ibid., 14:396.

25. Ibid., 14:397. This is a clear reference to the attitude taken by such as Theodor Heckel who, as has been seen, objected to ecumenical bodies "interfering" in "internal" German affairs.

26. Ibid.

27. Ibid., 14:398.

28. Ibid., 14:399.

29. Bonhoeffer's original German makes this clear in its lack of an indefinite article: "Ist die Ökumene in ihrer sichtbaren Vertretung Kirche?" DBW 13 (German version): 384. Likewise, in his thesis paper "The Church and the Peoples of the World," at Fanø 1934 (see above, ch. 6): "Das Schicksal des Weltbundes entscheidet sich daran, ob er sich als Kirche oder als Zweckverband versteht. Kirche ist er, wenn er im gehorsam . . ." (ibid., 13:295).

30. DBWE 14:400.

31. Ibid., 14:403.

32. Ibid., 14:407.

33. Ibid., 14:408.

34. Cf. above, ch. 2, 54.

35. DBWE 14:411f. Emphases Bonhoeffer's.

36. Ibid., 14:412.

37. DBWE 14:656–78. The paper also deals, albeit briefly, with the Confessing Church and ecumenism.

38. Ibid., 14:675.

39. John Wilcken, SJ, "Bonhoeffer: Church and Ecumenism," *The Heythrop Journal* 10, no. 1 (1969): 5–23.

40. Ibid., 23.

41. Ibid., 25.

42. See DBWE 13:289f.

43. See "Memorandum Concerning an Ecumenical Exchange of Young Theologians," DBWE 14:284–87.

44. See Bethge, *Bonhoeffer*, 506–514.

45. Ammundsen, however, died on 1 December 1936, a major loss to the ecumenical movement.

46. For full accounts, see Bethge, *Bonhoeffer*, 472–86, 546–61; Armin Boyens, *Kirchenkampf und Ökumene 1933–39. Darstellung und Dokumentation* (Munich: Chr. Kaiser Verlag, 1969), 46–52, 119–22, 197–201, 217–28.

47. On Oldham's suspicions of Heckel, see Clements, *Faith on the Frontier*, 299, 303.

48. See DBWE 14:287f., 292–94, 295f., 299f.

49. Technically, Bonhoeffer's resignation from the Youth Commission would presumably not have affected his status as a member of the executive committee of Life and Work, to which he had been coopted at Fanø in 1934. George Bell, it should be noted, was no longer president of the council of Life and Work after Fanø, though he remained chair of its administrative committee for four years. It may be that this affected the weight he could exert on the decision making of the Geneva staff.

50. "War and Peace," DBWE 14:297f.

51. *The Churches Survey Their Task: Report of the Conference at Oxford, July 1937, on Church, Community and State* (London: George Allen & Unwin, 1937), 275.

52. W. A. Visser't Hooft and J. H. Oldham, *The Church and Its Function in Society* (London: George Allen & Unwin, 1937).

53. W. A. Visser't Hooft, "Dietrich Bonhoeffer and the Self-Understanding of the Ecumenical Movement," *Ecumenical Review* 28 (1976): 201.

54. Ibid.

55. W. A. Visser't Hooft, "The Church as an Oecumenical Society," in *The Church and Its Function in Society*, 98.

56. *The Churches Survey Their Task*, 31.

57. On the genesis of this term at Oxford, see Ruth Rouse and Stephen Charles Neill, *A History of the Ecumenical Movement 1517–1948* (London: SPCK, 1967), 591 and n.2.

58. *The Churches Survey Their Task*, 169.

Chapter 8: Christian, Ecumenical, German

1. See ch. 7, 160.

2. As distinct from the *Schutzstaffel* ("SS") which, originating as a small Nazi paramilitary organization in the 1920s, grew into Hitler's bodyguard and then into a one million-strong Nazi army alongside the regular *Wehrmacht*.

3. For the ecumenical history of this period, see esp. W. A. Visser't Hooft, "The Genesis of the World Council of Churches," in Ruth Rouse and Stephen C. Neill, *A History of the Ecumenical Movement 1517–1948* (London: SPCK, 1967), 697–724; and Visser't Hooft, *Memoirs*, 2d ed. (Geneva: WCC, 1987), 76–112.

4. See above, ch. 7, 161.

5. See above, ch. 7, 161f.

6. See above, ch. 6, 146-148.

7. See above, ch. 7, 161f.

8. See Eberhard Bethge, *Dietrich Bonhoeffer: A Biography* (Minneapolis: Fortress Press, 2000), 669. According to Nils Ehrenström, "Movements for International Friendship and Life and Work 1925–1948," in Rouse and Neill, *History*, 579, Schönfeld's appointment to Geneva dated from 1929, when he was delegated to the Research Council by the German Evangelical Church Federation (see ch. 2, above).

9. See Visser't Hooft, "Genesis of the World Council of Churches," 709f.

10. There was by now a well-established tradition of refugee work based in Switzerland. The Federation of Swiss Protestant Churches had been pioneers in international and ecumenical relief work since the end of the 1914–18 war, and under the leadership of the ecumenist Adolf Keller (1872–1963) in 1922 set up the European Central Bureau for Relief (Inter-Church Aid), in close cooperation with Protestant churches in the USA. See Marianne Jehle-Wildberger, *Adolf Keller: Ecumenist, World Citizen, Philanthropist*, trans. Mark Kyburz with John Peck (Eugene, OR: Cascade, 2013). Recent research is also throwing more light on the fact that through the 1930s a considerable international network of concern for refugees was developing in Europe and the USA, involving both church-related and Jewish organizations with a significant amount of collaboration and information sharing, and in which Geneva was an important communications nexus. See Victoria J. Barnett, "Track Two Diplomacy, 1933–1939: International Responses from Catholics, Jews, and Ecumenical Protestants to Events in Nazi Germany," *Kirchliche Zeitgeschicte* (Fall 2014).

11. See above ch. 7, 165-167.

12. Visser't Hooft, "Genesis of the World Council of Churches," 708.

13. Visser't Hooft, *Memoirs*, 85.

14. Ibid., 98.

15. Ibid., 120.
16. Ibid., 106f.
17. Ibid., 106.
18. Ibid., 111.
19. For this period, see Bethge, *Bonhoeffer*, 587–635.
20. See Bethge, *Bonhoeffer*, 607.
21. Vice chairman of the WCC Provisional Committee.
22. See above, 188f.
23. Visser't Hooft, *Memoirs*, 98.
24. Bethge, *Bonhoeffer*, 640.
25. Ibid., 636.
26. DBWE 15:156.
27. Bonhoeffer would have had Hans Schönfeld particularly, if not wholly, in mind here.
28. See above, ch. 7, 165.
29. DBWE 15:154. Emphases mine.
30. See above, ch. 3, 79.
31. See above, ch. 7, 167.
32. See above, ch. 7, 171f.
33. DBWE 15:158.
34. See above, ch. 3, 000 MS p10; ch. 4, 000 MSp7.
35. In addition, at this distance in time Hodgson's insistence that there could be no German place on the Faith and Order continuation committee because no Germans had been present at the Edinburgh 1937 conference appears incomprehensibly legalistic since it took no account of the dire political reasons for that absence.
36. See Bethge, *Bonhoeffer*, 642–44. Hodgson and Temple, encouraged by Schönfeld in Geneva, were above all concerned to maintain an "impartiality" toward the German groups; and, if the Confessing representatives and Lutherans were invited with Heckel but refused to attend with him, were prepared to countenance the presence of only Heckel on the continuation committee since they would have demonstrated their "impartiality."
37. DBWE 15:155.
38. See above, ch. 7, 179f.
39. Visser't Hooft, *Memoirs*, 107. Visser't Hooft's account of the meeting is among the most vivid of all episodes in his autobiography.
40. Letter, 13 April 1934, DBWE 15:160.
41. See above, ch. 6, MSp13f.
42. DBWE 15:163.
43. DBWE 15:226f.
44. Leiper, "The Acts of the Apostle," in Wolf-Dieter Zimmermann and Robert Gregor Smith, eds., *I Knew Dietrich Bonhoeffer* (London: Collins, 1973), 93.
45. Reinhold Niebuhr, "The Death of a Martyr," *Christianity and Crisis* 5, no. 11 (25 June 1945): 6–7. It was reprinted in Britain in the *Christian News-Letter* of 14 November 1945 and is cited in Bethge, *Bonhoeffer*, 655.
46. See above, ch. 1, MSp9.
47. Eberhard Bethge, "True Ecumenism," in idem, *Bonhoeffer: Exile and Martyr*, ed. John de Gruchy (London: Collins, 1975), 79.
48. DBWE 15:438–62.
49. Ibid., 448.
50. Bethge, *Bonhoeffer*, 658f., suggests that Bonhoeffer in 1939 was more able to empathize with the American ethos as his own and as a new experience of existential

insecurity: "This time the refugee and person turning back home could appreciate the nation of refugees."

51. DBWE 15:438f.

52. See above, ch. 7, 168-172.

53. DBWE 15:439.

54. See above, ch. 2, 60f.

55. DBWE 15:462.

56. Visser't Hooft, *Memoirs*, 114.

57. Ibid.

58. The French Protestant leader Marc Boegner refused to sign. See ibid., 118.

59. Ibid., 119f.

60. Ibid., 123.

61. "The Genesis of the World Council of Churches," in Rouse and Neill, *A History*, 709.

Chapter 9: In Ecumenical Conspiracy: 1939–1943

1. Eberhard Bethge, *Dietrich Bonhoeffer: A Biography* (Minneapolis: Fortress Press, 2000), 670.

2. For the most comprehensive account of the German resistance in its various manifestations and its international relationships, see Klemens von Klemperer, *German Resistance Against Hitler. The Search for Allies Abroad, 1938–1945* (Oxford: Clarendon Press. 1992), on which this chapter draws.

3. See above, ch. 8, 185.

4. In fact, the group was only so-named by the Gestapo, after the arrests of 1944.

5. See later in this chapter.

6. This aspect of the resistance is conspicuously underplayed in Mark Thiessen Nation, Anthony G. Siegrist, and Daniel P. Umbel, *Bonhoeffer the Assassin: Challenging the Myth, Recovering His Call to Peacemaking* (Grand Rapids: Baker Academic, 2013), in an evident attempt to demonstrate that Bonhoeffer's activities as an *Abwehr* agent were not only unconnected with any of the actual assassination attempts on Hitler, but of very marginal significance in the conspiracy as a whole.

7. See Klemperer, *German Resistance*, 8.

8. Ibid., 9.

9. Ibid., 12.

10. Ibid., 46, 171–80. See also Owen Chadwick, *Britain and the Vatican during the Second World War* (Cambridge: Cambridge University Press, 1986).

11. See Chadwick, *Britain and the Vatican*, 86–100.

12. Klemperer, *German Resistance*, 27.

13. See Neal H. Petersen, ed., *From Hitler's Doorstep: The Wartime Intelligence Reports of Allen Dulles 1942–1945* (University Park: Pennsylvania State University Press, 1996).

14. See W. A. Visser't Hooft, *Memoirs* (London: SCM Press, 1973/Geneva: WCC, 1987), esp. chs. 21, 22.

15. Klemperer, *German Resistance*, 29.

16. Victoria J. Barnett, "Communications between the German Resistance, the Vatican and Protestant Ecumenical Leaders," in Christian Gremmels and Wolfgang Huber, eds., *Religion im Erbe. Dietrich Bonhoeffer und die Zukunftsfähigkeit des Christentums* (Gütersloh: Chr. Kaiser Gütersloher Verlagshaus, 2002), 61.

17. "It Was Not Shame: The Bethges Remember," in Keith Clements, *What Freedom? The Persistent Challenge of Dietrich Bonhoeffer* (Bristol: Bristol Baptist College, 1990), 37.

18. See Bethge, *Bonhoeffer*, 726–37, 755–57; DBWE 16:165–79, 215–24, 274–88.

19. Jacques Courvoisier, "Theological Existence," in Wolf-Dieter Zimmermann and Robert Gregor Smith, eds., *I Knew Dietrich Bonhoeffer* (London: Collins, 1966), 174.

20. See above, ch. 7.

21. DBWE 16:169.

22. Ibid., n.6.

23. W. A. Visser't Hooft, "Notes on the State of the Church in Europe," DBWE 16:175–79.

24. W. A. Visser't Hooft, "Some considerations concerning the post-war settlement," in Armin Boyens, ed., *Kirchenkampf und Ökumene*, vol. 2, *1939–1945* (Munich: Chr. Kaiser Verlag, 1973), 353–55. For reasons which are not entirely clear, Klemens von Klemperer, *German Resistance*, 271, seems to regard this as largely Bonhoeffer's work: "High-minded, if not high-flown, Bonhoeffer's memorandum . . ." But Visser't Hooft is quite clear (letter to William Temple, DBWE 16:171f.; and *Memoirs*, 152) that this document arose out of discussion between himself, Ehrenström, and very probably Kirkpatrick as well as Bonhoeffer, and that the final version, like the first draft, was his work.

25. G. K. A. Bell, *Christianity and World Order* (London: Penguin, 1940), 106.

26. DBWE 16:224.

27. William Paton, *The Church and the New Order* (London: SCM Press, 1941).

28. See Keith Clements, *Faith on the Frontier: A Life of J. H. Oldham* (Edinburgh: T & T Clark/Geneva: WCC, 1999), 363–405.

29. "The Church and the New Order in Europe," DBWE 16:528–39.

30. Ibid., 16:538.

31. See above, ch. 7, 168-172.

32. See above, ch. 8, 203-205.

33. DBWE 16:211.

34. Visser't Hooft, *Memoirs*, 153.

35. Adolf Freudenberg, "Visit to Geneva," in Zimmermann and Gregor Smith, *I Knew*, 168.

36. Visser't Hooft, *Memoirs*, 153.

37. Freudenberg, "Visit to Geneva," 168.

38. See above, ch. 8, 206, on Berggrav's efforts for negotiated peace, 1939–40.

39. Bethge, *Bonhoeffer*, 754.

40. DBWE 16:270.

41. See Bethge, *Bonhoeffer*, 757–70; Ferdinand Schlingensiepen, *Dietrich Bonhoeffer 1906–1945* (London: T & T Clark, 2010), 290–92; Klemperer, *German Resistance*, 281–93. See also Sven-Erik Brodd, "Sigtuna 1942: On the Structural Factors of Political Ecclesiology among Swedish Theologians," in Kirsten Busch Nielsen and Ralf Karolus Wüstenberg, eds., *A Spoke in the Wheel: The Political in the Theology of Dietrich Bonhoeffer* (Gütersloh: Gütersloh Verlagshaus, 2013).

42. George Bell, "The Church and the Resistance Movement," in Zimmermann and Gregor Smith, eds., *I Knew*, 196–211.

43. In many later accounts "Johannson" is anglicized to "Johnson"

44. Bell, "The Church and the Resistance Movement," 201.

45. Ibid., 202.

46. Ibid., 203.

47. "English Address: The Right Rev. The Lord Bishop of Chichester, Dr Bell," in Eberhard Bethge, ed., *Bonhoeffer Gedenkheft* (Berlin: Verlag Hus und Schule GMBH, 1947), 8.

48. DBWE 16:311f.

49. Ibid., 16:312 n.1.

50. Cf. Bonhoeffer's reply to Dohnanyi's question about taking the sword, see above, 221.

51. See above, ch, 2, 30f.

52. DBWE 16:89. Cf. also his letter to H.-W. Jensen, one of his former ordinands, DBWE 16:112.

53. DBWE 16:115.

54. Barnett, "Communications . . . ," 58.

55. DBWE 16:89.

56. DBWE 16:87.

57. DBWE 16:95. According to the editor of DBWE 16, this was probably Father Simon Scherzl. Bonhoeffer was keen to acquaint Bethge with the Redemptorist methods in view of his current work as inspector with the Gossner Mission. Bethge later asked Bonhoeffer to get more literature on the Redemptorists from the bishop's office in Munich; see DBWE 16:211.

58. DBWE 16:126. This has to be read against the background of the Nazi programme of "eradication of unworthy life." Bonhoeffer treats of euthanasia in *Ethics*, DBWE 6:189–96.

59. DBWE 16:148.

60. DBWE 6:171–218.

61. See above, ch. 1, 21f, 22-24, 36f.

62. DBWE 16:83f.

63. Ibid.

64. Visser't Hooft, *Memoirs*, 174.

65. Bell, *Christianity and World Order*, 197.

66. Visser't Hooft, *Memoirs*, 182.

67. "Draft Proposal for a Reorganization of the Church after the 'End of the Church Struggle,'" DBWE 16:574–80.

68. Ibid., 16:577.

69. See *Ethics*, DBWE 6:138–41.

70. DBWE 16:572–74.

71. Bethge, *Dietrich Bonhoeffer*, 776.

72. DBWE 16:502–28.

73. Placed in *Ethics*, DBWE 6:352–62.

74. Barnett, "Communications . . . ," 65.

75. *Ethics*, DBWE 6:257ff.

76. Ibid., 6:275.

77. Ibid., 6:352f.

78. See above, ch. 3 (MSp11).

79. *Ethics*, DBWE 6:357.

Chapter 10: Ecumenism from Prison

1. DBWE 16:513.

2. On Bonhoeffer's life in prison, see Eberhard Bethge, *Dietrich Bonhoeffer: A Biography* (Minneapolis: Fortress Press, 2000), ch. 13, "Tegel 1943–1944; Ferdinand Schlingensiepen, *Dietrich Bonhoeffer 1906–1945* (London: T & T Clark, 2010), ch. 11, "In Prison 1943–1945"; Charles Marsh, *Strange Glory: A Life of Dietrich Bonhoeffer* (New York: Knopf, 2014), ch. 14, "The Greatest of Feasts on the Journey to Freedom."

3. See above, ch. 9.
4. Bethge, *Bonhoeffer*, 768.
5. DBWE 8:199.
6. Ibid., 8:223.
7. See above, ch. 9.
8. DBWE 8:234.
9. On Bonhoeffer's work in the World Alliance for Friendship through the Churches, see esp. above, chs. 2, 3, 4, and 6.
10. See DBWE 8:234 n.36.
11. See above, chs. 1 and 2.
12. DBWE 8:271.
13. Ibid., 8:305.
14. Ibid., 8:81.
15. Ibid., 8:98.
16. Ibid., 8:104.
17. Ibid., 8:105.
18. Ibid., 8:201f., 206, 225f., 229f., 242f.
19. Based on Eph. 1:10: ". . . as a plan for the fullness of time, to gather up all things in [Christ], things in heaven and things on earth." See DBWE 8:230.
20. DBWE 8:306. Bonhoeffer uses as illustration the incompleteness of J. S. Bach's masterpiece *Art of Fugue*, which Bach could only conclude with the chorale "Before thy throne I come O Lord."
21. Ibid., 8:155.
22. Ibid. From his cell window the monk wistfully watches a party of knights setting off for the promised land: "I am like you a pilgrim yet, though I but stay at home."
23. Ibid., 8:145.
24. Ibid., 8:360.
25. Ibid., 8:425 n.10.
26. Ibid., 8:320f.
27. DBWE 7:167f.
28. DBWE 8:321f.
29. Ibid, 8:172.
30. "With a grain of salt." Ibid., 8:173.
31. Ibid., 8:213.
32. Ibid., 8:189.
33. Ibid.
34. Ibid., 8:323.
35. Dietrich Bonhoeffer and Maria von Wedemeyer, *Love Letters from Cell 92* (London: HarperCollins, 1994), 190.
36. Ibid., 192.
37. See above, ch. 5.
38. DBWE 8:362.
39. Ibid., 8:364.
40. Ibid., 8:372.
41. Ibid.
42. Ibid., 8:406.
43. Ibid., 8:451.
44. Ibid., 364 (emphases mine).
45. Ibid., 426.
46. Ibid., 502.

47. DBWE 16, 83f. See above, ch. 9.

48. DBWE 8:389.

49. Ibid.

50. DBWE 8:499–504.

51. See above, introduction.

52. DBWE 8:364.

53. See above, ch. 1.

54. See above, ch. 4.

55. See esp. "The Structure of Responsible Life," DBWE 6:257ff.

56. DBWE 4:285.

57. DBWE 8:205.

58. Ibid., 8:343–47. Hase was the military commandment of Berlin.

59. Ibid., 8:462–70.

Chapter 11: Still Ahead of Us?

1. Otto Dudzus, "Arresting the Wheel," in Wolf-Dieter Zimmermann and Robert Gregor Smith, eds., *I Knew Dietrich Bonhoeffer* (London: Collins, 1966), 91. See ch. 6, above.

2. Victoria Barnett, "Dietrich Bonhoeffer's Ecumenical Vision," *Christian Century* (26 April 1995): 454–57. Tendencies toward alleged hagiographical treatments of Bonhoeffer are critically examined by Stephen R. Haynes in *The Bonhoeffer Phenomenon: Portraits of a Protestant Saint* (Minneapolis: Fortress Press, 2004).

3. Reinhold Niebuhr, "The Death of a Martyr," *Christianity and Crisis* 5, no. 11 (25 June 1945): 6–7. It was reprinted in Britain in the *Christian News-Letter* of 14 November 1945.

4. In Eberhard Bethge, ed., *Bonhoeffer Gedenkheft* (Berlin: Verlag Haus und Schule GMBH, 1947), 8f.

5. G. K. A. Bell, *The Kingship of Christ* (London: Penguin, 1955), 173.

6. Eberhard Bethge, *Dietrich Bonhoeffer: A Biography* (Minneapolis: Fortress Press, 2000).

7. On this poem, see ch. 10, 267f, above.

8. W. A. Visser't Hooft, "Dietrich Bonhoeffer and the Self-understanding of the Ecumenical Movement," *Ecumenical Review* 28 (1976): 202.

9. Eberhard Bethge, *Friendship and Resistance: Essays on Dietrich Bonhoeffer* (Geneva: WCC/Grand Rapids: Eerdmans, 1995), 8.

10. Ibid.

11. As in the constitution of the early YMCA, which provided the model for the basis of subsequent interdenominational and ecumenical organizations. See ch. 2, above.

12. Keith Clements, "Barmen and the Ecumenical Movement," *Ecumenical Review* 59 (April-July 2007); and "Beginning All Over Again: Barmen 1934 and the Ecumenical Movement Questioned," ch. 6 in idem, *Ecumenical Dynamic: Living in More than One Place at Once* (Geneva: WCC, 2013).

13. WCC Central Committee, Minutes of 51st Meeting, Potsdam, Germany, 28 January–6 February 2001, 179f.

14. Dietrich Werner, "Missionary Structure of the Congregation," in Nicholas Lossky, et al., eds., *Dictionary of the Ecumenical Movement* (Geneva: WCC, 2002), 793.

15. *The Church for Others and the Church for the World: A Quest for Structures for Missionary Congregations* (Geneva: WCC, 1967). See also accounts in Harold C.

Fey, ed., *A History of the Ecumenical Movement 1948–1968* (Geneva: WCC, 1986), 193f., 406–409.

16. See, e.g., John W. de Gruchy and Charles Villa-Vicencio, eds., *Apartheid Is a Heresy* (Grand Rapids: Eerdmans, 1983); John W. de Gruchy, *The Church Struggle in South Africa*, 2d ed. (Grand Rapids: Eerdmans, 1986); idem, *Bonhoeffer and South Africa* (Grand Rapids: Eerdmans, 1984); Allan Boesak, "What Dietrich Bonhoeffer Has Meant to Me," in Guy Carter, et al., eds., *Bonhoeffer's Ethics: Old Europe and New Frontiers* (Kamden: Kok Pharos, 1991), 21–29.

17. See, e.g., Len Hansen and Robert Vosloo, eds., *Oom Bey for the Future: Engaging the Witness of Beyers Naudé* (Stellenbosch: Sun Press, 2006).

18. Ulrich Duchrow, *Global Economy: A Confessional Issue for the Churches?* (Geneva: WCC, 1987).

19. In 2010, the Alliance united with the Reformed Ecumenical Council to form the World Communion of Reformed Churches.

20. See ch. 6, 141, above.

21. The first English edition of Bonhoeffer's *Nachfolge* ("Discipleship"), by which he first became widely known, was titled *The Cost of Discipleship*, thereby giving special emphasis to the book's themes of "costly grace" and "costly discipleship" in contrast to "cheap grace," etc., and to the author's own path of suffering and martyrdom.

22. Thomas F. Best and Wesley Granberg-Michalson, eds., *Costly Unity: Koinonia and Justice* (Geneva: WCC, 1993). Cf. Thomas Best and Martin Robra, *Costly Commitment: Ecclesiology and Ethics* (Geneva: WCC, 1995). Note again that the title of General Secretary Philip Potter's report to the WCC Central Committee in 1974 (see n.12, above) was "Costly Ecumenism."

23. See "Violence, Non-Violence and the Struggle for |Social Justice," in *Ecumenical Review* 25 (1973): 4, 430–54. A section is reproduced in Michael Kinnamon and Brian E. Cope, eds., *The Ecumenical Movement: An Anthology of Key Texts and Voices* (Geneva: WCC, 1997), 216–18.

24. "Violence and the Use of Violence in Society," *Ecumenical Review* 25 (1973): 4, 458f.

25. E.g., José Miguez Bonino, "Por quénos interesa Bonhoeffer," in *Testimonium* 11 (1963): 86–91. Gustavo Guttíerez, "Theology from the Underside of History"; and "The Limitations of Modern Theology: On a Letter of Dietrich Bonhoeffer," in idem, *The Power of the Poor in History* (Maryknoll, NY: Orbis, 1983).

26. For a recent German analysis, see Wolf Krötke, "Ökumenische Ungeduld. Das Drängen Dietrich Bonhoeffers auf die Einheit der Kirche im Geiste Jesu Christi" (2014), http://wolf-kroetke.de/vortraege/ansicht/eintrag/126.html.

27. DBWE 5:107.

28. Michael Kinnamon, "New Contours of Ecumenism: Challenges to the Next Generation," *Ecumenical Review* 66, no. 1 (March 2014): 17.

29. DBWE 11:356.

30. DBWE 14:399.

31. See ch. 3, above.

32. See ch. 7, above.

33. See ch. 7, above.

34. See text of the statement in Kinnamon and Cope, *Ecumenical Movement*, 463–68.

35. For helpful background on the Toronto Statement, see Adrian Hastings, *Oliver Tomkins: The Ecumenical Enterprise 1908–92* (London: SPCK, 2001), 80f.

36. See L. Newbigin's reaction to the Toronto Statement in Kinnamon and Cope, *Ecumenical Movement*, 470.

37. William Nicholls, *Ecumenism and Catholicity* (London: SCM Press, 1951), 122.

38. Lukas Vischer, "Christian Councils—Instruments of Ecclesial Communion" (World Consultation of Christian Councils, 1971), in Kinnamon and Cope, *Ecumenical Movement*, 471–77.

39. Ibid., 473.

40. Jean-Marc R. Tillard, OP, "The Mission of Councils of Churches," *Ecumenical Review* 45 (1993): 276.

41. Alan Falconer, "An ecclesiological understanding of councils of churches," in Colin Podmore, ed., *Community–Unity–Communion: Essays in Honour of Mary Tanner* (London: Church House Publishing, 1998), 104–116.

42. See ch. 7, 171, above.

43. See ch. 4, 80, above.

44. DBWE 13:310.

45. As set out by Bonhoeffer in *Sanctorum Communio* (see ch. 1, above).

46. Ulrich Duchrow, *Conflict Over the Ecumenical Movement: Confessing Christ Today in the Universal Church*, trans. David Lewis (Geneva: WCC, 1981), 359.

47. Ulrich Duchrow, "The Confessing Church and the Ecumenical Movement," *Ecumenical Review* 35 (1981): 230.

48. See Keith Clements, *Ecumenical Dynamic: Living in More than One Place at Once* (Geneva: WCC, 2013), ch. 12, "Who Are We? Continuing Ecumenical Quest."

49. DBWE 8:358.

50. See ch. 1, above.

51. DBWE 8:364.

52. *The Church: Towards a Common Vision*, Faith and Order Paper no. 214 (Geneva: WCC, 2013).

53. Ibid., 33.

54. Ibid., 35.

55. Ibid., 36.

56. DBWE 8:51.

57. DBWE 4:284f.

58. DBWE 6:82–87.

59. DBWE 8:486.

60. DBWE 8:462–70. See ch. 10, above. The poem "The Death of Moses" (DBWE 8:531–41) likewise powerfully exemplifies this intercessory identification with his country's fate before God.

61. On intercession in Bonhoeffer, see Christiane Tjaden, "Die Fürbitte als zentrales politischen Handeln in der Theologie Bonhoeffers," in Kirsten Busch Nielsen, et al., eds., *A Spoke in the Wheel: The Political in the Theology of Dietrich Bonhoeffer* (Gütersloh: Gütersloher Verlagshaus, 2013), 123–36.

62. Nico Koopman, "How Do We Live Responsibly? Bonhoeffer and the Fulfilment of Dignity in Democratic South Africa," in ibid., 429.

63. Ibid., 431.

64. See ch. 9, "Bonhoeffer's Interfaith Encounters," in Stephen Plant, *Taking Stock of Bonhoeffer: Studies in Biblical Interpretation and Ethics* (Farnham: Ashgate, 2014), 115–19.

65. See ch. 1, above.

66. DBWE 6:117.

67. See ch. 6, above.

68. DBWE 4:285.

69. Frieda Haddad, "The Christian Community as sign and instrument for the renewal of human community: a Lebanese perspective," in Thomas F. Best, ed., *Faith and Renewal: Reports and Documents of the Commission on Faith and Order, Stavanger 1985, Norway* (Geneva: WCC, 1986), 187.

70. Ibid., 190.

71. DBWE 14:412.

Index

Abyssinian Baptist Church, Harlem, 40
Act and Being (book), 38, 54
Althaus, P., 52, 58f, 61, 62, 66, 74
Ammundsen, V., 57, 63, 72, 73, 89, 101, 103,134f, 168, 174

Baptist churches, 25, 33, 40, 126
Barcelona, 1928-1929, 35-38
Barmen Theological Declaration, 125, 259
Barmen, Free Synod of, 125, 128
Barnett, V., 6, 9, 220f
Barth, K., 223,6, 27f, 29, 41, 49, 53f, 60, 74, 86, 100, 109f, 119, 121, 123, 125, 159, 163, 171f, 188f, 190, 223, 227, 251
Barthian theology, DB, 27f, 54, 131
Beck, L., 185, 213, 215, 230, 272f
Bell, G.K.A., 1, 2, 3, 6, 63, 72, 89, 93, 95, 101, 114, 115, 116, 117-125, 126, 134, 139, 140, 168, 144-146, 158, 176, 188f, 192, 194, 198, 225, 225, 228, 230-234, 242, 251, 265, 275
Berggrav, E., 190, 206, 229f
Berlin theology faculty, 26f
Berneuchen movement, 258f
Bethge, E., 5, 7, 8, 13, 14, 162, 191, 193f, 203, 221f, 238, 250, 251-3
Boegner, M., 189, 192, 207, 224
Bonhoeffer, [later Leibholz] Sabine. 19, 191, 194, 198
Bonhoeffer, Karl, 19, 20, 50, 119
Bonhoeffer, Klaus, 21, 22, 37, 90, 233
Bonhoeffer, Walter, 21, 41
Brown, W. Adams, 39, 63, 93f, 103, 114, 161

Bruay Conference 1934, 158
Burroughs, E.A., 57f, 70, 82, 83f, 110, 113

Canaris, W., 185, 209
Chandler, A., 11f
Christ
    as centre of devotion, 259
    for us today, 260, 263
    man for others, 264
church,
    universality of, 3, 37, 41f, 67, 265f
    as "Christ existing as community", 31, 51, 62, 97, 266
    in world come of age, 263-265
    existing for others, 264, 267
    belonging wholly to world, 265, 292-299
Church of England 117
    visits to religious houses, 126, 159
Church Struggle, 91-93, 100-101, 120-123, 128, 163f
    and ecumenical movement, 93-97, 101-106, 276
Ciernohorské-Kúpele Youth Peace Conference (1932) 72, 77
coming of age of world, 260f
    ecumenical aspect to, 262
community, 13f, 29
Confessing Church, 125, 129, 157
    ecumenical movement, 158, 165-174, 175-177, 192-19
    See also Fanø Ecumenical Conference, Oxford Conference
Craske, F.W. T., 58, 67, 70, 113
Creation and Fall (book), 75

Deissmann, A., 50, 68, 89, 113, 285
Dickinson, W.H. 113
Diestel, M., 35f, 38, 39, 40, 42, 43, 51f,
    62, 68, 72, 76, 252, 285
Discipleship (book), 131, 164, 266f
"discipline of the secrets" (*disciplina
    arcana*), 263
Dohnanyi, H. von, 129, 185, 198, 209,
    221, 221f, 228, 230, 235, 235f, 237,
    242, 249
Duchrow, U., 9, 280, 291f
Dudzus, O., 141, 271

ecumenical bodies, ecclesial status of,
    288-292
"Ecumenical Council," 141, 172-174
ecumenical education/formation, 17-19
ecumenical movement
    in early 1930s 45-49
    and Church Struggle 111f, 117-125
    on eve of Second World War, 186-190
    in early period of Second World War,
        206-208
    international ecumenical dialogue in
        wartime 223,-225,225-227, 241-246
    as confessing, 275f
    theology of, 7, 62, 84-87, 100, 292f)
ecumenical organisations in 1930s
    Germany, 68f
ecumenism in world come of age, 266
Ehrenström, N. 93, 212, 223, 225, 231,
    232
Eidem, E., 63, 174, 176, 215, 230
Ethics (book) 10, 222, 247f, 234, 266

Faith and Order, 165-167, 195-197
faiths, dialogue with other, 297-299
fanaticism, 259f
Fanø Ecumenical Conference 1934,
    125, 127-148, 157
    Church Struggle/Confessing Church,
        133f, 138-140, 144-148
    DB's "Peace Sermon", 140-142
    DB's paper "The Church and the
        Peoples of the World", 135f, 142f,
        159f
    youth conference 136-138
Finkenwalde seminary, 162-164
Flossenbürg execution camp, 2
Fox, H.W., 113, 115
Freiburg Memorandum, 245f

Freudenberg, A., 186, 188, 221, 223,
    227, 228, 242

Gandhi, M.K., 72, 130, 159, 297
"German Christian" movement, 66f,
    75, 100
Gland Youth Conference (1932), 72f,
Goerdeler, C.F., 213, 215, 246
Guillion, C., 224

Haddad, F., 298f
Haeften, H.-B. von, 214
Harnack, A. von, 26, 27f, 215
Hassell, U. von, 213
Headlam, A.C., 115
Heckel, T., 96f, 100f, 106, 111, 112,
    132, 134, 138-140, 147f, 176, 178,
    188, 189, 192, 212
Henriod, H.L., 47, 48, 62, 67, 70, 90,
    93, 95, 100, 101, 113, 122, 132,
    133, 176, 177f, 186, 188, 224, 283
Hildebrandt, F., 55, 111, 119, 193, 272
Hirsch, E., 52, 59, 61, 66, 74
history, sense of, 10f, 255
Hitler, A., 65, 66, 90, 94, 121, 128,
    160, 184, 205f
Hodgson, L., 114, 165-167,187, 195-
    197, 283f
Holl, K., 28
Hossenfelder, J., 115

India, 130, 159, 297
    See also Gandhi
International Missionary Council, 46,
    48
Islam, DB, 25f, 297
Italy visit 1942, 234f

Jacobi, H., 69, 121
Jews
    persecution of, 41f, 66, 103, 184, 191
    Christian-Jewish post-Holocaust
        dialogue, 274, 297)
Justice, Peace and Integrity of Creation,
    280f

Keller, A., 86f, 188
Kerrl, H., 166, 178
Klemperer, K. von, 216
Koch, K. 134f, 168, 175, 177
Koch, W., 60

Koechlin, A., 122, 123, 207, 223,
Koopman, N., 296f

Lang, C. Gordon, 115f
Lasserre, J., 41
Lehmann, P and M 40, 92, 201
Leibholz, G., 191, 194, 198
Leiper, H.S., 63, 146-148, 177, 186,
200-201
Life and Work (Universal Christian
Council for) 6, 46f, 89, 122, 124
See also Fanø Ecumenical Conference
Life Together (book), 31, 164, 284
Lilje, H., 51, 76, 277
London pastorate 1933-1935, 109-126
ecumenical role 110, 112-117
and Church Struggle, 11f, 117-125
Luther, M., 28, 31f, 39, 61, 67, 163
Lutheran tradition, 21, 32, 257

Marty, M., 4 2n,
Metaxas, E., 4 3n
Methodist churches, 39f,, 126
"Missionary Structure of the Congrega-
tion" programme, 277f
Moltke, H.J. von, 214, 215, 229f
Moravian Brethren and "Watchwords"
(Losungen), 21, 163, 253
Müller, Josef., 215, 235, 236, 237
Müller, Ludwig., 91, 97, 106, 111, 115,
120, 123, 128, ,163

National Socialism/Nazi Party (NS-
DAP), 66
nationhood, 76f
Nazi revolution, 1933, 90
Newbigin, L., 287
Niebuhr, H. Richard, 203
Niebuhr, Reinhold, 6, 39, 198f, 200,
202, 271
Niemöller, M., 96, 111, 121, 134, 164,
277
Norwegian visit, 1942, 229-230
Novi Sad meeting, 1933, 100f, 104-106

Oikoumene (whole inhabited earth), 3,
247, 299, 300
Oldham, J.H., 6, 46, 48, 63, 114, 116,
123, 132, 160, 161, 169, 175, 176,
177, 179, 180f, 186, 226, 242, 277

"orders of creation", 74, 75f, 77
"orders of preservation" 75, 77
Oster, H., 185, 209, 213. 230, 235f
Oxford Conference "Church, Community and State" (1937), 132, 178-181,
286

pacifism, 41, 142
Paton, W., 186, 187, 189, 225, 226f,
241
peace, theological understanding of,
74, 77f
as God's commandment, 78, 140f)
Pentecost, 254
Perels, F.J., 243,246
Pius XII [Pope], 189, 217, 226, 235
Potter, P. 277
Programme to Combat Racism, 281

Raiser, K., 8, 9
Reich church, 125, 130
religion, 260
religionless Christianity, 261
as logic of ecumenism, 269
religionlessness, 260
resistance to Hitler, 185, 208-210,
213-222
Richter, J., 101, 103,
Rieger, J., 126, 198, 271
Roman Catholics Church, DB, 2, 22,
23f, 32f, 36, 235-239, 258
Rome, DB's visits to, 22-25, 234f, 252f
Rössler, H., 50, 60, 61

Sanctorum Communio (book), 28-35,
61f, 97
Schönfeld, H., 93, 123, 134, 135f,
142f, 176, 186, 192, 212, 214, 220,
230-233, 243
"sects", 25, 32, 33
Seeberg, R., 28
Siegmund-Schultze, F., 50, 52, 53, 55,
68, 72, 92f, 101, 103f, 223, 227, 285
Sigtuna (Sweden) meeting of DB and
Bell 1942, 230-240
Söderblom, N., 47, 48, 217
Sofia meeting 1933, 101-104
Stählin, W., 69, 70, 70, 71, 74, 258f
status confessionis
in Church Struggle, 100, 104

post Second World War instances,
278-280
Stellvertretung, see "vicarious representa-
tive action"
Student Christian Movement, 48, 49
Stuttgart Declaration, 1945, 275
Sutz, E., 41, 42, 60, 70, 223, 227
Switzerland, wartime visits to, 222-228

Temple, W., 114, 161, 185, 187, 189,
206f, 225, 226, 241
Tillard, J.-M., 288f
Toureille, P., 56, 57, 58, 67, 70, 101,
137
Troeltsch, E., 26, 29, 32
Trott, A. von, 214, 215, 220

Union Theological Seminary, New York,
38f
United States visit 1930-1931
black communities, 40
churches, 39f
Federal Council of Churches, 40, 50,
60
United States visit 1939, 199,205
"Protestantism without Reformation"
203-205
Unity of church(es), 33f, 41f, 54, 61f,
98f, 239-241, 247, 259

"vicarious representative action" (*Stellvertretung*), 30f, 234, 266f, 285, 300
Vischer, L., 288f
Visser't Hooft, W.A., 6, 9, 63, 161f,
179-181, 186, 188, 189, 192f, 197f,
206f, 218f, 220, 223-225, 226, 227,
228, 241f, 251, 275,m 276

war, false theological justification for, 76
War, First World, 21, 41
War, Second World, 183f, 205f
Wedemeyer, Maria von, 236, 250, 258f
Weimar Republic, demise of, 66
Weizsäcker, E.F. von, 214, 217, 219
Werner, F., 164, 188
Wilcken, J., 173
Williams, R., 10
Winterhager, J., 113, 132
World Alliance for Promoting Inter-
national Friendship through the
Churches, 6, 47f, 49, 53,

Cambridge conference (1931), 51,
55-58
theological basis, 78-81
Youth Commission, DB's work for,
58, 67-73, 132-135, 283f
See also Gland, Ciernohorské-Kúpele,
Sofia, Fanø, Bruay conferences.
World Council of Churches, 8, 45,
160f, 185-187, 191-193, 218-221,
246, 275f.
World Student Christian Federation, 6,
46, 48

Zoellner, W., 71, 79, 164